Lerone Bennett, Jr., was born in Clarksdale, Mississippi, in 1928 and educated in the public schools of Jackson, Mississippi, where he worked on the local Negro weekly, *The Mississippi Enterprise*. He attended Morehouse College and was Editor of the student newspaper, *The Maroon Tiger*. Upon graduation he joined the staff of the *Atlanta Daily World*, first as a reporter and then as City Editor. In 1960 he became the first Senior Editor of *Ebony*. Among his other books are *What Manner of Man: A Biography of Martin Luther King, Jr.; The Negro Mood;* and *Confrontation: Black and White* (now published in a Pelican edition). Mr. Bennett is married and the father of four children.

Before the Mayflower: A History of the Negro in America

1619-1964

REVISED EDITION

LERONE BENNETT, JR.

PENGUIN BOOKS BALTIMORE · MARYLAND

Penguin Books Inc, 3300 Clipper Mill Road,
Baltimore, Maryland, 21211 (USA)
Penguin Books Ltd, Harmondsworth, Middlesex, England
Penguin Books Pty Ltd, Ringwood, Victoria, Australia

First published 1962 by Johnson Publishing Company, Inc., Chicago

Penguin edition published 1966

Reprinted 1968

The lines from "Heritage" are reprinted from Countee Cullen's *Color*, copyright
1925 by Harper & Row, by permission of the publishers, Harper & Row; the lines
from "Fifty Years" are reprinted from James Weldon Johnson's *Saint Peter Relates An Incident*, copyright 1917, 1935 by James Weldon Johnson, by permission
of The Viking Press, Inc.; the lines from "If We Must Die" are reprinted from
Claude McKay's *Harlem Shadows*, copyright 1922 by Harcourt, Brace and Company, by permission of Twayne Publishers, Incorporated. Appreciation is also due
the following persons, institutions and corporations for permission to reproduce
photographs: Metropolitan Museum of Art, page 9; Chicago Historical Society,
pages 51, 61; Schoenfeld Collection, Three Lions, Inc., pages 76–7, 88, 102, 120,
135, 151, 190–1, 214–15; Carl Van Vechten, photograph of Bessie Smith, page 230;
Magnum Photos, Inc., page 231; Wide World Photos, Inc., page 309; United Press
International, pages 191, 283, 308, 320.

Printed in the United States of America

For the Negro Woman

For my Grandmother, Mother, and
  Wife

Lucy, Alma, and Gloria

Preface

THIS BOOK grew out of a series of articles which were published originally in EBONY magazine. The book, like the series, deals with the trials and triumphs of a group of Americans whose roots in the American soil are deeper than those of the Puritans who arrived on the celebrated "Mayflower" a year after a "Dutch man of war" deposited twenty Negroes at Jamestown.

This is a history of "the other Americans" and how they came to North America and what happened to them when they got here. The story begins in Africa with the great empires of the Sudan and Nile Valley and ends with the Second Reconstruction which Martin Luther King, Jr., and the "sit-in" generation are fashioning in the North and South. The story deals with the rise and growth of slavery and segregation and the continuing efforts of Negro Americans to answer the question of the Jewish poet of captivity: "How shall we sing the Lord's song in a strange land?"

This history is founded on the work of scholars and specialists and is designed for the average reader. It is not, strictly speaking, a book for scholars; but it is as scholarly as fourteen months of research could make it. Readers who would like to follow the story in greater detail are urged to read each chapter in connection with the outline of Negro history in the appendix.

Without the help and encouragement of many people, this book would not have been possible. John H. Johnson, president of Johnson Publishing Company, conceived the idea for the series and made it possible for me to spend fourteen months researching and writing it. The editors of Johnson Publishing Company were also helpful with suggestions and criticisms. I am especially indebted to the managing editors of EBONY, Herbert Nipson and Era Bell Thompson, and Doris Saunders, Lucille Phinnie, Basil Phillips, Norman Hunter, Ariel Strong, Herbert Temple, Lacey Crawford and Robert E. Johnson. I should like to express my appreciation to the personnel of the University of Chicago Library, the Johnson Publishing Company Library, the Hall Branch of the Chicago Public Library, and the Chicago Historical Society. My wife, Gloria, also has my thanks for her suggestions and understanding. Whatever virtues this book has are due to the help and encouragement of other people. The errors are my own.

When this material appeared in EBONY magazine in an abridged form, a great many readers—Negroes and whites—were surprised by the depth of involvement of Negroes in the American experience. They were surprised, for example, to discover that Negroes were at Lexington and Concord and that they stood with Andrew Jackson at the Battle of New Orleans and with William Lloyd Garrison in the battle against slavery. The reader, I believe, will be astonished by the richness of the Negro's heritage. He will also perceive, I hope, that this story is relevant to the struggle of all men and that it is a moving chapter in the whole human drama.

LERONE BENNETT, JR.

Chicago, Illinois

Contents

Illustrations

Before the Mayflower:

A History of the

Negro in America

1619–1964

1

The African Past

What is Africa to me:
Copper sun or scarlet sea,
Jungle star or jungle track,
Strong bronzed men, or regal black
Women from whose loins I sprang
When the birds of Eden sang?

COUNTEE CULLEN

A SERIES of revolutionary discoveries has spurred a radical re-evaluation of the strong bronzed men and regal black women from whose loins sprang one out of every ten Americans.

This re-evaluation has yielded a new perspective on African and human history. Africa, long considered the Dark Continent, is now regarded as the place where man first received light. Ancient Africans, long considered primitive and ignorant, are now revealed as creative contributors to Egyptian civilization and builders of powerful states in the Sudan.

From Olduvai Gorge in East Africa, from caves in the Sahara and excavations in the Nile Valley have come bits of bone and husks of grain which speak more eloquently than words of the trials and triumphs of the African ancestors of the American Negro. Consider the following items:

Olduvai Gorge: A series of startling discoveries in this area suggests that the most important and fascinating developments in human history took place in the Dark Continent. Discoveries by Dr. L. S. B. Leakey and other scholars indicate that man was born in Africa, that he began to use tools there and that this seminal invention spread to Europe and Asia.

The Nile Valley: Important finds in the Sudan and Nile Valley prove that peoples of a Negro type were influential contributors to that cradle of civilization—Egypt. Discoveries at excavations near Khartoum in the Sudan and at El Badari on the Nile indicate that Stone Age Negroes laid the foundation for much of the civilization of the Nile Valley and manufactured pottery before pottery was made in the world's earliest known city.

The Congo: Archeologists unearth remains of Ishongo people who lived some 8,000 years ago and used a primitive abacus or multiplication table, possibly the oldest in the world.

The Sahara: Henri Lhote, French explorer, discovers rock paintings which suggest to Author Basil Davidson that "peoples of a Negro type were painting men and women with a beautiful and sensitive realism before 3,000 B.C. and were, perhaps, the originators of naturalistic human portraiture."

"Later discoveries," W. M. Whitelaw writes, "all the way from Kenya to Transvaal not only of early human remains but also of advanced anthropoid types have brought the historical anthropologists to a state of confused expectancy. Considerably more evidence will have to be brought to light, however, before even the main outlines of man's early history in Africa can be drawn. It is already reasonable, however, to believe that such evidence may be forthcoming as will require a radical change of perspective on African history, if not on history itself."

When the human drama opened, Africans were on the scene and acting. For a long time, in fact, the only people on the scene were Africans. For some 600,000 years, Africa and Africans led the world. Were these people who gave the world fire and tools and cultivated grain—were they Negroes? The ancient bones are silent. It is possible, indeed, probable that they were dark-skinned. More than that cannot be said at this time.

Civilization started in the great river valleys of Africa and Asia, in the Fertile Crescent in the Near East and along the narrow ribbon of the Nile in Africa. In the Nile Valley, that beginning was an African as well as an Asian achievement. Negroes, or people who would be considered Negroes today, were among the first people to use tools, paint pictures, plant seeds and worship gods.

Back there, in the beginning, blackness was not an occasion for obloquy. In fact, the reverse seems to have been true. White men were sometimes ridiculed for the "unnatural whiteness of their skin."

Black people were known and honored throughout the ancient world. Ancient Ethiopia, a vaguely defined territory somewhere to the south of Egypt, was hailed as a place fit for the vacation of the gods. Homer praised Memnon, king of Ethiopia, and black Eurybates:

> Of visage solemn, sad, but sable hue,
> Short, wooly curls, o'erfleeced his bending head, . . .
> Eurybates, in whose large soul alone,
> Ulysses viewed an image of his own.

Homer, Herodotus, Pliny, Diodorus, and other classical writers repeatedly praised the Ethiopians. "The annals of all the great early nations of Asia Minor are full of them," Lady Flora Louisa Lugard writes. "The Mosaic records allude to them frequently; but while they are described as the most powerful, the most just, and the most beautiful of the human race, they are constantly spoken of as black, and there seems to be no other conclusion to be drawn, than that at that remote period of history the leading race of the Western World was a black race."

The Ethiopians claimed to be the spiritual fathers of Egyptian civilization. Diodorus Siculus, the Greek historian who wrote in the first century B.C., said: "The Ethiopians conceived themselves to be of greater antiquity than any other nation; and it is probable that, born under the sun's path, its warmth may have ripened them earlier than other men. They supposed themselves to be the inventors of worship, of festivals, of solemn assemblies, of sacrifices, and every religious practice."

However that may be, it is well established that black people *from somewhere* were an important element among the peoples who fathered Egyptian civilization. Badarian culture proves that black men camped on the banks of the Nile thousands of years before the Egypt of the Pharaohs. Bodies were excavated at El Badari amid artifacts suggesting a date of about 8,000 B.C. In the intestines of these bodies were husks of barley which indicated that the Badarians, a people of a Negro type, had learned how to cultivate cereals. The beautifully fashioned pottery the Badarians made was never surpassed, not even in Egypt's days of greatest glory.

A study of skulls provides additional evidence. Scholars who examined some 800 skulls of the predynastic Egyptians found that at least one-third of them were definitely Negroid.

"The more we learn of Nubia and the Sudan," Dr. David Randall-MacIver said, "the more evident does it appear that what was most characteristic in the predynastic culture of Egypt is due to intercourse with the interior of Africa and the immediate influence of that permanent Negro element which has been present in the population of Southern Egypt from the remotest times to our own day."

If Negroes were an important element among the peoples who fathered Egyptian civilization, what were the Egyptians? The question bristles with thorns. The only thing that can be said with assurance is that they probably were not Caucasians. The evidence suggests that they were a black-, brown-, and yellow-skinned people who sprang from a mixture of Negro, Semitic, and Caucasian stocks.

How did the Egyptians see themselves?

They painted themselves in three colors: black, reddish-brown, yellow. The color white was available to them, but they used it to portray blue-eyed, white-skinned foreigners. One of the great murals of Egyptian art is the procession from a tomb of Thebes in the time of Thotmes III. The Egyptians and Ethiopians in the procession are painted in the usual brown and black colors. Thirty-seven whites in the procession are rendered in white tones. Who were they? G. A. Hoskins said they were probably "white slaves of the king of Ethiopia sent to the Egyptian king as the most acceptable present."

Great Negro scholars (W. E. B. Du Bois, Carter G. Woodson, William Leo Hansberry) have insisted that the ancient Egyptians, from Menes to Cleopatra, were a mixed race which presented the same physical types and color ranges as American Negroes—a people, in short, who would have been forced to sit on the back seats of the busses in Mississippi. "If the Egyptians and the majority of the tribes of Northern Africa were not Negroes," Carter Woodson said, "then, there are no Negroes in the United States."

Most scholars deny that the Egyptians were Negroes, despite the testimony of an eyewitness. Herodotus, the Greek historian, visited the country some 500 years before Bethlehem. The Egyptians, he said, were "black and curly-haired."

Group identity aside, it is clear from the record that a large proportion of the ancient Egyptians—at least one-third—were undoubted Negroes. Many, perhaps most, of the soldiers were Negroes. Black peoples toiled on the pyramids, offered prayers to the sun-god and served with distinction in the state bureaucracy. "Ancient Egypt knew him [the Negro]," Alexander Chamberlain said, "both bond and free, and his blood flowed in the veins of not a few of the mighty Pharaohs."

Ra Nehesi and several other Pharaohs have been identified as Negroes by eminent scholars. So has Queen Nefertari, "the most ven-

Mural from Egyptian tomb illustrates color ranges of Ethiopians and Egyptians. Whites in the procession, G. A. Hoskins said, are probably slaves of the Ethiopian king sent to the Egyptian king as a present.

Black Egyptian queen, Nefertari, is pictured in this painting from ancient tomb with her husband, Aahmes I. She has been called one of the "most venerated figures" of Egyptian history.

erated figure," Sir Flinders Petrie said, "of Egyptian history." Nefertari was the wife of Aahmes I, Egypt's great imperial leader, and was cofounder of the famous Eighteenth Dynasty. She has been described as a "Negress of great beauty, strong personality, and remarkable administrative ability."

There was prolonged and intimate contact between the dark-skinned Egyptians and the dark-skinned Ethiopians. For fifty centuries or more, they fought, traded and intermarried. During the Middle Empire, Ethiopia was a tribute-paying dependency of Egypt. Then, in the middle of the eighth century B.C., the Ethiopians turned the tables and conquered Egypt. Kashta, a bold Ethiopian monarch, began the conquest which was completed by his son, Piankhy. When Piankhy returned to his capital at Napata, he had subdued sixteen princes and was master of both Egypt and Ethiopia. The legs of his enemies, he said, trembled "like those of women."

Piankhy was thoroughly aware of the value of good public relations. The celebrated stele in which he recounted his deeds of valor is one of the gems of Egyptology. A modern scholar, Sir Alan Gardiner, says it is "one of the most illuminating documents that Egyptian history has to show, and displays a vivacity of mind, feeling, and expression such as the homeland could no longer produce."

For more than a century, Ethiopian kings occupied the divine office of the Pharaohs. Shabaka, who succeeded Piankhy, attempted to restore the dwindling fortunes of Egypt. He sponsored a cultural revival, built a chapel at Karnak and restored a temple at Thebes. Diodorus Siculus said he "went beyond all his predecessors in his worship of the gods and his kindness to his subjects." Herodotus said he abolished capital punishment in Egypt.

Taharka, the greatest of the Ethiopian Pharaohs, ascended the throne about 690 B.C. at the age of forty-two. He was, from all accounts, a remarkable leader who improved the economic and cultural life of his realm. Sir E. A. Wallis Budge said Taharka (the Tirhakah of the Bible) was "a capable and energetic king, and under his able rule the country, notwithstanding his wars with the Assyrians, enjoyed a period of prosperity for about twenty-five years. That he should have been able to offer such steadfast resistance [to the Assyrians] says much for his capacity as a soldier and leader of men. There must have been something attractive in his personality . . . his deeds appealed so strongly to the popular imagination, at all events in Greek times, that they were regarded as the exploits of a hero."

This resourceful leader left inscriptions which indicate that he conquered the Hittites and the Assyrians—claims which most Egyptologists discount. His sway was so complete and his power was so absolute that he dubbed himself "Emperor of the World." A famous Egyptologist called his reign that "astonishing epoch of nigger domination." Dr. Randall-MacIver said: "It seems amazing that an African Negro should have been able with any sort of justification to style himself Emperor of the World."

Outmaneuvered by the Assyrians, Taharka retired to Napata, where Ethiopian kings continued to rule for several centuries. The capital was moved later farther south to Meroë where strong-willed queens called candaces ruled. One of these queens, a one-eyed woman "with masculine characteristics," led the Ethiopians in unsuccessful forays against the Romans.

The connection between this civilization and modern Ethiopia is far from clear. Some scholars call ancient Ethiopia "Kush" and begin the history of modern Ethiopia with the rise of the Axumite kingdom in what is now Eritrea and northern Abyssinia.

Modern Ethiopia, one of the oldest countries in the world, traces its lineage back to the famous visit the legendary Queen of Sheba ("black but comely") paid Solomon some 1,000 years before Christ. The Axumite kingdom reached the height of its power in the fifth century, when Christianity became the official religion. With the rise of Islam, the Ethiopians of Axum were isolated and slept, Edward Gibbon wrote, "for nearly a thousand years, forgetful of the world by whom they were forgotten."

During the early Christian Era, Negroes were scattered to the four corners of the world. For many centuries, Negro merchants traded with India, China and Europe. Other Negroes were sold as slaves in Europe and Asia. By the beginning of the Islamic Era, Negroes—as merchants and merchandise—had been introduced into many "white" countries. There was a Negro general in Japan, Sakanouye Tamuramaro. Negroes also lived in Venice in Europe and in the deserts of Arabia. The best known of the Arabised Negroes was Antar, the impassioned lover-warrior-poet. The son of an attractive slave woman and an Arab nobleman, Antar became a famous poet and was immortalized after his death as the "Achilles of the Arabian Iliad."

Fearless, impetuous, ready to fight, sing a lyric or drink wine, Antar won fame in the poetic contests which were common in pre-Islamic days. His fame spread and he was hailed as the greatest poet of his time. Like most Arabian poets, Antar had an eye for ladies and love.

> 'Twas then her beauties first enslaved my heart—
> Those glittering pearls and ruby lips, whose kiss
> Was sweeter far than honey to the taste . . .

Antar died about A.D. 615 and his deeds were recorded in literary form as *The Romance of Antar*. This book, Edward E. Holden wrote, "has been the delight of all Arabians for many centuries. Every wild Bedouin of the desert knew much of the tale by heart and listened to its periods and to its poems with quivering interest. His more cultivated brothers of the cities possessed one or many of its volumes. Every coffee-house in Aleppo, Bagdad, or Constantinople had a narrator who, night after night, recited it to rapt audiences. The unanimous opinion of the East has always placed *The Romance of Antar* at the summit of such literature. As one of their authors well says: '*The Thousand and One Nights* is for the amusement of women and children; *Antar* is a book for men.'"

When the Arabs exploded and carried Islam across North Africa and into Spain, Negroes went with them. As a religious ethic, Islam was unusually effective in cutting across racial lines. All Moslems, whatever their color, were brothers in the faith. "If a Negro slave is appointed to rule you," Mohammed said, "hear and obey him, though his head be like a dried grape."

In this climate, a man could be a slave today and a prime minister tomorrow. An extraordinarily large number of Negroes played heroic roles in the rise and spread of Islam—men like Mohammed Ahmad, the Sudanese Negro who claimed to be the Messiah; Abu'l Hasan Ali, the black sultan of Morocco and Bilal, the friend of Mohammed. There were also numerous black generals, administrators, and poets. The abundant and detailed descriptions of interracial relations in the *Arabian Nights* and other Oriental literature prove that race was not a crucial factor in the Islamic world.

Negroes went with crusading Islam into southern Europe, where a "learned and celebrated poet, a black of the Sudan, Abu Ishak Ibrahamin Al Kenemi" was a favorite at the court of Almansur in Seville, Spain.

In the Islamic Era, three powerful states—Ghana, Mali, and Songhay—emerged in the western Sudan, a broad belt of open country, sandwiched between the Sahara in the north and the rain forests of the Guinea Coast on the south. At one time, the peoples and rulers of these countries were classified out of the Negro race. It is now known that they were Negroes, some of whom were converted to Islam in the eleventh century. The extent of Moslem influence is debatable. But it seems probable that the upper classes and leaders, especially in the large cities, were black Moslems.

As political entities, Ghana, Mali, and Songhay do not suffer in comparison with their European contemporaries. In several areas, the Sudanese empires were clearly superior. "It would be interesting to know," Basil Davidson wrote, "what the Normans might have thought of Ghana. Anglo-Saxon England could easily have seemed a poor and lowly place beside it."

The economic life of these states revolved around agriculture, manufacturing, and international trade. Rulers wielded power through provincial governors and viceroys and maintained large standing armies. Chain-mailed cavalrymen, who carried shields and

Ancient Sudan empires reache[d]
peak of their power durin[g]
Middle Ages. Ghana dominate[d]
Sudan for almost three centurie[s]
Mali rose in thirteenth centur[y]
Songhay was Sudan power in t[he]
fifteenth and sixteenth centurie[s]

West African warrior
fought for medieval
African empire of
Kanem-Bornu. Cavaliers
were important part of
pomp and pageantry of
powerful Negro states
of the western Sudan.

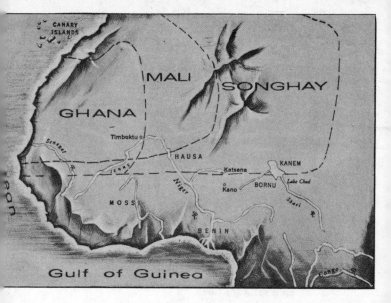

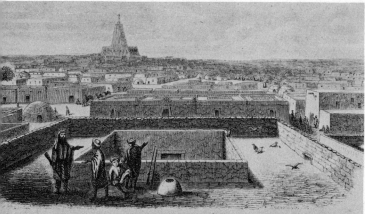

TIMBUKTU, FROM THE TERRACE OF THE TRAVELER'S HOUSE

Timbuktu, during fifteenth and sixteenth centuries, was one of
world's great cities. The intellectual center of black empire of
Songhay, Timbuktu was famed for its scholars and its social life.

fought with swords and lances, formed the shock troops of the armies.

Ibn Batuta, an Arab traveler who visited Mali in the fourteenth century, was impressed by the orderly flow of life. "Of all people," he said, "the blacks are those who most detest injustice. Their Sultan never forgives anyone who has been guilty of it."

Proud, a little haughty perhaps, the Sudanese were a formidable people. When the monarch of one state was overthrown, the women committed suicide because "they were too proud to allow themselves to fall into the hands of white men." Batuta was flabbergasted by the servile behavior of the whites in Mali. The black viceroy who received the merchants of the caravan with which Batuta was traveling remained seated while the whites stood before him. He spoke to the whites through an interpreter, although he understood their language. He did this, Batuta said, "solely to indicate his disdain for them."

Trade and commerce flourished in the great cities that sprang up in the Sudanese savannah. And the intellectual life was brisk and stimulating. Jenné and Timbuktu were known throughout the Moslem world as centers of culture and learning. The citizens were sophisticated and knowledgeable. Batuta said the black women were "of surpassing beauty." They were neither downtrodden nor meek, these women. Batuta said they were "shown more respect than the men." He added: "Their men show no signs of jealousy whatever . . . [the women] show no bashfulness before men and do not veil themselves."

The power and wealth of Ghana, Mali, and Songhay stemmed from the trans-Saharan trade, which exerted a profound influence on Sudanese civilization. The basis of this trade was gold. From the north came caravans of 12,000 or more camels, laden with wheat, sugar, fruit, textiles and salt which were exchanged in the Sudan for gold and other products. In the power politics of that day, the country which controlled this trade controlled the Sudan.

Ghana, which was old when the Arabs first mentioned it in A.D. 800, dominated the Sudan for almost 300 years. It flourished in the ninth and tenth centuries and reached the peak of its power in the early part of the eleventh century. The rulers of Ghana, which was one of the main suppliers of gold for North Africa and Europe, were fabulously wealthy. El Bekri, an Arab geographer who wrote in 1067, said the king owned a nugget of gold so large that he could tether his horse to it.

Tenkamenin, who ruled Ghana in the middle of the eleventh century, had an army of 200,000 men and lived in a castle decorated with sculpture and painted windows. "When he gives audience to his people," El Bekri said, "to listen to their complaints . . . he sits in a pavilion around which stand his horses caparisoned in cloth of gold; behind him stand ten pages holding shields and gold-mounted swords; and on his right hand are the sons of the princes of his empire, splendidly clad and with gold plaited into their hair. The governor of the city is seated on the ground in front of the king, and all around him are his viziers in the same position. The gate of the chamber is guarded by dogs of an excellent breed, who never leave the king's seat, they wear collars of gold and silver. . . ."

In the eleventh century, Ghana fell to a band of Moslem fanatics and the torch of Sudanese civilization passed to Mali, which began as a small Mandingo state on the left bank of the upper Niger River. Mali's history goes back to the seventh century, but it owes its fame to two men—Sundiata Keita and Gonga Musa. Keita transformed the small state into a great empire. Musa, the best known ruler of the ancient Sudan, came to power in 1307 and put together one of the greatest countries of the medieval world.

Musa is best known for a pilgrimage he made to Mecca in 1324. He went in regal splendor with an entourage of 60,000 persons, including 12,000 servants. Five hundred slaves, each of whom carried a staff of pure gold weighing some six pounds, marched on before Musa. Eighty camels bore 24,000 pounds of gold which the black monarch distributed as alms and gifts. Musa returned to his kingdom with an architect who designed imposing buildings in Timbuktu and other cities of the Sudan.

Mali declined in importance in the fifteenth century and its place was taken by Songhay, whose greatest king was Askia Mohammed. Askia, a general who had served as prime minister, seized power in 1493, a year after the discovery of America. He reigned for nineteen years and built the largest and most powerful of the Sudan states. His realm was larger than all Europe and included most of West Africa. "He was obeyed," a Sudanese writer said, "with as much docility on the farther limits of the empire as he was in his own palace, and there reigned everywhere great plenty and absolute peace."

A brilliant administrator and an enlightened legislator, Askia reorganized the army, improved the banking and credit systems and made Gao, Walata, Timbuktu, and Jenné intellectual centers. He has been hailed as one of the greatest monarchs of this period. Alexander Chamberlain said: "In personal character, in administrative ability, in devotion to the welfare of his subjects, in openmindedness towards foreign influences, and in wisdom in the adoption of non-Negro ideas and institutions, King Askia . . . was certainly the equal of the average European monarch of the time and superior to many of them."

Timbuktu, during Askia's reign, was a city of some 100,000 persons, filled to the top with gold and dazzling women. One of the most fabled and exotic cities in the medieval world, the Sudanese metropolis was celebrated for its luxury and gaiety.

The towering minarets of two great mosques dominated the face of the city. From the Great Mosque, flat-roofed houses (of wood covered with plaster) radiated in all directions. The older Sankore Mosque, to which was attached the University of Sankore, was the center of intellectual life. Both buildings were of cut stone and lime. Other buildings fronted the narrow streets: factories and shops where one could buy exotic goods from North Africa and faraway Europe. Leo Africanus, a Christianized Moor who visited the city in the sixteenth century, wrote: "It is a wonder to see what plentie of Merchandize is daily brought hither and how costly and sumptious all things be . . . Here are many shops of artificers and merchants and especially of such as weave linnen. . . ."

In the narrow streets of Timbuktu, scholars mingled with rich black merchants and young boys sat in the shade, reciting the Koran. Visiting Arab businessmen wandered the streets, looking, no doubt, for the excitement for which the city was famed. Perhaps, even at that early date, businessmen were traveling on expense accounts.

Youth from all over the Moslem world came to Timbuktu to study law and surgery at the University of Sankore; scholars came from North Africa and Europe to confer with the learned historians and writers of the black empire. Es Sadi, a Timbuktu intellectual who wrote a history of the Sudan, said his brother came from Jenné for a cataract operation at the hands of a distinguished surgeon. The operation, he said, was successful. Es Sadi, incidentally, had a private library of 1,600 volumes.

Timbuktu, during the reign of Askia the Great, was an intellectual's paradise. A Sudanese literature developed and Es Sadi, Ahmed Baba and other intellectuals wrote books. Leo Africanus said: "In Timbuktu, there are numerous judges, doctors and clerics, all receiving good salaries from the king. He pays great respect to men of learning. There is a big demand for books in manuscript, imported from Barbary. More profit is made from the book trade than from any other line of business." Since man first learned to write, few cities have been able to make such a claim.

The University of Sankore and other intellectual centers in Timbuktu had large and valuable collections of manuscripts in several languages. Scholars traveled to the Songhay city to check their Greek and Latin manuscripts. The seeds scattered here took deep roots. Hundreds of years later, Heinrich Barth met an old blind man in the Sudan. "This," he reported, "was the first conversation I had with this man . . . I could scarcely have expected to find in this out of the way place a man not only versed in all the branches of Arabic literature, but who had even read, nay, possessed a manuscript of those portions of Aristotle and Plato which had been translated into Arabic."

Sandstone column is part of the ruins of an Ethiopian temple. Ancient Ethiopia above second cataract of Nile abounds in monuments rivaling those of Egypt in grandeur and beauty.

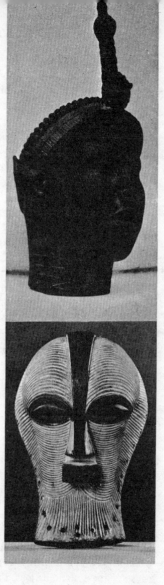

Naturalistic bronze head from Ife, West Coast art center, and abstract rendering of human face in mask (below) indicate great variety and strength of African sculpture.

How did the people of Timbuktu amuse themselves? If Songhay writers can be believed, Timbuktu was Paris, Chicago and New York blended into an African setting. Shocked Songhay historians said most of the people amused themselves with music, love and the pleasures of the cup. Music was the rage (orchestras with both male and female singers were preferred) and midnight revels were common. The dress of the women was extravagantly luxurious. Men and women were fond of jewels; and the women dressed their hair with bands of gold.

Dramatic displays, including dancing, fencing, gymnastics and poetic recitations, were popular. So was chess. The story is told of a Songhay general who bungled a military campaign and explained that he became so engrossed in a chess game that he paid no attention to the reports of his scouts.

Askia—a liberal man who had several wives and 100 sons, the last of whom was born when he was 90—was disturbed by the free and easy life of Timbuktu. He attempted, apparently without too much success, to curb the free intercourse between men and women.

Timbuktu and the civilization of which it was a flower declined in the seventeenth century and the reign of the great West African states came to an end. Why did Sudanese civilization collapse? W. E. B. Du Bois says it fell before the triphammer blows of two of the world's great religions: Islam and Christianity. Other students cite the difficulties of defense in the open Sudanese savannah, and the corrupting influence of the slave trade. Es Sadi, who wrote the *Tarikh es Sudan* in the dying days of the Songhay empire, has advanced another reason—social dissolution. The people, he said, had grown fat and soft on luxury and good living. "At this moment," he said, "faith was exchanged for infidelity; there was nothing forbidden by God which was not openly done. Men drank wine, they gave themselves up to vice. . . . As to adultery, it became so frequent that indulgence in it was almost accepted as permissible. Without it there was no elegance and no glory. . . . Because of these abominations, the Almighty in his vengeance drew upon the Songhai the victorious army of the Moors."

The age of the great Sudan empires ended, but several states to the east and south, notably Mossi, Hausa, Kanem-Bornu and Ashanti retained their political identities down to the eighteenth and nineteenth centuries. Great Zimbabwe and other stone cities in Southern Rhodesia suggest that strong states flourished inland. Vigorous centers of culture also existed on the East Coast where Negro and Arab merchants traded with India and China.

European penetration and the slave trade debased much that was vital in African culture. The popular myth depicts the conquering white man carrying the blessings of civilization to naked savages who sat under trees, filed their teeth and waited for fruit to drop into their hands. The truth is less flattering to the European ego. On the West Coast of Africa, from whence came most of the ancestors of American Negroes, there were complex socio-economic institutions. Political institutions ranged from extended family groupings to village states and territorial empires. Most of these units had all the appurtenances of the modern state—armies, courts, and internal revenue departments. Indeed, more than one scholar has paid tribute to "the legal genius of the African." Anthropologist Melville J. Herskovits has said: "Of the areas inhabited by nonliterate peoples, Africa exhibits the greatest incidence of complex governmental structures. Not even the kingdoms of Peru and Mexico could mobilize resources and concentrate power more effectively than could some of these African monarchies, which are more to be compared with Europe of the Middle Ages than referred to the common conception of the 'primitive' state."

Agriculture was the basis of economic life, although herding and artistry were important. Specialization was advanced, with one tribe, for example, concentrating on metallurgy and bartering with another tribe which specialized in weaving or farming. A money system based on the cowrie shell was in use before European penetration.

The concept of private property had not taken deep hold. The land belonged to the community and could not be alienated.

Iron was known and used from the Atlantic Ocean to Ethiopia.

With simple bellows and charcoal fires, the Africans smelted iron and manufactured beautiful implements. "It seems likely," Franz Boas said, "that at a time when the European was still satisfied with rude stone tools, the African had invented or adopted the art of smelting iron. . . . It seems not unlikely that the people who made the marvelous discovery of reducing iron ores by smelting were the African Negroes. Neither ancient Europe, nor ancient western Asia, nor ancient China knew iron, and everything points to its introduction from Africa."

The core of West African society was the family which was organized among many tribes on a matrilineal basis—that is, descent was traced through the mother. Polygamy was common, though, in practice, the poor, like poor people everywhere, contented themselves with monogamy. Some tribes, incidentally, were acquainted with the allegedly modern practice of birth control. Bantu tribes said it was not good for a woman to give birth to more than one child in a three-year period.

Social life was well organized. The old, the sick, the infirm were cared for. Spinsters were rare; prostitution was unknown. The villages and the surrounding gardens and fields were as safe as the streets of some American cities. Some tribes, as fantastic as it may seem, vaccinated for smallpox. Other Africans insisted that there was a cause and effect relationship between the mosquito and malaria. A European traveler in Abyssinia noted: "The Natives hereabouts say that Malaria is caused by the bite of the mosquito, but, of course, we know better—it is caused by the miasmas of the swamps!"

The West Africans were a bewildering mixture of various stocks. Centuries of contact and interbreeding had already produced different types. Some of the West Africans were short and broad-nosed. Some were tall, with straight hair and aquiline noses. They were of all colors: chocolate, asphalt, café au lait, persimmon, cream.

Although they spoke many tongues, there was a common substratum. Only four African languages were reduced to writing before the coming of the white man: Egyptian, Ethiopian, a variety

of Berber and an invention of the Vai people of Liberia. Though
not reduced to writing, African languages were far from simple.
Mario Pei has given a classic description of one African language,
Swahili. "Swahili," he wrote, "is a complete refutation of the rather
general belief that languages of 'primitive' peoples are necessarily
primitive, and consist largely of grunts, groans and mixed-up ideas.
Swahili has a euphony that is comparable to Italian, with clear, distinct sounds, vowel endings, and a most pleasing arrangement of
syllables that consist for the most part of consonant-plus-vowel. It
is capable of such absolute precision that the Swahili version of the
Pentateuch contains fewer words than the Hebrew original, without the slightest loss or distortion of meaning. Its grammatical and
syntactical structure is logical, almost to the point of being philo-
sophical. . . . Using Swahili roots, prefixes and suffixes, it would
be as easy to construct the vocabulary of nuclear fission (or of any
other science or philosophy) as it is in languages like the modernized Irish of Eire or the modernized Hebrew of Israel. . . ."

Of whatever tongue, of whatever color, Africans were a deeply
religious people. For a long time, African religion was written off
as a form of animism. We know now that it was a great deal more
complicated than that. Like advanced peoples everywhere, the Africans wrestled with the big questions. What is man? What hap-
pens to him after death? Is life a gigantic hoax or has it purpose
and meaning?

The answers Africans gave to these questions determined the
form of their religion. There was, to begin with, a supreme God
who created the earth. There was also a pantheon of lesser gods
identified sometimes with terrestrial objects. Intertwined with these
concepts were the cults of fate and ancestor worship. Undergir-
dling all was the basic concept of "life forces." The life force of
the Creator was thought to be present in all things, animate and in-
animate. This force, "a kind of individualized fragment of the Supreme Being itself," continued to exist, even after the death of the
individual. It continued, the African said, in a pure and perfect
state which could influence the lives of living things.

This sophisticated concept bears a striking resemblance to Henri

Bergson's *elan vital*. Bernard Fagg has found some parallels between African philosophy and modern subatomic physics. "African thought," he said, "is conditioned by their ontology, that is,
their theory of the nature of being; for them being is a process and
not a mere state, and the nature of things is thought of in terms of
force or energy rather than matter; the forces of the spirit, human,
animal, vegetable and mineral worlds are all constantly influencing
each other, and by a proper knowledge and use of them a man may
influence his own life and that of others."

Religion, to the African, was life. Every event was suffused with
religious significance; and the climax of life was death. The African's attitude toward death, anthropologists say, survived the Atlantic crossing and took root in the soil of Negro life. Another religious root, spirit possession, thrives, they say, in the shouting and
ecstasy complex of some American Negro churches.

Art, like religion, was a life expression. There were no art mu-
seums or opera houses in pre-white man Africa. Art and aesthetic
expression were collective experiences in which all the people participated. Art, in short, was not for art's sake, but for life's sake.

The different faces of beauty—line, color, sound, rhythm—fascinated the African ancestors of the American Negro. And their art
—embodied in cubistic masks, terra cotta pieces, gold figurines,
three dimensional objects and naturalistic representations of the
human body—is one of the great flights of the human spirit. Fascinated by the nonhuman geometry of African art, Picasso and other
modernists turned their backs on the Greco-Roman and Renaissance visions and immersed themselves in the vocabulary of Benin,
Ife and other West African art centers. In 1907, Picasso altered the
faces of his huge canvas, *Les Demoiselles d'Avignon*, to resemble
African masks. This was the beginning of cubism, a turning point
in Western art.

Before the coming of the white man, music and rhythm were
everyday things in Africa. Music was everywhere and it was
grounded in two techniques which survived in the New World:
polyrhythmic percussive technique and the call-and-response pat-

tern (leader and chorus alternating). The poetry of tom-toms, the symphonies of synchronized bodies: these ebbed and flowed with the rhythm of life. Men and women danced because dancing had a social and religious meaning. And more—because dancing *was* meaning, was life itself. This attitude came to America, too. The Afro-American dances from Afro-Cuba and the Afro-American dances from Afro-Harlem are rooted in an African *mystique*. It is of more than casual significance that films made in an African village contained a perfect example of the Charleston.

There was much, to be sure, that was mean and base in African life: slavery, for example, although it was a thousand times more moderate than American slavery; human sacrifice and, of course, the use of man by man. Men used other men in Africa, as they did in Greece and Rome. The only thing that can be said for human exploitation in Africa is that it was as well organized as it was in "more advanced" cultures.

The man who emerged from this African chrysalis was a courageous, warlike individual. He was not soft; he was hard. He had fought the tsetse fly, the mosquito and hundreds of nameless insects and he had survived. He had wrested from the hungry jungle gaps of land and he had found time to think beautiful thoughts and to make beautiful things. He was used to hard work and he was accustomed to an elaborate social code. If he were a nobleman or a rich merchant or a priest, if, in short, he belonged to the upper classes, as did many who came to America in chains, he was used to political responsibility, to giving orders and taking them, to making and altering rules, to governing. In fine, as Stanley M. Elkins has said, "he was the product of . . . cultural traditions essentially heroic in nature."

Was this rich cultural heritage transplanted and preserved in the American environment?

Some scholars find little in American Negro life that can be traced to the African past. Others, like Melville J. Herskovits, find Africanisms (survivals of African cultural patterns) in the family life, motor habits, religious practices and music of American Negroes. Lorenzo Turner has found a large number of survivals in the syntax, word-formations and intonations of American Negroes. Among the words he found "in fairly general use . . . especially in the South" were goober (peanut), gumbo (okra), ninny (female breast), tote (to carry), yam (sweet potato). Turner also found "several hundred" African names among Negroes on the South Side of Chicago. Among the names and their African derivation are:

> *Bobo*, one who cannot talk (Vai)
> *Geeji*, a language and tribe in Liberia
> *Agona*, a country in Ghana (Twi)
> *Ola*, that which saves (Yoruba)
> *Sambo*, name given the second son (Hausa)
> *Zola*, to love (Congo)

John Hope Franklin, the eminent modern-day scholar, says: "The survival of varying degrees of African culture in America does not suggest that there has been only a limited adjustment of the Negro to the New World situation. To the contrary, it merely points up the fact that he came out of an experience that was sufficiently entrenched to make possible the persistence of some customs and traditions. . . . After all, perhaps the survival of Africanisms in the New World was as great as it was because of the refusal of the members of the dominant group in America to extend, without reservations, their own culture to the Negroes whom they brought over."

Franklin's summation underlines the great number of answers which are available to students who echo the poet:

> *One three centuries removed*
> *From the scenes his fathers loved,*
> *Spicy grove, cinnamon tree,*
> *What is Africa to me?*

2

Before the Mayflower

. . . Ethiopia shall soon stretch out her hands unto God.

PS. 68:31

SHE CAME out of a violent storm with a story no one believed, a name no one recorded and a past no one investigated. She was manned by pirates and thieves. Her captain was a mystery man named Jope, her pilot an Englishman named Marmaduke, her cargo an assortment of Africans with sonorous Spanish names—Antony, Isabella, Pedro.

A year before the arrival of the celebrated "Mayflower," 113 years before the birth of George Washington, 244 years before the signing of the Emancipation Proclamation, this ship sailed into the harbor at Jamestown, Virginia, and dropped anchor into the muddy waters of history. It was clear to the men who received this "Dutch man of War" that she was no ordinary vessel. What seems unusual today is that no one sensed how extraordinary she really was. Few ships, before or since, have unloaded a more momentous cargo.

From whence did this ship come?

From somewhere on the high seas where she robbed a Spanish vessel of a cargo of Africans bound for the West Indies.

Why did she stop at Jamestown, the first permanent English settlement in America?

No one knows for sure. The captain "ptended," John Rolfe noted, that he was in great need of food; he offered to exchange his human cargo for "victualle." The deal was arranged. Antony, Isabella, Pedro, and 17 other Africans stepped ashore in August, 1619. The history of the Negro in America began.

It began, in a way, with Antony. And it began with a love story. Antony, who had no surname, fell in love with Isabella and married her. Isabella, in 1624, gave birth to the first Negro child born in English America. The proud parents named the boy William Tucker in honor of a local planter.

There were other ships, other William Tuckers, other Antonys and other Isabellas—millions after millions. This is a story about those millions and the way they came to the Americas. This is a story about the merchandising and marketing of human beings. This is a story about the "greatest migration in recorded history."

The story of Antony and Isabella is only an act in a larger drama—the European slave trade—which began in 1444 and continued for more than 400 years. During this period, Africa lost an estimated forty million people. Some twenty million of these men and women came to the New World. Millions more died in Africa during and after their capture or on the ships and plantations.

These figures, though instructive, do not say anything meaningful about the people involved. The slave trade was not a statistic, however astronomical. The slave trade was people living, lying, stealing, murdering and dying. The slave trade was a black man who stepped out of his hut for a breath of fresh air and ended up, ten months later, in Georgia with bruises on his back and a brand on his chest.

The slave trade was a black mother suffocating her newborn baby because she didn't want him to grow up a slave.

The slave trade was a kind captain forcing his suicide-minded passengers to eat by breaking their teeth, though, as he said, he was "naturally compassionate."

The slave trade was a bishop sitting on an ivory chair on a wharf in the Congo and extending his fat hand in wholesale baptism of slaves who were rowed beneath him, going in chains to the slave ships.

The slave trade was a greedy king raiding his own villages to get slaves to buy brandy.

The slave trade was a pious captain holding prayer services twice a day on his slave ship and writing later the famous hymn, "How Sweet the Name of Jesus Sounds."

The slave trade was deserted villages, bleached bones on slave trails and people with no last names.

The slave trade was Caesar negro, Angelo negro and Negro Mary.

Above all, the slave trade was Captain Tomba, who came to America, and Nealee, who didn't.

Nealee started out but she couldn't or wouldn't make it. She was being driven to the West African coast for sale when she became ill and refused to walk another step. Mungo Park, who was one of the last persons to see Nealee, said she was put on an ass "but the ass was so very unruly, that no sort of treatment could induce him to proceed with his load; and as Nealee made no exertion to prevent herself from falling, she was quickly thrown off, and had one of her legs much bruised. Every attempt to carry her forward being thus found ineffectual, the general cry of the coffle [slave caravan] was, *kang-tegi, kang-tegi,* 'cut her throat, cut her throat'; an operation I did not wish to see performed, and therefore marched onwards with the foremost of the coffle. I had not walked above a mile when one of Karfa's [the leader] domestic slaves came up to me, with poor Nealee's garment upon the end of his bow and exclaimed, 'Nealee *affeeleeta*.' (Nealee is lost.) I asked him whether the Slatees [black slave merchants] had given him the garment as a reward for cutting her throat; he replied that Karfa and the schoolmaster would not consent to that measure, but had left her on the road; where undoubtedly she soon perished, and was probably devoured by wild beasts."

Captain Tomba, who came to America, was first seen in a slave pen in Sierra Leone. John Atkins, a surgeon who saw him there, said he was a handsome man "who scorned looking at us, refusing to rise or stretch out his Limbs, as the Master Commanded." A few days later, Captain Tomba and a companion led a revolt on a slave ship and killed three sailors before they were subdued.

What happened to Captain Tomba?

"Why," says John Atkins, "Captain Harding weighing the Stoutness and Worth of the two slaves [Captain Tomba and a companion] did, as in other Countries they do by Rogues of Dignity, whip and scarify them only; while three others, Abettors, but not Actors, nor of Strength for it, he sentenced to cruel Deaths; making them first eat the Heart and Liver of one of them killed. The Woman he hoisted up by the Thumbs, whipped, and slashed her with Knives, before the other slaves till she died."

Captain Tomba living, Nealee dying, John Newton praying, the King of Barsally stealing, the fat bishop baptizing, Captain Harding torturing—these people and millions like them made the slave trade one of the darkest chapters in the history of man.

This dark chapter started in the fifteenth century but, in truth, it goes back to the dawn of history. Slavery, in one form or another, has been practiced in every country known to man. It was old when Moses was young. In Plato's Athens and Caesar's Rome, men—white, black and brown men—were bought and sold. Slavery existed in the Middle Ages in Christian Europe and in "pagan" Africa.

In the ancient world, almost anyone might become a slave. Slavery was so prevalent, in fact, that it was not considered a badge of shame. "The Israelites," Milton R. Konvitz reminds us, "in the Promised Land did not consider it a badge of shame that their forefathers had been slaves unto Pharaoh in Egypt. On the contrary, they were commanded to hold ever in their consciousness not only the fact that they had been led out of their bondage in Egypt, but also, and with equal importance, that before the Exodus they had been slaves. Slavery, then, like alienage, could serve as a bond to humanity. . . . The experience of slavery in the ancient world was so common that Plato ventured to suggest that every man has many slaves among his ancestors."

Cicero's letter to Atticus forms a curious comment on the changing fashions in race. "Do not obtain your slaves from Britain," he wrote, "because they are so stupid and so utterly incapable of being taught that they are not fit to form part of the household of Athens."

A charming story, which revolves around this letter, was recounted by the distinguished Britisher, Sir William Hamilton Fyfe. The incident, he said, happened in Sierra Leone. "A lecture had been arranged . . . and the lecturer took the line that the weight and structure of an African's brain was such that it was quite incapable of being developed by higher education. He thought his audience was wholly European. But when the time for questions came at the end, there rose at the back of the hall a tall, ebony figure, with that wide and winning African smile. It was one of the members of the staff of the old and famous missionary college at Fourah Bay. He thanked the lecturer very kindly for his interesting talk and he said, 'You know, it reminded me of what I happened to be reading last night in a volume of Cicero's letters. It was a letter that was written by Cicero to his friend Atticus, the millionaire employer of slave labour, and he says in the letter that of all his slaves the British were the ugliest and most stupid.' And then he added ingratiatingly, 'How you have come on!' and with that he sat down!"

There was a crucial difference between ancient slavery and modern slavery. Ancient slavery, which had little or nothing to do with race, was justified primarily by the rules of war. Christians and

Moslems added a new dimension to this ancient institution. "Members of each faith," Historian Kenneth M. Stampp writes, "looked upon the other as infidels, and hence felt doubly entitled to make slaves of the other when taken as captives. Moors captured in North Africa and in the Spanish peninsula were held in bondage in Italy, Spain, Portugal and France. Christian prisoners suffered the same fate in the lands of Islam. Christians and Moslems alike believed it just to hold heathens in servitude, and both found victims among the Negroes of Africa."

The Moslems got there first. For several centuries before the opening of the European trade, Moslem merchants dragged dark captives across the hot Sahara sands. Then, in the fifteenth century, Portugal diverted this trade to the Atlantic. The prime mover in this development was a devout, covetous prince named Henry the Navigator. Excited by stories of the great wealth of Africa and Asia, he ordered his ships to explore the coast of Africa. There, on a fateful day in 1444, Henry's men came upon the first large group of Africans. They tiptoed through the high grass and crept to the edge of the village and then, said a contemporary, "they looked towards the settlement and saw that the Moors, with their women and children, were already coming as quickly as they could out of their dwellings, because they had caught sight of their enemies. But they, shouting out 'St. James,' 'St. George,' 'Portugal,' attacked them, killing and taking all they could."

"And at last," the chronicler continued, "our Lord God who giveth a reward for every good deed, willed that for the toil they had undergone in his service, they should that day obtain victory over their enemies, as well as a guerdon and a payment for all their labour and expense; for they took captive of those Moors, what with men, women and children, 165, besides those that perished and were killed. . . ."

The pious Portuguese captured seventy more Africans, including a girl they found sleeping in a deserted village, and sailed home. The captives were promptly baptized and enslaved. Within ten years, Portugal was importing one thousand Africans a year. A century later, Negroes outnumbered whites in some sections of Portugal. There was a big demand for Negro domestics, stevedores and agricultural laborers, especially in the southern section. "By the middle of the sixteenth century," says Mary Wilhelmina Williams, "the inhabitants of the Algarve were largely Ethiopians, and even as far north as Lisbon blacks outnumbered whites. There was no marked color line, and the blood of the two races mingled freely, resulting eventually in Negroid physical characteristics in the Portuguese nation."

Christopher Columbus and sugar made the slave trade a big business.

Descendants of the first Negro slaves—black Christians born in Spain and Portugal—were among the first settlers of the New World. Negro explorers, servants and slaves accompanied French, Spanish and Portuguese explorers in their expeditions in North and South America. They were with Pizarro in Peru, Cortes in Mexico and Menendez in Florida. Thirty Negroes were with Balboa when he discovered the Pacific Ocean. Some authorities believe a Negro made the first trip; they say Pedro Alonso Niño, who piloted one of Columbus' ships, was a Negro.

Among the outstanding Negro explorers in the New World was Estevanico, who opened up New Mexico and Arizona for the Spaniards. Other Negroes, W. E. B. Du Bois says, "accompanied DeSoto and one of them stayed among the Indians in Alabama and became the first settler from the Old World."

Spaniards, who took the lead in the exploration, attempted at first to enslave Indians. But they died out so fast that Bishop Bartolomé Las Casas, a famous missionary, recommended in 1517 the importation of Africans. Las Casas lived to regret this recommendation. The development of large-scale sugar planting gave the slave trade a cruel twist. In a few years, droves of Negroes were crossing the Atlantic each year and the soil of Africa, America and Europe was drenched with their blood. "Strange," says Eric

Williams, "that an article like sugar, so sweet and necessary to human existence, should have occasioned such crimes and blood-shed!"

An estimated million of these Negroes found their way to the land that became the United States of America. But the first black immigrants (Antony, Isabella, and the Jamestown group) were not slaves. This is a fact of capital importance in the history of the American Negro. They came, these first black men, the same way that many, perhaps most, of the first white men came—under duress and pressure. They found a system (indentured servitude) which enabled poor white men to come to America and sell their services for a stipulated number of years to planters. Under this system, thousands of whites—paupers, ne'er-do-wells, religious dissenters, waifs, prisoners, and prostitutes—were shipped to the colonies and sold to the highest bidder. Some were sold, as the first Negroes were sold, by the captains of ships. Some were kidnapped on the streets of London and Bristol, as the first Negroes were kidnapped in the jungles of Africa.

In Virginia, then, as in other colonies, the first Negro settlers fell into a well-established socio-economic groove which carried with it no implications of racial inferiority. That came later. But in the interim, a period of forty years or more, the first Negroes accumulated land, voted, testified in court and mingled with whites on a basis of equality. They owned other Negro servants. And at least one Negro imported and paid for a white servant whom he held in servitude. Negro and white servants, Kenneth Stampp says, "seemed to be remarkably unconcerned about their visible differences. They toiled together in the fields, fraternized during leisure hours, and, in and out of wedlock, collaborated in siring a numerous progeny."

The racial situation, at this juncture, was fluid; it contained the seeds of several alternatives. Indentured servitude could have continued for Negro and white servants or both groups could have been reduced to slavery. Other possibilities were Indian slavery and a free labor system for Negroes and whites, Indians and immigrants. Socio-economic forces selected Negro slavery out of these alternatives. In the West Indies, sugar was decisive. In America, tobacco and cotton were the villains. A world-wide demand for these products and the rise of plantation-sized units to meet this demand focused attention on the labor force. How could men be *forced* to work?

The rulers of the early American colonies were not overly scrupulous about the color or national origin of their work force. Indian slavery was tried and abandoned. Many masters attempted to enslave white men and white women. When these attempts failed, the spotlight fell on the Negro. He was tried and he was found not wanting. Why were Negroes more acceptable than poor whites and poor Indians? White men, for one thing, were under the protection of strong governments; they could appeal to a monarch. White men, moreover, were white; they could escape and blend into the crowd. Indians, too, could escape; they knew the country and their brothers were only a hill or a forest away. Another element in the failure of Indian slavery was the fact that Indians tended to sicken and die.

Negroes did not have these disadvantages. They were strong: one Negro, the Spanish said, was worth four Indians. They were inexpensive: the same money that would buy an Irish or English indentured servant for ten years would buy an African for life. They were visible: they could run, but they could not blend into the crowd. Above all, they were unprotected. And the supply, unlike the supply of Irishmen and Englishmen, seemed to be inexhaustible. The rulers of early America fell to thinking. Why not?

Virginia and Maryland led the way in the 1660's. Laws made Negroes servants for life; intermarriage was forbidden; children born of Negro women were ruled bond or free, according to the status of the mother.

At first, religion was the rationalization; Negroes were good material for slavery because they were not Christians. Between 1667 and 1682, the basis shifted to race. Virginia said it first, in her law of 1667: ". . . the conferring of baptisme doth not alter the condition of the person as to his bondage or freedom." After that, it was easy. A series of laws stripped the Negro slave of all rights of personality and made color a badge of servitude. The Negro population, which had grown slowly during the twilight interim of freedom, lunged forward. By 1710, the number had increased to 50,000. When the Declaration of Independence was signed, there were 500,000. By 1860, the twenty Negroes who landed at Jamestown in 1619 had become 4,000,000.

Where did these people come from?

How did they come?

Why did they come?

Most of the Negro slaves came from an area bordering a 3,000-mile stretch on the West Coast of Africa. They came, chained two by two, left leg to right leg, from a thousand villages and towns. They came from many racial stocks and many tribes, from the spirited Hausas, the gentle Mandingos, the creative Yorubas, from the Ibos, Efiks and Krus, from the proud Fantins, the warlike Ashantis, the shrewd Dahomeans, the Binis and Sengalese.

Some slaves were captured in native wars and sold to *Slattees* (black slave merchants) who sold them to Europeans. Some were kidnapped by Europeans and Africans. Some were sold into slavery for infractions of native laws.

Driven by *Slattees*, some captives made forced marches of 500 miles to the coast where they were examined like cattle and packed into the holds of slave ships. They came, on these forced marches, across rivers and over mountains, barefooted and naked to their enemies, with chains on their ankles, burdens on their heads and fear in their hearts.

Were they—these people who gave to the world the American Negro—were they the dregs of society? No. The strong came and the weak, too. Priests, princes, warriors, merchants and nobles came. Slave traders testified that it was not unusual for an African to sell an African today and to be captured and sold himself tomorrow. The story is told of a slave merchant who sold a parcel of slaves and unwisely accepted a social drink to seal the transaction. One drink led to another—and to America. The slave merchant woke up the next morning with a hangover and a brand on his chest. He was in the hold of a slave ship with his victims and over him stood the captain, laughing to beat the band.

This story underlines a rather obvious fact: Africans as well as Europeans were involved in the slave trade. There has been a systematic attempt, however, to overemphasize the degree of African involvement. The picture of a whole continent of Africans kidnapping and selling each other for rum, guns and gew-gaws is wide of the mark. It is true that some Africans, corrupted by Europe's insatiable desire for human flesh, sold their countrymen. But many Africans like King Almammy and Captain Tomba loathed the whole business and forbade their subjects to take part in it.

European nations fought each other for the privilege of managing the trade. Portugal, who ran the first leg, was ousted by Holland who in turn surrendered supremacy on the African coast to France and England. Portugal, one trader said, "served for setting dogs to spring the game." Once the game was sprung, all Europe rushed to the playing field. Spain, barred from Africa by a papal bull which gave her most of the New World, made her money by giving other powers a contract to supply her colonies with slaves. This contract, the infamous Asiento, was the national status symbol of that day: it symbolized commercial and political supremacy. In the eighteenth century, when England held the Asiento, the slave trade was the basis of European commerce, the cause of most of her wars and the prize politicians competed for.

An intricate set of trading arrangements existed on the Guinea Coast (the West Coast of Africa) for processing Africans bought and stolen. Europeans—French, Swedish, Danish, Portuguese, Dutch, English and Prussian traders—dotted the coast with a series of forts and factories. Each fort and factory had a dungeon or "Negroe House" where slaves were confined until shipment.

Into these factories, Europeans poured a steady stream of goods—colorful cloth, trinkets, rum and "other strong water," blankets, old sheets—which were converted into human beings. Europeans, operating as representatives of powerful companies or as private traders, bartered these goods for men and women. A woman might change hands for a gallon of brandy and six beads. A man might bring eight guns, a wicker bottle, two cases of whiskey and twenty-eight old sheets.

Slaves were purchased from brokers at the forts and factories or in open markets. John Barbot, a famous trader, has described an open market on the Slave Coast. "As the slaves come down to Fida from the inland country, they are put into a booth, or prison, built for that purpose, near the beach, all of them together; and when the Europeans are to receive them, they are brought out into a large plain, where the surgeons examine every part of every one of them, to the smallest member, men and women being all stark naked. Such as are allowed good and sound are set on one side, and the others by themselves; which slaves so rejected are there called Mackrons, being above thirty-five years of age, or defective in their limbs, eyes or teeth; or grown grey, or that have the vene-real disease, or any other imperfection. These being so set aside, each of the others, which have passed as good, is marked on the breast, with a red-hot iron, imprinting the mark of the French, English or Dutch companies. . . . In this particular, care is taken that the women, as tenderest, be not burnt too hard."

The newly-purchased slaves, properly branded and chained, were rowed out to the slave ships for the dreaded Middle Passage across the Atlantic. They were packed like books on shelves into holds which in some instances were no higher than eighteen inches. "They had not so much room," one captain said, "as a man in his coffin, either in length or breadth. It was impossible for them to turn or shift with any degree of ease." Here, for the six to ten weeks of the voyage, the slaves lived like animals. Under the best conditions, the trip was intolerable. When epidemics of dysen-tery or smallpox swept the ships, the trip was beyond endurance.

"On many of these ships," a contemporary said, "the sense of misery and suffocation was so terrible in the 'tween-decks—where the height sometimes was only eighteen inches, so that the unfortunate slaves could not turn round, were wedged immovably, in fact, and chained to the deck by the neck and legs—that the slaves not infrequently would go mad before dying or suffocating. In their frenzy some killed others in the hope of procuring more room to breathe. Men strangled those next to them, and women drove nails into each other's brains."

It was not unusual, John Newton said, to find a dead and living man chained together. So many dead people were thrown overboard on slavers that it was said that sharks would pick up a ship off the coast of Africa and follow it to America.

All Negroes did not come this way. There was a trickle of free immigrants from the West Indies. And some black men and women got on boats in Africa and paid their way to America. In 1772, for example, the governor of Georgia issued a certificate to Fenda Lawrence, "a free black woman and heretofore a considerable trader in the river Gambia on the coast of Africa [who] hath voluntarily come to be and remain for some time in this province." The certificate gave Miss Lawrence permission to "pass and repass unmolested within the said province on her lawful and necessary occasions." Fenda Lawrence, of course, was an exception. Most Negroes came in chains, followed by wise and greedy sharks.

The survivors of this gruelling ordeal were sold either on the ships or in slave markets in American ports. In New England, where there was a large "retail" demand, slaves were sold in taverns, stores, and warehouses. Some were "shown," as the ads put it, in the merchants' homes.

Some slave merchants sold Negroes and whites, liquor, clothing and other goods. One merchant, for example, advertised: "Several Irish Maid Servants time/most of them for Five Years one/Irish Man Servant—one who is a good/Barber and Wiggmaker/also Four or Five Likely Negro Boys."

The price of men, like the price of butter, fluctuated. George Washington, for example, bought a man slave for $260 in 1754. But when he went to the market ten years later, he had to pay $285.

Slaves were sold for small down payments and "on reasonable

terms." An advertisement of 1726 noted that "the Buyer shall have 3, 6, 9 or 12 months Credit." There was also a mail-order business. One New Englander noted in his diary that "I wrote Mr. Salmon of Barbadoes to send me a negro."

The human factories in Africa struggled to keep up with the demand. In the eighteenth century, between 50,000 and 100,000 Negro slaves crossed the Atlantic each year. The greatest number, by far, went to the West Indies and Brazil. At least two million were shipped to the West Indies. João Pandiá Calogeras, the Brazilian historian, said at least eighteen million were shipped to Brazil. Arthur Ramos, another Brazilian, thinks this figure is too high. Five million, he says, is a more accurate estimate.

Large blocks of slaves were dropped off in Spanish colonies in the Caribbean and in Central and South America. As early as 1553, there were twenty thousand Negroes in Mexico. Some 200,000 slaves were imported before slavery was abolished in Mexico in the first quarter of the nineteenth century.

Hundreds of thousands of slaves were scattered over the areas of present-day Panama, Colombia, Ecuador, Chile, Peru, and Venezuela. In 1810, Venezuela had some 500,000 Negroes in a total population of 900,000. In 1847, there were 496,000 Negroes in Cuba and only 418,000 whites. In the same year, there were 4,400,000 Negroes in Brazil's population of 7,360,000. More than 1,000,000 of the Brazilian Negroes, incidentally, were free.

Widespread amalgamation and unreliable census data make it difficult to assess the impact of these millions on South American life. But in some South American countries people with "Negro blood" still comprise a considerable proportion of the population. What Gilberto Freyre, the Brazilian sociologist and philosopher, said of Brazil is true for a great part of the New World. "Every Brazilian, even if he is light skinned and has fair hair, bears in his soul . . . the shadow or the mark of the native or the Negro. Of the Negro particularly on the seaboard, from Maragnan to Rio Grande in the South and in the State of Mines. The influence of the African is direct or vague and remote. In our way of expressing tenderness, in our excessive mimicry, in our Catholicism which is a delight of the senses, in our way of walking and talking, in the songs which cradled our childhood, in short in all the sincere expressions of our life, the Negro influence is patent."

For the human chattel involved, the slave trade was a stupendous roulette wheel. The boats fanned out from Africa and scattered human freight over the Western Hemisphere; around and around the wheel went, stopping here and there, sealing, wherever it stopped, the fate of mothers and fathers and their children to the nth generation.

It made a great deal of difference to the slaves where the dice of fate fell—whether they landed, for example, in a country where *the* word was the Spanish *yo* or the French *je* or the English "I." Slavery, to be sure, was a form of hell wherever it existed. But there were gradations of hell, Dantesque circles, as it were, within circles. By all accounts, the British-Protestant colonies were the deepest pit. The Roman Catholic colonies, especially the Portuguese and Spanish colonies, were, by comparison, relatively mild. The French and Spanish could be cruel, and often were. But they did not seem to be driven by the same demons that pursued the Puritans. They did not, for example, interfere as much in the personal lives of the slaves. In the Roman Catholic colonies, African religious practices and other elements of African culture were not as vigorously opposed as they were in the Protestant colonies. The Protestant colonies, with an instinct for the jugular vein, rode herd on tom-toms and joyful noises unto the Lord. The difference this made in social cohesion is roughly the difference between the successful Haitian Revolution and the abortive Nat Turner insurrection. The final meeting of the Haitian Revolution was held at a *vodun* ceremony and the signal went out by tom-toms. Another difference, minor perhaps, but important to the people involved, was the texture of the different societies. The Catholic colonies were gay and colorful; the Protestant colonies, by comparison, were a dull shade of gray.

More important was the relative absence of color prejudice in

Spanish America and Portuguese Brazil. This fact gave a certain tone to social intercourse. And the life of a slave in these colonies was less hopeless and unhappy than the life of a slave in, say, South Carolina. In Brazil there was a state officer, a protector of slaves, who looked after the welfare of the disadvantaged.

Manumission was easier in Brazil and Spanish America. And a manumitted slave inherited the rights and privileges of citizens. There were several ways in which a slave could win freedom. If he could earn his purchase price, he could walk up to his master and hand him the money—and the master had to accept it. He could earn money on Sundays and religious holidays. Another means of salvation was childbearing. If slave parents had ten children in Hispanic America, the whole family went free.

The difference between Hispanic America and Protestant America reduces itself, as so many racial problems do, to the problem of sex. For reasons that are not entirely explicable, the Spanish and Portuguese were willing to marry Negroes. In America, white men drew the line—at marriage, that is.

In America, in the French, English, Spanish, Dutch, and Danish colonies, the slaves were given a new conception of themselves—according to the different lights of their captors. This process, whether it took place in liberal Brazil or harsh South Carolina, was a painful, mind-reversing operation in which two or three out of every ten died. In one form or another, every slave from Africa went through a "breaking-in" period. During this period, which varied from one to three years, the slave was taught pidgin English or French or Spanish. He got a new name and began to look at himself and others in a different manner. Yahweh took the place of Olorum; Legba became St. Peter; the Mass or hymnal replaced voodoo.* The strain was too much for tens of thousands. Some died

---

* Melville J. Herskovits and other students have analyzed the process by which African slaves blended African and Western religious figures. In some cases, Western saints and rituals were identified with African gods and rituals. Legba, the African trickster-god, was sometimes identified with St. Peter. Domballa, the snake-god, was sometimes identified with St. Patrick. In some cases, an African deity was given the name of a Roman Catholic saint as well as an African name.

from old and new diseases; some refused to give up Shango and wasted away; others ran away and died of exposure; still others committed suicide—drowning was popular in liberal Brazil. Charles S. Johnson has given an excellent description of the "breaking-in" process in South Carolina.

"In the early days of the plantation regime, when a gang of fresh Africans were purchased, they were assigned in groups to certain reliable slaves who initiated them into the ways of the plantation. These drivers, as they were called, had the right of issuing or withholding rations to the raw recruits and of inflicting minor punishments. They taught the new slaves to speak the broken English which they knew and to do the plantation work which required little skill. . . . At the end of a year, the master or overseer for the first time directed the work of the new Negro who now had become 'tamed,' assigning him to a special task of plantation work along with the other seasoned hands who had long since learned to obey orders, to arise when the conch blew at 'day clean,' to handle a hoe in listing and banking, to stand still when a white man spoke."

The merchandising and marketing of men made millionaires in England and America. And many people shared in the profits. "On the eve of the American Revolution," says Dr. Lorenzo J. Greene, "it [the slave trade] formed the very basis of the economic life of New England; about it revolved, and on it depended, most of her other industries. The vast sugar, molasses and rum trade, shipbuilding, the distilleries, a great many of the fisheries, the employment of artisans and seamen, even agriculture—all were dependent upon the slave traffic."

Liverpool in England, Newport in Rhode Island, Nantes in France prospered as slave trading centers. "It was a common saying," Eric Williams reports, "that several of the principal streets of Liverpool had been marked out by the chains, and the walls of the houses cemented by the blood of the African slaves, and one street was nicknamed 'Negro Row.' The red brick Customs House was blazoned with Negro heads. The story is told of an actor in the town, who, hissed by the audience for appearing before them, not for the first time, in a drunken condition, steadied himself and declared with offended majesty: 'I have not come here to be insulted by a set of wretches, every brick in whose infernal town is cemented with an African's blood.' "

"The Western World," Williams contends, "is in danger of forgetting today what the Negro has contributed to Western civilization. . . . London and Bristol, Bordeaux and Marseilles, Cadiz and Seville, Lisbon and New England, all waxed fat on the profits of the trade in the tropical produce raised by the Negro slave. Capitalism in England, France, Holland and colonial America received a double stimulation—from the manufacture of goods needed to exchange for slaves, woolen and cotton goods, copper and brass vessels, and the firearms, handcuffs, chains and torture instruments indispensable on the slave ships and on the slave plantation. . . . This contribution of the Negro has failed to receive adequate recognition. It is more than ever necessary to remember it today. England and France, Holland, Spain and Denmark, not to mention the United States, Brazil and other parts of South America are all indebted to Negro labor."

Africans helped build Liverpool, Nantes and Newport. They helped finance the industrial revolution in England. They helped clear the forest in America. They did these things, but they protested every step of the way. Protests began in Africa, where mutinies on ships were common, and continued in America, where revolts were common. "The negroes," Captain Thomas Phillips said, "are so willful and loth to leave their own country, that they have often leap'd out of the canoes, boat and ship, into the sea, and kept under water till they were drowned, to avoid being taken up and saved by our boats, which pursued them; they having a more dreadful apprehension of Barbadoes than we can have of hell, tho' in reality they live much better there than in their own country; but home is home, etc. . . ."

Home being home, etc., many slaves revolted, brained the captain and crew and escaped to the shore. Rebellions on ships were so common that a new form of insurance was introduced—insurrection insurance.

Many slaves refused to eat when well, and refused to take medicine when ill. One man, for instance, attempted to cut his throat. After the wound was sewed up, he ripped out the sutures with his fingernails. He was patched up again but refused to eat and died ten days later of starvation.

In the West Indies and on the mainland, there were many revolts. A long series of conspiracies and revolts culminated in the great Haitian Revolution which played an important part in the abolition of the trade. Pushed by fear of the unmanageable slaves and pulled by humanitarian motives stemming from the American and French Revolutions, politicians abolished the trade in the nineteenth century. It continued surreptitiously, however, until the final abolition of slavery in the United States.

The slave trade left a bloodstained legacy. During the four centuries the trade was pursued, it wrecked the social and economic life of Africa, set tribe against tribe and village against village. The trade was no less disastrous in Europe and America where it left a legacy of ill will and guilt and a potentially explosive racial problem.

"Raphael painted," W. E. B. Du Bois has said, "Luther preached, Corneille wrote, and Milton sang; and through it all, for four hundred years, the dark captives wound to the sea amid the bleaching bones of the dead; for four hundred years the sharks followed the scurrying ships; for four hundred years America was strewn with the living and dying millions of a transplanted race; for four hundred years Ethiopia stretched forth her hands unto God."

3

The Negro in the

American Revolution

'Tis not the concern of a day, a year, or an age; posterity are virtually involved in the contest, and will be more or less affected even to the end of time. . . . Freedom hath been hunted around the Globe. . . . O! receive the fugitive, and prepare in time an asylum for mankind.

THOMAS PAINE

THERE LIVED in Connecticut in the days preceding the Revolution a patriotic preacher who was given to making pretty speeches about liberty or death. This preacher owned a slave named Jack. The preacher preached and Jack slaved and listened and wondered. One day Jack went to his master and said:

"Master, I observe you always keep preaching about liberty and praying for liberty, and I love to hear you, sir, for liberty be a good thing. You preach well and you pray well; but one thing you remember, Master—Poor Jack ain't free yet."

An irony of fate made Poor Jack and his master polar symbols of one of history's greatest paradoxes: the American Revolution.

Consider the background of that great event. A colony with a half-million slaves decides to go to war in support of the theory that all men are created equal and are "endowed by their Creator with certain unalienable Rights, that among these are Life, Liberty and the pursuit of Happiness."

Consider the prologue. A bold Negro decides to strike a blow for liberty and becomes the first martyr of the Revolution.

Consider the climax. Black men, some of them slaves, enter the lines and sign the Declaration of Independence with their blood. "It was not," Harriet Beecher Stowe said, "for their own land they fought, not even for a land which had adopted them, but for a land which had enslaved them, and whose laws, even in freedom, oftener oppressed than protected. *Bravery, under such circumstances, has a peculiar beauty and merit*." [Emphasis supplied.]

Behind the Revolutionary rhetoric, behind the bombast, behind the living and dying and bleeding is the irony: black men toiled and fought so that white men could be free. This fact was not lost on the Revolutionary generation. It worried good men and women so much that they made Negro freedom an "inevitable corollary" of American freedom. James Otis and Tom Paine, the great propagandists of the Revolution, thundered against British tyranny *and* slaveholder tyranny. Abigail Adams told her husband John: "It always appeared a most iniquitous scheme to me to fight ourselves for what we are daily robbing and plundering from those who have as good a right to freedom as we have."

Thomas Jefferson, a worried slaveholder, inserted a clause in the Declaration of Independence which indicted the King of England for promoting slavery: "He has waged cruel war against human nature itself, violating its most sacred rights of life and liberty in the person of a distant people who never offended him, captivating and carrying them into slavery in another hemisphere, or to incur

Negro patriots were conspicuous in the fighting
the Battle of Bunker Hill. Two Negroes, Peter Sale
and Salem Poor, were outstanding soldiers in t
battle. Poor was later commended for his val

Boston Massacre was one of the events
which led to Revolutionary War.
Several Negroes were in the group
which fought British soldiers on the
night of March 5, 1770. Crispus Attucks
(below, right) was the first person shot
by the soldiers.

miserable death in their transportation thither. . . ." This clause was struck out in deference to slaveholders and slave-carriers who had grave doubts about the meaning of the sentence: "All men are created equal. . . ."

What precisely did the word "all" mean?

This question agitated the minds of men before and after the Revolution; and it played an important role in the prewar jockeying between Patriots and Loyalists (Colonials who sided with Great Britain). Ingenious Patriots called on the poor and unenfranchised for support and these classes, having tasted power, became increasingly independent. Having nothing to lose in a reshuffle of power, sailors, artisans and Negroes rioted against British officials, stoned the houses of Loyalists and voiced open demands for representation and property *in America*. "The Revolution," one historian noted, "was not merely a question of 'home rule'; it was also a question of who should rule at home."

An untold story of this era is the part Negroes played in the agitation which isolated the Loyalists and forced an open break with England. Negroes were prominent in the tumultuous Stamp Act riots. John Miller has described one of these riots. "For a fortnight, the tension in Boston continued to increase, until, on the night of August 28 [1765], boys and Negroes began to build bonfires in King Street and blow the dreaded whistle and horn that sent the Boston mob swarming out of taverns, houses and garrets. A large crowd immediately gathered around the bonfires, bawling for 'Liberty and Property.' "

When British troops were dispatched to Boston to awe the populace, Negroes and whites drove them out. Several months before the Boston Massacre, British soldiers tangled with Bostonians. One Boston newspaper commented: "In the morning nine or ten soldiers of Colonel Carr's regiment were severely whipped on the Commons. To behold Britons scourged by Negro drummers was a new and very disagreeable spectacle."

All through the long winter of 1769, soldiers and citizens fought a cold war. There were provocations on both sides and innumerable street brawls and tavern fights. In the spring of 1770, tension reached the explosion point. On Friday, March 2, three soldiers got into a scrape with the ropemakers. The soldiers were driven off, but they returned with reinforcements headed by a lanky Negro man. A townsman upbraided the Negro. "You black rascal," he called out, "what have you to do with white people's quarrels?" The Negro replied sweetly, "I suppose I may look on."

The Negro looked on—and threw a few punches. Despite his help, the soldiers were driven off. They stalked away, nursing their wounds, shouting curses and threats. Rumors and predictions of disaster swept the town. By Sunday night, Boston was boiling.

Monday morning dawned cold and grey. There was a film of ice on the ground. Toward evening, the sky cleared and a young moon bobbled up over Beacon Hill. Lights and eerie shadows played across the streets which were filled now with boys and men spoiling for a fight.

A little after eight, soldiers emerged from a barracks near the center of town. They were armed with cudgels and tongs. Townsmen gathered in front of the barracks and waited to see what the hour would demand of them. In the center of this group stood a giant who was no stranger to "white people's quarrels." He was six-feet-two and looked taller. Although his "knees were nearer together than common," he moved gracefully. He had large powerful arms and big hands. His name was Crispus Attucks, but some men called him "the mulatto." He was a native of Framingham, Massachusetts, where he was born some time around 1723. A Negro with some Indian blood, Attucks had spent several years as a slave and had escaped. After his escape in 1750, he went to sea as a sailor. Tall, brawny, with a look that "was enough to terrify any person," Attucks was well known around the docks in lower Boston.

Attucks was not a proper Bostonian, a fact which has pained innumerable historians. He was a drifter of sorts, a man who loved freedom and knew what it was worth. He was about forty-seven, fearless and commanding. When he spoke, men listened. When he commanded, men acted.

"The mulatto" was the hero on the memorable night of the Boston Massacre. He moved among the people, urging them to stand their ground. They stood firm; so did the soldiers. Insults were exchanged. A fight flared. Attucks led a group of citizens who drove the soldiers back to the gate of the barracks. The soldiers rallied and drove the people back. The sound of clubs striking on human flesh could be heard for several blocks away. Someone ran to the Old Brick Meeting House and rang the fire bell. People poured out of houses.

A small boy ran through the crowd holding his head and screaming, "Murder! Murder!" He told the people that the sentry in front of the custom house had bashed him across the head with his musket. The furious crowd moved to the custom house in three groups. One group, holding clubs over their heads, huzzaing and whistling, followed the intrepid mulatto, Crispus Attucks.

The crowd gathered before the sentry in the square facing the custom house. The boy came up and said, "This is the . . . who hit me." Someone said, "Kill him. Knock his head off." Another voice said: "Burn the sentry box. Tear it up."

Backing off, the sentry climbed the steps of the custom house and called for help. Down King (now State) Street came seven soldiers, clearing the way before them with bayonet thrusts. The soldiers made a semicircle around the sentry box. Captain Thomas Preston joined them.

"Do not be afraid," Attucks and his group cried. "They dare not fire."

The people took up the cry.

"Fire! Fire! and be damned!"

Bells clanged. The air vibrated with curses and threats.

"Fire!" the crowd shouted. "Fire, and be damned!"

Attucks and the men following him gave three cheers and moved to the front of the crowd. A stick sailed over their heads and struck Private Hugh Montgomery who fell back, lifted his musket and fired. Attucks pitched forward in the gutter. Sam Gray, a ropemaker, made a step toward Attucks. Another soldier fired. Gray spun around on his heel and fell on his back. When the smoke cleared several persons lay bleeding in the white snow.

The die was cast.

"From that moment," Daniel Webster said, "we may date the severance of the British Empire." John Adams, America's second President, said: "Not the Battle of Lexington or Bunker Hill, not the surrender of Burgoyne or Cornwallis were more important events in American history than the battle of King Street on the 5th of March, 1770."

One hundred and eighteen years later, a handsome monument was erected to the victims. Poet John Boyle O'Reilly contributed a spirited poem to the occasion.

And honor to Crispus Attucks, who was leader and voice that day:
The first to defy, and the first to die, with Maverick, Carr, and Gray.
Call it riot or revolution, or mob or crowd as you may,
Such deaths have been seed of nations, such lives shall be honored for
    ay . . .

"Attucks little thought," wrote Dr. Samuel Green, "that in future generations a monument of granite and bronze on a public site would be erected in honor of himself and his comrades for the part they took in the State Street fight; and that his own name, cut in stone, would lead the list of those who fell on that eventful evening. 'Thus the whirligig of Time brings in his revenges,' and verifies the Gospel saying: 'But many that are first shall be last; and the last shall be first.'"

Having played an important role in precipitating the conflict, Negroes were in the front ranks in the first battles. When Paul Revere galloped through the Massachusetts countryside, he alerted Negro and white minutemen. Negroes were at Lexington and at the bridge in Concord. Lemuel Haynes was there and Samuel Craft and Peter Salem and Pomp Blackman and Job Potomea and Isaiah Barjonah. Lemuel Haynes was also at Ticonderoga when Ethan Allen invoked Great Jehovah and the Continental Congress. So were Primas Black and Epheram Blackman, two members of the famous Green Mountain Boys.

When British troops stormed up Breed's Hill in the battle mistakenly called Bunker Hill, Negro Patriots were in the ranks with white Patriots. One of the heroes of that hot June afternoon was Peter Salem who shot Major Pitcairn when he popped up and announced, a trifle prematurely, "The day is ours." Among the many Negro soldiers who fought at Bunker Hill were Prince Hall, Pomp Fisk, Cuff Hayes, Caesar Dickerson, Caesar Weatherbee and Salem Poor. The two Salems—Peter Salem and Salem Poor—were among the great heroes of the war. Poor was later commended by fourteen officers who said he "behaved like an experienced officer, as well as an excellent soldier. To set forth particulars of his conduct would be tedious . . . in the person of this said Negro centres a brave and gallant soldier."

The Battle of Bunker Hill was fought in June. In July, George Washington took command of the American troops. An order went out immediately from his headquarters forbidding the enlistment of Negroes.

Several factors entered into the decision to bar Negroes. Despite the evidence of their eyes, some officers insisted that Negroes were poor soldiers. Others said it was shameful to ask Negroes to die for white men. Still others said it was dangerous to use Negro troops. If America used Negroes, they reasoned, so would England.

The argument raged through the fall of that year. It was debated in Congress and in coffeehouses and manors. General Washington summoned his general officers and they sat down in October to debate the question. It was decided finally to bar all Negroes, slave and free. Washington issued an order to this effect on November 12, 1775.

Seven days earlier, however, Lord Dunmore, the deposed royal governor of Virginia, had taken a step which eventually forced Washington to reconsider. From his ship in Norfolk harbor, Dunmore proclaimed freedom to all male slaves who were willing and able to bear arms. Thousands of slaves immediately deserted their masters to fight for *their* freedom. At Kemp's Landing in Virginia, they proved their mettle by defeating a group of Virginians. When the white men broke ranks and retreated into the swamps, the former slaves gave chase. At this point occurred one of those little incidents that illuminate a whole era. One Colonel Hutchings, a proper Virginian, was cornered by a Negro man he recognized as one of his escaped slaves. Naturally, the colonel was indignant. He fired at his ex-slave. But the bullet missed. The ex-slave closed in and whacked his former master across the face with a saber. Then, in the greatest humiliation of all, Colonel Hutchings was led into the British lines by his own former slave.

Thoroughly alarmed by the Dunmore proclamation, Virginians attempted to pacify their slaves. One paper ran a long editorial under the heading: "CAUTION TO NEGROES." The *Virginia Gazette* said: "Be not then, ye Negroes, tempted by this proclamation to ruin yourselves . . . whether we suffer or not, if you desert us, you most certainly will."

General Washington was also alarmed. He reversed himself and permitted the enlistment of free Negroes who had fought in the early battles. Congress approved this order, but again refused to countenance the enlistment of slaves.

Circumstances, however, made this a moot point. For one thing, it was very difficult to coax white men into the Continental Line. Although there were some one million men of fighting age in the colonies, the Continental Line never exceeded fifty thousand soldiers at one time. Bounties of land and money were offered to volunteers. Some states even offered bounties of Negroes. Nothing, however, flushed the backsliders. "Such a dearth of public spirit," Washington said, "and want of virtue, such stock-jobbing and fertility in all the low arts to obtain advantage of one kind or another . . . I never saw before, and I pray God I may never be a witness to again. Such a dirty mercenary Spirit pervades the whole that I should not be at all surprised at any disaster that may happen." Washington went into the terrible ordeal of Valley Forge in December, 1777, with some nine thousand men. By March of 1778, more than three thousand men had deserted.

After Valley Forge, every able-bodied man, Negro or white,

slave or free, was welcome in the Continental Army. Washington sent an officer from Valley Forge in 1778 to ask the Rhode Island Assembly to authorize the enlistment of Negro slaves. In February, the Assembly took this precedent-shattering step. Two months later, Massachusetts followed. By the end of the war, some five thousand Negroes, slaves and freemen, had shouldered arms in defense of American liberty. There were Negro soldiers from every one of the original thirteen states, including South Carolina and Georgia. Most of these soldiers served in integrated units, although there were a few all-Negro groups, notably the ones from Rhode Island, Connecticut, and Massachusetts. Colonel Middleton, a Negro, commanded a group of Negro volunteers from Massachusetts.

Several witnesses remarked on the integrated character of the American Army. In the first months of the war, British writers taunted Americans with this jingle:

> *The rebel clowns, oh! what a sight*
> *Too awkward was their figure*
> *'Twas yonder stood a pious wight*
> *And here and there a nigger.*

A Southern soldier serving in the Army around Boston in 1775 wrote: "Such Sermons, such Negroes, such Colonels, such Boys and such Great Great Grandfathers." A few years later, a Hessian officer said: "The Negro can take the field instead of the master; and therefore, no regiment is to be seen in which there are not Negroes in abundance and among them there are able bodied, strong and brave fellows."

Negro soldiers fought in practically all the big battles of the war. They were at Monmouth, Red Bank, Saratoga, Savannah, Princeton, and Yorktown. Two Negroes, Prince Whipple and Oliver Cromwell, made the famous Delaware Crossing. Another Negro participated in the daring capture of General Prescott in Rhode Island.

Negro soldiers fought and they fought brilliantly. A memorable tableaux of the war is of the bloody battlefield at Eutaw, South

Carolina, where a Negro soldier and a British soldier were found dead, each impaled on the bayonet of the other. At the Battle of Rhode Island, a regiment of Negro soldiers repulsed the vaunted Hessians three times. "Had they been unfaithful," one soldier said, "or even given away before the enemy all would have been lost."

No less valiant were the heroic defenders of Fort Griswold in Connecticut. When the British officer, Major Montgomery, was lifted over the walls, Jordan Freeman ran him through with a pike. Then, when Colonel Ledyard was murdered with his own sword, Lambert Latham immediately avenged his death by slaying the British officer. The Redcoats pounced on Latham, who fell dead, pierced by thirty-three bayonet wounds.

Negro seamen, sailors and pilots distinguished themselves in the infant Navy. Caesar Terront piloted the Virginia vessel, the "Patriot," and was cited for his gallantry in action. Captain Mark Starlin, the only Negro naval captain in Virginia's history, made daring night raids on British vessels in Hampton Roads. Starlin was reclaimed by his master after the war and died in slavery.

There were also Negro spies and undercover agents in the Revolutionary War. A slave named Pompey was largely responsible for Anthony Wayne's capture of the Stony Point, New York, fort in 1779. Feigning ignorance, he obtained the British password and helped a detachment of Americans overpower the British lookout. Perhaps the greatest of all Negro spies was James Armistead, a Virginian who helped trap Cornwallis. General Lafayette told Armistead to go into Cornwallis' camp and learn his strength and battle plans. Armistead was so successful that General Cornwallis asked him to spy on Lafayette. The Negro spy shuttled between the British and American camps, carrying false information to the Cornwallis camp and bona fide information to Lafayette.

Every schoolboy knows that Lafayette and Kosciusko answered America's call for help. Not so well known is the fact that Negroes from Haiti came to America to fight. The Haitians, who called themselves the Fontages Legion, did yeoman service at the siege of Savannah and helped prevent a rout of the American forces.

With Washington when he crossed the Delaware were at least two Negroes, Prince Whipple and Oliver Cromwell. Whipple was bodyguard to Washington's aide, General William Whipple of New Hampshire.

Richard Allen, Phillis Wheatley, and Prince Hall were outstanding Negroes in the Revolutionary and post-Revolutionary periods. Allen organized the AME Church. Wheatley became an internationally known poet. Hall (right) organized the first Negro Masonic Lodge.

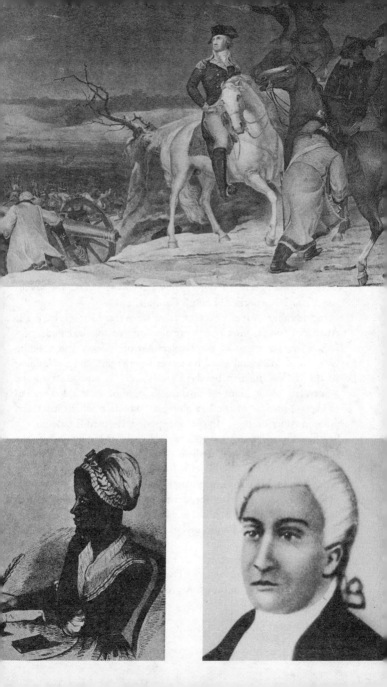

More than 100,000 Negro slaves received their freedom as a direct result of this war for freedom. Aptheker believes that at least 100,000 voted with their feet. Some of these slaves made their way to Canada or Florida. Others took refuge in Indian camps. Still others were befriended by the British. When the Redcoats embarked in 1782 and 1783, several thousand Negroes went with them.

A large number of escaped slaves hid in the swamps and made guerrilla raids on their former masters. In 1781, a Virginia slaveholder wrote: "We have had most alarming times this Summer, all along the shore, from a set of Barges manned mostly by our own Negroes who have run off—These fellows are really dangerous to an individual singled out for their vengeance whose Property lay exposed—They burnt several houses." As late as 1786, a group of ex-slaves who called themselves the King of England's Soldiers were fighting guerrilla actions against slaveowners along the Savannah River in Georgia and South Carolina.

In addition to slaves who escaped or were freed for service in the American forces, thousands were manumitted by slaveholders infected by the magic of the Declaration of Independence. Philip Graham of Maryland freed his slaves in 1787 and said the holding of his "fellow men in bondage and slavery is repugnant to the golden law of God and the unalienable right of mankind as well as to every principle of the late glorious revolution which has taken place in America. . . ." In the same period, Richard Randolph, the brother of the famous John Randolph, came of age and wrote the following letter to his guardian. "With regard to the division of the estate, I have only to say that I want not a single Negro for any other purpose than his immediate liberation. I consider every individual thus unshackled as the source of future generations, not to say nations, of freemen; and I shudder when I think that so insignificant an animal as I am is invested with this monstrous, this horrid power."

Scores of Negroes, moreover, turned the Rights of Man movement to their own advantage. They peppered courts and legislatures with petitions and suits. A group of slaves told the Massachusetts Assembly in 1777 "that every principle from which America has acted, in the course of her unhappy difficulties with Great Britain, bears stronger than a thousand arguments in favor of your humble petitioners."

Slavery died in the North as a direct result of forces set in motion by the Rights of Man movement. By legislative decrees and by court action, Negro slaves were declared free men. In some states, legislative emancipation was a gradual process extending over several years. The preamble of the Pennsylvania act for the gradual abolition of slavery accurately reflected the spirit of the age. The preamble said it was the duty of Pennsylvanians to give proof of their gratitude for deliverance from the oppression of Great Britain "by extending freedom to those of a different color by the work of the same Almighty hand."

It seemed for a time that slavery would die in the South, but the invention of the cotton gin and other mechanical devices cooled the Revolutionary ardor of Southern patriots.

The period in which slavery died in the North was a crucial period in the history of the American Negro. For a short spell in the North and for an even shorter spell in the South, it seemed that good men might solve the classic American Dilemma. Baptists and Methodists strongly condemned slavery. Negroes like Joshua Bishop of Virginia and Lemuel Haynes of New England pastored white churches. Haynes, who was probably the first Negro to preach regularly to white audiences, was a Congregationalist. The son of a white woman and an African native, he was fair-skinned and eloquent. When he was appointed pastor of a church in Torrington, Connecticut, a leading citizen was so displeased with "the nigger minister" that he decided to sit through the sermon with his hat on. "He had not preached far," the man said later, "when I thought I saw the whitest man I ever knew in that pulpit, and I tossed my hat under the pew."

During this period, Phillis Wheatley became an internationally-known poet and Benjamin Banneker became a celebrated mathematician. Banneker and Wheatley, in different ways and in different places, dramatized the possibilities and limitations of the age. In an age in which few women—or men for that matter—read books, Phillis Wheatley wrote one. Her book, *Poems on Various Subjects, Religious and Moral*, was the first volume by a Negro woman and the second book by an American woman.*

Phillis Wheatley did not write as a Negro; she wrote as an eighteenth-century Bostonian, a *proper* eighteenth-century Bostonian. When George Washington was appointed commander in chief of the American Army, she celebrated the event in heroic couplets. Washington was delighted. On February 28, 1776, he acknowledged receipt of the poems in a letter addressed to "Miss Phillis":

"Thank you most sincerely for your polite notice of me, in the elegant lines you enclosed; and however undeserving I may be of such encomium and panegyric, the style and manner exhibited a striking proof of your poetical talents; in honor of which, and as a tribute justly due to you, I would have published the poem, had I not been apprehensive that, while I only meant to give the world this new instance of your genius, I might have incurred the imputation of vanity."

Phillis Wheatley visited the American commander at Cambridge and was entertained by the general and his staff.

Above everything else, the Boston poet sang songs of Thanksgiving. She was grateful for the gift of Christianity, grateful even that a slave ship brought her to it:

> *'Twas mercy brought me from my Pagan land,*
> *Taught my benighted soul to understand*
> *That there's a God, that there's a Saviour too:*
> *Once I redemption neither sought nor knew.*

A delicate wisp of a woman, black, slight of build, with great glimmering eyes, a pert nose and a mystic air, Phillis Wheatley was born in Africa in an unknown place. She came to America in 1761,

* Jupiter Hammon, a New York slave, was probably the first Negro author. His poem, *An Evening Thought: Salvation by Christ, with Penetential Cries*, was printed as a broadside in 1760.

remembering nothing save that her mother poured out water each morning "before the sun at its rising." She was seven or eight when the slave ship deposited her in Boston. John Wheatley, a rich merchant and tailor, saw her shivering on a Boston slave block, stark naked except for a dirty piece of carpet around her loins. Wheatley bought her and took her home to his wife, Susannah. Within sixteen months, the slave girl was reading and writing fluent English. She read every book she could lay hands on: the Bible, Milton and Alexander Pope's translation of Homer. Pope, the neoclassic Englishman, was her special favorite. Timidly at first and then with increasing confidence, she put down words in the Pope manner. Within six years after her arrival in America, Phillis Wheatley was writing poetry. Her first poem, written at the age of fourteen, was a blank verse eulogy of Harvard University. Six years later, the slim girl from Africa was an internationally-known poet. In 1773, she visited England and was hailed as a prodigy. An English publisher brought out her slim volume.

Her poems do not excite modern critics. The verdict is practically unanimous: too much Pope and not enough Wheatley. But her ease with words, her genius for sound and color and rhythm: these still excite awe and wonder.

Phillis Wheatley lived in the State Street house with the white Wheatleys and moved in a white world, apparently as an equal. Upon the death of her patron, Susannah Wheatley, the Negro poet came face to face with racial reality. She married John Peters, a handsome grocer who "wore a wig, carried a cane, and quite acted out 'the gentleman.'" The marriage didn't work. Proud and, some say, irresponsible, Peters alienated his wife's white friends. The couple drifted from place to place, carrying with them the first child and then the second child. Poverty and disease dogged them; the first child died and then the second. After the birth of the third child, Phillis was reduced to earning her bread in a mean boarding house. She had never been too strong and the exertion and the cold and the wretchedness were too much for her. On a cold day in December, 1784, mother and child died within a few hours of each other.

Phillis Wheatley said nothing of her personal griefs in her poems that survive; nor did she say much about the trials and tribulations of Negroes. But on at least one occasion she abandoned Pope and Homer and the Greeks and said words from a woman's heart. The poem was to the Earl of Dartmouth:

> *Should you, my lord, while you peruse my song,*
> *Wonder from whence my love of* Freedom *sprung,*
> *Whence flow these wishes for the common good,*
> *By feeling hearts alone best understood,*
> *I, young in life, by seeming cruel fate*
> *Was snatch'd from* Afric's *fancy'd happy seat:*
> *What pangs excruciating must molest,*
> *What sorrows labour in my parent's breast?*
> *Steel'd was that soul and by no misery mov'd*
> *That from a father seiz'd his babe belov'd:*
> *Such, such my case. And can I then but pray*
> *Others may never feel tyrannic sway?*

Benjamin Banneker, like Phillis Wheatley, was a child of an age of birth pains. He was born in Maryland, the grandson of an Englishwoman and an African native. The Englishwoman, Molly Welsh, came to America as an indentured servant, worked her time out and bought a farm and two slaves. She freed the slaves and married one of them. Banneker's mother, Mary, was one of four children born to this union. Banneker's father was an African native.

Banneker attended a local school with Negro and white children. Like Phillis Wheatley, he hungered and thirsted after books. His forte, however, was science—mathematics and astronomy. He became so proficient in these subjects that he was named to the commission which surveyed the territory which became Washington, D.C. The Georgetown *Weekly Ledger* of March 12, 1791, noted the arrival of the commission. Banneker, the paper said, was "an Ethiopian whose abilities as surveyor and astronomer already prove that Mr. [Thomas] Jefferson's concluding that that race of men were void of mental endowment was without foundation."

Beginning in 1791, Banneker issued an annual almanac which has been compared with Benjamin Franklin's *Poor Richard's Almanac.*

He also continued the study of astronomy and other scientific subjects.

His was an idyllic life. He lived on a farm, about ten miles outside Baltimore. A confirmed bachelor, he studied all night, slept in the morning and worked in the afternoon. He washed his own clothes, cooked his own meals and cultivated gardens around his log cabin. He had an early fondness for "strong drink," but later became a teetotaler.

His habits of study were odd, to say the least. Of a night, he would wrap himself in a great cloak and lie under a pear tree and meditate on the revolutions of the heavenly bodies. He would remain there throughout the night and take to his bed at dawn.

A contemporary has left a portrait of the stargazer. "His head was covered with a thick suit of white hair, which gave him a very dignified and venerable appearance. . . . His dress was uniformly of superfine broadcloth, made in the old style of a plain coat, with straight collar and long waistcoat, and a broad-brimmed hat. His color was not jet-black, but decidedly Negro. In size and personal appearance, the statue of Franklin at the Library of Philadelphia, as seen from the street, is a perfect likeness. Go to his house when you would, either by day or night, there was constantly standing in the middle of the floor a large table covered with books and papers. As he was an eminent mathematician, he was constantly in correspondence with other mathematicians in this country, with whom there was an interchange of questions of difficult solution."

Banneker, unlike Wheatley, boldly lashed out at the injustices of the age. In a famous letter of 1791, he reminded Thomas Jefferson that words were one thing and slavery was another. "Suffer me to recall to your mind that time, in which the arms of the British crown were exerted, with every powerful effort, in order to reduce you to a state of servitude; look back, I entreat you . . . you were then impressed with proper ideas of the great violation of liberty, and the free possession of those blessings, to which you were entitled by nature; but, sir, how pitiable is it to reflect, that although you were so fully convinced of the benevolence of the Father of

Mankind, and of his equal and impartial distribution of these rights and privileges which he hath conferred upon them, that you should at the same time counteract his mercies, in detaining by fraud and violence, so numerous a part of my brethren under groaning captivity and cruel oppression, that you should at the same time be found guilty of that most criminal act, which you professedly detested in others."

Banneker and Wheatley demonstrated, in their own ways, latent possibilities in the burgeoning American Dream. To be sure, things were not rosy in this period. But some men, a very few men, had room to dream and dare and hope.

Then the roof caved in. When did this happen? No man can say. It happened at different times in different ways in different places. Caste lines hardened; racial hostility increased. Free Negroes were taunted, insulted, assaulted and driven off the streets. Slaves were hemmed in by restrictive rules designed to deny them even the rudiments of human personality.

Several factors entered into the change. There was, first of all, the conservative reaction which followed the Revolution. The increase in the number of free Negroes and the failure of various plans to get rid of them alarmed laborers and aristocrats. Then the Haitian Revolution of 1791 and the Gabriel conspiracy in Virginia frightened liberals and conservatives.

The Haitian Revolution, the invention of the cotton gin, slave conspiracies in America, the increase in the number of free Negroes—all these things played a part in the birth of the American Negro. It would not be too much of an exaggeration to say that the American Negro, as a group, did not exist before the Revolution. The first Negro churches were founded in 1773 in South Carolina and in 1776 in Virginia. There then followed the conservative reaction which forced Negroes North and South to look around them and ask the question of the Jewish poet of captivity: "How shall we sing the LORD'S song in a strange land?"

Richard Allen and Absalom Jones were trying to sing that song within the dominant society when they were pulled off their knees in a white church in Philadelphia. They immediately organized the Free African Society. Out of this society came the African Methodist Episcopal Church. There was a similar development in New York City. The withdrawal of Negroes from the John Street Methodist Episcopal Church led to the establishment of the AME Zion church. Taunted, ridiculed, insulted and abused, Negroes in New York, Philadelphia, Boston and other Northern centers withdrew and formed their own organizations.

What did it mean to be a Negro in the America of that period?

Listen to Prince Hall, son of an English father and a Negro mother, a Revolutionary War veteran who later became a Methodist and organized the first Negro Masonic Lodge. Listen to his charge to Boston's African Lodge.

"Patience, I say; for were we not possessed of a great measure of it, we could not bear up under the daily insults we meet with in the streets of Boston, much more on public days of recreation. How, at such times, are we shamefully abused, and that to such a degree, that we may truly be said to carry our lives in our hands, and the arrows of death are flying about our heads."

The arrows of death and humiliation whistled about the head of Colonel Middleton, another Revolutionary War veteran. During a Boston riot, a group of whites attacked Negroes in front of his home. The old soldier stuck a musket out of his door and threatened to kill any white man who approached. One of his neighbors, a white man, asked the whites to leave. Then he approached Colonel Middleton and begged him to put away his gun. Colonel Middleton stood silent for a moment. Then he turned and tottered off, dropping his gun and weeping as he went.

Colonel Middleton's America, Prince Hall's America and Thomas Jefferson's America tottered into the nineteenth century, divided and afraid.

4

Behind the Cotton Curtain

Slavery time was tough, boss. You just don't know how tough it was.

TINES KENDRICKS, AN EX-SLAVE

FOR TWO HUNDRED YEARS, black, brown and yellow men and women were held in bondage in America. During these two hundred years, "a social system as coercive as any yet known," was erected on the flimsy framework of "the most implacable race-consciousness yet observed in virtually any society."

A curtain of cotton rang down on some four million human beings. It became a crime to teach these men and women to read and write; it became a crime to give them a Bible.

Behind this Cotton Curtain, four million human beings were systematically deprived of every right of personality. Vice, immorality and brutality were institutionalized. The sanctity of the family was violated; children were sold from mothers and fatherhood, in effect, was outlawed. The rape of a slave woman, a Mississippi court ruled, is an offense unknown to common or civil law. The "father of a slave," ruled a Kentucky court, "is unknown to our law."

Out of this system came the American Negro and, though some would like to forget it, the American white man; for everyone—Negroes and whites, free men of color and slaves, slaveholders and nonslaveholders—was stained by it. In this system, in this back alley of American history, the American Dream was temporarily derailed for millions and fear, hate, prejudice and guilt were generated for millions more. It is not possible to know much about the Negro or the white man unless one knows a little about those terrible two hundred years through which they came together. "The pro-slavery theory of the *ante-bellum* South," Gunnar Myrdal writes, "is basic to certain ideas, attitudes, and policies prevalent in all fields of human relations even at the present time."

Until quite recently, it was fashionable to view this era through the mint julep glasses of *Gone With the Wind*. A radical re-evaluation in scholarly circles has largely destroyed this myth. One of the most encouraging facets of this re-evaluation is the new stress being placed on American Negro slavery as a moving chapter in the human drama. In an era of resurgent totalitarianism, in an era of big lies and big whips, scholars are going back to this dark alley to find answers relevant to the questions of today. Historian Stanley M. Elkins has reminded us that the only "mass experience that Western people have had within recorded history comparable in any way with Negro slavery was undergone in the nether world of Nazism. The concentration camp was not only a perverted slave system; it was also—what is less obvious but even more to the point—a perverted patriarchy."

Another historian, Kenneth M. Stampp, has underlined with clarity and power the relevance of Aunt Hagar to all men. Stampp, whose book (*The Peculiar Institution*) destroyed the intellectual props of plantation apologists, says: "The record of slave resistance forms a chapter in the story of the endless struggle to give dignity to human life. Though the history of southern bondage reveals that men *can* be enslaved under certain conditions, it also demonstrates that their love of freedom is hard to crush. The subtle expressions of this spirit, no less than the daring thrusts for liberty, comprise one of the richest gifts the slaves have left to posterity."

Let us go back in time to *The Peculiar Institution* which stamped these people. Let us feel the lash which broke their skins and sing the "sorrow songs" which soothed their hearts. "O Lord, O my Lord! O my good Lord, keep me from sinking down." Let us visit the houses and the fields where all the trouble started.

The big white house stands in colonnaded splendor on a hill which overlooks fields fleeced with cotton or lined with tobacco or sugar cane or rice. Near this house, which oftentimes was neither big nor very white, huddle two rows of "log-and-daub" cabins. Other houses and buildings dot the landscape: the overseer's quarters, the stables, the corn cribs, the gin and press. The center of this agricultural factory is the "big house." From it radiate like spokes the fields and gardens: the sweet potato field, the watermelon patch, the cornfield, the pews of cotton or sugar cane or tobacco or rice. This is a plantation. This is where the trouble started.

Not all Negroes were slaves (there was a substantial free population, even in the South); nor did all slaves work on plantations. (Some 500,000 worked in cities as domestics, skilled artisans and factory hands.) Some Negroes even owned slaves. Benjamin O. Taylor of King George County, Virginia, owned seventy-one bondsmen and ruled from his own big house. And two Negroes in South Carolina owned eighty-four slaves apiece. But they were exceptions. Most Negro slaves worked on plantation-sized units in seven states of the Deep South.

Plantations and planters varied. There were small farmers with two or three slaves, planters with ten to thirty slaves and big planters who owned a thousand or more slaves. Scholars generally agree that slaves received better treatment on the small farms and plantations which did not employ overseers or general managers. Almost half of the bondsmen, however, lived, worked and died on plantations where the owners delegated much of their authority to overseers. And the plantation and its fleecy flower, King Cotton, gave tone and direction to the whole society.

The plantation was a combination factory, village and police precinct. Totalitarian regimentation was pushed to a point which would have pleased the most ardent Fascist. Slave women, for example, usually had little or nothing to do with the raising of their children. They went to the fields in the mornings and left their children at the plantation nurseries. The woman who cared for the Negro children was commonly designated "Aunty," to distinguish her from the "Mammy," the nurse of white children. Sometimes, one woman cared for both white and Negro children. Nannie Williams, an ex-slave, has described a Negro "children's house" directed by Aunt Hannah who weighed "nigh onto three hundred pounds."

"I was Ant Hannah's helper, and each mornin' mama would drap me past Ant Hannah's house. Guess dey was 'bout fo'teen chillun she had to look after, all of 'em black babies. Deed, chile, you ain't gonna believe dis but it's de gospel truth. Ant Hannah had a trough in her back yard—jus' like you put in a pig pen. Well, Ant Hannah would just po' dat trough full of milk an' drag dem chillun up to it. Chillun slop up dat milk jus' like pigs."

Children—boys and girls—flopped around in a state of near nudity until they reached the age of toil. On some plantations they were issued tow-linen shirts; on others they wore guano bags with holes punched in them for the head and arms. Children were never issued shoes until they were sent to the fields, usually at the age of six or seven. Young workers were broken in as water boys or in the "trash gang." At the age of ten or twelve, children—boys and girls—were given a regular field routine.

"Children had to go to the fiel' at six on our place," an ex-slave recalled. "Maybe dey don't do nothin' but pick up stones or tote water, but dey got to get used to bein' dere. Uncle Zack had fit de injuns an' had a twisted leg. Used to set in de shade lookin' at de chillun goin' to de field and mutter, 'Slave young, slave long.' "

Cooking, in many instances, was also a communal concern. Food was prepared in a common kitchen and sent to the workers in the field. In most cases, however, slaves were expected to cook the evening meal in their cabins. The food, which was issued once a week, was generally coarse and lacking in variety. Each adult was given a peck of corn and three or four pounds of bacon or salt pork. Fractional amounts, usually one-half, were allotted to each child in the family. Most slaves supplemented this meager fare by trapping coons and opossums in the fields or by stealing corn from the master's corn cribs and chickens from his chicken coops. Slaves, it should be noted, made a distinction between "taking" and "stealing." It was considered right and proper to "take" anything that belonged to white folk. It was considered wrong to "steal" the property of other slaves.

Twice a year, the regimented slave was issued a clothes ration. A South Carolina planter described a typical allowance in his plantation manual. "Each man gets in the fall 2 shirts of cotton drilling, a pair of woolen pants and a woolen jacket. In the spring 2 shirts of cotton shirting and 2 pr. of cotton pants . . . Each woman gets in the fall 6 yds. of woolen cloth, 6 yds. of cotton drilling and a needle, skein of thread and ½ dozen buttons. In the spring 6 yds. of cotton shirting and 6 yds. of cotton cloth similar to that for men's pants, needle, thread and buttons. Each worker gets a stout pr. of shoes every fall, and a heavy blanket every third year."

Clothes came in two sizes, large and small. And women and men apparently were issued the same kind of shoes. Ex-slaves say "the Negro brogans" burned and blistered in the summer and "got stiff as a board in cold weather." And they seldom fitted. On some plantations, the same man shod slaves and horses. West Turner, an ex-Virginia slave, remembered Old Black Jack Fly, a blacksmith, who would "trace yo' foot in the dirt wid a stick, but it didn't do no good, 'cause he ain't never made de shoes like de dirt say."

Most slaves lived in family-type log cabins, but some lived in large barracks "literally alive with slaves, of all ages, conditions and size." Some of the family cabins were two- and three-room brick or frame structures with windows and brick fireplaces. The vast majority, however, were dark, dank holes built flat on the ground. Five or six were crowded in one room. "Everything," an ex-slave said, "happened in that one room—birth, sickness, death—everything."

There was considerable specialization on the larger plantations. The basic division, of course, was between "field Negroes" and "house Negroes." But there were also artisans, nurses, and drivers. The drivers were slaves appointed to assist the overseer in the field and were charged with keeping order in the quarters. Thoroughly detested by most of their fellow bondsmen, the drivers were an integral part of the plantation command hierarchy. They were, in effect, master sergeants under a lieutenant (overseer), under a captain (master). When there were two or more drivers, one of them was named head driver. "The head driver," one planter said, "is the most important negro on the plantation, and is not required to work like other hands. He is to be treated with more respect than any other negro by both master and overseer. . . . He is to be required to maintain proper discipline at all times; to see that no negro idles or does bad work in the field, and to punish it with discretion on the spot."

The usual punishment was thirty-nine lashes with a cowskin whip. It was not unusual, however, for slaves to receive one hundred or more lashes in one day. Few slaves, no matter how obedient or humble, reached old age without receiving at least one lashing. Masters who were psychotic, sadistic or otherwise mentally unbalanced devised ingenious methods of punishment. And "kind" masters whipped the skin off slaves' backs and washed them down with brine.

"No slave," ex-slave Austin Steward said, "could possibly escape being punished—I care not how attentive they might be, nor how industrious—punished they must be, and punished they were."

Slaves were often punished for oversleeping and impudence. And what was impudence? "Impudence," Frederick Douglass said, might mean "almost anything, or nothing at all, just according to

Slave coffles, driven by "soul-drivers," marched down streets of Washington, D.C., in shadow of the Capitol. Washington was a famous American slave market until 1850

Men, women and children worked in the fields during the slave regime. The large plantation was a combination factory, village and police precinct. For some two hundred years, Negroes were held in bondage in America.

An invoice of ten negroes sent this day to John B Williamson by Geo Kremer named & cost as follows

To wit
Betsey Kackley	$410.00
Nancy Aulick	515.00
Harry & Helen Miller	1200.00
Mary Kootz	600.00
Betsey Ott?	560.00
Isaac & Fanny Brent	992.00
Lucinda Luckett ?	467.50
George Smith	510.00
Amount of my traveling expences & boarding	254.50
of lot No 9 not included in the other bills	39.50
Kremers expences Transporting lot N 9 to Richd	51.00
Carryall hire	6.00
	$5351.00

I have this day delivered the above named negroes costing including my expences and other expences five thousand three hundred & fifty dollars this May 26th 1835

John. W. Pittman

I did intend to leave Nancy child but she made such a damned fuss I had to let her take it I could of got fifty Dollars for so you must add forty Dollars to the above

Invoice lists prices paid for slaves. Seller noted at bottom: "I did intend to leave Nancy child (sic) but she made such a damned fuss I had to let her take it. . . ."

the caprice of the master or overseer, at the moment. But, whatever it is, or is not, if it gets the name of 'impudence,' the party charged with it is sure of a flogging. This offense may be committed in various ways; in the tone of an answer; in answering at all; in not answering; in the expression of the countenance; in the motion of the head; in the gait, manner and bearing of the slave."

"House Negroes," artisans, nurses, and "slave drivers" were the slave elite. They were not necessarily, however, the leaders of slave society. On most plantations, there were two or three slaves whom the other slaves looked to for guidance and direction. These natural leaders received their credentials from strength, age, practical wisdom, or religion. Not a few of these leaders were women. A Louisiana planter, for example, complained that Big Lucy was a leader who "corrupts every young negro in her power." On a South Carolina plantation, Sinda prophesied the end of the world and for a long time no slave on the plantation would work.

"Thus," to quote Kenneth Stampp again, ". . . a slave might reach the upper stratum of his society through intimate contact with his master, by learning to ape his manners, and by rendering him personal service, as well as by being a rebel or a leader of his people. And a bondsman, in his own circle, was as highly sensitive to social distinctions as ever was his master. In a society of unequals —of privileged and inferior castes, of wealth and poverty—the need to find some group to feel superior to is given a desperate urgency."

Older slaves, commonly called uncle or aunt, demanded and received respect and veneration. Douglass has left a memorable description of plantation etiquette. "Strange, and even ridiculous as it may seem," he wrote, ". . . there is not to be found, among any people, a more rigid enforcement of the law of respect to elders, than they [slaves] maintain. . . . A young slave must approach the company of the older with hat in hand and woe betide him, if he fails to acknowledge a favor, of any sort, with the accustomed 'tank'ee,' &c."

There was a systematic attempt to divide the slaves into groups and to play one group off against the other. House slaves were encouraged to remain apart from the other slaves and to identify themselves with the interests of the masters.

Despite strong cross-currents, there was a bond of sympathy between slave groups. And house slaves, no matter how many airs they put on, had a deep interest in the activities in the slave quarters. Not everyone, it should be noted, wanted to be a house slave. In the quarters, a man had a certain amount of freedom which was denied to his brother in the house. It is not surprising, therefore, that the deep and brooding spirituals came not from the house but from the field.

Frederick Law Olmsted, the tireless reporter of the foibles of the South, understood the different textures of house life and field life. "Slaves brought up to house work," he wrote, "dread to be employed at field-labour; and those accustomed to the comparatively unconstrained life of the negro-settlement detest the close control and careful movements required of the house-servants. It is a punishment for a lazy field-hand to employ him in menial duties at the house . . . and it is equally a punishment to a neglectful house-servant, to banish him to the field-gangs."

In the slave quarters, bondsmen developed their own society which differed in many ways from the society of the masters. On most plantations, there were two parties: "the dancing party" and "the praying party." The dancing party apparently commanded the allegiance of the bulk of the slaves. On holidays, especially Christmas, the slaves kicked up their heels in joyous dances, drank strong liquor and persimmon beer and sang "devil songs." Most members of the dancing party were non-Christians or at best nominal Christians. It comes as something of a surprise to find that some of them were anti-Christians who spoke the language of existential absurdity.

> Our father, who is in heaven
> White man owe me eleven, and pay me seven,
> Thy kingdom come, thy will be done,
> And if I hadn't took that, I wouldn't have none.

Saturday night was the dancing party's night. In barns and open fields and in slave row shacks, slaves did jigs, shuffles and "set de flo." They danced to the fiddle or the banjo and beat out rhythms with sticks and bones or by clapping their hands and stomping their feet. The slaves had a word for it, even then. A "cool cat" in those days was a "ring-clipper." If he were aware or, in the jazz idiom, if he were "hip," he was "no bug-eater." On most plantations there were shapely lasses like Miss Lively, a Louisiana belle who had a "well-earned reputation," Solomon Northup said, "of being the 'fastest gal' on the bayou."

The praying party held forth on Sundays. The religion taught the slaves was a censored pablum which dwelt almost always on the duties of obedience. J. W. Fowler of Coahoma County, Mississippi, told his overseer that he had no objection to his slaves hearing the gospel if they heard it in its "original purity and simplicity." What did this mean? Ephesians, 6:5, usually: "Servants, be obedient to them that are *your* masters. . . ."

Few slaves accepted this version of Christianity. Their God was the God who delivered the Israelites.

> *Didn't my Lord deliver Daniel,*
> *And why not every man.*

Ex-slaves say they slipped away to the fields and in "hush-harbors" told God all their troubles. Out of these proscribed meetings and the wakes and other mournful events of the slave quarters came the spirituals which were created, James Weldon Johnson said, by "black and unknown bards."

> *Oh, Mary, don't you weep, don't you moan;*
> *Pharaoh's Army got drownded,*
> *Oh, Mary, don't you weep.*

There were joyful noises unto the Lord:

> *I went down in the valley to pray*
> *My soul got happy and I stayed all day*

There were laments:

> *I'm gonna tell God all my troubles,*
> *When I get home . . .*

> *I'm gonna tell him the road was rocky*
> *When I get home.*

And regrets:

> *Don't know what my mother wants to stay here fuh,*
> *Dis ole world ain't been no friend to huh.*

And tears:

> *I know moon-rise, I know star-rise*
> *Lay dis body down.*
> *I walk in de moonlight, I walk in de starlight,*
> *To lay dis body down.*
> *I'll walk in de graveyard, I'll walk through de graveyard*
> *To lay dis body down.*
> *I'll lie in de grave and stretch out my arms;*
> *Lay dis body down.*
> *I go to de judgement in de evenin' of de day,*
> *When I lay dis body down;*
> *And my soul and your soul will meet in de day*
> *When I lay dis body down.*

I'll lie in de grave and stretch out my arms. The words made shivers run down Thomas Wentworth Higginson's back. "Never," he said, "it seems to me, since man first lived and suffered, was his infinite longing for peace uttered more plaintively than in that line."

An interesting feature of some slave religious meetings was the "ring shout," which has been called an adaptation of the West African circle dance. Anthropologist Ernest Borneman called it "a straight adaptation of African ceremonialism to Christian liturgy." The practice survives, incidentally, in some shouting churches. A celebrated description of the ring shout appeared in the *Nation*.

. . . the benches are pushed back to the wall, when the formal meeting is over, and old and young, men and women, sprucely-dressed young men, grotesquely half-clad field hands—the women generally with gay handkerchiefs twisted about their heads and with short skirts, boys with tattered shirts and men's trousers, young girls bare-footed—all stand up in the middle of the floor, and when the "sperichil" is struck up, begin first walking and by-and-by shuffling round, one after the other, in a ring. The foot is hardly taken from the floor, and the progression is mainly due to a jerking, hitching motion which agitates the entire shouter, and soon brings out streams of perspiration. Sometimes he dances silently, sometimes as he shuffles he sings the chorus of the spiritual, and sometimes the song itself is also sung by the dancers. But more frequently a band, composed of some of the best singers and of tired shouters, stand at the side of the room to "base" the others, singing the body of the song and clapping their hands together or on the knees. Song and dance are alike extremely energetic, and often, when the shout lasts into the middle of the night, the monotonous thud, thud of the feet prevents sleep within half a mile of the praise-shout.

Slave society revolved around the slave family, an unusually fragile institution. Slave marriages had no standing in law. At any time, the wife or the husband or the children could be sold to another master in another city, county or state. The tenuousness of the thing lent itself to levity. Preachers often joined couples "until death or distance do you part." Charles Grandy, an ex-slave in Virginia, said his master was good-humored about the situation.

"Marsa," he said, "used to sometimes pick our wives fo' us. If he didn't have on his place enough women for the men, he would wait on de side of de road till a big wagon loaded with slaves came by. Den Marsa would stop de ole nigger-trader and buy you a woman. Wasn't no use tryin' to pick one, 'cause Marsa wasn't gonna pay but so much for her. All he wanted was a young healthy one who looked like she could have children, whether she was purty or ugly as sin. Den he would lead you an' de woman over to one of de cabins and stan' you on de porch. He wouldn't go in. No, sir. He'd stan' right dere at de do' and open de Bible to de first thing he came to an' read somethin' real fast out of it. Den he close up de Bible an' finish up wid dis verse:

> Dat yo' wife
> Dat yo' husban'
> I'se yo' marsa
> She yo' missus
> You married."

Some masters sanctioned polygamy and polyandry. Others kept "stud Negroes" and bred slaves for the market. That some planters—the number of planters and the extent of the practice is debatable—used selected individuals as breeding machines cannot be doubted. The evidence, to be sure, is vague—planters would hardly leave written records. But plantation tradition is shot through with reports on the practice. Stories were whispered in the quarters. And some cases emerged from the secrecy and shame of the Cotton Curtain. On one occasion, a white man was questioning a fugitive slave. He wanted to know why the slave—a handsome, intelligent-looking man—ran away from his master. Was he badly treated? No, the slave couldn't say that he was. Well, why did he run away? The slave said he didn't like his work. What line of work was he in? With a great deal of reluctance, the slave explained that he was kept "as a breeding man in order to improve the stock of little niggers for the market."

Apologists for the slave regime deny that slave breeding—sustained efforts to produce the maximum number of slave children—occurred, but there is abundant evidence to the contrary. The subject was bruited about by men and women, Negroes and whites. Travelers in the South—Harriet Martineau, Frederick Law Olmsted and others—frequently mentioned the subject. Olmsted, a perceptive observer, believed that slave breeding was common. "Most gentlemen of character," he wrote, "seem to have a special disinclination to converse on the subject. . . . It appears to me evident, however, from the manner in which I hear the traffic spoken of incidentally, that the cash value of a slave for sale, above the cost of raising it from infancy to the age at which it commands the highest price, is generally considered among the surest elements of a planter's wealth. . . . That a slave woman is commonly esteemed least for her laboring qualities, most for those qualities which give value to a brood-mare, is, also, constantly made apparent."

Southerners admitted as much. In a letter to Olmsted, a slaveholder said: "In the states of Md., Va., N.C., Ky., Tenn. and Mo., as much attention is paid to the breeding and growth of negroes as to that of horses and mules. Further South, we raise them both for use and for market. Planters command their girls and women (married or unmarried) to have children; and I have known a great many negro girls to be sold off, because they did not have children. A breeding woman is worth from one-sixth to one-fourth more than one that does not breed."

Another planter, a Virginian, told Olmsted that his slave women "were uncommonly good breeders; he did not suppose there was a lot of women anywhere that bred faster than his; he never heard of babies coming so fast as they did on his plantation; it was perfectly surprising; and every one of them, in his estimation, was worth two hundred dollars, as negroes were selling now, the moment it drew breath."

Advertisements listing slave women for sale were brutally frank. A South Carolina advertisement of 1796 offered fifty "prime" Negroes for sale. "They were purchased," the advertisement said, "for stock and breeding Negroes, and to any Planter who particularly wanted them for that purpose, they are a very choice and desirable gang." Another advertisement of May 16, 1838, offered a slave "girl of about 20 years of age [who] is very prolific in her generating qualities and affords a rare opportunity for any person who wishes to raise a family of strong and healthy servants . . ." Other advertisement abounded in suggestive terminology: "She is a No. 1 girl." "This is truly a No. 1 woman." "Breeding slaves," "child-bearing women," and "breeding period" were also stock advertising terms.

Planters were frank and open about their desire for the maximum number of slave children. By sins of omission and commission, they encouraged "reckless propagation." When they visited the slave quarters, they usually asked first about new births and new pregnancies. When they discussed shop with other planters, the talk often turned to "rattlin' good breeders" and "the annual rate of increase." John C. Reed, a Georgia lawyer who had access to high planter circles, said "the greatest profit of all was what the master thought of and talked of all the day long,—the natural increase of his slaves, as he called it."

Breeding, like the economics of farming, was reduced to statistics. A planter figured on an annual increase of about 5 per cent. If the increase topped 5 per cent, he was pleased—naturally. But if it dropped below that figure, well—

To reach and top the figure established as a standard for well-conducted businesses, various inducements were offered to nubile slave women. Frances Anne Kemble, who lived on a Georgia plantation, said "many indirect inducements [are] held out to reckless propagation, which has a sort of premium offered to it in the consideration of less work and more food counterbalanced by none of the sacred responsibilities which hallow and ennoble the relation of parent and child; in short, as their lives are for the most those of mere animals, their increase is literally mere animal breeding, to which every encouragement is given, for it adds to the master's live-stock and the value of his estate."

The inducements varied. James H. Hammond of South Carolina gave a bounty of five dollars to "first marriages." Other planters sent delicacies from the kitchen to new mothers. Bright new dresses and baubles were also tendered to the mothers of fat, $200 babies. One planter was direct: he gave a small pig to the mother of each new baby. The most effective inducement was a promise of freedom when the mother had a certain number of babies. Ten was the usual figure; but when the market value of Negroes was high, some planters settled for five.

The plantation sexual syndrome placed a premium on fertility. On some plantations, it was common for girls of sixteen to have children. On Frances Kemble's plantation, it was not unusual for a woman to be a grandmother at thirty. Some slave women began their families at the age of thirteen and begat thirteen, fourteen and fifteen children. Helen Catterall cited a court record of a woman named Nancy who bore seventeen children in eighteen or nineteen years. A Lynchburg, Virginia, paper ran a report on a woman who probably established a record.

VERY REMARKABLE: There is now living in the vicinity of Campbell, a negro woman belonging to a gentleman by the name of Todd; this woman is in her forty-second year and has had forty-one children and at this time is pregnant with her forty-second child, and possibly with her forty-third, as she has frequently had doublets.

Great fortunes were founded on slave fecundity. It worked like this, an Alabamian said: "As soon as a man had the money he bought a girl, and before many years she had a family that was worth $10,000." Another Alabamian said he knew of "a single negro couple [who] brought a $25,000 increase in forty years."

It was not unusual in those days of blurred sensibilities for churches to invest in the fecundity of slaves. Some members of Presbyterian churches in Prince Edward County, Virginia, bought two slave women in 1767. The women and their descendants were hired out and the money was appropriated "to the payment of the salaries of the (common) pastor." This arrangement continued for sixty-eight years by which time the two women had increased to seventy. In 1835, the seventy slaves were sold and the money reinvested. "It was," Frederic Bancroft said with biting sarcasm, "a very lucrative religious enterprise."

One needs to be especially dense to miss the fact that some slaves enjoyed this system of permissive promiscuity. One needs to be even denser to miss the point that this promiscuity—enforced or permissive—was socially destructive.

Fatherhood, under this system, was a monstrous joke; fatherhood, in fact, was virtually abolished. Masters sometimes made the husband subject to the wife. The husband, for example, lived in "Dinah's cabin" and he was often called "Dinah's Tom." Despite these centrifugal forces, many slaves established stable homes. And many mothers strove to protect their daughters, especially if they had "that which is ever a curse to a slave girl"—personal beauty.

"Practical amalgamation" was a reality in most slave communities. Masters sought and found mistresses in their human chattel. Some of these liaisons were casual rapes, but others assumed the permanency of common-law arrangements. Numerous divorce petitions by white wives who were ousted from bed and board by comely slave girls indicate that many masters found it impossible to confine love to the narrow channels of the slave system.

"It is to be noted," James Hugo Johnston wrote, "that the white woman also reacted in a human way. The records of Virginia divorces give interesting evidences of jealousies, hatreds and suspicions that were both natural and human; but these records of divorce cases make it plain that the white woman in the slave period, in many cases, succumbed to the same human weaknesses, lusts, and temptations that white men seemed too human to overcome."

After an exhaustive study of miscegenation in the South, Johnston concluded that the birth of a mulatto child to a white woman was not uncommon in the slave South. In a typical case, the guilty wife said "that she had not been the first nor would she be the last guilty of such conduct, and that she saw no more harm in a white woman's having been the mother of a black child than in a white man's having one, though the latter were more frequent."

Some of these relationships continued for several years. In a Virginia divorce petition, the husband complained that "in spite of the remonstrances and persuasions of your petitioner, she has lived for the last six or seven years and still continues to live in open adultery with a negro man, a slave, the property of one of your petitioner's neighbors. . . . That your petitioner believes and such is the belief of all living in the neighborhood, as your petitioner will show that the said negro man has had by her two children, one of whom is now alive." Similar cases in other Southern states indicate that slavery was a problem to master and slave, male and female.

Within the restrictive limits of the slave system, some Negroes rose to commanding positions of authority. Several were overseers on plantations. Others worked as drivers under overseers, but were *de facto* managers.

For most slaves, however, life was a nightmare of drudgery. An ex-slave has said that it seemed that the fields stretched "from one end of the earth to the other." Men, women and children worked. Women cut down trees, dug ditches and plowed. The old and the ailing worked; old men and women fed poultry, cleaned the yard, mended clothes and cared for the young and the sick. Male and female, the quick and the halt worked the traditional hours of slavery—from can (see) to can't (see).

On most plantations, a horn ("dat ole fo' day horn") or bell

Religion was a source of solace for many slaves. One writer said slaves poured all their emotion into religious services "with an intensity . . . almost terrible to witness."

Fugitive slaves are shown arriving at the home of Levi Coffin, "the president of the Underground Railway." Many slaves escaped from plantations and rode "Underground Railroad" to freedom in the Promised Land—Canada.

sounded about four in the morning. Thirty minutes later, the field hands were expected to be out of their cabins and on their way to the fields. Stragglers and late-sleepers were lashed with the whip. An ex-slave in Virginia recalled seeing women scurrying to the fields "with their shoes and stockings in their hands, and a petticoat wrapped over their shoulders, to dress in the fields the best way they could."

Overseers and drivers, armed with whips, drove the work force, which was divided into hoe gangs and plow gangs. The overseer might also carry a bowie knife and a pistol. He often rode a horse, accompanied by a vicious dog.

Solomon Northup, a free Negro who was kidnapped and sold into slavery, said the hands worked steadily and "with the exception of ten or fifteen minutes, which is given them at noon to swallow their allowance of cold bacon, they are not permitted to be a moment idle till it is too dark to see, and when the moon is full, they often labor till the middle of the night."

After work, Northup continued, "each must then attend to his respective chores. One feeds the mules, another the swine—another cuts the wood, and so forth. . . . Finally, at a late hour, they reach the quarters, sleepy and overcome with the long day's toil. Then a fire must be kindled in the cabin, the corn ground in the small hand-mill, and supper, and dinner for the next day in the field prepared. . . . When the corn is ground, and fire is made, the bacon is taken down from the nail on which it hangs, a slice cut off and thrown upon the coals to broil. The majority of slaves had no knife, much less a fork. They cut their bacon with the axes at the woodpile. The corn meal is mixed with a little water, placed in the fire, and baked. When it is 'done brown,' the ashes are scraped off, and being placed upon a chip, which answers for a table, the tenant of the slave hut is ready to sit down upon the ground to supper. By this time, it is usually midnight. The same fear of punishment . . . possesses them again on lying down to get a snatch of rest. It is the fear of oversleeping in the morning. Such an offense would certainly be attended with not less than twenty lashes. With a prayer that he may be on his feet and wide awake at the first sound of the horn, he sinks to his slumbers nightly."

Fear, toil and the lash, hard words and a little ash cake and bacon, and fields stretching around the world—for most slaves, this was life, day in and day out, season after season, with a half-day off on Saturday perhaps and a whole day on Sunday. Small wonder that the burdened bondsman eased his weary frame down and addressed God in stark eloquence: "Come day, go day, God send Sunday."

Why did they do it?

Why didn't they revolt?

Why didn't they run away? Commit suicide? Or stand like a man and be cut down?

Slaves did all these things and more. They did them so often that it is nothing short of amazing that the myth of the docile Negro persists. There were repeated insurrections and there is solid evidence that the South lived in constant fear of the "docile" slaves. Bondsmen ran away in droves. They fled to Canada and Mexico and to Florida and Louisiana before these territories became a part of the United States of America; they fled to the Indians and joined them in their wars against the white man.

Young and old ran, mulattoes and pure blacks, Uncle Toms (in the modern sense) and radicals. Following the North Star, some made their way to the North and on to Canada. Many, aided by slaves and liberal whites, traveled the famed Underground Railway. But many were recaptured or returned voluntarily when they found the odds against them too great. A large number, however, remained in the South, living in swamps and raiding nearby plantations. Frederick Law Olmsted was told that escaped slaves lived, bred and died in the swamps. "What a life it must be!" he wrote, "born outlaws; educated self-stealers; trained from infancy to be constantly in dread of the approach of a white man as a thing more dreaded than wildcats or serpents, or even starvation."

In the mountains, swamps, and forests, slaves, slavehunters and vicious "Negro dogs" matched wits. A Virginia court record illustrates the problems of the pursued and the pursuer. A deputy, sent out to capture a runaway slave, saw his man standing neck deep in a dangerous recess of the swamp. The deputy went back to the courthouse and scratched the slave's name off the book. He wrote across the warrant: "Seeable but not Comeatable."

Another runaway, cornered by his pursuers, chose death. A contemporary newspaper account says that when pursuers found him he was standing "at bay upon the outer edge of a large raft of driftwood, armed with a club and a pistol. In this position he bade defiance to men and dogs—knocking the latter into the water with his club, and resolutely threatening death to any man who approached him. Finding him obstinately determined not to surrender, one of his pursuers shot him. He fell at the third fire, and so determined was he not to be captured, that when an effort was made to rescue him from drowning he made battle with his club, and sunk waving his weapon in angry defiance at his pursuers."

Arson was the favorite and most-feared method of revenge. In many slave areas, there were periodic epidemics of house-, gin-, and crop-burning. The big towns were not exempt. As early as 1723, fifty-three years before the Declaration of Independence, Boston was terrorized by a series of fires. On April 18, 1723, the Rev. Joseph Sewell of Boston preached a sermon on "The Fires that have Broken out in Boston, supposed to be set purposely by ye Negroes."

Fires and rumors of slave-set fires bedeviled Albany, Georgia, and Albany, New York; Newark and Elizabeth City, New Jersey; Baltimore and Charleston; Augusta and Savannah, Georgia. The South was definitely a bad risk area. An official of the American Fire Insurance Company of Philadelphia sent the following letter to a Savannah, Georgia, man on February 17, 1820: "I have received your letter of the 7th instant respecting the insurance of your house and furniture in Savannah. In answer thereto, I am to inform you, that this company, for the present, decline making insurance in any of the slave states."

Arrayed against rebellious slaves was a police apparatus of unparalleled severity. Each slave state had a slave code which was designed to keep slaves ignorant and in awe of white power. Slaves were forbidden to assemble in groups of more than five or seven away from their home plantation. They were forbidden to leave plantations without passes and they could not blow horns, beat drums or read books. Slave preachers were proscribed and hemmed in by restrictions; and slaves were forbidden to hold religious meetings without white witnesses. Other provisions forbade slaves to raise their hands against whites and gave every white person police power over every Negro, free or slave. A free Negro, when challenged by a white person, was obliged to produce papers proving that he was free. The presumption in most slave states was that a colored person was a slave. Slave patrols or "paderollers," as the slaves called them, were authorized to make periodic searches of slave cabins and to chastise bondsmen found off plantations without passes.

The police power of the state, the state militia, and the U.S. Army stood behind these onerous provisions. But power alone could not uphold them. More was needed; the slave, if slavery were to be successful, had to *believe* he was a slave. Anticipating the devious tactics of the modern police state, masters laid hands on the minds of their human chattel. Each slave was taught, by various methods and with varying success, that he was totally helpless and that his master was absolutely powerful. Each slave was taught that he was inferior to the meanest white man and that he had to obey every white man without thinking, without questioning. Finally, if these lessons were learned, the slave looked at himself through the eyes of his master and accepted the values of the master.

Masters, with few exceptions, recognized the necessity of mind control. A Louisiana planter told Olmsted that he wanted to buy the land of poor whites who lived near his plantation. "It was better," he said, "that they [slaves] never saw anybody off their own plantation; they should, if possible, have no intercourse with any other white man than their owner or overseer; especially, it was desirable that *they should not see white men who did not command their respect, and whom they did not always feel to be superior to themselves, and able to command them.*" [Emphasis supplied.]

That some slaves succumbed to this assault on the mind is not unusual. Faced with absolute power in a closed system, American white men and Europeans succumbed in concentration camps in Korea and Germany. The interesting thing about slavery is that so many saw through the shell game and fought back.

There were many proud and defiant rebels who could not be broken. At one time or another, most planters ran afoul of the "bad Negro," fabled in the traditions of slavery, who vowed that no white man would whip him. Some of these rebels who could not and would not be whipped by one man were overpowered by groups and killed. Many were sent to "professional Negro breakers" and broken. Several "persisted in their folly." They poisoned masters and mistresses with arsenic, ground glass and "spiders beaten up in buttermilk." They chopped them to pieces with axes and burned their houses, gins and barns to the ground. Not a few "bad Negroes" were women.

Court records speak for these "bad Negroes" whom some historians would like to forget.

One slave said:

"He would be damned if he did not kill his master, if he ever struck him again."

Another was ecstatic as he dug his master's grave.

"I have killed him at last."

Patrick vowed revenge.

"Their master had attempted to whip Patrick . . . and it took five persons to hold him. That Patrick said that he was not done yet, that he was a good Negro when he was let alone, but if he was raised he was the devil."

A woman slave prodded a timid male.

"If she, the witness, were a man, she would murder her master."

Another woman was frank.

"If old mistress did not leave her alone and quit calling her a bitch and a strumpet, she would take an iron and split her brains out."

The court records of this period yield ample evidence that a large number of slaves refused to play the game of slavery: they would neither smile nor bow. Some bowed but would not smile. Many, perhaps the majority, went through the ritual of obeisance. What about them? What did they think of slavery?

What they thought can be inferred from what they did. Stampp and other historians have uncovered a mass of material relating to their passive, "day-to-day resistance to slavery." They worked no harder than they had to, put on deliberate slowdowns, staged sit-down strikes and fled to the swamps en masse at cotton picking time. They broke implements, trampled the crops and "took" silver, wine, money, corn, cotton and machines.

"If slaves yielded to authority most of the time," says Stampp, "they did so because they saw no other practical choice. Yet few went through life without expressing discontent, somehow, sometime. Even the most passive slaves, usually before they reached middle age, flared up in protest now and then. The majority, as they grew older, lost hope and spirit. Some, however, never quite gave in, never stopped fighting back in one way or another. . . . Such rebels seldom won legal freedom, yet they never quite admitted they were slaves. . . . True, these rebels were exceptional men, but the historians of any group properly devotes much attention to those members who did extraordinary things, men in whose lives the problems of their age found focus, men who voiced the feelings and aspirations of the more timid and less articulate masses. As the American Revolution produced folk heroes, so also did Southern slavery—heroes who gave much for the cause of human freedom."

5

Slave Revolts and Insurrections

. . . *Denmark Vesey, a Negro who resisted slavery and led an insurrection in the effort to throw off the oppression, is a type which contradicts the assumption that Negroes are innately docile as a race and were content with slavery. In a sense, Vesey represents the spirit of independence for which the founding fathers of America are praised—an insurrection is merely an unsuccessful revolution. But Denmark Vesey is a symbol of a spirit too violent to be acceptable to the white community. There are no Negro schools named for him, and it would be extremely poor taste and bad judgement for the Negroes to take any pride in his courage and philosophy. There is, indeed, little chance for Negro youth to know about him at all.*

CHARLES S. JOHNSON

I_T WAS a long hot summer.

On colonnaded verandas in the French possession of Haiti (Saint-Domingue), planters sipped tall cold drinks and looked into the apocalyptic sun. Black men—slaves—served the drinks, bowing, scraping, listening. The planters sipped the cool liquid, fondled the tall glasses and chewed over the revolution then raging in the mother country.

Liberté, Fraternité, Egalité.

What precisely did these words mean?

The planters speculated. The black men bowed, scraped, listened.

The planters were going to die, but they did not speculate about death in the red summer of 1791. Lush summers and cold drinks do not lend themselves to reflections on blood and doom; nor do men situated as these men were situated look gift horses in the mouth. They ruled a half-million slaves. God, they reasoned, made the sugar cane to grow and He sent black men from Africa to cultivate it and white men from Europe to divide the profits. It had always been so, they reasoned; it would always be so. But weren't they playing with fire? To prattle about liberty, equality and fraternity in the presence of slaves—wasn't this suicidal? No, of course not. Slaves were not men; they didn't have the same desires as Europeans. They were primitives. Like children, really.

The planters speculated. The black men sharpened their knives.

Liberté, Fraternité, Egalité.

What precisely did these words mean?

All summer long, the tom-toms talked in the hills. If a visitor remarked on the rumbling, the planters had a ready answer. The servants were worshipping their tribal gods. They were a superstitious people. Like children, really.

The boom-boom-boom continued, summoning slave leaders to secret meetings in the hills. On August 14, men moved noiselessly through the night, responding to the insistent telegraphy of the tom-toms. They came from a hundred plantations, slave foremen and black men of distinction. Noiselessly, they assembled in a glade in a forest called Bois Caïman.

They sat in a great half circle, facing a fire, behind which, magnified by the flames, stood a tall man who leaned on an improvised altar. The man answered to the name Boukman. He was a *houngan*, a celebrated voodoo priest who had come to Haiti via Jamaica. Boukman seemed pleased, as well he might. Overhead, lightning zigzagged through the sky and the heavens rolled with thunder. It was a good sign: *Bon Dieu*, the good God, was angry. Moreover, as Boukman pointed out to the delegates, *Bon Dieu* demanded action; a slave revolt; now. Boukman, speaking for *Bon Dieu*, vowed vengeance for the wrongs of his people. Speaking in a deep, hollow voice, playing the strings of his listeners' emotions, Boukman raised the assembly to a pitch of religious frenzy. The only problem, it turned out, was the time of D-Day. Some there were who wanted to do it that night; but cooler heads prevailed. Eight days were set aside for deliberation and planning.

Boukman gave a sign and acolytes brought a black pig. A gleaming knife flashed through the air. Every man present moved forward, dipped his hands in the blood of the animal and, holding them up, swore *Liberté ou mort*. A streak of lightning seared the sky; the heavens thundered and rolled. Boukman, observing this, was pleased; it was a good sign: *Bon Dieu* was giving his approval.

The ceremony continued.

A statuesque young virgin, stark naked save for red laurels twined about her brow, weaved through a religious dance. As she danced, swaying from side to side, moving her hands, her arms, her entire body, she chanted a strange song of prophecy, of a land laid waste, of a people finding themselves and rising to greatness through inspired leadership. She finished at last and Boukman, a master of crowd psychology, fell to his knees and improvised—or did the wily old Jamaican have it all written out—the famous Creole prayer—*Bon Dieu*.

"Good God, who makest the sun to light us from on high, who raisest up the sea and makest the storm to thunder—good God who watches over all, hidden in a cloud, protect and save us from what the white men do to us.

"Good God, the white men do crimes, but we do not.

"Good God, give us vengeance, guide our arms, give us help. Negroes show the image of the good God to the white men, that we thirst not.

"Good God, grant us that freedom which speaks to all men!"

Down below in the valley, all was quiet. Here and there, white men sat on the wide porches and watched the play of the lightning in the heavens.

Liberté, Fraternité, Egalité.

What precisely did these words mean?

Eight days later—at midnight on August 22, 1791—an answer, of sorts, came.

"In an instant," a writer said, "twelve hundred coffee and two hundred sugar plantations were in flames; the buildings, the machinery, the farmhouses, were reduced to ashes; and the unfortunate proprietors were hunted down, murdered or thrown into the flames, by the infuriated Negroes. The horrors of a servile war universally appeared. The unchained Negro signalized his ingenuity by the discovery of new methods and unheard of modes of torture."

More than 100,000 slaves were in revolt, hacking, burning, murdering. For three weeks, the slaves continued the work of death. For three weeks, the fires burned. A French planter named Carteau was there. "Picture to yourself," he said, "the whole horizon a wall of fire, from which continually rose thick vortices of smoke, whose huge black volumes could be likened only to those frightful storm-clouds which roll onward charged with thunder and lightning. The rift in these clouds disclosed flames as great in volume, which rose darting and flashing to the very sky. Such was their voracity that for nearly three weeks we could barely distinguish between day and night, for so long as the rebels found anything to feed the flames, they never ceased to burn."

Thus began a revolution which shook the world and had profound repercussions in America where planters took to sleeping with pistols under their pillows. Fear, a deep, miasmic fear, seeped into the consciousness of planters everywhere. There had been earlier revolts, scores of them, in the Caribbean, in South America, in North America; but these revolts had been quickly suppressed and the details expunged from memory. The Haitian revolt reopened old wounds and magnified old phobias.

Historians, armed with hindsight, have written a great deal of romantic nonsense about the docility of the Negro slave. The planter who lived with the Negro slave knew him better. He knew from bitter experience that the Negro was a dangerous man because he was a wronged man. The Negro smiled; yes. But he also cut throats, burned down houses and conceived plots to rise up and kill every white person within reach. This happened so often that many white men weakened under the strain. Some died of heart failure. Some went insane.

"These insurrections," a Virginian wrote during a period of panic, "have alarmed my wife so as really to endanger her health, and I have not slept without anxiety in three months. Our nights are sometimes spent in listening to noises. A corn song, or a hog call, has often been the subject of nervous terror, and a cat, in the dining room, will banish sleep for the night. There has been and there still is a *panic* in all this country. I am beginning to lose my courage about the melioration of the South. Our revivals produce no preachers; churches are like the buildings in which they worship, gone in a few years. There is no principle of life. Death is autocrat of slave regions."

Fear fed by guilt made men do strange things. Two poor whites told Frederick Law Olmsted how it was in the South's palmiest days. "Where I used to live [Alabama]," the husband said, "I remember when I was a boy—mus' ha' been about twenty years ago —folks was dreadful frightened about the niggers. I remember they built pens in the woods where they could hide, and Christmas time they went and got into the pens 'fraid the niggers was rising." This man's wife had seen similar scenes. "I remember," she said, "the same time where we was in South Carolina, we had all our things put in a bag so we could tote 'em, if we heard they was coming our way."

This all-embracing fear played a big part in precipitating the Civil War and is still an important element in race relations. "Small most of the revolts were," Melville J. Herskovits writes, "yet in their aggregate and persistence over the entire period of slaving, they give point to the comments made by a recent Netherlands observer of the interracial situation in America, that today one of the keys to an understanding of the South is fear of the Negro, a legacy of slavery."

Herbert Aptheker (*American Negro Slave Revolts*) has listed 250 slave revolts and conspiracies within the area of the continental United States. The first of these revolts occurred ninety-four years before the "Mayflower." Aptheker writes:

"The first settlement within the present borders of the United States to contain Negro slaves was the locale of the first slave revolt. A Spanish colonizer, Lucas Vasquez de Ayllon, founded, in the summer of 1526, a community whose probable location was at or near the mouth of the Pedee River in what is now South Carolina. The settlement consisted of about five hundred Spaniards and one hundred Negro slaves. Trouble soon beset it. Illness caused numerous deaths, carrying off, in October, Ayllon himself. Internal dissension arose, and the Indians grew increasingly suspicious and hostile. Finally, probably in November, several of the slaves rebelled, and fled to the Indians. The next month what was left of the adventurers, some one hundred and fifty souls, returned to Haiti, leaving the rebel Negroes with their Indian friends—as the first permanent inhabitants, other than the Indians, in what was to be the United States."

There were scores of uprisings and threatened uprisings in Colonial America. In 1712, for example, slaves in New York City revolted and killed at least nine whites. And a Virginia plot of 1730 prompted the lieutenant governor to order white men to take their pistols to church with them. A few years later, in South Carolina,

Condemned slave is burned at the stake after "Negro Plot of 1741." Citizens believed Negro and white conspirators intended to burn New York City and kill the white citizens. Thirteen slaves were burned and eighteen were hanged.

Toussaint L'Ouverture was the leader of the Haitian Revolution. Negro general, who won freedom for Haitian slaves, has been called "greatest Negro produced in Western Hemisphere."

After passage of Fugitive Slave Act of 1850, Negroes became increasingly militant. In Christiana, Pennsylvania, Negroes defeated a group of slave hunters.

a group of slaves killed several whites, fired several buildings and
set out for Florida, which was held then by Spain. They "called
out Liberty," a contemporary account says, "marched on with
Colours displayed, and two drums beating." Some twenty-five
whites were killed.

The flood of ideas released by the American and French Revolutions stirred slaves greatly. The rhetoric of Thomas Jefferson and
Patrick Henry, both slaveholders, also impressed slave conspirators. But the biggest influence in the slave cabins was a small black
man who once made a four-word speech on liberty. Holding up
his musket, he told Haitian slaves, "There is your liberty!" In Brazil, in the Caribbean, in Charleston, wherever slaves chafed under
chains, this man's name was whispered. The name was François
Dominique Toussaint L'Ouverture. The man was one of the great
men of an age that abounds in greatness.

"You think me a fanatic," thundered Wendell Phillips, "for you
read history not with your eyes, but with your prejudices. But
fifty years hence, when Truth gets a hearing, the Muse of history
will put Phocion for the Greek, Brutus for the Romans, Hampden
for the English, Lafayette for France; choose Washington as the
bright, consummate flower of our earliest civilization; and then,
dipping her pen in the sunlight, will write in the clear blue, above
them all, the name of the soldier, the statesman, the martyr, Toussaint L'Ouverture."

When the Haitian Revolution began, Toussaint was an obscure
carriage driver on the Bréda plantation in the northern province of
Haiti. He had lived the life of a slave, had married, sired children
and gained some local fame from his skill in mixing herb potions.
A devout Roman Catholic, he was literate in French and could roll
out a few Latin phrases. He was, it seems, a model slave. His master
trusted him implicitly and had given him a succession of important
jobs. Now, in the autumn of his life, Toussaint drove his master's
carriage, sitting barefooted on the box, smiling and bowing at the
proper times. He was almost fifty and it seemed that his life was
almost over. Yet, in a few years, this grey-haired carriage driver

electrified the world and sent shivers down the backs of American slaveholders. He defeated the English and Spanish armies, unified Haiti and held his own in slippery maneuvering with the wily Napoleon.

The Haitian Revolution began, as we have seen, with the firing of the plantations and the slaughter of the whites. Toussaint, who did not participate in this phase, saw that more, a great deal more, was needed if the slaves were to gain and keep their freedom. There were dangers on all sides. The whites, driven from the fertile plains, were plotting in the seacoast towns. Spain and England, having declared war on France, were demanding a division of the Haitian spoils.

In this volatile situation, Toussaint realized, superior firepower would prevail. Moreover, as Ralph Korngold points out, he seemed determined "not to permit a white man to claim the honor of having freed the slaves."

Joining the tattered rebel army, Toussaint quickly became the man of the hour. He preached the virtues of discipline and dry gunpowder, trained and hardened a crack corps of black troops. Then he took to the field, first as an ally of Spain against France, then as an ally of France against England and Spain. Playing off the Spanish against the French and the French against the English, he outmaneuvered the best diplomats of his day and gained freedom for the slaves.

Toussaint was a military genius. He had complete control over his men and he moved them about with a rapidity that seemed miraculous. Antoine Métral said: "He disappears—he has flown—as if by magic. Now he reappears again where he is least expected. He seems to be ubiquitous. One never knows where his army is, what it subsists on, how he manages to recruit it, in what mountain fastness he has hidden his supplies and his treasury. He, on the other hand, seems perfectly informed concerning everything that goes on in the enemy camp."

Moving with incredible speed, Toussaint outfoxed General Maitland and forced the withdrawal of the English Army. Historians say England lost some 40,000 men in a vain attempt to take the island from the black general.

Having subdued external foes, Toussaint annexed the eastern two-thirds of the island (now the Dominican Republic) and squashed a dissident force of mulattoes. By 1801, he was at the height of his power. He was then in his middle fifties, a lean, wiry man, small of stature, very black, with large eyes, a broad uptilted nose and thick lips. He was not, by any standard, handsome; yet there was something about the man. The face was strong, magnetic, noble even; and he had that without which actors and generals are mere puppets: personal presence. A French general said: "Nobody can approach Toussaint without fear or leave him without emotion."

The black general had an eye for drama. Almost always he wore a yellow madras handkerchief, carelessly knotted about his head. When he entered Santo Domingo at the head of a triumphant army, he was dressed in a blue uniform with gold-embroidered cuffs and large gold epaulettes.

Toussaint had all the gifts of greatness: an incisive mind, reckless courage and unbounded self-confidence. He despised flattery and was contemptuous of titles and empty show. He was also, it seems, something of a Puritan; he forbade divorce and kept a stern eye on the moral tone of the country. When an attractive young French girl appeared at a social function in a low-cut dress, Toussaint modestly covered the exposed flesh with his handkerchief and asked the girl's mother to take her home. He was puritanical, cynical historians say, "at least as far as other people's morals were concerned." This is a veiled reference to reports that Toussaint had at least three white mistresses—Madame Valabrègue, Madame Lartigne and Madame Lartigne's daughter. However that may be, it is established beyond doubt that the Haitian dictator remained devoted to Suzanne, the wife of his captivity, and their two sons.

Having unified the island, Toussaint embarked on an extraordinary career as an administrator. Roads were built; buildings were repaired; the administrative machinery was overhauled. With enemies all about him, with the major powers waiting for him to make a mistake, Toussaint decreed total mobilization. Every citizen, he said, was a soldier. A heavy tax schedule financed an ambitious program of arms procurement.

Colonel Poyen, the French military historian, said Toussaint "was responsible for the most extraordinary activity in all departments of the administration. He busied himself with the building of the fortifications, the stocking of the arsenals, the acquisition of supplies, the instruction and discipline of the army. He spurred the agricultural inspectors to intense activity. He restored and embellished the cities and built bridges. He administered justice, kept an eye on the exercise of religion, visited schools and distributed prizes to the best scholars. He frequently visited hospitals and barracks. It is difficult to sum up the amazing activity of this extraordinary Negro, who slept only two hours out of twenty-four. His body, accustomed to privations, was entirely under the control of his will."

Perhaps the most outstanding accomplishment of Toussaint's reign was the integration of the white minority into the life of the country. He had a way with whites. "Races," General Vincent said, "melt beneath his hand." Feeling that the country needed the technical know-how of the whites, Toussaint went out of his way to quiet their fears. The whites, out of fear *and* love, reciprocated. When the black general made a triumphant entrance into Port-au-Prince, the whole populace turned out. Little white girls, carrying baskets of flowers, lined the parade route and pelted Toussaint and his staff. Priests, planters and city officials walked up the road to greet the triumphant general. Behind these functionaries were white women in elegant carriages and an honor guard, composed of the planters' sons. The next day a delegation of planters, headed by the mayor, gave Toussaint a gold medal bearing his likeness and the fantastic words: "AFTER GOD—HE." Later, during a similar welcome to Le Cap, white men chose the most beautiful white woman in the city to place a laurel on Toussaint's head. The woman eulogized Toussaint in verses in which he was compared to

Hercules and Alexander the Great. When she finished, Toussaint rewarded her with a kiss and white men led the applause.

Though Toussaint ruled nominally in the name of France, he was in reality the military and political dictator of Haiti. This fact pained Napoleon, another small-statured man of great military ability. Napoleon did not think highly of men with dark skins. "I will not leave an epaulette," he said, "upon the shoulders of a single black."

There were other considerations. The French empire was not big enough for two Napoleons. It irritated the First Consul when men compared him with the Black Consul and found parallels in their careers. Toussaint, to be blunt, was in Napoleon's way. Napoleon had dreams of a vast empire in the Western Hemisphere; he needed Haiti and slave labor to complete the plans he had for the Louisiana Territory. Toussaint was thwarting these plans; Toussaint, therefore, had to go. Napoleon sent his brother-in-law, Victor Emanuel LeClerc, and some 25,000 soldiers to do the job.

Toussaint fell back into the mountains and harried LeClerc with a scorched-earth campaign. "Raid the roads," Toussaint instructed his subordinates, "throw the bodies of dead horses in all the springs; destroy and burn everything. May they find an image of the hell they deserve!"

The scorched-earth campaign continued until Christophe, one of Toussaint's top generals, defaulted and went over to the French. Toussaint, always a realistic man, sued for a temporary peace and retired to his plantation. The French believed and many modern historians say that the cagey general was waiting for yellow fever to decimate the ranks of his enemies.

Toussaint was a devout Roman Catholic, but it seems that his faith weakened near the end. His nephew is authority for the story that the deposed general walked up to an altar in a village church and denounced it. "You! You are the God of the white man, not the God of the Negroes! You have betrayed men, and deserted me! You have no pity for my race!" He then hurled a marble crucifix to the floor.

Like most men, Toussaint was vain. There came to his plantation one day a letter calculated to appeal to his vanity. The letter, couched in deferential, respectful terms, was from General Brunet, one of LeClerc's aides. Could Toussaint come to Brunet's headquarters for an important conference? He would not find all the comforts Brunet would like to put at his disposal, but he would find a "frank and honest man, whose only ambition is to promote the welfare of the colony and your happiness." Toussaint, normally a cautious, suspicious man, gobbled the bait. When he reached Brunet's headquarters, he was arrested, hurried on a ship and dispatched to France. Napoleon, taking no chances, had him locked up in a dark cell in a medieval fortress high in the Jura Alps on the French-Swiss borders. There, one day in April, 1803, death came to the greatest Negro produced in the Western Hemisphere. He was alone when he died, sitting in a straight-backed chair, in a dank, dark cell far from the Haitian sun. William Wordsworth, the great English poet, saw him as "the most unhappy of men."

> O miserable Chieftain! where and when
> Wilt thou find patience! Yet die not; do thou
> Wear rather in thy bonds a cheerful brow:
> Though fallen thyself, never to rise again,
> Live, and take comfort. Thou hast left behind
> Powers that will work for thee: air, earth, and skies:
> There's not a breathing of the common wind
> That will forget thee; thou hast great allies;
> Thy friends are exultations, agonies,
> And love, and Man's unconquerable mind.

Noble words, these; but Toussaint had a horror of mere words; and his friends, in the first instance, were the friends he always relied on—muskets. After his capture, the farmers he had organized into a mass militia and the officers he had trained sprang into revolt. Harried by the heat, yellow fever, and black soldiers who materialized from nowhere and disappeared into nowhere, LeClerc resorted to wholesale slaughter and terror.

If LeClerc and his successor, Rochambeau, wanted to play with fire, Jean-Jacques Dessalines was their man. A slim, handsome general with a fondness for elegant uniforms and a knack of always saying and doing the thing that electrifies and moves masses, Dessalines was mercurial and ruthless. He had suffered in slavery and he had scars to prove it. In him was a loathing for all Frenchmen. As Toussaint's aide, he had demonstrated a military genius second only to the master. Now, as Toussaint's successor, he hurled a defiant challenge: "war for war, crime for crime, atrocity for atrocity." Dessalines was not talking for literary effect. He later organized and led a systematic extermination of the white population. One day, so the story goes, he stood watching a group of whites who were marching to their death. Suddenly, a man darted from the line. "Governor!" the white man shouted. "They are going to kill your bootmaker. Save me!" Dessalines saved the man—vengeance was one thing and ill-fitting boots another.

The war continued—blow for blow, crime for crime. LeClerc bombarded Napoleon with appeals for help. "The [black] men," LeClerc wrote, "die with a fanaticism that is unbelievable. They laugh at death." One Haitian soldier, unfortunately nameless, immolated and immortalized himself by walking into a fire. "He was greater," a French officer wrote, "than Mucius Scaevola. The Roman hero burned his own hand. The Negro thrust his whole body into the fire to show his enemies that he knew how to die. And those were the men we had to fight!"

Time—it was only a matter of time. The hours ran out on Napoleon's men one day in 1803 at Vertieres outside Le Cap. Rochambeau sent in a white flag, and Dessalines ripped the white from the French tricolor, joined the red and blue and proclaimed the second republic in the Western Hemisphere. The venture was doubly disastrous for Napoleon. The French lost some 60,000 men and a rich colony, and Napoleon soured on the Western Hemisphere and sold the Louisiana Territory to America for four cents an acre—the biggest real estate bargain in history.

"Thus," said De Witt Talmadge, "all of Indian Territory, all of Kansas and Nebraska, Iowa and Wyoming, Montana and the Dakotas, and most of Colorado and Minnesota, and all of Washing-

ton and Oregon states, came to us as the indirect work of a despised
Negro. Praise, if you will, the work of a Robert Livingstone or a
Jefferson, but today let us not forget our debt to Toussaint L'Ouverture, who was indirectly the means of America's expansion by
the Louisiana Purchase of 1803."

No monument was needed to remind nineteenth-century Americans of Haiti and Toussaint L'Ouverture. Every hint, every rumor of slave disaffection called back the memory of the little black
man who made a revolution and made it stick. And the names of
Gabriel Prosser, Denmark Vesey and Nat Turner turned memory
into a nightmare.

The first of this triumvirate was a young man, only 24, when he
burst upon the guilty consciousness of the slave power. He stood
six-feet-two and he wore his hair long in imitation of his Biblical
idol, Samson. Like most leaders of American Negro slave revolts,
Gabriel was a deeply religious man. The Old Testament, particularly the blood and doom passages, fascinated him. Gabriel medi-
tated on the Bible, and dreamed dreams of a Negro state—not in the
Caribbean, but in Virginia, the land of Jefferson and Washington.

Gabriel laid plans for his uprising in the spring and summer of
1800. For four or five months, he held meetings at fish fries and
barbecues. Every Sunday, Gabriel slipped into Richmond and studied the town, making a mental note of strategic points and the lo-
cations of arms and ammunition.

Among Gabriel's associates were his brothers, Martin and Solomon, and his wife, Nanny. Martin was a religious exhorter and a
firebrand. When a cautious slave advised delay, Martin exploded:
"Before he would any longer bear what he had borne, he would
turn out and fight with a stick."

Gabriel's plan was simple. Three columns would attack Richmond; the right wing would grab the arsenal and seize the guns;
the left wing would take the powder house; the key, central wing
would enter the town at both ends simultaneously and would cut
down every white person, except Frenchmen, Methodists and
Quakers. After Richmond was secured, Gabriel planned lightning-

like attacks on other cities in the state. If the plan succeeded, he was to be named King of Virginia. If it failed, the insurgents were to flee to the mountains and fight a guerrilla war.

By August, 1800, several thousand (estimates range from 2,000 to 50,000) slaves had been enlisted. A date—midnight, August 30—had been selected. Weapons—scythe swords, pikes, guns—had been assembled. On the Saturday selected, Gabriel and his aides reviewed their plans and sweated out the hours. On that very day, they were betrayed. Two slaves informed their master, who, in turn, communicated the intelligence to the authorities. The governor was so impressed with the magnitude of the danger that he shifted to a war footing. He appointed three aides-de-camp, shored up the guard at vital installations and called out the militia.

Gabriel, unaware of the betrayal, pushed forward with his plans. Some one thousand slaves assembled that night at the rendezvous point, six miles outside Richmond. Many historians believe they would have carried the day had not nature interceded. Thunder rent the sky and rain poured down in sheets. Bridges were washed away; roads were inundated. It was impossible to get into Richmond.

Virginians said later that an act of God saved them. What Gabriel called the deluge is not recorded. He looked into the angry sky and postponed the invasion; the postponement was fatal. Before he could reassemble his army, the state struck. Gabriel and some thirty-four of his men were arrested, convicted and hanged. At the trial, one of the defendants, perhaps Gabriel, made a stirring speech. "I have nothing more to offer," he said, "than what General Washington would have had to offer, had he been taken by the British and put to trial by them. I have adventured my life in endeavouring to obtain the liberty of my countrymen, and am a willing sacrifice to their cause; and I beg, as a favour, that I may be immediately led to execution. I know that you have pre-determined to shed my blood, why then all this mockery of a trial?"

When details of the plot leaked out, a deep fear spread through the populace. "They could scarcely have failed of success," wrote the Richmond correspondent of the Boston *Chronicle*, "for, after all, we could only muster four or five hundred men, of whom not more than thirty had muskets." Another correspondent wrote to the Philadelphia *United-States Gazette:* "Let but a single armed negro be seen or suspected, and, at once, on many a lonely plantation, there were trembling hands at work to bar doors and windows that seldom had been even closed before, and there was shuddering when a grey squirrel scrambled over the roof, or a shower of walnuts came down clattering from the overhanging boughs."

Denmark Vesey and Gabriel were cast in the same mould. In the year of Gabriel's defeat, Vesey won a lottery and purchased his freedom. From that date until 1822, he worked as a carpenter in Charleston, South Carolina. He accumulated money and property and was respected by Negroes and whites. He was, by his own admission, satisfied with his own condition; yet he risked everything in a bold effort to free other men. Offered a chance to emigrate to Africa, Vesey balked. He said, a witness reported, "that he did not go . . . to Africa, because he had not a will, he wanted to stay and see what he could do for his fellow creatures."

There burned in Vesey's breast a deep and unquenchable hatred of slavery and slaveholders. A brilliant, hot-tempered man, he was for some twenty years the slave of a slave trader. He traveled widely and learned several languages; he learned also that slavery was evil and that man was not meant to slave for man. Vesey reached a point, it is said, where he could not bear to have a white person in his presence.

The conspiracy this firebrand conceived is one of the most elaborate on record. For four or five years, he patiently and persistently played the role of an agitator. Men, he saw, must not only be dissatisfied; they must be so dissatisfied they will *act*. Denmark Vesey was interested in *action*. He told slaves their lives were so miserable that even death would be an improvement.

Vesey buttressed his arguments with quotations from abolitionists, Toussaint L'Ouverture and the Bible. He would read to the slaves "from the Bible *how the children of Israel were delivered out of Egypt from bondage.*" But he warned that God helped those who helped themselves. It was necessary to strike the first blow. Always, everywhere, the words of Joshua were on his lips.

"And they utterly destroyed all that was in the city, both man and woman, young and old, and ox, and sheep, and ass, with the edge of the sword."

This "volcanic man," witnesses say, never rested. If he saw slaves bowing to white men in the street, he would rebuke them. When the slaves replied, "But we are slaves," Vesey would comment with biting sarcasm, "You deserve to be slaves." If he were asked, "What can we do?" he would tell the story of Hercules and the man whose wagon stuck at the bottom of the hill. The waggoner began to cry and pray; Hercules told him, Vesey would say, "to put the whip to the team and his shoulder to the wheel."

Always, everywhere, Denmark Vesey was teaching. "I know Denmark Vesey," a slave said; "on one occasion he asked me, what news? I told him, none. He replied, 'We are free, but the white people here won't let us be so; and the only way is to raise up and fight the whites.'" Another witness said: "If it had not been for the cunning of the old villain Vesey, I should not now be in my present situation. He employed every strategem to induce me to join him. He was in the habit of reading to me all the passages in the newspapers that related to St. Domingo [Haiti], and apparently every pamphlet he could lay his hands on, that had any connection with slavery."

Ridiculing, taunting, threatening, Vesey gained a vise hold on the minds of Negroes in Charleston and surrounding areas. Many slaves feared him more than they feared their masters. One man said he feared Vesey more than he feared God.

Having reached this point, Vesey switched from the role of agitator to the role of organizer. Around Christmas in the year 1821, he chose lieutenants and perfected his organization. He was then in his early fifties, a vigorous big-bodied man with a keen insight into human nature. "In the selection of his leaders," said the judges, "Vesey showed great penetration and sound judgment." He enlisted slave artisans and class leaders in the Methodist church. He did not disdain the darker arts. A valuable functionary in his organization was Gullah Jack, an African-born sorceress who was considered invulnerable. If Gullah Jack could not convince a potential recruit, the talents of Blind Phillip were available. Phillip reportedly could see ghosts and other invisible phenomena. Timid recruits were carried to his house. Phillip would run his unseeing eyes over them and inquire: "Why do you look so timorous?" The abashed recruits, thunderstruck that a blind man should know how they looked, would remain silent. Blind Phillip would quote Holy Scripture, "Let not your heart be troubled."

The chief lieutenant of this remarkable organization was Peter Poyas, a "first-rate ship carpenter" who displayed an organizing ability bordering on genius. Ice water ran in Peter Poyas' veins; he was undoubtedly the coolest gambler in the history of American slave revolts. Like a good poker player, Peter was a blend of caution and recklessness. Characteristically, he volunteered for the most difficult and important assignment: the surprise and capture of the main guardhouse. The plan called for Peter to advance alone, surprise the sentinel and quietly slit his throat.

Vesey recognized Peter's talents and gave him large responsibilities. Peter was in charge of organization; he decided who should be approached and who shouldn't. It was Peter who pinpointed the greatest danger to a slave revolt: house servants. He told one of his recruiting agents to "take care and don't mention it to those waiting men who receive presents of old coats, etc., from their masters, or they'll betray us: *I will speak to them.*"

Vesey and Peter perfected a cell-like organization. Each leader had a list of recruits and an assignment. Only the leaders knew the details of the plot; the average recruit knew nothing except the name of his leader and vague outlines of the plan. If a single recruit was arrested, he was not in a position to endanger the whole plot.

For four or five months, the Vesey organization recruited slaves in Charleston and surrounding areas. Whole plantations were signed up. Weapons were constructed. A barber was hired to make Caucasian disguises. It has been estimated that some 9,000 slaves were recruited.

Plans were discussed at secret meetings in Vesey's house. On Sunday, July 16, the slave army was to strike at six points, taking possession of arsenals, guardhouses, powder magazines, naval stores. All whites were to be killed.

Vesey's house on the eve of the insurrection was a beehive of activity. Under cover of darkness, agents slipped in, conferred and slipped out. One conspirator left an interesting account of a cell meeting. "I was invited to Denmark Vesey's house," he said, "and when I went, I found several men met together, among whom was Ned Bennett, Peter Poyas, and others, whom I did not know. Denmark opened the meeting by saying he had an important secret to communicate to us, which we must not disclose to anyone, and if we did, we should be put to instant death. He said, we were deprived of our rights and privileges by the white people . . . and that it was high time for us to seek for our rights, and that we were fully able to conquer the whites, if we were only unanimous and courageous, as the St. Domingo people were. He then proceeded to explain his plan, by saying that they intended to make the attack by setting the governor's mills on fire, and also some houses near the water, and as soon as the bells began to ring for fire, that they should kill every man, as he came out of his door, and that the servants in the yard should do it, and that it should be done with axes and clubs, and afterwards they should murder the women and children, for he said, God had commanded it in the Scriptures. At another meeting at Denmark's, Ned Bennett and Peter Poyas and several others were present in conversation, some said, they thought it was cruel to kill the ministers and the women and children, but Denmark Vesey said, he thought it was for our safety, not to spare one white skin alive, for this was the plan they pursued in St. Domingo."

On a Saturday in the last week of May, the disaster Peter tried to prevent, materialized. An unauthorized slave, William Paul, attempted to recruit a house servant. Within five days, the authorities were in possession of the bare outlines of the plot.

There then followed one of the most extraordinary poker games in the history of slave conspiracies. At one end of town, the mayor and other city officials worked feverishly in a frantic effort to crack the plot. In another room, at the other end of town, Vesey and his aides worked feverishly in a frantic effort to spring their trap. The city officials and Vesey were working under certain difficulties; neither side knew what cards the other side held. The city officials did not know the names of the leaders or the details of the plot; but Vesey did not know this. With incredible boldness, he continued to hold meetings and walked the streets as though nothing had happened.

For two weeks, the game continued. The two rooms buzzed with activity; tension mounted. Word came through the grapevine that city officials were getting close; two of the top leaders—Peter Poyas and Mingo Harth—were under suspicion. A weak organization would have crumbled at this point; men and leaders would have scurried to the hills. But the Vesey organization didn't work that way. Peter and Mingo ran not to the hills but to the mayor's office. They were indignant; their honor, their fidelity had been questioned. Justice demanded that they be questioned and cleared. The authorities were confounded; guilty slaves didn't act that way. Peter and Mingo were released and the cops-and-robbers game continued. Vesey, in his rooms on Bull Street, read the signs and moved D-Day up. Then, on the Friday before D-Day, another slave went over to the enemy. This slave, unlike the others, knew what he was talking about. He was privy to the plans and he knew the names of some of the leaders. Thoroughly alarmed now, the officials beefed up the guard and alerted the militia. Vesey and most of the leaders were arrested, tried and hanged. They behaved nobly, eyewitnesses say. Only one leader confessed; the rest remained silent in the face of abuse, threats, promises and torture. Peter Poyas, the official report said, was splendid in defeat. His only anxiety, the report said, was "to know how far the discoveries had extended; and the same emotions were exhibited in his conduct. He did not appear to fear personal consequences, for his whole behaviour indicated the reverse. . . . His countenance and behaviour were the same when he was sentenced; and his only words were, on retiring, 'I suppose you'll let me see my wife and family before I die?' and that not in a supplicating tone. When he was asked, a day or two after, if it was possible he could wish to see his master and family murdered, who had treated him so kindly, he only replied to the question with a smile."

So cool, so carefree was Peter that he spurned last-minute pleas for additional information. "Do not open your lips," he said to the other leaders. "Die silent as you shall see me do." Archibald Grimke said such "words, considering the circumstances under which they were spoken, were worthy of a son of Sparta or of Rome, when Sparta and Rome were at their highest levels as breeders of iron men."

Gabriel Prosser plotted and was betrayed. Denmark Vesey plotted and was betrayed. Nat Turner plotted and executed.

"No ante-bellum Southerner," Historian Kenneth Stampp writes, "could ever forget Nat Turner. The career of this man made an impact upon the people of his section as great as that of John C. Calhoun or Jefferson Davis. Yet Turner was only a slave in Southampton County, Virginia—during most of his life a rather unimpressive one at that."

The man called the Prophet was born in the year Gabriel died—1800. His mother, an African-born slave, could not bear the idea of bringing a slave into the world and was "so wild . . . that she had to be tied to prevent her from murdering him." The son survived and demonstrated his hatred of slavery in his own way.

A mystic with blood on his mind, a preacher with vengeance on his lips, a dreamer, a fanatic, a terrorist, Nat Turner was a fantastic mixture of gentleness, ruthlessness and piety. Of middling stature, black in color, in demeanor commanding and bold, Nat was five feet, six inches tall, a little dumpy perhaps, running to fat around the middle, with a mustache and a little tuft of hair on his chin.

Early in life, Nat came to the view that God had set him aside for some great purpose. And he worked hard to help God. Systematically ascetic, he forswore tobacco, liquor and money. He avoided crowds and close companionships and wrapped himself in mystery. "Having soon discovered [that] to be great, I must appear so, [I] studiously avoided mixing in society and wrapped myself in mystery, devoting my time to fasting and prayer."

In a lesser man, this would have been cant and bombast. But Nat was clearly no ordinary man. At an early age, he demonstrated a facility with the alphabet. And he was inventive with his hands. Using pieces of wood and metal, he cast different things in moulds made of earth and attempted "to make paper, gunpowder, and many other experiments."

When Nat reached maturity, he was a person of some importance in Southampton County. Slaves in the neighborhood looked to him for advice and direction. Even whites were affected. An overseer fell under Nat's influence and so far overstepped the bounds of propriety that he let Nat baptize him. The conversion took; the overseer gave up his bad habits. The whites were so scandalized that they hounded the overseer out of the state.

With maturity and increasing recognition came understanding. Nat became convinced that he was destined to lead his people out of bondage. Like Gabriel, like Denmark Vesey, he found food for insurrection in the Bible. He immersed himself in religion; he even prayed at the plow. He saw visions and heard voices. One day, he had an unusual vision: he saw black and white spirits wrestling in the sky; the sun grew dark and blood gushed forth in streams.

Ordinary things appeared to the mystical slave in a strange light. While plowing the field, he saw drops of blood on the corn. On the leaves in the woods, he found hieroglyphic characters and numbers. He concluded that the day of judgment for slaveholders was nigh. Another vision confirmed this conclusion. The "spirit," he said, told him that on the appearance of a sign "I should arise and prepare myself and slay my enemies with their own weapons." The sign appeared in the form of a solar eclipse in February, 1831.

Nat chose four disciples, Henry Porter, Hark Travis, Nelson Williams and Samuel Francis, and set his face towards Jerusalem. Some historians believe he found a warrant in the famous passage:

Planning 1831 slave
uprising, Nat Turner
(above, center)
outlines plans at
secret meeting in the
woods. Capture of
Turner (left) ended
Southampton
insurrection. He was
hanged on
November 11, 1831.

Trail of terror traveled by Nat Turner and his men is
indicated on map by gray line. Some sixty whites
were killed in the insurrection.

"From that time began Jesus to show unto his disciples, that he must go unto Jerusalem, and suffer many things of the elders and chief priests, and scribes, and be killed."

In Virginia in that year there was a Jerusalem; it was the county seat of Southampton. The parallel was not lost on the mystical slave. He resolved to strike on July 4, but he became ill and the day passed. There then came another sign—the peculiar color of the sun on August 13. Nat set another date: Sunday, August 21. He promised to meet his disciples on that day at a wooded retreat near his master's farm.

On the appointed day, Nat's disciples gathered on the banks of Cabin Pond. They ate barbecue, drank brandy and discussed death. Nat, a nondrinking man who appreciated the value of a dramatic entrance, did not join them until late in the afternoon. Then he appeared suddenly and assumed control. He ran his eyes over the group; two additional slaves were present at the invitation of his disciples. Nat asked one of them, Will, "how came he there." Will replied that "his life was worth no more than others, and his liberty as dear to him." Six feet tall, or nearly so, well-developed, with a back covered with whip scars, with a face disfigured by a scar extending from his right eye to his chin, Will was the slave of a cruel master. He was said to be the strongest man in the county and he bore a special grudge: his master had sold his wife to a Negro trader. Will later handled the broadax with such ferocity that Nat dubbed him, "Will, the executioner."

Having assured himself of the steadfastness of his men, Nat outlined his plans. They would strike that night, beginning at the home of his master and proceeding from house to house, killing every man, woman and child. In this way, he explained, they would terrorize the whites and stampede them. Then, he said, women and children would be spared and "men too who ceased to resist."

About 10 P.M., the conspirators left their retreat and moved to the home of Joseph Travis. They were seven men, armed with one hatchet and a broadax. Twenty-four hours later, there would be seventy men and at least fifty-seven whites would be dead.

Nat climbed through the window of his master's house and opened the front door. He then led his men to the bedroom of his master and mistress. Nat struck the first blow, but his aim was faulty. Will finished the job. Two boys in an upstairs bedroom were also killed. Nat's band appropriated guns and powder. Leaving the house, Nat recalled that a baby had been spared. Remarking that "nits make lice," he detailed two men to kill the infant.

Moving quietly and swiftly through the night, the little band cut a swath of red, chopping down old, young, male, female. At almost every stop, additional slaves joined them.

"I took my station in the rear," Nat said later, "and, as it was my object to carry terror and devastation wherever we went, I placed fifteen or twenty of the best armed and most to be relied on in front, who generally approached the houses as fast as their horses could run. This was for two purposes—to prevent their escape, and strike terror to the inhabitants. . . ."

All through that terrible night, men, women and children died. No one with a white skin was spared except a family of poor whites who owned no slaves.

Monday morning dawned and Nat rode on.

When the first bodies were discovered, a nameless dread seized the white citizenry. Women, children, and men fled to the swamps and hid under the leaves. Other citizens flocked to public buildings and barricaded the doors. Some whites left the county; others left the state.

Nat rode on, picking up recruits at each stop, moving closer and closer to Jerusalem. On Monday afternoon, he reached the Parker farm, only three miles from Jerusalem. Nat wanted to bypass the farm and push on to the city. His men, some of whom were groggy from periodic raids on cider stills, wanted to stop. Nat gave in—a fatal mistake. While waiting, he met his first opposition. A group of eighteen or twenty whites advanced with guns drawn. Nat ordered a charge. The whites held their ground for a moment and then turned and fled. Nat gave chase, crossed a hill and discovered that the whites had been reinforced by a larger group from Jerusalem. It was now his turn to retreat. He decided to retrace his steps and recruit more men. The next day he was defeated and his men dispersed. Nat retired to Cabin Pond and waited for his disciples to regroup. After waiting for a day or so, he dug a cave and went into hiding.

By this time, soldiers were flocking to the county from all points. Three companies of artillery from Fort Monroe and detachments of men from the warships "Warren" and "Natchez" arrived. Hundreds of soldiers and militiamen from North Carolina and other Virginia counties thronged into the area. All in all, some three thousand armed men came to Southampton to put down the insurrection.

A massacre followed. The enraged whites shot down innocent Negroes who smiled and innocent Negroes who did not smile. The editor of the *Richmond Whig* said: "Men were tortured to death, burned, maimed and subjected to nameless atrocities. The overseers were called upon to point out any slaves whom they distrusted; and if any tried to escape they were shot down."

Nat eluded capture for almost two months. While he was at large, a panic seized large parts of Virginia, North Carolina, and Maryland. General W. H. Broadnax reported to the governor: "The consternation unfortunately was not confined to the county where the danger existed, but extended over all immediately about it. Not a white family in many neighborhoods remained at home, and many went to other counties, and the rest assembled at different points in considerable numbers for mutual protection. Numerous females, with their children, fled in the night with but one imperfect dress and no provisions. I found every hovel at Hicks' Ford literally filled with women and children, with no way to lodge but in heaps on the floors, without any article of food or the means of procuring or cooking provisions. . . ."

In North Carolina, too, people feared Nat Turner more than they feared starvation. An eyewitness said: "It was court week [in Murfreesboro], and most of our men were twelve miles away, in Winton. Fear was seen in every face; women pale and terror-stricken, children crying for protection, men fearful and full of foreboding, but determined to be ready for the worst." A boy rode into the town and reported falsely that a hostile force was within eight miles. The town went up in hysteria. An old man keeled over and died. At least two other white men died of heart failure in the state.

The panic rolled over a large part of the South. A niece of George Washington wrote that the hysteria was "like a smothered volcano—we know not when, or where, the flame will burst forth but we know that death in the most horrid form threatens us. Some have died, others have become deranged from apprehension since the Southampton affair."

When Nat was finally captured, guns were fired all over Southampton County. The women, thinking Nat had assembled another force, fled to the swamps, misinterpreting the cry, "Nat is caught!" for "Nat is coming!"

Nat Turner was taken to Jerusalem in chains. At his trial, he pleaded not guilty, saying that he did not *feel* guilty. Judge Jeremiah Cobb pronounced sentence. "The judgement of the court, is that you be taken hence to the jail from whence you came, thence to the place of execution, and on Friday next, between the hours of ten a.m. and 2 p.m. be hung by the neck until you are dead! dead! dead! and may the Lord have mercy upon your soul."

On November 11, the dark, buddha-bellied man called The Prophet dangled from the end of a rope in a town called Jerusalem. Author W. S. Drewry said Nat prophesied that it would grow dark and rain after his execution. "It did actually rain," Drewry wrote, "and there was for some time a dry spell. This alarmed many whites as well as Negroes."

Parables should not be taken literally.

The darkness Nat saw, came. It came in a generation of crisis in which the issue of Negro slavery almost severed the nation. Nat Turner's "dark arm of vengeance" did much to bring that crisis to a head. In this, Drewry is correct. Nat Turner's insurrection, he wrote, "was a landmark in the history of slavery. . . . It was the forerunner of the great slavery debates, which resulted in the abolition of slavery in the United States and was, indirectly, most instrumental in bringing about this result. Its importance is truly conceived by the old negroes of Southampton and vicinity, who reckon all time from 'Nat's Fray' or 'Old Nat's War.'"

6

The Generation of Crisis

Let our posterity know that we their ancestors, uncultured and unlearned, amid all trials and temptations, were men of integrity; recognized with gratefulness their truest friends dishonoured and in peril; were enabled to resist the seductions of ease and the intimidations of power; were true to themselves, the age in which they lived, their abject race, and the cause of man; shrunk not from trial, nor from sufferings—but conscious of Responsibility and impelled by Duty, gave themselves up to the vindication of the high hopes, and the lofty aims of true Humanity!

ALEXANDER CRUMMELL

THE WHOLE STORY is in three boys and an old man. In the years of hope and promise, in the years before the big war, before the blood and the rats and the bleached bones, the old man and the three boys dreamed dreams and made prophecies.

The old man heard fire bells ringing in the night.

Before old age downed him, he had spoken the language of desperation and death. This is "a reprieve only, not a final sentence," he had said, adding: "This momentous question, like a fire bell ringing in the night, awakened and filled me with terror." He was talking about the Missouri Compromise, a thing of lines and words, and slavery, a thing of words and compromises. The old man knew whereof he spoke: he himself was involved in the compromise he himself had made impossible. He had, when his blood was hot, put words on paper.

We hold these truths to be self-evident, that all men are created equal, that they are endowed by their Creator with certain unalienable Rights, that among these are Life, Liberty and the pursuit of Happiness.

He had written these words in a room in Philadelphia when he was thirty-three. Now, in another room, in another age, fifty years to the date after the signing of the Declaration of Independence, Thomas Jefferson, the sage of Monticello, the architect, the philosopher, the humanitarian, lay dying in a house filled with rare books and old slaves. All his life, he had wrestled with the awful presence of *his* slaves and the noble sound of *his* words and he had gone down in defeat. He was not a small man and so his defeat gives no man joy. In him was the strength and the weakness of America. He died on July 4, 1826, and went to his grave, borne by weeping slaves.

In that same year, over in Little Pigeon Creek, Indiana, a big awkward boy of seventeen, all arms and legs, was reading books and chopping down trees. He was dirt poor, a descendant of poor people who left Europe running and came to America looking for something better than the life they had. Some of his kin signed their names with an X, but he was dreaming bigger things. He read books in an area where few people read books. People said, "There's suthin' peculiarsome about Abe."

"Peculiarsome," too, was Frederick Augustus Washington Bailey, a nine-year-old slave in Baltimore, Maryland. Frederick and Abe were two of a kind. Both would climb out of their narrow prisons on ladders of words; both would climb steep mountains and walk lonely paths; and both would grapple with the revolutionary implications in Thomas Jefferson's words. Fate had sent their forefathers across the same ocean. Abe's folks had been pushed out of Europe by need and want, and Frederick's folks had been pulled out of Africa by greed and gold. Fate had implanted in both their bosoms a hunger for letters. Frederick's mistress wanted to teach him the alphabet, but his master forbade it. "Give a nigger an inch," he said, "and he will take an ell. . . . Learning would spoil the best nigger in the world." Listening, thinking, dreaming, Frederick came to the conclusion that words were power. He hid dirty pages in his pockets and when no one was looking he extracted the pages and spelled out the magic words. Like Abe, Frederick was a comer.

Up the country a bit, another comer was deep in the happy world of books and dreams. Jefferson Davis, eighteen, the grandson of an illiterate Welsh immigrant, a namesake of the great Thomas Jefferson, was studying war at West Point. Like Abraham Lincoln, like the slave who would take the name Frederick Douglass, Jefferson Davis was ambitious. It would be said of him later that he was "ambitious as Lucifer and cold as a lizard."

In these three boys, in their hopes, in their dreams, in their fears, is the whole story of the crisis which reached a climax in a Civil War and the emancipation of four million slaves with a book value of four billion dollars. The crisis was a compound of many things, of machines and turnpikes and railroad tracks; of sin, sex and salvation; of the restless yearnings of poor whites and the volcanic stirrings of poor blacks; of the fear, guilt and anxiety which lay like a slave chain across the American soul. Abraham Lincoln, Frederick Douglass, and Jefferson Davis did not make the crisis, but they would stand in the eye of the storm and each, in his own way, would symbolize latent possibilities in the American Dream.

How did the crisis come about?

It came about because millions of men made choices, acted and were called upon finally to back up their acts. It came about because men said words, wrote them and were called upon finally to back up their words.

The crisis had been a long time coming. It went back to the Founding Fathers who gave in to Southern threats, compromised and wrote slavery into the Constitution. They were not little men, the Founding Fathers, and they were ashamed of what they were doing: they could not bring themselves to write the ugly word "slave"; they used instead weasel words like "persons held to service or labor" (Art. IV, sec. 2) and they contented themselves with the idle hope that slavery would wither and die. But slavery did not die. A machine, a thing of brushes and cylinders and wire teeth, made black men and white fibers big business. Year by year, the evil spread until it ate into the ganglia and tendons of American life.

The Missouri Compromise made men look at the monster they had created. A line was scratched on a map and slavery was forbidden to the north of that line; but, as it turned out, nothing had been settled. Far off on the horizon, a storm was rising; but men were walking in the streets without umbrellas. Men with eyes to see, saw it. Thomas Jefferson saw it and cried out in despair. John Quincy Adams saw it and told his diary that the bargain between slavery and freedom in the U.S. Constitution was "morally and politically vicious." Other men saw it and moved with a vague sense of disquiet to contain the monster. Step by step, act by act, compromise by compromise, men moved toward the great antislavery drama which brought the issue to a head.

The antislavery crusade, one of the great social movements of modern history, did not begin in 1831 with William Lloyd Garrison; nor was it a crusade in which white men led and Negroes followed. This crusade, like so many other things in American life, went back to Jefferson's massive ALL. Negroes were in the vanguard of the Rights of Man movement which resulted in the manumission of thousands of slaves and the abolition of slavery in the North. Prince Hall, the Masonic leader and Revolutionary War veteran, and other Negro leaders presented petitions, raised money for test cases and protested against taxation without representation *in America.*

On the second day of the nineteenth century, the free Negroes of Philadelphia, led by Absalom Jones, an Episcopalian priest, and James Forten, a wealthy manufacturer, submitted an antislavery petition to Congress. Eight months later, King Gabriel made an abortive attempt to establish a Negro state in Virginia. Alarmed whites organized a colonization society and made frantic efforts to settle free Negroes ("a dangerous and useless element") in Liberia. Many white abolitionists were fooled, but Negroes perceived that the colonizationists were generally anti-Negro and proslavery. One Negro put the case against the colonizationists with admirable bluntness. "The Colonizationists," he said, "want us to go to Liberia if we will. If we won't go there, we may go to hell."

Neither place excited the imagination of nineteenth-century Negroes. In state and local meetings, in pamphlets, papers and books, free Negroes told whites that the Negro was in America and that he was in America to stay. "This is our home," a Negro convention said, "and this is our country. Beneath its soil lies the bones of our fathers; for it, some of them fought, bled, and died. Here we were born, and here we will die."

A decade of anticolonization agitation gave free Negroes of the North a sense of community. Out of this agitation came the pioneer Negro abolitionists, the Negro convention movement and the first Negro newspaper, *Freedom's Journal*, which was published for the first time on March 16, 1827, by Samuel E. Cornish, a Presbyterian minister, and John B. Russwurm, the first Negro college graduate (Bowdoin, 1826). Richard Allen, the great AME bishop, was the leader of the first Negro convention which met in Philadelphia in 1830, three years before the founding of the American Anti-Slavery Society.

Perhaps the greatest of the pioneer Negro abolitionists was James Forten, a fair-skinned Philadelphian who fought in the American Revolution and later amassed a fortune of $100,000 as a sail manufacturer. Forten was a major abolitionist angel. He pulled Garrison out of several financial crises and assumed a large part of the indebtedness of Garrison's *Liberator*.

Although pioneer Negro leaders spurned colonization and made sporadic protests against slavery, the antislavery crusade did not begin until the end of the second decade of the century. It began with the words of a free Negro and the acts of a slave. David Walker, the John the Baptist of the antislavery crusade, was a product of the emerging group consciousness of American Negroes. Born free in Wilmington, North Carolina, he decided that the air of a slaveholding community was noxious. "If I remain in this bloody land," he said, "I will not live long. As true as God reigns, I will be avenged for the sorrows which my people have suffered. This is not the place for me—no, no. I must leave this part of the country. . . . Go, I must."

Walker moved to Boston, opened a secondhand clothing store and started peddling incendiary ideas. In 1828, he appeared on the Boston scene as a radical agitator; a year later, he published *Walker's Appeal*, one of the great abolition pamphlets. Into this slim volume, Walker poured the accumulated disgust of his people. He scornfully dismissed the slaveholding Christians of "this Republican Land of Liberty!!!!!!" and urged slaves to cut their tormentors' throats from ear to ear. "Kill," he said, "or be killed."

These words, like a cry of fire in a crowded theater, constricted hearts and made sweat run down men's backs. The governors of Virginia, Georgia, and North Carolina called their legislatures into secret sessions. Consternation turned into fear two years later when Nat Turner added a bloody period to *Walker's Appeal*. Nat Turner's 1831 ride marked a turning point in Negro history. After Nat, events hurried forward with the portentousness of a Greek drama.

A major actor in this drama was William Lloyd Garrison, a brilliant young journalist who published the first issue of his famous *Liberator* in 1831. His first editorial sang with indignation. "I will be as harsh as truth, and as uncompromising as justice. On this subject [slavery] I do not wish to think, to speak, or write, with moderation. No! No! Tell a man whose house is on fire to give a moderate alarm; tell him to moderately rescue his wife from the hands of the ravisher; tell the mother to gradually extricate her babe from the fire into which it has fallen; but urge me not to use moderation in a cause like the present! I am in earnest—I will not equivocate— I will not excuse—I will not retreat a single inch—AND I WILL BE HEARD."

Two years later, Garrison and other abolitionists organized the American Anti-Slavery Society in Philadelphia. Among the Negroes who helped organize this society were Robert Purvis, a wealthy young man who lived a life of leisure in a Philadelphia suburb; James McCrummell, a Philadelphia dentist; and James G. Barbadoes, a Boston reformer. Three Negroes served on the society's first executive committee—Samuel E. Cornish, the minister and editor; Theodore S. Wright, a New York minister; and Peter S. Williams, an Episcopalian priest. Interestingly enough, David Walker, Garrison, and the American Anti-Slavery Society took their stand on the rock of Thomas Jefferson's Declaration.

Crises breed big men. They come forth like diamonds, perfected by the pressures they have been subjected to. It is true today in Africa; it was so 120 years ago in Negro America. Never before or since have so many great men and women crowded the stage of history. In the early days of the antislavery struggle, men like Purvis, Cornish, Wright, and Forten fought shoulder to shoulder with Garrison and Theodore D. Weld. They fought with the traditional weapons of agitation: pamphlets, books, resolutions, petitions and the spoken word. Hundreds of unsung Negroes also manned the Underground Railroad, a complex network of barns, stables and big-hearted men and women.

The fugitives who traveled the Underground Railroad were the greatest of the abolitionists. Far from being passive, as they are usually portrayed, they were major antagonists in the sectional drama. As much as William Lloyd Garrison, as much as John Brown, they made men face up to the evils of the slave system. In an age when most people wanted to forget, "running abolitionists" made them remember.

Fugitive slaves scaled mountains, forded creeks and threaded the

William Lloyd Garrison, one of major figures of abolitionist movement, worked closely with Negro abolitionists like James Forten and Charles Lenox Remond.

Frederick Douglass, one of the great men of the nineteenth century, was a leading abolitionist, politician and editor. Born a slave in Maryland in 1817, Douglass escaped in 1838.

Pennsylvania Hall, erected by abolitionists in Philadelphia, was burned on May 17, 1838, by Northerners who opposed the antislavery crusade. There were five major anti-Negro riots in Philadelphia between 1832 and 1849.

forests; they came across the Ohio River and the Chesapeake Bay; they came with ailing women and sick children; softly sometimes and sometimes imperiously they rapped on windows and begged help: a piece of bread, a spoon of medicine, directions to the next town. Wherever they rapped, wherever they stopped, men and women had to make a decision—either for or against slavery. Fugitive slaves reached people who were cool or hostile to the "speaking abolitionists." Whigs helped them and Democrats, too; Quakers helped them, and Southern Baptists. Frederick Douglass said "we seldom called in vain upon Whig or Democrat for help. Men were better than their theology, and truer to humanity than to their politics, or their offices."

"It was said long ago," the *Boston Commonwealth* commented, "that the true romance of America was not in the fortunes of the Indian, where Cooper sought it; nor in New England character, where Judd found it; nor in the social contrasts of Virginia planters, as Thackeray imagined, but in the story of the fugitive slaves."

Thousands of fugitive slaves—estimates range from 40,000 to 100,000—escaped from the South in the years of crisis. In the background of each succeeding crisis—the fight over the Wilmot Proviso, the Kansas-Nebraska Bill, the Compromise of 1850—was the constant irritant of intrepid slaves who lectured with their feet.

The road these slaves traveled ran from the sunny South to the snow-white shores of Canada. One great route ran through Ohio and Indiana; the other went through Maryland, Delaware, and Pennsylvania. Following the North Star, fugitives made their way along these routes to the "Promised Land" of Canada. Along the way, they were aided by "a company of godly men"—some of them white, some of them black, a great many of them women.

White abolitionists like Levi Coffin, Thomas Garrett and thousands of gentle Quakers were brilliant as undercover agents who hid slaves and slipped them through to the next Underground Railroad station. No less brilliant were scores of Negro agents who did the same thing at far greater risks. Two Negroes, David Ruggles and William Still, were in charge of the key Underground Railroad stations in New York City and Philadelphia, respectively. James G. Birney, the great white abolitionist, said the Underground Railroad in his area was "almost uniformly managed by the colored people. I know nothing of them generally till they are past." Levi Coffin, the "president of the Underground Railroad," said that fugitive slaves generally stopped at the homes of Negro agents.

Was it true what they said about Dixie?

This question was the core of the slavery dialogue. And no one could answer the question better than fugitive slaves. In the forties, fugitive slaves moved into the front lines of the antislavery battle. No abolitionist meeting was complete without the presence of a Negro speaker or a Negro exhibit (a fugitive slave). Audiences would accept a white speaker, if necessary; but they preferred the real thing, a speaker like Henry Highland Garnet who could say: "I was born in slavery, and have escaped, to tell you, and others, what the monster has done, and is still doing."

"Oh," Sarah Grimké cried out, "that the slaves could write a book!"

In the two decades preceding the Civil War, a great many slaveholders expressed hopes that slaves would stop writing books. Scores of slaves escaped and told; and the abolitionist audience increased. Slave narratives became a new form of literature. An English clergyman, Ephraim Peabody, observed that "America had the mournful honor of adding a new department to the literature of civilization—the autobiography of escaped slaves."

The pioneer Negro abolitionists gave way in the forties to the giants of the movement, Charles Lenox Remond, the first Negro to take the platform as a professional antislavery lecturer; Samuel Ringgold Ward, the eloquent black man who pastored a white church; Henry Highland Garnet, the bitterly brilliant Thomas Paine of the movement; Martin R. Delany, the Harvard man who was the first major Negro nationalist; William Wells Brown, the grandson of Daniel Boone (he said) and the first Negro to write a novel and a play. There were others: the big-souled, God-intoxi-cated women, Sojourner Truth and Harriet Tubman; and scholars like J. W. C. Pennington, the minister who received a D.D. degree from the University of Heidelberg while he was still a fugitive slave; Alexander Crummell, the erudite Episcopal priest; and James McCune Smith, the New York physician who graduated from the University of Glasgow.

Frederick Augustus Washington Bailey, the giant of the giants, graduated from no school. He escaped from Baltimore in 1838 by borrowing a sailor suit and an official-looking paper with a big American eagle on it. Grabbing a train, young Bailey traveled to New York, flashing his eagle-stamped paper as he went. Three years later, he stood on a platform with a new name, Douglass, and an old story. The story was old, but no one had ever told it that way before. By turns humorous, dolorous, and indignant, Douglass transported his audiences to slave row. A master mimic, he could make people *laugh* at a slaveowner preaching the duties of Chris-tian obedience; could make them *see* the humiliation of a black maiden ravished by a brutal slaveowner; could make them *hear* the sobs of a mother separated from her child. Through him, peo-ple could cry and curse and *feel;* through him, people could *live* slavery. "White men and black men," William Wells Brown said, "had talked against slavery, but none had ever spoken like Fred-erick Douglass."

The Garrisonians hired Douglass and sent him on speaking tours. It was a trying experience: life was not easy, in this age, for white agitators; it was impossible for Negroes. There were riots and other disorders and young toughs came charging to the platform, scream-ing, "Kill the nigger," "Get the god-damned nigger." Douglass was pelted with eggs and thrown down steps; but he stood his ground and took his knocks. People came, listened and went away con-vinced. More important, for Douglass anyway, they left singing his praises.

Douglass grew in the job; so did his ambition; so did his prob-lems. To some abolitionists, the Negro was an exhibit, not an advocate. Douglass disturbed these people; he did not fit into the usual pattern; he not only recited evils but he also denounced them. "People won't believe that you were a slave, Frederick," one abolitionist said, "if you keep on in this way." Another abolitionist told Douglass: "Better have a little of the plantation speech than not; it is not best that you seem too learned." More blunt were the repeated exhortations: "Give us the facts, we will take care of the philosophy." Douglass refused to be stereotyped. "I could not always follow the injunction," he wrote, "for I was now reading, and thinking. New views of the subject were being presented to my mind. It did not entirely satisfy me to narrate wrongs; I felt like denouncing them. . . . Besides, I was growing and needed room."

England gave Douglass and other Negro abolitionists the room they needed. Lords, Ladies, and earls welcomed them to suburban estates; ambassadors feted them in Regent's Park; average people flocked to their lectures in Exeter Hall and Finsbury Chapel. The *New York Herald* was indignant. "It is good," the paper said, "to be dyed black if you come up to London, for Negro love is filling all ranks, from Prince Albert and the Queen, down to the poorest subjects."

One hundred years later, America would pay England back by drooling over English-oppressed Africans, but, in the middle of the nineteenth century, it was fashionable to receive American-oppressed Negroes. The Negro abolitionists were unusually successful, not only for themselves but also for America. The seeds they sowed may have saved the American Union. During the Civil War, the English government sympathized with the Confederacy but did not dare extend official recognition because of the antislavery convictions of the great mass of people.

Douglass and other Negro abolitionists were good for England and England was good for them. Douglass spent nineteen months in England. "I seem to have undergone a transformation," he wrote. "I live a new life." Tall, well-made, with an impressive mane of hair, a throbbing baritone voice, and a vast forehead over deep-set smoldering eyes, Douglass created something of a sensation in England. One white man found him "touchy, huffish, haughty" with "many of the characteristics of the man of genius." Another abolitionist wrote: ". . . you can hardly conjure how he is noticed." Douglass' female admirers, he added, "exceed the bounds of propriety or delicacy as far as appearances are concerned."

The famous Negro abolitionist crisscrossed England and Ireland, winning friends and influencing people for the antislavery cause. His reception was so warm that he was tempted to remain abroad. But, in an eloquent Farewell Speech at London Tavern, he said: "I choose rather to go home; to return to America. I glory in the conflict, that I may hereafter exult in the victory. I know that victory is certain. [Cheers.] I go, turning my back upon the ease, comfort, and respectability which I might maintain even here, ignorant as I am. Still, I will go back, for the sake of my brethren. I go to suffer with them; to toil with them; to endure insult with them; to undergo outrage with them; to lift up my voice in their behalf; to speak and write in their vindication; and struggle in their ranks for that emancipation which shall yet be achieved by the power of truth and of principle for that oppressed people."

So, turning his back on ease, Douglass returned to America. For almost six years, he had labored in the Garrison vineyard. Now, he stepped out on his own. In 1847, the year that Abraham Lincoln entered the House of Representatives, the year that Jefferson Davis, the Mexican War hero, entered the Senate, Frederick Douglass started publishing the *North Star* in Rochester, New York. From that year until the abolition of slavery, he was in the forefront of the abolitionist ranks.

Frederika Bremer, the Swedish traveler, saw Douglass in Rochester when he was about thirty. "I found him," she wrote, "to be a light mulatto . . . with an unusually handsome exterior, such as I imagine should belong to an Arab chief. Those beautiful eyes were full of dark fire." Douglass, at the time, employed a white governess. The Swedish traveler wondered why a white woman would expose herself to the scorn of the community. "But," said she, "possibly has that former slave, now the apostle-militant of freedom, that greatness of character which makes such a sacrifice easy to an ardent soul."

Douglass, Remond, Ward, Garnet and other Negro abolitionists played a major role in shaping the crisis which led to the Civil War. They, too, fought with Garrison and Wendell Phillips; but some of them, the greatest of them, thought their own thoughts and went their own way. They came in all shapes and sizes and colors, these men and women; and they ranged the spectrum from pre-M. L. King, Jr., passive resisters to post-Paine radicals.

Charles Lenox Remond, the first Negro to rise to prominence in the abolitionist movement, leaned toward the Garrison tenets of nonviolence and nonvoting. Born in Salem, Massachusetts, the free son of a free West Indian hairdresser who got on a boat and paid his way to America, Remond was an elegant little man in elegant clothes—a lover of fine horses and the New England air, fastidious, spare, with a long deeply-furrowed face and an aquiline nose. Remond began his career as a professional abolitionist in 1838 and shot to fame after a triumphant tour of England. He was an ardent Garrisonian, but he later abandoned nonviolence and championed slave revolts.

One of the seventeen members of the first antislavery society in America, Remond later served as vice-president of the New England Anti-Slavery Society and president of his county unit. A bitter foe of intolerance, he lectured against slavery until its abolition. In the forties and fifties, however, he was overshadowed by the rising star of Frederick Douglass—and he was human enough to resent it.

Remond was not a lucky man; and history, largely the story of lucky men, has passed him by. He did not have the firsthand knowledge of slavery that Douglass had; and his speeches lacked Douglass' concreteness and fire. In Remond's later years, illness, bad luck and frustration made him somewhat peevish and petulant. When Douglass broke with Garrison, Remond supported Garrison and

Henry "Box" Brown escaped from slavery in a box lined with
baize. A friend locked him in the box and shipped it from
Richmond to Philadelphia. Brown stepped from the box
and sang: "I waited patiently for the Lord, and he heard
my prayer."

Among the outstanding women in the antislavery ranks were Harriet Tubman (left), who helped three hundred slaves escape from the South, and Sojourner Truth, who was an abolitionist lecturer.

publicly thanked God that he was not a slave or the son of a slave. Douglass, stung to the quick, retorted: "I thank God that I am neither a barber nor the son of a barber."

Samuel Ringgold Ward, one of the most eloquent men of an age of eloquence, was a fugitive slave and the son of a fugitive slave. Unlike Remond, who was allied with the Massachusetts Garrisonians, Ward was a New Yorker who advocated a militant, political brand of abolitionism. Born in 1817 in Maryland, Ward was carried to New York at an early age by his fugitive slave parents. He was educated there, became a Presbyterian minister and pastored a white church in South Butler, New York. He became a professional antislavery agent in 1839 and was one of the first Negroes to join the Liberty party.

Big-framed, eloquent, "so black that when he closed his eyes you could not see him," Ward was an effective lecturer and propagandist. He was advertised as "The Black Daniel Webster," but some men thought him a better speaker than Webster or Frederick Douglass. Unlike Douglass, however, Ward lacked staying power. He fled America in 1851, went to England and then to Jamaica where he died in poverty.

Sojourner Truth and Harriet Tubman had staying power. Both were fanatically religious, but they expressed their religion in different ways. John Brown liked to make a rough distinction between "talking" abolitionists and "acting" abolitionists. Sojourner Truth was a "talking" abolitionist—a preacher, seer and teacher. She was complex; so complex, in fact, that no one paragraph or book, for that matter, will cover her. She burned for love of the whole world; but, like many world-savers, she was bored by domesticity and left her children at the drop of a cause. She loathed slavery, but she bore five children for her master. She was a religious fanatic, but she was associated with a scandalous religious movement which dissolved in charges of adultery, incest and murder.

Perhaps her background had something to do with it.

Born Isabella in upstate New York in 1797 or thereabouts, she inherited a deep mysticism from her mother—Mau Mau Bett. At an early age, she was sold; thereafter, she had an interesting succession of masters. One family was coarse and profane; from them, Isabella learned to curse and smoke. Another master was sensuous; for him, Isabella had the children.

By 1827, when she became free under New York's gradual emancipation act, Isabella had been through the wringer. With hardly a deep breath, she headed straight for another one. In New York City, she fell in with a group of eccentrics who preached a "religious" doctrine of "match spirits"—every person was entitled to choose a new mate who "matched" his or her spirit. As a maid and religious exhorter, Isabella followed this group to Sing Sing, New York, where it disintegrated amid wild headlines of murder and loose sexual goings-on. Isabella was not involved in the shady sexual experiments—not, however, because of strength of character. Isabella was frank; she was lucky; it proved impossible to find a "match" for her spirit.

At this point, an interesting thing happened: Isabella became a new person. One day in 1843, she walked out of New York City with a bag of clothes, twenty-five cents and a new name: Sojourner Truth. From that date until her death, she walked the land, preaching, teaching, lecturing. The great and the near great sang her praises and quoted her strong, striking utterances.

Harriet Beecher Stowe could never forget the looks of her—a gaunt, misty-eyed black woman in a gray dress, a white turban and a sunbonnet, calm and erect, like "one of her native palm trees waving alone in the desert." Novelist Stowe said she had never met anyone who had more personal presence. "She seemed perfectly self-possessed and at her ease; in fact, there was almost an unconscious superiority in the odd, composed manner in which she looked down on me."

On a platform, Sojourner was unforgettable. Though illiterate, she had power and a quick, incisive mind that reduced things to their essentials. Once, at a religious meeting, a speaker praised the U.S. Constitution. Sojourner stood up, all six feet of her, and dropped her sunbonnet on the platform. "Children," she said, "I talks to God and God talks to me. I goes out and talks to God in de fields and de woods. Dis morning I was walking out, and I got over de fence. I saw de wheat a holding up its head, looking very big. I goes up and takes holt of it. You b'lieve it, dere was *no* wheat dare. I says, 'God, what *is* de matter wid *dis* wheat?' and he says to me, 'Sojourner, dere is a little weasel [weevil] in it.' Now I hears talkin' bout de Constitution and de rights of man. I come up and I takes holt of dis Constitution. It looks *mighty big,* and I feels for *my* rights, but dere ain't any dare. Den I says, 'God, what *ails* dis Constitution?' He says to me, 'Sojourner, dere is a little *weasel* in it.'"

Harriet Tubman attacked the "weasel" with boldness and directness. She was John Brown's kind of man; he called her "the most of a man naturally that I ever met with." Harriet was born in Maryland and escaped when she was about twenty-five. She went with a threat in her heart. "I had reasoned dis out in my mind," she said; "there was one or two things I had a *right* to, liberty or death; if I could not have one, I would have the other; for no man should take me alive; I should fight for my liberty as long as my strength lasted, and when de time come for me to go, de Lord would let dem take me."

And how did it feel when she touched free land?

"I looked at my hands to see if I was the same person now I was free. Dere was such a glory over everything, de sun comes like gold through the trees. . . ."

Freedom felt so good that Harriet Tubman returned to the South nineteen times and brought out more than three hundred slaves. Rewards for her capture mounted to an astronomical figure: $40,000. No matter. The short black woman continued her dangerous work, bringing out her brothers and sisters, her aging parents and anyone else who wanted to go. By 1852, she was a legend in antislavery circles. "A more heroic soul," Professor Hopkins said, "did not breathe in the bosom of Judith or of Jeanne D'Arc."

Like Harriet Tubman, like Samuel Ringgold Ward, like Benja-

min Banneker and Frederick Douglass, Henry Highland Garnet
was born in Maryland, that early nursery of Negro greats. He was
the grandson, tradition said, of an African chieftain; this was said
of almost everyone in those days; but in Garnet's case, it could have
been true—he was that kind of man. When he was ten, his family
escaped and carried him to New York, where he received an education and became a Presbyterian minister. Even then, the "Thomas
Paine of the abolitionist movement" was a striking figure; tall,
commanding, black, broad-nosed with "eyes that look through
you."

Garnet was a sufferer; he suffered more than any other figure
in abolitionist circles. Like John Brown, he could not stand to
hear the word slavery. In 1840, at the age of twenty-five, he attracted attention with a slashing attack on slavery at the American
Anti-Slavery Convention. Three years later, he made one of the
most eloquent speeches ever uttered by an American Negro. Speaking to a national convention of colored men in Buffalo, New York,
he suggested a national slave strike.

"Brethren," he said, speaking directly to the slaves, "the time
has come when you must act for yourselves. . . . Look around
you, and behold the bosoms of your loving wives heaving with
untold agonies! Hear the cries of your poor children! Remember
the stripes your fathers bore. Think of the torture and disgrace of
your noble mothers. Think of your wretched sisters, loving virtue
and purity, as they are driven into concubinage and are exposed to
the unbridled lusts of incarnate devils. Think of the undying glory
that hangs around the ancient name of Africa—and forget not that
you are native born American citizens, and as such, you are justly
entitled to all the rights that are granted to the freest. Think how
many tears you have poured out upon the soil which you have cultivated with unrequited toil and enriched with your blood; and
then go to your lordly enslavers and tell them plainly, that you
are determined to be free. . . . Do this, and for ever after cease to
toil for the heartless tyrants, who give you no other reward but
stripes and abuse. If they then commence the work of death, they,

and not you, will be responsible for the consequences. You had better all die—*die immediately*, than live slaves and entail your wretchedness upon your posterity. If you would be free in this generation, here is your only hope . . . there is not much hope of redemption without the shedding of blood. If you must bleed, let it all come at once—rather *die freemen, than live to be slaves.*"

In an age of danger and doubt, Garnet, Douglass and other black abolitionists came to grips with dilemmas which lie deep in the Negro's heart. Frederick Douglass asked the old and insistent questions: "How can I sing the Lord's song in a strange land?" The answers revolved around the traditional trilogy: ballots, bullets or Bibles, and Iago's injunction: "Go, make money." The Garrisonians, led by the Philadelphians and Charles Lenox Remond, condemned "complexional institutions" (Negro churches, lodges, schools, newspapers and conventions). The Garrisonians also abandoned political action and advocated a campaign based on passive resistance and moral force.

The hard-boiled New Yorkers (Ward, Garnet and, after 1851, Douglass) favored ballots, if possible, and bullets, if necessary. The New Yorkers were opportunists on the issue of "complexional institutions." They were in favor of complete integration, but if circumstances made this impossible they unhesitatingly recommended special institutions. Douglass, for example, anticipated Booker T. Washington with his plan for a manual training college.

The New Yorkers also favored Negro conventions and Negro newspapers. At stake here was a bitter issue of power. Douglass, Ward and Garnet were independent men who felt uncomfortable in subsidiary roles; they demanded a share in the "generalship" of the movement. Douglass broke with Garrison on this issue. In a statement reminiscent of Toussaint L'Ouverture, he said: "No people that has solely depended on foreign aid, or rather, upon the efforts of those, in any way identified with the oppressor, to undo the heavy burdens, ever stood forth in the attitude of Freedom." He also lashed out at the "colored mail-wrappers" in the Garrisonian camp and said, "Our oppressed people are wholly ignored, in one sense, in the generalship of the movement."

Douglass believed that he and other black abolitionists could make a positive contribution by proving that Negroes were active rather than passive cogs in the antislavery machinery. He said that ". . . the man who has *suffered the wrong* is the man to *demand redress,*—that the man STRUCK is the man to CRY OUT—and that he who has *endured the cruel pangs of Slavery* is the man to *advocate Liberty.* It is evident that we must be our own representatives and advocates, not exclusively, but peculiarly—not distinct from, but in connection with our white friends."

Black abolitionists were also divided over words. When Daniel Payne, the AME leader, uttered the plaintive cry, "Who am I, God? And what?" there was no dearth of possible answers. Early Negro leaders ("Sons of Africa") identified themselves in African terms (African Lodge, Free African Society, African Baptist Church). When the campaign to send Negroes back to Africa moved into high gear, a Negro convention, dominated by Philadelphians, urged Negroes to "abandon use of the word 'colored,'" and "especially to remove the title of African from their institutions." Philadelphia leaders later recommended the use of the term "Oppressed Americans." This got a laugh in New York circles. "Oppressed Americans!" snorted Samuel Cornish, "*who are they?* Nonsense brethren!! You are COLORED AMERICANS. The Indians are RED AMERICANS, and the white people are WHITE AMERICANS and *you are as good as they, and they are no better than you.*" A complicating factor was the presence of Negro nationalists like Martin R. Delany of whom Douglass said: "I thank God for making me a man simply; but Delany always thanks him for making him a black man." Delany said no people could gain respect unless they retained their identity. He urged Negroes to identify as Africans, Blacks, Mulattoes and Coloreds. A short, brilliant man of a "most defiant blackness," Delany was one of the backers of a Negro convention which made the surprisingly mod-

John B. Russwurm was one of the founders of the Negro press. Russwurm and Samuel E. Cornish founded the first Negro newspaper, *Freedom's Journal*, in 1827.

Henry Highland Garnet, minister and editor, was called the "Thomas Paine of the abolitionist movement." In famous speech of 1843, he called for a slave revolt.

Fugitive slaves played significant role in the events which led to the Civil War. Some cities refused to return fugitive slaves. Some 2,000 soldiers were required to escort Anthony Burns, captured slave, to Boston ship which returned him to his master.

ern prediction that the "question of black and white" would one day decide the future of the world.

This intramural debate among Negro abolitionists took place against a backdrop of deepening crisis. Negroes in the North were nominally free, but they were hemmed in by restrictions. As free men, they were wanted neither in the South nor in the North. They lived along the docks and wharves and in dark alleys—on "Nigger Hill" in Boston, in Little Africa in Cincinnati. Wherever they lived, people wanted them to go away. Some states like Illinois and Ohio refused free Negroes admittance unless they could post large bonds. Outside New England, free Negroes were generally denied the ballot and were barred from the jury box. They could not testify against whites and they could not enter certain trades.

Bread, in this age, was crucial. A potato famine in Ireland and political complications on the Continent sent millions of poor white immigrants to America. The Irish settled in the big cities and fought Negroes for elbow room in the slums and working space in kitchens and on the docks. In some cases, this contest approached an open war—the worst kind of war, a war for bread and milk and potatoes. It was a dreadful contest, but it was a contest which, in the nature of things, could only go one way; after all, the white immigrants *were* white.

In the two decades preceding the Civil War, white immigrants depressed wages and eliminated Negroes as serious competitors in several fields. The situation was alarming; some Negroes were actually starving; and behind the danger of starvation lay the danger of mob violence at the hand of desperately insecure immigrants. Fred Douglass, reading the signs of the times, sat down and wrote an editorial.

LEARN TRADES OR STARVE!

. . . White men are becoming house-servants, cooks and stewards on vessels—at hotels.—They are becoming porters, stevedores, wood-saw-yers, hod-carriers, brick-makers, white-washers and barbers, so that the blacks can scarcely find the means of subsistence—a few years ago, and a *white* barber would have been a curiosity—now their poles stand on every street. Formerly blacks were almost the exclusive coachmen in wealthy families: this is so no longer; white men are now employed, and for aught we see, they fill their servile station with an obsequiousness as profound as that of the blacks. The readiness and ease with which they adapt themselves to these conditions ought not to be lost sight of by the colored people. The meaning is very important, and we should learn it. We are taught our insecurity by it. Without the means of living, life is a curse, and leaves us at the mercy of the oppressor to become his debased slaves. Now, colored men, what do you mean to do, for you must do something? The American Colonization Society tells you to go to Canada. Others tell you to go to school. We tell you to go to work; and to work you must go or die."

This was easier said than done. Negroes were excluded from some trades by unions; and it was extremely difficult for them to get apprenticeship training. On one occasion, for instance, the president of a Cincinnati mechanic association was tried for the crime of helping a Negro youth to learn a trade.

Neither fish nor fowl, neither slave nor free, Negroes in the North existed on a precarious ledge. At any moment, they could be shelved off. Seldom in any country have men lived in such a vale of anxiety. Time and time again, whites herded Negroes into groups and pointed to the city boundaries. Time and time again, immigrants, fresh from the boats, cracked the skulls of Negroes and burned their homes and churches. Some men said openly that the only solution to the "Negro problem" was the "Indian solution." An Indianian said, "It would be better to kill them off at once, for there is no other way to get rid of them." He added ominously: "We know how the Puritans did with the Indians, who were infinitely more magnanimous and less impudent than the colored race."

Standing outside the pale of justice, enslaved in the South, despised in the North and patronized by his friends, the nineteenth-century Negro tasted the dregs of bitterness. "What stone," cried New York Negroes in 1860, "has been left unturned to degrade us? What hand has refused to fan the flame of popular prejudice against us? What American artist has not caricatured us? What wit has not laughed at our wretchedness? What songster has not made merry over our depressed spirits? What press has not ridiculed and condemned us? Few, few, very few. . . ."

Why did they take it? Why didn't they give up the fight and flee? The answer is noble in its simplicity; they believed in America. Their forefathers, they said, had settled the land and "manured it" with blood. The land was theirs; the country was theirs; they were willing to fight for it.

Listen to Henry Highland Garnet, Douglass' most formidable rival. At a Negro convention, Garnet rises and limps to the lectern. His right leg has been amputated, but he moves gracefully, with dignity and pride. He stands before the audience, a tall, princely man, black, erect, famous at twenty-eight. He is silent for a moment. He is thinking perhaps of his father who escaped from slavery and hurried to New York with his family. Slavery is no abstraction to Henry Highland Garnet; it is personal, terribly personal. He came home one day and discovered that slavecatchers had kidnapped his sister. Something died in him that day. He opened a knife and put it into his pocket and walked down Broadway, hoping that a slavecatcher would approach him. He stands now, looking out into the audience, and the fury rolls out of him. "Brethren," he says, thinking perhaps of his sister, "arise, arise! Strike for your lives and liberties. Now is the day and the hour. . . . *Rather die freemen than live to be slaves.* . . . Let your motto be resistance, *resistance!* RESISTANCE!"

(*They came out of the darkness, across swamps, across rivers, across mountains. They came in twos, threes, twelves. One came all the way from Alabama, traveling, the report said, "only by night, feeding on roots and berries," swimming every river between Tuscaloosa and Pennsylvania. Ellen and William Craft came from Macon, Georgia, stopping at first-class hotels on the way, the light-skinned Ellen posing as a Southern planter, the dark-skinned William acting the part of a devoted manservant. Henry Box Brown came from Richmond, Virginia, locked in a box marked THIS*

SIDE UP. He came via Adams' Express and when the box was opened he stepped out and sang the song he had said he would sing: "I waited patiently for the Lord, and He heard my prayer.")

Listen to Sojourner Truth. She stands on an Indiana platform, braving the taunts of proslavery Northerners. A local doctor rises and says there is some doubt about the sex of the speaker. He asks Sojourner to submit to an inspection by local ladies. The meeting goes up in an uproar; there are shouts, screams, coarse laughs. Sojourner looks out into the audience and shouts: "My breasts have suckled many a white babe, even when they should have been suckling my own." She stabs a bony finger. "Some of those white babes are now grown men, and even though they have suckled my Negro breasts, they are in my opinion far more manly than any of you appear to be." Suddenly, without warning, she rips open the front of her dress. "I will show my breasts," she says, "to the entire congregation. It's not my shame but yours. Here then, see for yourself." Her eyes lock on the face of the doubting doctor and she says quietly, "Do you wish also to suck?"

(They came across a river, armed with bowie knives and guns, refugees from words and compromises. "Nearly all the waiters in the hotels," a Pittsburgh paper said, "have fled to Canada. Sunday, thirty fled; on Monday, forty; on Tuesday, fifty; on Wednesday, thirty. . . . They went in large bodies armed with pistols and bowie knives, determined to die rather than be captured." They came from all over, some 3,000 of them, in the first three months after passage of the Fugitive Slave Bill of 1850. But some remained at home. In Boston, Negroes crashed into a courtroom and rescued a slave who was being returned to slavery. In Syracuse, New York, Negroes rammed the door of the courtroom with a log and spirited away another fugitive. Down in Christiana, Pennsylvania, slave-catchers, led by a man named Gorsuch, surrounded the home of a free Negro named William Parker. The Negroes asked the slave-catchers to go away, but Gorsuch said he would "go to hell, or have his slaves." When the smoke cleared, Gorsuch lay dead and his supporters were hiding in the tall corn. In Washington, Daniel

Webster cried, "Treason!" Henry Clay wondered "whether gov-
ernment of white men is to be yielded to a government of blacks.")

Listen to Samuel Ringgold Ward. He sits on a platform in New
York City listening to William Lloyd Garrison. A proslavery
Northerner interrupts Garrison. What does Garrison know about
slavery? He is a white man; he has been free all his life. Frederick
Douglass leaps up and presents himself for inspection. Is he not a
Negro and a man? The heckler laughs: Douglass is light brown,
the son of a white man and a Negro woman; he is only half-Negro.
Samuel Ringgold Ward rises and moves to the front of the platform "like a dark cloud." "Well," the scoffer exclaims, "this is
the original nigger." Ward raises big, black, eloquent hands and
stills the crowd. "My friends," he says, "hear me for my cause
and be silent that you may hear me. . . . I have often been called
a nigger, and some have tried to make me believe it; and the only
consolation that has been offered me for being called nigger was
that when I die and go to heaven, I shall be white. But, if I cannot
go to heaven as black as God made me, let me go down to hell and
dwell with the Devil forever."

(They came across a river, a woman, a man and three children,
tiptoeing on the ice. The slave hunters caught them the next morn-
ing, but Margaret Garner was too quick. Out came the gleaming
butcher knife and slash—across the throat of her beloved daughter.
The daughter died and Margaret Garner rejoiced. Slavery, she said,
was hell for a Negro woman; and she was glad her daughter would
never know. The slavecatchers carried Margaret Garner to court
and she begged the judge to kill her; she said she would "go singing
to the gallows rather than be returned to slavery.")

Listen to Frederick Douglass. In Rochester, New York, he
moves to the front of the platform. He is the featured speaker at a
Fourth of July celebration. Douglass begins in a low key. "Fellow-
citizens, pardon me, and allow me to ask, why am I called upon to
speak here today?" Perhaps, he says, you mean to mock me. For
what have I to do with your celebration? "What, to the American
slave, is your fourth of July? I answer; a day that reveals to him,

more than all other days in the year, the gross injustice and cruelty
to which he is the constant victim. To him, your celebration is a
sham; your boasted liberty, an unholy license; your national greatness, swelling vanity; your sounds of rejoicing are empty and heartless; your denunciation of tyrants, brass-fronted impudence; your
shouts of liberty and equality, hollow mockery; your prayers and
hymns, your sermons and thanksgivings, with all your religious
parades and solemnity, are to him, mere bombast, fraud, deception,
impiety, and hypocrisy—a thin veil to cover up crimes which would
disgrace a nation of savages."

(*They came out of swamps, woods, rivers—men, women and
babies led by a bold woman. A baby whimpered; the woman
poured opium down its throat. A man said he was tired, sick; he
couldn't make another step. The woman cocked her pistol. "Dead
niggers," she said, "tell no tales. You go on or die." The man
went on. They came to a road. Something told the woman there
was danger ahead. The woman talked to God: "You been wid me
in six troubles, Lord, be wid me in the seventh." The Lord spoke
to Harriet Tubman; he told her to turn right. Harriet turned right
and carried her passengers to the Promised Land—Canada.*)

Frederick Douglass speaks again. He stands on a stage, saying he
no longer believes in words. He calls for a slave revolt. He recites
the wrongs inflicted on his people, the whips, the chains, the taunts,
the cracked skulls, the—"

"Frederick!" The big, booming voice comes from out of nowhere. "*Is God dead?*"

Sojourner Truth's question electrifies the audience and no one
hears Douglass' answer. "No, God is not dead and therefore
slavery must end in blood."

(*They came out of the darkness, thirteen white men, five Negroes and an old man. Talk. Talk. Talk. John Brown was tired of
talk; he was on his way to the gallows. With him was Dangerfield
Newby, forty-four. Newby was a free Negro who had a wife and
seven children in slavery about thirty miles from Harpers Ferry.
His wife had written him a letter: she had begged him to buy her*

*and the baby who had just "commenced to crawl" for "if you do
not get me somebody else will." The letter ended with a passionate
plea: "Oh, Dear Dangerfield, come this fall without fail, money or
no money, I want to see you so much." Dangerfield made it as far
as Harpers Ferry where he was the first of John Brown's men to
die.)*

Frederick Douglass protests again. A brilliant, self-made aristo-
crat named Jefferson Davis has been elected president of a Confederacy founded on the "great corner-stone" of human slavery.
An eloquent commoner named Abraham Lincoln has been named
President of the not-so-United States. Lincoln says slavery is
wrong, but he also says he is opposed to giving Negroes social and
political equality. Who is this man Lincoln? What does he stand
for? Douglass writes an editorial. "With the single exception of the
question of slavery extension, Mr. Lincoln proposes no measure
which can bring him into antagonistic collision with the traffickers
in human flesh."

*(Men were marching, flags were flying, banks were closing,
stocks were falling. Death was in the air and not many wanted to
die for the Negro. The South turned in on itself in an agony of
fear and guilt; some Southerners denounced the Declaration of Independence and demanded that free Negroes and poor whites be
enslaved; some Southerners went so far as to deny that Negroes
and whites belonged to the same species. The North tied itself up
in an orgy of appeasement. The Negro, "the cause" of it all, bore
the brunt of the emotional frenzy. Already stripped of his citizenship by the Dred Scott decision, he stood naked before his enemies. South Carolina, anticipating Nazi Germany, required free
Negroes to wear diamond-shaped badges. In Boston, in New York,
in Washington, men scurried to and fro with the word compromise
on their lips. Northern governors promised to repeal the Personal
Liberty Laws which made slave-catching difficult. Congress passed
a constitutional amendment which guaranteed slavery forever in
the South: A Springfield, Massachusetts, paper asked: "What Shall
Be Done With the Darkies?" A man in a lunatic asylum ran scream-*

ing through the wards, shouting, "I've got it, I've got it, Let the niggers be white-washed.")

Frederick Douglass grows weary. Despair grips him. Disappointed by Lincoln's inaugural address, alarmed by public persecution, he fears for his people. For the first time in twenty years, he loses faith in the American Dream. Maybe, a still voice whispers, maybe Negroes would be better off somewhere else. Douglass decides to investigate Haiti as a possible haven for Negroes. A boat is chartered. He writes an editorial announcing his proposed trip. The words are put into metal. Then comes a shattering announcement. Douglass yanks out a fistful of type and inserts an announcement below his editorial.

Since this article upon Haiti was put into type, we find ourselves in circumstances which induce us to forego our much desired trip to Haiti, for the present. The last ten days have made a tremendous revolution in all things pertaining to the possible future of the colored people in the United States. We shall stay here and watch the current of events. . . ."

What gave Douglass heart, what made him shout, "God be praised," was the firing on Fort Sumter and the beginning of the Civil War.

7

Black, Blue, and Gray:

The Negro in the Civil War

Mine eyes have seen the glory of the coming of the Lord,
He is trampling out the vintage where the grapes of wrath
    are stored,
He hath loosed the fateful lightning of his terrible swift
    sword,
His truth is marching on!

JULIA WARD HOWE

FAR OFF to the east, far out over the Atlantic Ocean, the first faint glow of the sun tinged the blue-black sky. In a ravine near Richmond, Virginia, black men in blue hugged the ground and watched the bloody blotch of red widen and glow. Shells howled and burst over their heads, bullets whined and whacked into the trees, wounded men cried out and blabbered in pain.

The men waited, watched, listened.

A general came and said words, said the Confederate redoubt over the hill must be taken and that they—the Third Division of the Eighteenth Corps of the Army of the James—must do it. The men checked their muskets, fixed their bayonets and listened to the words and the heavy beating of their hearts. They waited a few minutes more for the coming of the sun and then moved out, winding their way through a forest of young pines to the crest of the hill. It was 4:30 A.M. It was Thursday, September 29. It was 1864.

Benjamin Franklin Butler, the Union general, watched the soldiers climb the hill. He had a big stake riding on the throw. A political general with a genius for agitating the explosive "Negro issue," Butler was cordially despised by many of his aides. It was said that he couldn't command a Sunday School class. Ben Butler intended to show them. He had drawn up an elaborate plan for a two-pronged attack on Richmond which was cordoned by a meandering maze of slave-built fortifications. As the black division moved to the attack on New Market Road, a column of white troops was advancing on the Varina Road, a mile or so to the west. Behind Butler now, another column (which included a brigade of Negro troops) was waiting for the black division to take the strong redoubt on New Market Heights. This redoubt commanded the New Market Road down which Butler wanted his second column to march. If all went well, Butler would establish a toe hold in the suburb of Richmond. If he got a little luck, he would go all the way. In either case, he would have a laugh on people who said he couldn't command and Negroes couldn't fight.

A great deal depended on the action of the Negro division which was moving now over the brow of the hill. The land before the Negro troops sloped down to a swamp and a shallow brook, then rose sharply to the crest of a hill on which were a Confederate redoubt and some one thousand troops. The Confederates, seeing the Negro troops on the opposite hill, gave a wild whoop and opened fire. They were understandably confident. Their artillery swept the narrow neck of land over which the Union soldiers had to charge. Fifty yards down the hill from their entrenchments was an abatis (a barricade of felled trees with sharpened branches pointing toward the attackers); one hundred yards below this was another abatis. The storming party would have to cross the brook, come uphill under artillery and musketry fire and wait at the first and second lines of abatis until axmen could cut a way through. While waiting, they would be sitting ducks. The rebels gave another wild whoop and urged the Negro soldiers on. On they came, getting mired in the muck of the swamp, splashing across the brook with their guns held over their heads, faltering, reforming and moving up the hill, one man falling and another man replacing him in line, the whole column swept by grape, shot and canister, the ground wet with the blood, the entrails and the brains of the dead.

Axmen dashed to the first barricade and hacked away; rebel sharpshooters leisurely picked them off. Other men seized the axes. A hole was made; the men streamed through. Only 150 yards to go. Could they make it? Most of the white officers were wounded now or dead. Negro sergeants commanded companies, Negro corporals commanded platoons. Cursing, pleading, threatening, they drove the men on. On they went, stepping over the wounded, to the second abatis. Axmen sprang forward; steel ate into wood; men dashed through the opening. Corporal Miles James spun around suddenly. What had been his arm was a dripping mass of blood and pulpy tissue. Corporal James dropped to his knees, loaded and fired his gun with one hand and cheered his men on. A rebel officer was equally gallant. He leaped upon the parapet, waved his sword and shouted, "Hurrah, my brave men." Private James Gardiner rushed forward, shot the officer and ran him through with his bayonet. The rebel soldiers abandoned their posts and ran up the road to Richmond. With a resounding cheer, the black men in blue sprang over the parapet of the dearly purchased real estate on New Market Heights. Behind them on the hill running down to the swamp lay 543 of their comrades. It had been a bloody thirty minutes work. But on this day and largely in these thirty minutes, twelve Negroes (Corporal James, Private Gardiner and ten others) won Congressional Medals of Honor.

With the New Market Road secured, the column moved on Richmond. A white division seized Fort Harrison, but the advance ground to a halt at Fort Gilmer where General William Birney's Negro brigade made a daring but unsuccessful assault. Despite this repulse, Union soldiers were too close to Richmond for comfort. General Robert E. Lee, President Jefferson Davis and other Confederate dignitaries came out to the battlefield and peered through field glasses. The next day Lee sent ten of the South's finest brigades against the Union soldiers in Fort Harrison. The first charge and the second charge were neatly repulsed. And then someone—was it Lee?—had a bright idea. The rebel soldiers came back again, but this time the charge was against Brigadier General Charles J. Paine's New Market veterans. The long gray lines swept forward, came to the very edge of the earthwork; and Negro and rebel soldiers fought hand to hand. For an agonizing moment, the issue hung in dispute. White soldiers stood with their mouths agape, oblivious to shot and shell. So great was "their realization of the danger," wrote R. B. Prescott, a white Union officer, "so keen the anxiety, so doubtful the issue, that every eye was riveted upon [the scene], unmindful of the storm of lead and iron that the Confederate sharpshooters and artillery poured upon us from every available point. It seemed impossible in such a storm for any to escape, but happily in a few moments, the Confederates broke in disorder and sought safety under the protecting guns of Fort Gilmer, while the Union troops shouted themselves hoarse with delight."

It was a bitter moment for the South: Robert E. Lee had failed to retake an important position within sight of the steeples of Richmond. Lieutenant Prescott stood cheering on the parapet of Fort Harrison and he believed he could see "the beginning of the end."

That Negro soldiers should play an important role in this action seems somehow poetic. For in the beginning, in the middle and in the ending of the Civil War, the Negro—as soldier and civilian— was central.

William H. Carney of the Fifty-fourth Massachusetts Volunteers received Congressional Medal of Honor for bravery in the assault on Fort Wagner, South Carolina, July 18, 1863.

John H. Lawson won the Congressional Medal of Honor for his heroism in the Battle of Mobile Bay. At least three other Negroes received Medals of Honor for bravery in naval battles.

Making famous charge on Fort Wagner in Charleston,
South Carolina, Harbor, soldiers of Fifty-fourth
Massachusetts Volunteers are repulsed by Confederate
defenders. The charge won plaudits in the North.

In the beginning, men tried hard to get around this fact. In the first blast of emotion which followed the fall of Fort Sumter, Abraham Lincoln tried to get around it. He issued a call for men who loved the Union. White and Negro patriots rallied to the flag. Negroes hired halls, drilled and formed military units like the Hannibal Guards of Pittsburgh and the Crispus Attucks Guards of Albany, Ohio. In Philadelphia, in New York, in Boston, Negroes came forward. The Lincoln Administration thanked the Negro volunteers and sent them home with an understanding that the war was a "white man's war."

Dr. G. P. Miller, a Negro physician of Battle Creek, Michigan, asked the War Department for authority to raise "5,000 to 10,000 free men to report in sixty days to take any position that may be assigned to us (sharpshooters preferred)." He received, in reply, a wonderfully comic bureaucratic masterpiece. "The War Department," the letter said, "fully appreciates the patriotic spirit and intelligence which your letter displays, and has no doubt upon reflection you will perceive that there are sufficient reasons for continuing the course thus far pursued in regard to the important question upon which your letter is based."

What Dr. Miller perceived upon reflection is not recorded, but it is a matter of record that the Lincoln Administration continued "the course thus far pursued." Black men were barred from the army and some Union commanders returned fugitive slaves to rebel masters. Some generals, in fact, said that if slaves rose behind enemy lines they would stop fighting the enemy and start fighting the slaves. They would, in the words of General George McClellan, put down slave insurrections with "an iron hand." It occurred to some people that this was a novel way to fight a war. Congressional liberals, abolitionists, Negro leaders, and "hard-war" Unionists asked Lincoln to stop the "military slave hunt" and hit the South where it would hurt the most: free the slaves and give them guns. What kind of war was the President fighting anyway? What was he trying to do? Lincoln said he was trying to save the Union. What then was to be done with slaves who abandoned their masters in droves and flocked to the Union lines? Lincoln said his policy was to have no policy. John C. Frémont, a Union general, issued a proclamation freeing the slaves of Missouri rebels. Lincoln revoked the proclamation and kicked up a storm of abuse. Congressional liberals, abolitionists, Negro leaders, and "hard-war" Unionists said he was weak-kneed, vacillating, spineless, dumb.

Morning, noon and night, Lincoln was pressed by the one problem he was determined to ignore. A White House visitor reported that the mere mention of the word "slave" made Lincoln nervous. For almost two years, Lincoln appeased the slaveholding Border States. For almost two years, he maintained the official fiction that the war was a polite misunderstanding between white gentlemen, a war in no way related to the Negro and slavery. "The soul of old John Brown may have been marching," Dudley Taylor Cornish wrote, "but it marched in exclusively white company."

That this policy was changed at all is due not to Union humanitarianism but to rebel battlefield brilliance—the South knew what it was fighting for—and the daring and hope of fugitive slaves. By digging in and fighting, the South brought the North to a realization that it was in a real brawl and that it needed all the weapons it could lay hands on. It came to some soon and to others late that all men, at the very least, are buried equal. By flocking to the Union lines, by leaving bed and cabin and rallying to the flag, fugitive slaves made the North define its terms. It came to some in 1861 and to others in 1863 that the Negro was inextricably involved in the root cause of the war and that the war could not be fought without taking him into consideration; nor, and this was most frightening, could the war be ended without coming to grips with the meaning of the Negro and the meaning of America.

It came fairly soon to Ben Butler, an odd character who seemed to be everywhere in this war. Ben Butler was a Massachusetts politician who wangled a general's commission and went down to Virginia to fight. He got there at a good time. The Union was in a dither over fugitive slaves who persisted in leaving their masters and seeking refuge under the American flag. Nobody knew what to do with these people. Ben Butler acted; he welcomed slaves into his line, put them to work and grandly dubbed them "contraband of war." The word "contraband" caught on; the word—and a great many people had been waiting for a word—permitted the North to strike at slavery without using that dangerous word—slavery. The first step had been taken; Congress and Robert E. Lee did the rest. Congress, pushed by liberals like Charles Sumner, Ben Wade, Henry Wilson, and Thaddeus Stevens, forbade Union officers to return fugitive slaves to rebels, emancipated District of Columbia slaves, declared free the slaves of all rebels and gave Lincoln discretionary power to use Negro troops. Robert E. Lee and other rebel generals taught the Union that war, in Sherman's pithy phrase, was hell.

It came to Lincoln in the summer of 1862 that the Union, in his phrase, could not escape history. "Things," he explained later, "had gone from bad to worse, until I felt that we had reached the end of our rope on the plan of operations we had been pursuing; that we had about played our last card." On Tuesday, July 22, Abe Lincoln called his Cabinet together and put his "last card" on the table. It was a good one; a draft of a preliminary Emancipation Proclamation. The thing was discussed pro and con until Secretary of State William H. Seward came to the heart of the matter. The timing, he said, was bad. "The depression of the public mind," Seward said, "consequent upon our repeated reverses, is so great that I fear the effect of so important a step. It may be viewed as the last measure of an exhausted government, a cry for help; the government stretching forth its hand to Ethiopia, instead of Ethiopia stretching forth her hands to the government." There was truth in this. Lincoln put the document into his desk drawer and waited for the Union to win a battle.

While Lincoln waited, three generals stretched out their hands to Ethiopia. Without waiting for official approval, David (Black David) Hunter and Jim Lane started organizing Negro regiments. Hunter organized the First South Carolina Volunteers, the first Negro regiment, and Jim Lane organized the First Kansas "Col-

ored" Volunteers. The government did not get around to extending official recognition to these regiments until January, 1863.

Down in New Orleans, in this long hot summer, Ben Butler was
thinking. He needed men, and black men were all around him.
Why not use them? Butler turned the problem over in his fertile
mind. There was a prejudice against the use of Negro troops. This
prejudice, however, was crumbling. The sons of thousands of white
mothers were dying, and people were beginning to say that Negroes could stop bullets as well as white men. Humorist Miles
O'Reilly marked the shift in a poem: "Sambo's Right to be Kilt."

> *Some say it is a burnin' shame*
> *To make the naygurs fight,*
> *An' that the thrade of bein' kilt*
> *Belongs but to the white;*
>
> *But as for me upon my sowl'*
> *So liberal are we here,*
> *I'll let Sambo be murthered in place o' meself*
> *On every day in the year.*

The wind was changing and Ben Butler was an excellent weather
vane. In New Orleans at that very moment were fourteen hundred
free Negroes who had organized a regiment of free black Confederate soldiers. Butler sent for the leaders of the regiment and plied
them with questions. He wanted to know if Negroes would fight.

"General," the spokesman said, "we come of a fighting race. Our
fathers were brought here because they were captured in war, and
in hand to hand fights, too. We are willing to fight. Pardon me,
General, but the only cowardly blood we have got in our veins is
the white blood."

Butler issued the necessary papers and the First Louisiana Native
Guards became the first Negro regiment to receive official recognition in the Union Army.

While Butler was organizing his Negro regiment, Lincoln was
polishing the phrases of the preliminary Emancipation Proclamation. On September 22, 1862, five days after the Battle of Antietam,

Negro sailors served on famous Union ironclad, the "Monitor." Large number of Negroes served on Union vessels. Negro sailors held all ranks below petty officer, were stewards, cooks, seamen and pilots.

Soldiers of Second U.S.C.T. artillery participated
in the Battle of Nashville. There were twelve
Negro heavy artillery units in Union Army.
Union recruited some 100,000
Negro soldiers in the South.

he notified the South that he would free all slaves in states in rebellion on January 1, 1863. The one hundred days between the issuance of the preliminary proclamation and the signing of the real thing were anxious ones for Negro Americans. Would Lincoln go through with his threat? No man knew. On the issue of Negro rights, Lincoln was an unknown and unpredictable quantity. In Illinois, he had opposed granting Negroes social and political equality. In Washington, he had plumped for gradual emancipation and abrupt (voluntary) emigration of free Negroes. To most liberals and militant Negro leaders, the President was something of an enigma; a good man, to be sure, honest, decent and kind, but slow, timid, vacillating even in his approach to the supreme moral issue of the age. As the moment of truth approached, many people said Lincoln would never go through with it. Nor was this all speculation. The Rev. Byron Sunderland told Lincoln one day that people were saying he would never sign the proclamation. "Well, Doctor," Lincoln replied obliquely, "you know Peter was going to do it, but when the time came, he did not." It was an ominous sign in the dying days of 1862 that Abraham Lincoln was dwelling on the example of Peter and the cock that crowed thrice.

Wednesday, December 31, 1862, was a day of anticipation and rumor. People gathered in little knots and tried to read the signs of the time. That night, Negroes gathered in churches and prayed the Old Age out and the New Age in. There was no doubt about what Lincoln would do at the "watch meeting" held in the Washington, D.C., "Contraband Camp." An eloquent old "contraband" got up and told the gathering what time it was. "Onst, the time was," he said, "dat I cried all night. What's de matter? What's de matter? Matter enough. De nex morning my child was to be sold, and she was sold; and I never spec to see her no more till de day ob judgement. Now, no more dat! no more dat! no more dat! Wid my hands agin my breast I was gwine to my work, when de overseer used to whip me along. Now, no more dat! no more dat! no more dat! . . . We'se free now, bress de Lord! [Amen! Amen! said the audience.] Dey can't sell my wife an' child no more, bress de Lord! [Glory! Glory!] No more dat! no more dat! no more dat, now!" A few minutes before midnight, the people went to their knees and greeted the New Age in prayerful silence..

Down South, on the Sea Islands off South Carolina, Negroes and whites celebrated at the camp of the First South Carolina Volunteers. Boats brought the celebrants from the mainland and a makeshift platform was erected in a grove on the edge of the camp. There, under the giant oaks, Lincoln's preliminary proclamation was read. There were more words, too many words, and finally when Colonel T. W. Higginson got up to speak, unfolding a new flag as he collected his thoughts, an old dry voice came from the audience. The old man carried it by himself for a little while. Then two women joined in and another man and another until the words swelled out:

> My country, 'tis of thee,
> Sweet land of Liberty,
> Of Thee I sing.

A few whites chimed in, but Colonel Higginson waved them silent. "I never," he said later, "saw anything so electric; it made all other words cheap. It seemed the choked voice of a race at last unloosed."

On the night of the first day of January in "the Year of Jubilee," Negroes and whites gathered at Boston's Tremont Temple. Lincoln had not yet signed the proclamation and the group waited impatiently as speaker after speaker mounted the platform. Frederick Douglass spoke and others, but the words lacked fire; all minds were locked on Lincoln. Eight o'clock came and nine and nine-thirty and ten, and still there was no word from Washington. People who were given to saying, "I told you so," said it; even Frederick Douglass began to doubt. Finally, when the most sanguine began to droop, a man ran screaming into the room, "It is coming! It is on the wires!" Suddenly, everyone was on his feet, shouting, laughing, weeping. The meeting went on all night and it seemed, Frederick Douglass recalled later, "that almost everything seemed to be witty and appropriate to the occasion."

The morning after was a little more prosaic. Examining the proclamation in the hard glare of daylight, Douglass and others were disappointed. The document was as dry as a brief in a real estate case. There was in it none of the King James nobility that Lincoln carried to Gettysburg; nor, it seemed, did the proclamation do much emancipating. It did not apply to slaves in the loyal Border States and in sections under federal control in the South. Still, there was something about the piece of paper. In spite of its matter-of-fact dryness, in spite of its repeated pleas of "military necessity," in spite of its many exceptions, the document became one of the great state papers of the century. And it converted a vague war for Union into something men could get their teeth into: a war for freedom.

Cryptic messages sped along the invisible telegraph wires that ran into every slave cabin and men, women and children went looking for President Lincoln's soldiers. Planters, in desperation, attempted to "run the Negroes," i.e., move them further into the interior away from the advancing Union Army. The mass migration continued. Although some slaves (mainly house servants) remained loyal to their masters, most slaves took advantage of the first opportunity to join a migration which reached mammoth proportions. There had never been anything quite like it, John Eaton said, a slave population "rising up and leaving its ancient bondage, forsaking its local traditions and all the associations and attractions of the old plantation life, coming garbed in rags or in silks, with feet shod or bleeding, individually or in families and larger groups." Eaton said it was like "the oncoming of cities." The slaves said it in a song:

> No more peck of corn for me,
>   No more, no more,
> No more peck of corn for me,
>   Many thousands gone.
>
> No more driver's lash for me,
>   No more, no more,
> No more driver's lash for me,
>   Many thousands gone.

Many slaves and free Negroes found employment in the Union Army. By the end of 1863, there were some 50,000 black soldiers in Union ranks. They were not, to be sure, accepted as brothers in arms by everyone. But at Port Hudson, Milliken's Bend, Fort Wagner, Poison Spring, Olustee, Nashville, Tupelo, Petersburg, Richmond and 440 other places they struck man-sized blows for their own freedom. They fought gallantly. But this, as Colonel N. P. Hallowell said, is not the most that can be said for them. Negro soldiers in this war, Colonel Hallowell said, demonstrated the "highest order" of courage which America demands of men with dark skins. He added: "They were promised the same pay, and, in general, the same treatment as white soldiers. No one expected the same treatment in the sense of courtesy, but everyone believed a great nation would keep faith with its soldiers in the beggarly matter of pay. They were promised thirteen dollars per month [the pay of white privates]. They were insulted with an offer of seven dollars."

Many regiments refused to accept seven dollars. When the Massachusetts legislature passed a bill providing the six dollars difference, the state's Negro regiments refused to accept the money. They were fighting, they said, for a principle, not money. Many Negroes fought for fourteen, sixteen and eighteen months (until the inequity was corrected) without accepting a penny from the government. There is a kind of bittersweet poetry in the fact that the Fifty-fourth Massachusetts Volunteers went into the Battle of Olustee with the cry, "Hurrah for Massachusetts and seven dollars a month."

Negro soldiers were paid less money, but they faced grimmer hazards. Some Negro POWs were accorded the rights of civilized warfare, but others were murdered and sold into slavery. "I hope," Jerome Yates of Mississippi wrote his mother, "I may never see a Negro soldier or I cannot be . . . a Christian soldier." Not a few white Southerners found it impossible to reconcile the conflicting claims of Christianity and white supremacy. In the ugliest incident of the war, a rebel force, commanded by Major General Nathan

Bedford Forrest, massacred a predominantly-Negro group at Fort Pillow, Tennessee. The rebels entered the fort, shouting, "Kill the god-damned niggers! Kill all the niggers!" A Congressional investigating committee said Forrest's men murdered three hundred persons after the fort surrendered. Negro soldiers were shot in cold blood; some were nailed to logs and burned; some were buried alive. Negro women and children were also murdered. General Forrest rode among the dead and the wounded, stopping here and there to say that he recognized some of the Negroes. "They've been in my nigger-yard in Memphis," the ex-slave trader said.

One Negro soldier died at Fort Pillow in a hopeless cause, but he died with rare nobility. Private Woodford Cooksey, a white soldier, testified: "I saw one of them [Forrest's men] shoot a black fellow in the head with three buckshot and a musket ball. The man held up his head, and then the fellow took his pistol and fired that at his head. The black man still moved, and then the fellow took his sabre and stuck it in the hole in the Negro's head and rammed it way down, said: 'Now, god-damn you, die.' The Negro did not say anything, but he moved, and the same fellow took his carbine and beat his head soft with it. That was the next morning after the fight."

At Memphis, a few days after the Fort Pillow Massacre, Negro soldiers dropped to their knees and swore remembrance. After April 12, 1864, Negro soldiers entered battle with the cry, "Remember Fort Pillow."

Bull Run I and Bull Run II were over, Shiloh had been fought and New Orleans had been taken when Negro soldiers became important military factors in the war. But the game was far from over. Robert E. Lee had not gone to Gettysburg and Ulysses S. Grant had not gone to Vicksburg when Negro soldiers proved what many men professed to disbelieve: that Negroes would fight. Negro soldiers handled themselves brilliantly in minor actions at Island Mound, Missouri, in October, 1862, and in skirmishes in Georgia and Florida in November, 1862. They did not come into their own, however, until the summer of 1863. In that summer, in

May, June and July, at Port Hudson, Milliken's Bend and Fort Wagner, black men in blue became a part of the big war.

At Port Hudson, an important Confederate fort commanding a stretch of the Mississippi River, and at Fort Wagner, a Confederate fort commanding a stretch of the Charleston Harbor, Negro troops made seven of the most gallant charges of the war. Six times did the troops of the First and Third Louisiana Native Guards assault the elaborate fortifications at Port Hudson. They dashed across a treacherous sweep of land into the very mouth of artillery mounted on the parapet of Port Hudson. Some soldiers plunged into a bayou under the parapet and attempted to swim across. Almost all of them were killed. They tried it again and some got across and fought the rebels. But they received little support and were repulsed.

In this assault, on May 27, 1863, Captain André Cailloux, a prominent Catholic layman from New Orleans, was conspicuous in his gallantry. A well-to-do man who liked to boast of his blackness, Cailloux was all over the field. Speaking now in French and now in English, he urged his men on, leading the way himself. When his left arm was shattered by a bullet, he remained on the field and rallied his men for a final charge. Cailloux dashed to his death like a brave and reckless matador. As he sprinted across the field, with his broken arm flopping crazily, his voice could be heard above the thunder of battle. "Follow me," he said in English and French, "*Suivez-moi.*" He fell mortally wounded some fifty yards from the fort.

Black men, led by white officers, were equally courageous at Fort Wagner. Colonel Robert Gould Shaw led his men across a half-mile of sand, mounted the parapet and struggled with the defenders. Shaw and a brave Negro color sergeant were mortally wounded. They fell from the parapet and lay close together, integrated in death.

Milliken's Bend was not a classic charge. It was a last-ditch, hand-to-hand, cutting, gouging, brain-busting brawl. Ten days after the Port Hudson assault, two thousand Texans attacked the Union fort

Confederate troops, under command of General
Nathan Bedford Forrest, killed some three hundred
soldiers and civilians in the Fort Pillow Massacre. A
predominantly Negro force held the Tennessee fort.

In triumphant ride through Richmond, Virginia, on April 4, 1865, Abraham Lincoln received wide acclaim from the freed slaves. Lincoln issued Emancipation Proclamation on January 1, 1863. The Thirteenth Amendment ended slavery in America.

at Milliken's Bend, about twenty miles up the river from Vicksburg. The fort was held by one thousand soldiers, all but 160 of them
Negroes. The Texans drove the Union soldiers back to the banks
of the river. As the Texans advanced, they murdered captured Negro soldiers. Enraged by atrocities committed before their eyes,
helped at the last moment by a Union gunboat, the troops rallied
and charged. For ten or fifteen minutes, the Negro and white soldiers stood toe to toe. Men gave out of bullets, clubbed each other,
baseball fashion, with the butts of muskets and gouged with bayonets. Finally, the Texans broke and fled.

Milliken's Bend was a sideshow of the big war. In 1864, Negro
soldiers entered the big tent. When Ulysses S. Grant crossed the
Rapidan and began his bloody duel with Robert E. Lee, a Negro
division accompanied him. Moving at the same time, the omnipres-
ent Ben Butler advanced on Richmond from the Virginia peninsula, taking with him five thousand Negro foot soldiers and
eighteen hundred Negro cavalrymen. Grant wheeled around
Lee's right flank to Spotsylvania Court House and Cold Harbor
and then sent General W. F. Smith down to Petersburg to make
a sneak attack. On June 15, Smith attacked the undermanned Petersburg's defenses with a mixed force. The attack succeeded; the
Negro division which spearheaded the attack knocked a mile-wide
hole in the Petersburg defenses, captured seven guns and two hundred prisoners. Petersburg lay open. But Smith dallied and the Petersburg defenses were reinforced. Grant settled down for the ten-
month siege which ended in April, 1865, with the fall of Petersburg
and Richmond. Some thirty-four Negro regiments played a part in
this famous siege. Negro troops were especially prominent in the
disastrous Battle of the Crater and engagements at Darbytown
Road, Fair Oaks, Deep Bottom, Hatcher's Run, New Market
Heights, and Fort Gilmer.

Negro soldiers were in on the kill. The Second Division of the
all-Negro Twenty-fifth Corps was one of the Union divisions
which chased Lee's tattered army from Petersburg to Appomattox
Court House. When the end came, the Negro and white troops

were moving forward at double quick and Lee's men were retreating in confusion. At the appearance of the white flag, Union soldiers whooped it up with a vengeance. Cheers went up from hill to hill and the air was filled with thousands of blue caps.

Negro soldiers and civilians had something to cheer about. With the defeat of Lee and the surrender of Joseph Johnston, the freedom of words, of the Emancipation Proclamation and the Thirteenth Amendment, became a freedom involving concrete realities. To the ex-slave, freedom was a serious thing. Freedom was getting married before a preacher and signing a paper and knowing that it was for always and not until the next cotton crop. Freedom was Bibles, freedom was churches, freedom was gin. Freedom was two names. A man sat for awhile and decided on a name and if he didn't like it he could change it again tomorrow. (Some ex-slaves chose the last names of their late masters, but some decided they "had nuff o' old massa" and looked further for family identification.)

Freedom was getting up when you wanted to and lying down when the spirit hit you. Freedom was doing nothing, too. How was a man to know he was free if he couldn't sit still and watch the sun and pull on his pipe when he didn't want to do anything else? Freedom was all this and more, but mostly it was books and legs: an opportunity to learn and the right to pick up and go. With a yearning born of centuries of denial, ex-slaves worshipped the sight and the sound of the printed word. Old men and women on the edge of the grave could be seen in the dark of the night, poring over the Scripture by the light of a pine knot, painfully spelling out the sacred words.

The right to pick up and go was less complicated. With a need born of centuries of close confinement, hundreds of thousands of Negroes walked the roads and flocked to the cities and towns, testing that strange word called freedom. They did this with a startling lack of bitterness. More Negroes than historians would care to remember told their late masters that "answering bells was out," but most Negroes apparently were willing to let bygones be bygones, if whites would let them.

A whole generation, black and white, is vignetted in William Colbert, an ex-slave in Georgia. When the war came Colbert's master sent his three boys off to whip the Yankees and none of them ever came home again. Misfortune piled on misfortune. The old man lost his money, his house began rotting away, his wife died. Then his slaves began to leave. William Colbert left, too.

"The last time I seed the home plantation," Colbert said, "I was a-standing on a hill. I looked back on it for the last time through a patch of scrub pines, and it looked so lonely. There wasn't but one person in sight, the massa. He was a-setting in a wicker chair in the yard looking out over a small field of cotton and corn. There was four crosses in the graveyard in the side lawn where he was a-setting. The fourth one was his wife." William Colbert stood there on the hill for a long time, looking down on the bent old man, feeling sorry for him. The old white man was mean as sin; he had owned slaves and he had used them badly, but he was a human being and it grieved Colbert to see him brought so low. Standing there on the hill, looking down through the scrub pine, Colbert gave the old man what the old man had never given him: human sympathy. Colbert shook his head finally, more in sorrow than anger; and he walked on down the road to freedom. For William Colbert, for William Colbert's children and his grandchildren and his great-great-grandchildren, freedom was a long road.

8

Black Power in Dixie

> *The attempt to make black men American citizens was in a certain sense all a failure, but a splendid failure. It did not fail where it was expected to fail. It was Athanasius contra mundum, with back to the wall, outnumbered ten to one, with all the wealth and all the opportunity, and all the world against him. And only in his hands and heart the consciousness of a great and just cause. . . .*
>
> W. E. B. DU BOIS

NEVER BEFORE had the sun shone so bright.

An ex-slave, Blanche Kelso Bruce, was representing Mississippi in the United States Senate. Pinckney Benton Stewart Pinchback, young, charming, daring, was sitting in the governor's mansion in Louisiana.

In Mississippi, in South Carolina, in Louisiana, Negro lieutenant governors were sitting on the right hand of power. A Negro was secretary of state in Florida; a Negro was on the state supreme court in South Carolina. Negroes were superintendents of education, state treasurers, adjutant generals, solicitors, judges and major generals of militia. Robert H. Wood was mayor of Natchez, Mississippi, and Norris Wright Cuney was running for mayor of Galveston, Texas. Seven Negroes were sitting in the House of Representatives.

Negroes and whites were going to school together, riding on street cars together and cohabiting, in and out of wedlock (Negro men were marrying white women in the South, but it was more fashionable, investigators reported, for white men to marry Negro women). An interracial board was running the University of South Carolina where a Negro professor, Richard T. Greener, was teaching white and black youth metaphysics and logic.

These things were happening on the higher levels. What of the masses? How was it with them? They were struggling, as they had always struggled, with the stubborn and recalcitrant earth. But there was a difference. Now there was hope. Never before—never since—had there been so much hope. A black mother knew that her boy could become governor. The evidence of things seen, the evidence of things heard fired millions of hearts. Black mothers walked ten, fifteen and twenty miles to put their children in school. They sacrificed and stinted. They bowed down and worshipped the miraculous ABC's from whom so many blessings flowed. The sky, or at the very least, the mountain top was the limit. Had not Blanche Kelso Bruce been suggested as a possible vice-presidential candidate? Was it not clear that a black boy could go as far as nerve, energy and ability would carry him? Black mothers, bending over washtubs, could hope. Black boys, in cotton fields, could dream. The millennium hadn't come, of course, but there were some who believed it was around the next turning.

A man, in this age, went to mail a letter, and the postmaster was black. A man committed a crime, and, in some counties, was arrested by a black policeman, prosecuted by a black solicitor, weighed by a black and white jury and sentenced by a black judge. It was enough to drive some men mad; it was enough to warp some men's judgment. Come with James S. Pike, a Northern reporter, into the South Carolina House of Representatives, the first Western assembly of its kind with a black majority. "The Speaker," Pike reports, "is black, the clerk is black, the doorkeepers are black, the little pages are black, the chairman of Ways and Means is black, and the chaplain is coal black."

There had never been an age like this one before and there would never be one again—not in 90 years anyway. Up in Maine, in these Democracy-in-Wonderland days, James Augustine Healy, the first and only American Negro Catholic bishop, was tending his flock and his Irish communicants were chanting a pagan ditty, "Glurry be to God, the Bishop is a Nee-gar!" Farther South, in Washington, D.C., the bishop's brother, Patrick Francis Healy, was sitting in the presidential chair at Georgetown, America's oldest Catholic university.

Farther south, in New Orleans, Bourbons were doing what they would do again ninety years later. Policemen were escorting Governor Pinchback's children to a high school where organized gangs were making their lives miserable. "They were good enough niggers," one of the ringleaders would say, "but still they were niggers."

Farther east, in Columbia, South Carolina, men were sampling democracy and finding it to their liking. The fabulous Rollins sisters —three *café au lait* descendants of a Negro-white union—were operating a Paris-type salon for movers and shakers and hostile critics were saying that more legislation was passed there than in the legislature. On hot nights, Negroes and whites walked the wide streets arm in arm and went perhaps to Fine's Saloon for a cold drink. The social life was gay, glittering and interracial. A dashing young militia captain gave a ball and Negroes and whites—some of them native South Carolinians—glided across the polished floor. At official balls, receptions and dinners, Negroes and whites sat down together and got up in peace. Years later, a renegade Republican would poke fun at these affairs. "The colored band," he would write, "was playing 'Rally 'Round the Flag.' . . . There was a mixture of white and black, male and female. Supper was announced, and you ought to have seen the scramble for the table. Social equality was at its highest pitch. It was amusing to see Cuffy reach across the table and swallow grapes by the bunch, champagne by the bottle, and turkey, ham and poundcake by the bushel."

These things, improbable as they may seem now, happened in America during the ten improbable years (1867–77) of Black Reconstruction. W. E. B. Du Bois called them the "mystic years." Mystic they were, and, in retrospect, a trifle mad. Intoxicated perhaps by the emotional bang of the big war, taunted by the arrogance of the conquered South, spurred on by economic and political forces, the North took the longest stride America has ever taken: it decided to try democracy. The decision was not a conscious one and it was not made all at once. At war's end, few politicians—Charles Sumner and Thaddeus Stevens were exceptions—knew what to do with the emancipated slaves. As late as April, 1865, Abraham Lincoln was dallying with the idea of voluntary deportation. Ben Butler, the ex-Union general and Massachusetts politician, said Lincoln asked him to figure out the logistics of deporting the freedmen to another land. Butler came back two days later with a sad story. "Mr. President," he said, "I have gone carefully over my calculations as to the power of the country to export the Negroes of the South and I assure you that, using all your naval vessels and all the merchant marine fit to cross the seas with safety, it will be impossible for you to transport to the nearest place . . . half as fast as Negro children will be born here."

The Negro, in short, was in America to stay. What was to be done with him? Frederick Douglass, the Negro leader, had an answer: ". . . do nothing with [him]. Your *doing* with [Negroes] is their greatest misfortune. . . . The Negro should have been let alone in Africa . . . let alone when the pirates and robbers offered him for sale in our Christian slave markets . . . let alone by the courts, judges, politicians, legislators and slave drivers. . . . If you see him plowing in the open field, leveling the forest, at work with a spade, a rake, a hoe, a pick-axe, or a bill—let him alone; he has a right to work. If you see him on his way to school, with spelling book, geography and arithmetic in his hands—let him alone; . . . If he has a ballot in his hand, and is on his way to the ballot-box to deposit his vote for the man whom he thinks will most justly and wisely administer the Government which has the power of life and death over him, as well as others—let him *alone*. . . ."

What was to be done with the Negro?

Charles Sumner, the Massachusetts senator, had an answer: Give him the ballot and treat him like a man.

What was to be done with the Negro?

Thaddeus Stevens, the Pennsylvania congressman, had an answer: Give him forty acres of land and treat him like a human being.

Most Americans were not willing to go that far. While men debated, while public opinion was congealing, Congress passed a stopgap measure which created the Freedmen's Bureau. This bureau, the first federal welfare agency, did the work of Hercules in building bridges from slavery to freedom. During its short life (1865–72), the Freedmen's Bureau was an Urban League, CIO, WPA and Rosenwald Foundation all rolled up into an early NAACP. It stood between the freedman and the wrath of his ex-master. It gave direct medical aid to some one million freedmen, established hospitals and distributed over twenty-one million rations, many of them to poverty-stricken whites. The bureau also established day schools, night schools and industrial schools. Practically all the major Negro colleges (Howard, Fisk and Morehouse) were founded or received substantial financial aid from the bureau. Handicapped by inadequate appropriations, a poorly trained staff and the bitter hostility of white Southerners, the bureau did not do all it could have done. What it did, however, was absolutely indispensable to four million freedmen who were protected neither by law, love, nor greed.

For the freedmen, emancipation was a catastrophic social crisis.

Tens of thousands died of privation, disease and want. In some communities, one out of every four Negroes died. "The child is already born," crowed the *Natchez Democrat*, "who will behold the last Negro in the state of Mississippi." Dr. C. K. Marshall, a learned and wealthy minister, was more precise. "In all probability," he said, "New Year's Day, on the morning of the 1st of January, 1920, the colored population in the South will scarcely be counted."

The freedmen tightened their belts and—to the consternation of mourners—their tribe increased. Painfully, in fear and trembling, Negroes picked up the threads of a social life which had been shattered hundreds of years before in Africa. In slavery, Negro males had been systematically emasculated. They had no say over their children or their women. Now suddenly they were heads of households. Negro women, who were not accustomed to taking orders, submitted to male authority with a great deal of self-consciousness. Some men gave the whole thing up as a bad joke and wandered around the country. Some women, proud, independent, headstrong, drove their men away.

During slavery, mothers had been sold from children, husbands from wives, brothers from sisters. In the first sweet flush of freedom, men and women trudged dusty roads asking sad questions. Has anyone here seen Sarah? Do you know a man named Sam? Many stories from this era tell of men who married only to discover later that they had married a cousin or a sister.

What did the freedmen want? What did freedom mean to them? The evidence is incontrovertible: there was a mania for land and education. The Freedmen's Bureau and heroic New England schoolma'ams satisfied the hunger for letters. But no one—and this is the great tragedy of Reconstruction—no one satisfied the hunger for land. Some men said the freedmen were entitled to retributive and compensative justice. Retributive and compensative were big words to the ex-slaves: all they wanted was a little back pay. They saw what only the wisest saw: that freedom was not free without a firm economic foundation.

Charles Sumner saw it.

So did Thaddeus Stevens. To Stevens, more than to any other man, the freedmen owed their undying faith in the magical phrase, "Forty Acres and a Mule." In and out of Congress, the crusty old Pennsylvanian demanded that large plantations be broken up and distributed to the freedmen in forty-acre lots. Congress refused to budge and Stevens, always a realist, admitted that the dream was stillborn. He was 74, old and gnarled like an oak tree, on the day he rose in the House and pronounced the eulogy. "In my youth," the Great Commoner said, "in my manhood, in my old age, I had fondly dreamed that when any fortunate chance should have broken up for a while the foundation of our institutions [that we would have] so remodeled all our institutions as to have freed them from every vestige of human oppression, of inequality of rights. . . . This bright dream has vanished 'like the baseless fabric of a vision.'"

Charles Sumner made a similar fight in the Senate. When that body refused to countenance homes and land for the freedmen, Sumner, the elegant Harvard man, the scholar, the orator, the passionate advocate of human freedom, went home and wept.

There were tears, too, in South Carolina. When officials tried to reclaim land that had been distributed with temporary titles, the Negroes picked up stones and drove them away. General O. O. Howard, the head of the Freedmen's Bureau, went to South Carolina to explain the situation. The land had been given in good faith, but President Johnson had pardoned the owners and the land was to be returned to them. General Howard called a large assembly and stood on the platform looking out into the sea of black faces. He tried to say it, but the words wouldn't come. How does one tell a people that they have been taken *again?* To cover his confusion and shame, General Howard asked the people to sing him a song. One old woman on the edge of the crowd was up to the occasion. She opened her mouth and out came words tinged with insufferable sadness. "Nobody Knows The Trouble I've Seen." Howard, a gentle, one-armed humanitarian, broke down and wept.

Men, women and children attended primary schools established for the freedmen. Some Southerners opposed the schools, said Northern missionaries were teaching freedmen "the three P's"—politics, pulpit and penitentiary.

Thaddeus Stevens is regarded as the architect of the Radical Reconstruction program. Stevens proposed a plan which would have given each adult freedmen a forty-acre lot.

Freedmen voted for the first time in elections of 1867–68. Ex-slaves showed unusual interest in politics. A South Carolina newspaper said "the polls were thronged with eager crowds of Negroes."

There were tears, there were rivers of tears, but there was little land and no mules. Without land, without tools, without capital or access to credit facilities, the freedmen drifted into a form of peonage: the sharecropping system.

The land problem was intertwined with the larger problems of the South and the Negro. Nothing could be done with the conquered South until the status of the Negro was settled. The reverse was also true. Nothing could be done with the Negro until the status of the conquered South was settled. Lincoln's answer to this thorny problem was liberal to the South. He proposed to readmit the late rebellious states as soon as 10 per cent of the prewar electorate had qualified by taking an oath of allegiance to America. Lincoln's successor, Andrew Johnson, was substantially of the same mind. Neither man came to grips with the status of the Negro, although Lincoln suggested that "very intelligent" Negroes and Union veterans be given the right to vote.

Stevens and Sumner were aghast at the presidential innocence. To turn the ex-slaves over to their ex-master without adequate safeguards, they contended, would be madness. Subsequent events tended to support their position. Ignoring Congress, President Johnson appointed provisional governors who organized lily-white governments on the basis of lily-white electorates.

These governments enacted the Black Codes (1865–66) which indicated that the South intended to re-establish slavery under another name. The codes generally restricted the freedmen's movements under vagrancy and apprenticeship laws. South Carolina forbade freedmen to follow any occupation except farming and menial service; a special license was required to do other work. The legislature also gave "masters" the right to whip "servants" under eighteen years of age. In other states, Negroes could be punished for "insulting gestures," "seditious speeches" and the "crime" of walking off a job. Negroes could not preach in one state without police permission. A Mississippi law enacted late in November required Negroes to have jobs before the second Monday in January.

Even more serious was the vindictive attitude of Southerners who vented their frustration on unarmed Negroes. General Carl Schurz, who made a special investigation for the President, was astonished by postwar conditions in the South. "Some planters," he said, "held back their former slaves on their plantations by brute force. Armed bands of white men patrolled the country roads to drive back the Negroes wandering about. Dead bodies of murdered Negroes were found on and near the highways and by-ways. Gruesome reports came from the hospitals—reports of colored men and women whose ears had been cut off, whose skulls had been broken by blows, whose bodies had been slashed by knives or lacerated with scourges. A number of such cases, I had occasion to examine myself. A . . . reign of terror prevailed in many parts of the South."

The South looked back in anger. Hundreds of freedmen were massacred in "riots" staged and directed by policemen and other government officials. In the Memphis, Tennessee, "riot" of May, 1866, forty-six Negroes (Union veterans were a special target) were killed and seventy-five were wounded. Five Negro women were raped by whites, twelve schools and four churches were burned. Two months later, in New Orleans, policemen returned to the attack. Some thirty-five Negroes were killed and more than one hundred were wounded.

"The emancipation of the slave," General Schurz concluded, "is submitted to only in so far as chattel slavery in the old form could not be kept up. But although the freedman is no longer considered the property of the individual master, he is considered the slave of society. . . . Wherever I go—the street, the shop, the house, the hotel, or the steamboat—I hear the people talk in such a way as to indicate that they are yet unable to conceive of the Negro as possessing any rights at all. Men who are honorable in their dealings with their white neighbors will cheat a Negro without feeling a single twinge of their honor. To kill a Negro, they do not deem murder; to debauch a Negro woman, they do not think fornication; to take the property away from a Negro, they do not consider robbery. The people boast that when they get freedmen's affairs in their own hands, to use their own expression, 'the niggers will catch hell.' "

The South's intransigence changed the national mood. Here and there, men fell into step with Sumner and Stevens. They did so for many reasons. Some believed it would be a major tragedy to hand the freedmen over to their ex-masters. Others saw a chance to insure the continued supremacy of the Republican party. Still others believed it would be dangerous to return ex-Confederates to national power. For various reasons, some of them contradictory, some of them noble, some of them base, men began to march by the sound of a different drummer.

Emboldened by the national mood, Stevens struck. He wrested control of Reconstruction from President Johnson and vested it in the Joint Congressional Committee of Fifteen. This committee reported legislation which put the South under military control and authorized new elections in which all males, irrespective of color, could participate. When the tallies were in, it was discovered that Negro voters outnumbered whites in five states—Mississippi, South Carolina, Louisiana, Alabama and Florida. In some counties, Negro voters outnumbered whites by majorities of seven, eight and nine to one.

Stevens and Sumner pushed on. Prodded by these two men and others, Congress enacted the Fourteenth and Fifteenth Amendments and enabling legislation which sent troops into the South to protect the rights of Negroes.

Day in and day out, Sumner and Stevens prodded, criticized, demanded. They made men squirm; even today they make men uncomfortable. No white men in American public life have ever had a more profound understanding of the Declaration of Independence. Some there were who wanted to do it next week. Some there were who wanted to do it tomorrow. Sumner and Stevens wanted to do it NOW. They were men of different styles and temperaments. Sumner was an idealist, a lover of the classics, a declaimer of poetry. "I am in morals," he said, "not politics."

Stevens was in politics. A tart-tongued, tough-minded old Pennsylvanian with a clubfoot and a burning passion for the poor, the disadvantaged and the driven against the wall, Stevens loved the give and take of politics. He dominated men not by quotations but by strength of will. Men tried to dismiss him: they said he was a bitter, vindictive old fanatic. "There may be fanatics," Stevens replied, "in false religion, in superstition. But there can be no fanaticism, however high the enthusiasm, however warm the zeal, in true religion, or in the cause of national, universal liberty." Men said that Stevens not only preached social equality but that he practiced it. This was a sly dig at Lydia Smith. For twenty-two years, she was Stevens' devoted housekeeper. She kept his house in Lancaster, Pennsylvania, and when Stevens went to Washington, she went with him. Men said there was more to their relationship than met the eye. Stevens was a bachelor; Lydia Smith was a comely Negro widow. On this slim foundation and the fact that Stevens called his housekeeper "Mrs. Smith," the rumors grew. Indifferent to and contemptuous of public opinion, Stevens disdainfully ignored the gossips and went his lonely way.

To Stevens and Sumner, as much as to Lincoln, Negroes owed their freedom. Long before Lincoln was ready, Sumner was demanding freedom for the slaves. Long before Lincoln was ready, Stevens was demanding that he arm them and let them fight. A Kentucky representative ridiculed the idea of "Sambo" serving as a soldier and commanding white men. Stevens replied: "The distinguished gentleman from Kentucky and his allies from Ohio have talked of 'Sambo's' commanding white men. Sir, the bill contains no such provisions. They are to be employed only as soldiers or non-commissioned officers. I do not expect to live to see the day when, in this Christian land, merit shall counterbalance the crime of color. True, we propose to give them an equal chance to meet death on the battlefield. But even then their great achievements, if equal to those of Dessalines, would give them no hope of honor. The only place where they can find equality is in the grave. There all God's children are equal."

Two men—Sumner in the Senate, Stevens in the House. Only

two; and when they died, the dream died with them. Sumner went to his death fighting for a national Civil Rights Bill which would have banned discrimination and segregation in schools, churches, cemeteries, public conveyances, inns, hotels. On his death bed, surrounded by Frederick Douglass and other Negro friends, he whispered his last words: "Take care of my Civil Rights Bill—take care of it—you must do it." Historian Benjamin Quarles has said: "Negroes whose sense of honoring their benefactors exceeded their knowledge of history might name their sons after Lincoln, but [Frederick] Douglass, with a truer appreciation, knew that if Negroes wished to honor the greatest friend they ever had in public life, they should place wreaths on the tomb of Charles Sumner."

Thad Stevens had said that he intended to die "hurrahing." And he did. He was buried in a Negro cemetery. The stone above the ground bears the words he wrote:

> I repose in this quiet and secluded spot,
> not from any natural preference for solitude,
> but finding other cemeteries
> limited by charter rules as to race,
> I have chosen this that I might illustrate in my death
> the principles which I advocated through a long life,
> Equality of Man before his Creator.

The principles which animated Stevens and Sumner turned the South upside down. "The bottom rail," freedmen would say, "is on top." During the summer and fall of 1867, the Negro masses were stirred by an unparalleled ferment of political activity. Negroes flocked to huge open-air meetings, registered and organized political groups. Leaders emerged from the masses and demanded political and civil equality. The white South was stunned. It was believed at first that "Sambo" would fall flat on his face. But the freedmen disappointed their late masters: they demonstrated a real genius for what one writer called "the lower political arts."

The South revised its strategy. The baby had not begun to walk when the men sat down to plan the funeral. In the beginning, naïve men say, it was an organization for fun and social profit. The name: Ku Klux Klan. The first national meeting: April, 1867. Room 10, the Maxwell House, Nashville's big new hotel. Confederate generals, colonels, substantial men of church and state, from Georgia, from Alabama, from all over. The leader: Nathan Bedford Forrest, the strong man of the Fort Pillow Massacre. The plan: reduce Negroes to political impotence. How? By the boldest and most ruthless political operation in American history. By stealth and murder, by economic intimidation and political assassinations, by whippings and maimings, cuttings and shootings, by the knife, by the rope, by the whip. By the political use of terror, by the braining of the baby in its mother's arms, the slaying of the husband at his wife's feet, the raping of the wife before her husband's eyes. By *Fear*. Soon the South was honeycombed with secret organizations: the Knights of the White Camelia, the Red Shirts, the White League, Mother's Little Helpers and the Baseball Club of the First Baptist Church.

The secret organizations ran underground. Above ground, there was a different strategy. In every state, Democrats attempted to control the votes of their late slaves. There was real humor in the situation: ex-slaveholders and racists sitting on platforms with Negroes, "reminding" Negroes that Southern white men had always been their friends and that the North was "responsible" for slavery. An interracial meeting was held at Terry, Mississippi, with former governor A. G. Brown presiding and a Negro, Alfred Johnson, acting as vice-president. The group decided to have a picnic and the committees named to arrange the affair were blatantly interracial: three Negroes and three whites on each committee. The Negroes came, ate, listened and went away and voted Republican. Constitutional conventions were elected in which Negroes constituted from 10 per cent (Texas) to 61 per cent (South Carolina). The results were so unpalatable to one Mississippian that he called for a day of prayer to God who, he said, had permitted Negroes to attain political power because the white folk had forgotten him.

When the constitutional conventions met, some Southerners again put their heads into the sand. Surely "Sambo" would make a fool out of himself. After all, what did he know about the whereases and therefores of Anglo-Saxon government? Again the South was disappointed. The constitutions were excellent documents. They were so good, in fact, that some states were content to live under them for several years after the Democrats regained power.

The constitutions were not entirely the work of Negroes. The much-maligned "carpetbaggers" (Northern-born white men) and "scalawags" (white Southerners) were dominant elements in all of the conventions. But Negroes played important roles, especially in the Big Three—South Carolina, Louisiana and Mississippi.

South Carolina's Constitution, like most Reconstruction constitutions, made the state a much more positive force in the lives of the peoples. It eradicated every form of slavery, abolished imprisonment for debt, authorized universal male suffrage and gave the state its first divorce law. White women and poor white Southerners, it should be remembered, were emancipated with the slaves.

Negro delegates were largely responsible for the most important innovation in Reconstruction governments—the establishment of a public school system for poor and rich, black and white. In Mississippi, Louisiana, and South Carolina, incidentally, the laws called for interracial school systems. Louisiana was most explicit. "There shall be no separate schools or institutions of learning established exclusively for any race by the state of Louisiana."

Dixie politics during Reconstruction did not differ markedly from Dixie politics after Reconstruction—a fact which does not necessarily recommend the era highly. Negro leaders shared power with "carpetbaggers" and "scalawags." Only in Mississippi, Louisiana, and South Carolina did Negroes rise to the summit of power. Even in South Carolina, however, Negroes were outnumbered in the state senate. It is a mistake, therefore, to speak of the Reconstruction era as one of "Negro domination." Negroes had power, Negroes used power, but they showed no desire to "dominate whites." State by state the political situation was this: *

---

* Texas, Tennessee and Arkansas did not send Negroes to Congress. Negroes, as a group, did not wield much power in these states. Negroes, however, served in the legislatures of these states and held local offices. J. C. Corbin was superintendent of education in Arkansas. Mifflin W. Gibbs was elected city judge in Little Rock, Arkansas, in 1873.

SOUTH CAROLINA: 1860 population: 412,000 Negroes, 291,-000 whites. Voter registration, 1867 (males): 80,000 Negroes, 46,000 whites. Negro voters were in majority in 21 of 31 counties. Reconstruction constitutional convention: 76 Negro delegates, 48 whites. First Reconstruction legislature: 84 Negroes, 73 whites. Negroes were in majority in every legislative session except one. A. J. Ransier, R. H. Gleaves, lieutenant governors. F. L. Cardozo, secretary of state (1868–72), treasurer (1872–76). J. J. Wright, associate justice, state supreme court. R. B. Elliott, S. J. Lee, speakers of House of Representatives. Robert Smalls, major general, state militia. South Carolina sent eight Negroes to Congress during Reconstruction and post-Reconstruction eras: R. B. Elliott, J. H. Rainey, Robert DeLarge, A. J. Ransier, R. H. Cain, Robert Smalls, T. E. Miller, G. W. Murray. Rainey, first Negro in the House of Representatives, was sworn in December 12, 1870.

MISSISSIPPI: 1860 population: 353,000 whites, 437,000 Negroes. Registration, 1867: 60,000 Negroes, 46,000 whites. Negro voters were in majority in 30 counties. Constitutional convention, 16 Negroes, 84 whites. First legislature: 40 Negroes, 75 whites. A. K. Davis, lieutenant governor. James Hill, secretary of state. T. W. Cardozo, superintendent of education. Two Negro senators, Hiram Revels (1870–71), B. K. Bruce (1875–81). One congressman: John Roy Lynch. Two speakers, House of Representatives: J. R. Lynch, I. D. Shadd.

LOUISIANA: 1860 population: 350,000 Negroes, 357,000 whites. Registration, 1867, 84,000 Negroes, 45,000 whites. Constitutional convention: 49 Negroes, 49 whites. First legislature, 49 Negroes, 88 whites. P. B. S. Pinchback, governor, 43 days, on impeachment of former governor. Three lieutenant governors: O. J. Dunn, P. B. S. Pinchback, C. C. Antoine. P. G. Deslonde, secretary of state. Antoine Dubuclet, state treasurer. W. B. Brown, superintendent of education. One congressman: Charles E. Nash. Pinchback and James E. Lewis were elected to U.S. Senate, which refused to seat Pinchback. Lewis did not press his case.

FLORIDA: 1860 population: 77,000 whites, 62,000 Negroes. Registration, 1867: 16,000 Negroes, 11,000 whites. Constitutional convention: 18 Negroes, 27 whites. First legislature: 19 Negroes, 57 whites. Jonathan C. Gibbs, secretary of state (1868–72) and superintendent of education (1872–74). One congressman: J. T. Walls.

NORTH CAROLINA: 1860 population: 629,000 whites, 361,000 Negroes. Registration, 1867: 106,000 whites, 72,000 Negroes. Constitutional convention: 15 Negroes, 118 whites. First legislature: 19 Negroes, 135 whites. Four congressmen: J. A. Hyman, J. E. O'Hara, H. P. Cheatham, George H. White.

ALABAMA: 1860 population: 526,000 whites, 437,000 Negroes. Registration, 1867: 104,000 Negroes, 61,000 whites. Constitutional convention: 18 Negroes, 90 whites. First legislature: 26 Negroes, 58 whites. Three congressmen: B. S. Turner, J. T. Rapier, J. Haralson.

GEORGIA: 1860 population: 465,000 Negroes, 591,000 whites. Registration, 1867: 95,000 Negroes, 96,000 whites. Constitutional convention: 33 Negroes, 137 whites. First legislature: 32 Negroes, 214 whites. One congressman: J. F. Long.

VIRGINIA: 1860 population: 548,000 Negroes, 1,000,000 whites. Registration, 1867: 105,000 Negroes, 120,000 whites. Constitutional convention: 25 Negroes, 80 whites. First legislature: 27 Negroes, 154 whites. One congressman: J. M. Langston.

To justify the revolutionary methods by which these governments were overthrown, Southerners manufactured and perpetuated the twin myths of corruption and ignorance. Negro politicians, so the myths run, were corrupt or ignorant. So many Negroes stole so much that it was necessary to cheat and kill in order to restore "honest" governments. Not only historians but Negroes accepted the myths. Not a white but a Negro poet made the most withering comment on the Negro leaders of Reconstruction.

"Some people," Paul Laurence Dunbar said, "are born great, some achieve greatness, others lived during the Reconstruction period."

Greatness, political greatness, is a slippery concept. The great Negro leader during Reconstruction would have had the hardness of Nkrumah, the ascetic brilliance of Nehru, the Machiavellian adroitness of Franklin Delano Roosevelt, and the love-thy-neighbor vocabulary of Martin Luther King, Jr. No such person emerged. No such person, in fact, has ever emerged in America. Judged by American standards, the major Negro leaders of Reconstruction were leaders like the leaders of other eras: men who just missed greatness because they failed to solve the problem no American has solved—the fear and anxiety of the white man and the presence and birth rate of the Negro.

But, say the critics, Negro leaders were corrupt. The evidence on this subject is so confusing as to be almost worthless. Nine-tenths of the evidence is hearsay, innuendo, ex parte. Most of the rest would not be admissible in the meanest police court. The ex parte reports on which historians rely were produced by men who lied, stole, cheated and killed in order to take over the state governments—men, in short, who had to believe their enemies were barbarians in order to believe that they themselves were Christians. What evidence there is suggests that white men—Northern white men and Southern white men, South Carolinians, Georgians and Louisianians—got most of the money. Take Mississippi, for example. James Garner, after an exhaustive study of reconstructed Mississippi, concluded that there were only two thefts on the state level: a Negro was accused of stealing books from the state library, a white man misappropriated $7,000. This is in marked contrast to Mississippi before and after Reconstruction. In 1866, for example, a Democratic treasurer stole $61,000. Years later, after white men had restored "honest" government, a treasurer made off with $315,000.

The conclusion is inescapable. The monstrous crime of Reconstruction was equality. A Southern historian has said as much. "The worst crime of which they have been adjudged guilty," said F. B. Simkins of Reconstruction governments, "was the violation of the

American caste system. The crime of crimes was to encourage
Negroes in voting, office-holding, and other functions of social
equality. This supposedly criminal encouragement of the Negro is
execrated even more savagely as with the passing years race prejudices continue to mount. . . . Attempts to make the Reconstruction governments reputable and honest have been treated with
scorn, and the efforts of Negroes to approach the white man's
standards of civilization are adjudged more reprehensible than the
behaviour of the more ignorant and corrupt. Social equality and
Negroism have not a chance to be respectable."

It would be a mistake, however, to imply that no Negroes stole:
that would be making the same mistake as some white historians
who imply that all Negroes stole. In an era where some men were
bought and sold in New York (Boss Tweed), in an era in which
some men were bought and sold in Washington (Crédit Mobilier
scandal), it seems reasonable to conclude that some men were also
bought and sold in South Carolina. Only the naïve, or what turns
out to be the same thing, the cynical are horrified when some Negroes do what some white men are doing. The key word here is
some. There were Negro scoundrels. There were Negro reform-
ers. And there were Negro wheelers and dealers whose morals
were no better—and no worse—than the morals of politicians in
contemporary Chicago, New York or Washington.

Not corruption but honesty, not ignorance but brilliance horrified racists during the Reconstruction era. If there was anything
Southern whites feared more than bad Negro government, it was
good Negro government. If there was anything they feared more
than an ignorant Negro, it was a brilliant one. There were many
brilliant Negro politicians, Dunbar to the contrary notwithstanding: O. J. Dunn of Louisiana, Jonathan Gibbs of Florida, James T.
Rapier of Alabama, J. J. Wright of South Carolina, and Francis L.
Cardozo, John Roy Lynch, B. K. Bruce, R. H. Cain, J. M. Langston, Robert Smalls. Smalls, a man of limited education, was worshipped by his constituents. One day, so the story goes, two of
his constituents got into an argument. One man insisted that Smalls

was a political genius. The second man countered, "Smalls ain't so hot. He ain't God." "Yes," replied the first man in a line that would be applied to Marcus Garvey, "that's true. But give him time. He's a young man yet."

It has been said that the Negro leaders of Reconstruction were uneducated. This is a false way to state the issue. Although a degree may be necessary for writing about politics or teaching it, a degree is not at all necessary for practicing the game. A politician needs drive, energy, the ability to deal with people, the skills of the conference table and the smoky room, nerve, cheek and an eloquent tongue. Many Negro leaders had these requisites. There were literate, cultured Negro politicians—but that's beside the point. Robert Brown Elliott, a graduate of Eton, was a brilliant politician, but his English education does not seem to have helped him any more than the common school education of P. B. S. Pinchback who, if anything, was more brilliant. James T. Rapier of Alabama was more polished than most white men of his day, but S. D. Smith, an authority on Negroes in Congress, believed that the uneducated Jeremiah (Jere) Haralson ("black as an ace of spades and with the brogue of the cotton field") was a better natural politician. Men admired Rapier's learning and literacy, but they cleared political matters with "Jere." It is enough to state the obvious: most of the major Negro leaders had more formal education than Abraham Lincoln. Ten of the twenty-two Negroes who served in Congress had attended college; five were lawyers. Both Negro senators had attended college. Both handled themselves well in the Senate. And both were infinitely superior to Bilbo and several others Mississippi would send to the Senate. Revels, a minister, was a lucid speaker and a fair politician. After his Senate career, he spent a great deal of time conciliating the white people of Mississippi. He spent so much time conciliating the whites that he alienated the Negroes. When the Democrats drove the Republicans out of the Statehouse, Revels, a timid, conservative man, supported them. As a reward, he was returned to his old post as president of Alcorn College. Bruce was cut out of different timber. A handsome, elegant man "with a

Ku Klux Klan and other secret
organizations undermined
Reconstruction with a revolutionary
campaign of terror and intimidation.
Klan was organized in 1866 in
Pulaski, Tennessee.

Among the leading
Reconstruction politicians were
Robert Brown Elliott (left),
the South Carolina congressman;
Blanche K. Bruce (center), the
only Negro to serve a full term
in the U.S. Senate; and P. B. S.
Pinchback, who served briefly
as governor of Louisiana.

magnificent physique," he made a good record in the Senate and later became Register of the Treasury.

On some issues, at some times, Negro leaders followed "carpet-baggers" and "scalawags." On many issues, however, Negroes went their own way. Against the advice of party leaders, Negroes enacted strong civil rights provisions in Mississippi, Louisiana, and South Carolina. When the first South Carolina Republican convention met, white men advised Negroes that it would be diplomatic to elect a white chairman; R. H. Gleaves, a Negro, was elected. In Louisiana, Negro leaders revolted against H. C. Warmoth, who was wooing Democrats. In Mississippi, Negro leaders revolted against J. L. Alcorn, the aristocratic "scalawag" who opposed radical innovations in interracial living. In Louisiana, no politician, not even the governor, could operate without considering the wishes of Pinchback. The same thing was true in South Carolina, where the governor was under some pains to determine the desires of Elliott. Even in Mississippi, where Negro leaders were most conciliatory, the tide changed. By 1873, Mississippians were demanding an equal division of the loaves and the fishes. The *Vicksburg Plaindealer*, a Negro paper, put it bluntly. Some white men, the paper said, believed Negroes should do all the voting and white men should do all the directing. "This thing," the paper said, "has played out."

If Negroes were so militant, why didn't they elect a governor? The answer is fairly simple. In the first period of Reconstruction, Negro leaders attempted to assuage the fears of the white men. Many people, some of them sincere liberals, told Negroes that it would not be politic to shock unduly the sensibilities of whites. This gambit was accepted everywhere except Louisiana where Pinchback and Francis E. Dumas were nominated when the Republican convention met. Since nomination at that time was tantamount to election, there was considerable interest in the contest. Pinchback, believing it would be impolitic to nominate a Negro the first time, withdrew, a decision he would later regret. Dumas stood his ground. He was a free Negro, fair-skinned, wealthy, a Union veteran who had carried his slaves into the Union Army and had been commissioned a major. On the first ballot, no one had a majority. The real contest, it turned out, was between Dumas and H. C. Warmoth, a talented, unscrupulous "carpetbagger." Negro delegates were in the majority, but most of the Negro delegates were ex-slaves who had no love for ex-slaveholders, especially Negro ex-slaveholders. Between the first and second ballots, Warmoth made good use of the fact that his opponent, a Negro, had owned slaves. On the second ballot, Warmoth won—45 to 43. It seems, therefore, that the only Negro who had a good chance to be elected governor was defeated, ironically enough, because he had owned slaves. Later, when Pinchback and Elliott panted and thirsted after the governor's chair, white men were in control of the election machinery and Negroes were divided into several factions.

Some Negro politicians, perhaps most Negro politicians, were willing to sit on the right hand of power. The two most brilliant Negro politicians in this era wanted to sit in the chair itself. Robert Brown Elliott and P. B. S. Pinchback were as unlike as two men could be. Elliot was a scholar, a linguist, a brilliant lawyer, the owner of one of the largest private libraries in South Carolina. Pinchback, on the other hand, was an ex-cabin boy, shrewd, capable, vain, a gambling type, a man who would put everything on an ace and, losing, walk away with a smile. Elliott was dark-skinned, the son of West Indian immigrants. Pinchback was fair-skinned, the son of a Mississippi planter and a Negro woman who bore him ten children. To Pinchback and Elliott, racists would apply their most telling adjective, "dangerous." Both men understood the uses and, critics said, the "misuses" of power. There are conflicting reports on the political morality of both men, but there is unanimity on their ability in the political arena.

Elliott was elected to the South Carolina legislative assembly at twenty-six and to Congress at twenty-eight. But the House of Representatives bored him. He was elected twice and resigned both times to return to South Carolina where there was power to be used. An implacable foe of racism and intolerance, Elliott supported Sumner's Civil Rights Bill and made what was probably the most eloquent speech ever uttered by a Negro in Congress. The situation was dramatic and Elliott, who had an eye for drama, made the most of it. On January 5, 1874, Alexander H. Stephens, former vice-president of the Confederacy, attacked the Civil Rights Bill. When he finished, Elliott seized the floor and held it until adjournment, thereby earning the right to continue the next day. The word went out: a Negro would answer the former vice-president of the Confederacy. People came early the next morning to get seats; senators came over from the Senate chamber.

The stage was set when Stephens, elderly and ailing, was brought into the chamber in his chair.

All eyes turned to Elliott.

He was an impressive man, deep-chested, broad-shouldered, with abundant hair worn *au naturel* in the African style. "Face to face," a contemporary said, "stood the Anglo-Saxon and the undoubted African. The issue was between them; the contest began." Elliott stood silent for a spell, savoring the moment. Then he began: "I regret, sir, that the dark hue of my skin may lend color to the imputation that I am controlled by motives personal to myself in my advocacy of this great measure of national justice. Sir, the motive that impels me is restricted to no such narrow boundary, but is as broad as your Constitution. I advocate it, sir, because it is right."

Elliott reviewed the history of the Negro in America. Black men had shown their mettle in the Revolutionary War, had proved a decisive factor in the Civil War and had been praised by Andrew Jackson in the War of 1812. They had earned their civil rights, in tears and blood. And what were civil rights? Like a teacher in a graduate seminar, Elliott explained civil rights, quoting Francis Lieber, Alexander Hamilton and the French Constitution.

He scornfully dismissed Stephens. It ill behooved a man who tried to wreck the Constitution to read lectures to men who fought for it. ". . . I meet him only as an adversary; nor shall age or any other consideration restrain me from saying that he now offers his Government, which he has done his utmost to destroy, a very poor return for its magnanimous treatment, to come here and seek to continue . . . the burdens and oppressions which rest upon five millions of his countrymen who never failed to lift their earnest prayers for the success of this government when the gentleman was seeking to break up the Union of these states and to blot the American Republic from the galaxy of nations. (Loud applause.)

To another adversary, Elliott offered the back of his hand. "To the diatribe of the gentleman from Virginia, who spoke on yesterday, and who so far transcended the limits of decency and propriety as to announce upon this floor that his remarks were addressed to white men alone, I shall have no word of reply. Let him feel that a Negro was not only too magnanimous to smite him in his weakness, but was even charitable enough to grant him the mercy of his silence. (Laughter and applause on the floor and in the galleries.)

Elliott pleaded for the bill. "The Constitution warrants it; the Supreme Court sanctions it; justice demands it." Negroes, moreover, had earned it as soldiers in the Union Army. He was mindful, however, that "valor, devotion, and loyalty are not always rewarded according to their just deserts, and that after the battle some who have borne the brunt of the fray may, through neglect or contempt, be assigned to a subordinate place, while the enemies in war may be preferred to the sufferers." Still, he was hopeful. Negroes were like the faithful Ruth who labored in the fields of Boaz. "The last vestiture only is needed—civil rights. Having gained this, we may, with hearts overflowing with gratitude, and thankful that our prayer has been granted, repeat the prayer of Ruth: 'Entreat me not to leave thee, or to return from following after thee; for whither thou goest, I will go; and where thou lodgest, I will lodge; thy people shall be my people, and thy God my God; where thou diest, will I die, and there will I be buried; the Lord do so to me, and more also, if aught but death part thee and me.' " (Great applause.)

The black South Carolinian sat down in triumph. For almost an hour, he held court on the floor of the House. Even the Democrats were impressed. The Republicans were ecstatic. Ben Butler compared Elliott to John Hancock, to John Adams and that other South Carolinian, John C. Calhoun.

The applause was still ringing in Elliott's ears, he was at the height of his fame when he resigned from the House to return to South Carolina, where he became speaker of the legislative assembly. Applause and empty honors did not impress Elliott. Rumor had it that he intended to become governor. When he made an unsuccessful bid for the Senate, some racists hoped he would win. It was felt at the time that the Senate would satisfy his ambition and moderate his militancy. Elliott's motto, a reporter said, was: "I am what I am and I believe in my own nobility."

Pinchback was of like mind: he was what he was. A Congressional investigating committee asked him if the governor acknowledged his strength. Pinchback was frank. "Oh, yes; he always acknowledged he couldn't get along without me. I have to tell you the truth." Bold, elegantly turned out, daring, Pinchback made his mark in Reconstruction Louisiana. By turns a senator, lieutenant governor, and governor, he held more offices than any other Negro in American history. In the fall of 1872, he was elected to the House of Representatives. In January, 1873, he was elected to the Senate. He went to Washington, therefore, with the extraordinary distinction of being both a congressman-elect and a senator-elect. (There were also disquieting rumors that Pinchback intended to make himself vice-president.)

Pinchback did not go as a beggar. "Sir," he told the Senate, "I demand simple justice. I am not here as a beggar. I do not care so far as I am personally concerned whether you give me my seat or not. I will go back to my people and come here again; but I tell you to preserve your own consistency. Do not make fish of me while you make flesh of everybody else."

For three years, the Senate grappled with Pinchback's case. Almost the whole of an extra session of Congress was devoted to the senator-elect from Louisiana. Finally, after reams of debate, he was rejected. The real reason, some authorities insist, was that the sena-

tors' wives told them that they did not intend to associate with
Mrs. Pinchback. During the controversy, "Pinch," as he was called,
became a national figure. Washington women, charmed by his
"Brazilian" good looks, went out of their way to meet him and
Pinchback stories made the rounds.

The Washington correspondent of the *New York Commercial
Advertiser* was impressed with the senator-elect. "Aside from the
political view of the question [two factions in Louisiana were com-
peting for national recognition]," he wrote, "Pinchback's presence
in the United States Senate is not open to the smallest objection, except the old Bourbon war-whoops of color. He is about thirty-
seven years of age, not darker than an Arab. . . . His features are
regular, just perceptibly African, his eyes intensely black and brilliant, with a keen, restless glance. His most repellent point is a sar-
donic smile which, hovering continuously over his lips, gives him
an evil look, undeniably handsome as the man is. It seems as though
the scorn which must rage within him, at sight of the dirty ignorant
men from the South who affect to look down upon him on account
of his color, finds play imperceptibly about his lips. . . . Mr.
Pinchback is the best dressed Southern man we have had in Congress from the South since the days when gentlemen were Democrats."

Even more remarkable than the rise of Pinchback and Elliott and
other major leaders was the mushroom growth of local leaders.
"There is something fascinating," Vernon Wharton wrote, "about
the suddenness with which, all over the state [Mississippi], they
emerged from the anonymity of slavery to become directors and
counselors of their race. In general, it can be said that they were
not Negroes who had held positions of leadership under the old
regime; the characteristics which made a man a slave driver or fore-
man were not those which would allow him to organize a Loyal
League. Almost none of them came from the small group who had
been free before the war. Such men, as barbers, artisans or small
farmers, had depended too long on the favor of the whites for the
maintenance of their existence. Servility had become a part of

them. . . . A large proportion of the minor Negro leaders were preachers, lawyers, or teachers from the free states or from Canada. . . . There was a general tendency for them to combine preaching with their politics; as Sir George Campbell has said, they were rather preachers because they were leaders than leaders because they were preachers."

Local leaders bore the brunt of the sustained assault by which whites undermined Reconstruction. The word went out: "Forget Pinchback. Forget the big boys. Let them prance around in New Orleans, Columbia, Jackson and Washington. Concentrate on the local leaders. Destroy the foundation and leave the big boys dangling in mid-air."

It was done.

One by one, the local leaders were killed, driven out of the state or compromised. In Mississippi, to cite only one case, Charles Caldwell, the courageous state senator, was killed in broad daylight and his body was "grotesquely turned completely over by the impact of innumerable shots fired at close range." At least five thousand Negroes died for their political beliefs. What did this mean in personal terms? John Childers of Alabama was on the witness stand.

How long after the whipping did she die?
In eight days.
How old was she?
She would have been ten years old on the 26th of next August.
What was she whipped for?
She was hired out as a nurse to see to the baby; she had taken the baby out to the front yard among a parcel of arbor vitae; and, being out there, the baby and she together, she was neglectful, so as to leave the baby's cap out where it was not in place when the mother of the child called for the cap. When I came home . . . I saw the rest of the children playing in the yard, and she was in the door sitting there, and I thought that was strange, because she was a mighty playful chap, and I asked, "What are you sitting here for?" And she says, "Pap, Mr. Jones has beat me nearly to death." (The witness weeping) . . .

Where a colored man is known as a Democrat, and votes the Democratic Party, is he ever whipped or interfered with?

Not at all, sir.

So it is only the radicals that are whipped, and their children killed?

Yes, sir; these men that contends for their equal rights for person and property with white men.

They are the men singled out and punished, are they?

Yes, sir.

How many of your people in this country do you think have been whipped or otherwise outraged because of their political sentiments?

O, hundreds. I could not number them to you, sir.

By 1874, only South Carolina, Florida, Louisiana, and Mississippi were still in the Republican column. In the Big Three (Mississippi, South Carolina, Louisiana) Negro voters were so deeply entrenched that nothing short of a revolution could dislodge them. Southern Democrats were up to the demands of the hour. "Organize! Organize! Organize!" screamed a Charleston, South Carolina, paper. "We must render this a white man's government," another paper said, "or convert the land into a Negro man's cemetery." General Martin W. Gary, the South Carolina strong man, said: "Never threaten a man individually, if he deserves to be threatened, the necessities of the time require that he should die." General John McEnery, the Louisiana strong man said, "We shall carry the next election if we have to ride saddle-deep in blood to do it."

It was done.

Wavering Democrats were whipped into line. Newspapers which had been indifferent to or amused by the antics of Negro politicians turned mean. Now all Negro politicians were devils: "the shameless, heartless, vile, grasping, deceitful, creeping, crawling, wallowing, slimy, slippery, hideous, loathsome, political pirates." Now all Negroes were barbarians: "Does any sane man believe the negro capable of comprehending the Ten Commandments? The miraculous conception and birth of our Saviour. . . . Every effort to inculcate these great truths but tends to bestialize his nature, and by obfuscating his little brain unfits him for the duties assigned him as a hewer of wood and drawer of water. The effort makes him a demon of wild, fanatical destruction, and consigns him to the fatal shot of the white man."

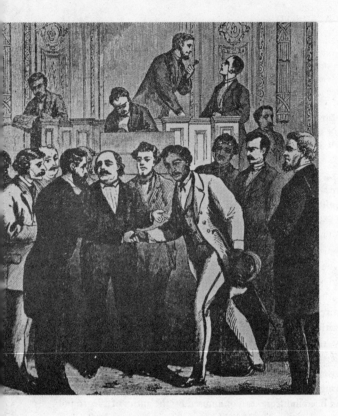

First Negro elected to House of Representatives,
John W. Menard, received premature
congratulations from congressmen on
December 21, 1868. Menard, who was elected
from Louisiana, received an ovation, but was
denied a seat in the House.

L. A. Wiltz took possession of the speaker's chair in the Louisiana Statehouse on January 4, 1875. Last Southern states were "redeemed" by whites in 1876–77.

The white population organized for war. The Negro population, at the same time, was systematically disarmed. By hook and crook, on any and every pretext, the homes of Negroes were searched and arms were systematically appropriated. Adroitly playing on the fears of white governors, who dreaded a race war, Democrats succeeded in disarming or emasculating the Negro militia.

Ballot box manipulations reached an artistic height. Polling places were located in bayous and on islands, in barns and fodder houses. Armed white men were stationed on the roads leading to the polls "to prevent Negroes from seizing arms." In one Louisiana county, the polling place was located in an isolated wilderness. The whites gathered at the white church and were told, in whispers, how to reach the polls. In another county, the polls opened in the dark of morning and whites voted by the light of candles. When the Negro voters showed up, the polls were closed for the day. In Mississippi, white men from Alabama and Louisiana streamed across the state line and voted early and often. In South Carolina, "citizens" came from North Carolina and Georgia.

In this age, a cannon was a necessary part of the canvassing equipment of every self-respecting Democratic club. They were very useful. In the skirmishes and guerrilla wars fought by Negro and white voters, the cannon was the "convincer." On election days, the cannons were sometimes rolled out and trained on the polls.

Economic power was brought to bear. Negro Republicans could not find work, their wives could not buy supplies, their children could not get medical attention.

Social artillery was rolled up. White Republicans were ostracized. Their children were hounded in school. Their wives were cut to the quick at church. Near the end, there was an exodus of whites from the Republican party. Knowing Democrats called the party-switching "crossing Jordan."

Negro Republicans counterattacked. Negro women refused to marry, talk to or cohabit with Negro men who weakened and deserted the Republican party. Landladies evicted Negro Democrats. Enraged women pulled the clothes off "Uncle Toms" who wore the distinctive red shirts of the Democratic party. Wives showed their husbands to the door. A South Carolina wife was frank. She did not, she said, intend to sleep with a "Democratic nigger."

Negro Republicans and their allies put up a good fight, but their resources were meager. White Democrats controlled the money, the land and the credit facilities. When the showdown came, Negroes were unarmed and unorganized. The climax came in South Carolina and Louisiana in 1876. The Republican governments did not collapse. It would take another generation to teach Negro voters their political place. But a beginning, a good beginning, from the standpoint of the Bourbons, was made in 1876. In South Carolina and Louisiana, Republicans and Democrats claimed the 1876 elections. Both sides organized governments. If Washington insisted on fair play, if troops were used to support the Republican governments, if federal officials protected the Negro voters, the Republican governments would prevail. If, on the other hand, Washington chose to look the other way, if Washington countenanced the violence and fraud of the secret organizations, then the Democrats would prevail.

The center of decision shifted to Washington.

As it happened, the presidential race between Republican Rutherford B. Hayes and Democrat Samuel J. Tilden hinged on the disputed elections in South Carolina, Louisiana, and Florida. Hayes claimed these states and the Presidency and an Electoral Commission sustained him.

The center of decision shifted to the House of Representatives.

There had been a radical shift in public opinion. The North was tired of "the eternal nigger"; businessmen wanted to get back to business as usual; the violence in the Southern states was playing havoc with profits. These currents were reflected in the House of Representatives which had a Democratic majority. A group of Democrats launched a filibuster which prevented the orderly counting of the electoral votes. If the Democrats could hold out until inauguration day, America would not have a President. And disorder, perhaps war, would be inevitable.

The center of decision shifted to certain small rooms.

Men scurried to and fro, speaking the word "compromise." The South was willing to compromise, the South was willing to get on with the electoral count—if. Men scurried to and fro, exploring the possibilities of "if." Representatives of Hayes and representatives of the South huddled together in smoky rooms. The price—that was the question. How much? The South wanted certain economic concessions, but most of all it wanted "home rule": the right to deal with the Negro in its own way, a suspension, in fact, of constitutional safeguards which protected the Negro. *Quid pro quo*—something for something. "Home Rule" for the South, withdrawal of troops, an end to agitation of the Negro question, a tacit agreement that the South would be allowed to deal with the Negro in its own way. And for Hayes? The Presidency.

The bargain was arranged in a series of conferences which reached a climax, ironically enough, in a fashionable hotel owned by James Wormley, a well-to-do Negro businessman. After the Wormley Hotel Conference of February 26, 1877, Hayes's representatives handed Southern representatives a signed letter which represented the core of the bargain. The agreement, which shaped the future of the American Negro as much as the Fourteenth and Fifteenth Amendments, read:

GENTLEMEN: Referring to the conversation had with you yesterday in which Governor Hayes's policy as to the status of certain Southern States was discussed, we desire to say in reply that we can assure you in the strongest possible manner of our great desire to have adopted such a policy as will give to the people of the States of South Carolina and Louisiana the right to control their own affairs in their own way; and to say further that we feel authorized, from an acquaintance with and knowledge of Governor Hayes and his views on this question, to pledge ourselves to you that such will be his policy."

The bargain was signed, sealed and delivered. The Southerners called off the filibuster, Hayes was elected, the troops were with-

drawn, and the South began the long process of whipping the
Negroes into submission. The North began a precipitate retreat
from racial reality. The scornful smile of Pinchback, the incisive
mind of Elliott, the screams and groans of the lacerated thousands: these were too painful to bear. Instead, men, North and
South, immersed themselves in racial myths. There emerged, as
Sterling A. Brown has shown, the myths of The Contented Slave
and The Wretched Freedman. Soon all ex-slaves would say, "Dey
was good ole days, dose times befoah de wah!" Soon all freedmen
would say, "Marse Lincoln gun me freedom. Whar' my Chris'-
mus?" Soon the Civil War would be sucked of all possible meaning and would become an agency of reconciliation between the
North and South. Soon, the *Nation*, an influential Northern peri-
odical, would say: ". . . the Negro will disappear from the field
of national politics. Henceforth, the nation, as a nation, will have
nothing more to do with him."

9

The Birth of Jim Crow

I have no protection at home, or resting-place abroad. . .
I am an outcast from the society of my childhood, and an
outlaw in the land of my birth. "I am a stranger with thee
and a sojourner as all my fathers were."

T<small>HOMAS</small> <small>DARTMOUTH</small> <small>RICE</small>, one of the white pioneers
in comic representation of the Negro, saw James Crow somewhere
in Kentucky or Ohio and immortalized him in dialect.

> *Weel a-bout and turn a-bout*
> *And do just so*
> *Every time I weel a-bout*
> *I jump Jim Crow.*

Wheeling about and turning about and jumping just so, "Daddy"
Rice shuffled across the stage at New York's Bowery Theatre in
1832 and gave America its first international song hit.

By 1838, Jim Crow * was wedged into the language as a synonym for Negro. A noun, a verb, an adjective, a "comic" way of life.

By 1839, there was an antislavery book about him: *The History of Jim Crow.*

By 1841, there was a Jim Crow railroad car—in Massachusetts of all places.

By 1901, Jim Crow was a part of the marrow of America. But he was no longer singing. He had turned mean. The song-and-dance man had become a wall, a way of separating people from people. Demagogue by demagogue, mania by mania, brick by brick, the wall was built. Interracial riding, interracial drinking and interracial dying were banned.

The cornerstones of the great wall were two taboos: interracial eating and intermarriage. Anything approaching interracial eating was proscribed. Anything which might by any stretch of the imagination lead to intermarriage was interdicted. One law led to a hundred. One fear became a nightmare. Out came the rope. Out came the signs:

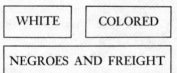

Out came the rationalizations. Cole L. Blease, the South Carolina demagogue, said it. "Whenever the Constitution comes between me and the virtue of the white women of the South, I say to hell with the Constitution."

Fear. Frenzy. White Womanhood.

Brick by brick, bill by bill, fear by fear, the wall grew taller and taller. The deaf, the dumb and the blind were separated by color. White nurses were forbidden to treat Negro males. White teachers were forbidden to teach Negro students. South Carolina forbade

---

* James Crow is an unknown soldier. Some writers say he was a Cincinnati, Ohio, slave; others say he was a Charleston, S.C., slave. Some writers say the Crow came from old Mr. Crow, the slaveowner; others say the Crow came from the simile, black as a crow.

Negro and white cotton mill workers to look out the same window. Florida required "Negro" textbooks and "white" textbooks to be segregated in warehouses. Oklahoma required "separate but equal" telephone booths. New Orleans segregated Negro and white prostitutes. Atlanta provided Jim Crow Bibles for Negro and white witnesses.

In the last decade of the nineteenth century and the first decades of the twentieth, the wall went higher and higher. The thrust came from fear, from economic competition and political needs, from frustration, from an obsession with the cult of White Womanhood. In only two other countries—South Africa and Nazi Germany— have men's fears driven them to such extremes.

As the years rolled by the wall loomed so tall that men forgot that there was a time when there was no wall, a time when national law required equal treatment in inns, hotels and railroads, when whites and blacks rubbed shoulders together in streetcars, ate in the same dining rooms and drank bad gin in the same saloons.

The extraordinary thing about the wall that fear built is that it is of so recent an origin. There were no separate but equal privies in slavery time. Nor, as C. Vann Woodward has shown in his excellent book, *The Strange Career of Jim Crow*, were there separate but equal rest rooms for a considerable period thereafter. So long as Negroes were slaves, so long as they posed no threat to the political and economic supremacy of whites, men were content to live with them on terms of relative intimacy. But when the slave became a citizen, when he got a ballot in his hot hand and a wrench and pencil and paper—well, something had to be done with him.

That something was a long time working itself out. For several years after whites undermined Black Reconstruction, Negroes and whites were served in the same inns and buried in the same graveyards. There were even some communities where Negro and white children read letters out of the same spelling books in the same classrooms. As late as 1879, Vernon Wharton reports, most of the saloons in Mississippi "served whites and Negroes in the same bar. Many of the restaurants, using separate tables, served both races in the same room."

In April, 1885, when T. McCants Stewart, a Negro lawyer and reporter, made the first Freedom Ride through the South, Jim Crow was a sometimes thing. "On leaving Washington, D.C.," he reported, "I put a chip on my shoulder, and inwardly dared any man to knock it off." McCants was pleasantly surprised. He rode first class in a car in which several whites had to sit on their baggage for lack of seats. "Bold as a lion," he went into a station dining room in Virginia and was served at a table with whites. He wrote a dispatch. "Along the Atlantic Seaboard from Canada to the Gulf of Mexico—through Delaware, Maryland, Virginia, the Carolinas, Georgia and into Florida, all the old slave States with enormous Negro populations . . . a first-class ticket is good in a first-class coach. . . ." His dispatch from Columbia, South Carolina, was lyrical. "I feel about as safe here as in Providence, R.I. I can ride in first-class cars on the railroads and in the streets. I can go into saloons and get refreshments even as in New York. I can stop in and drink a glass of soda and be more politely waited upon than in some parts of New England." Stewart finally gave up: no news was good news. "For the life of [me]," he wrote, "I can't 'raise a row' in these letters. Things seem (remember I write *seem*) to move along as smoothly as in New York or Boston. . . . If you should ask me, 'Watchman, tell us of the night!'. . . I would say, 'The morning light is breaking!' "

The light Stewart saw was, in fact, the coming of the moon. Things were not what they seemed. There was still room for maneuvering, but a darkness was moving in. The road, at that time, ran through a swamp and forked off. America and the South had not yet decided which fork to take.

It seemed, for a spell, that all America would take the road leading to brotherhood and democracy. Congress, in fact, seemed determined to push America down the right fork. "Never before," Milton R. Konvitz has written, "in the history of any people was there such an obsessive concern with the establishment of fundamental rights for a minority which, until then, had had no rights at all. Congress was intent on not merely passing laws giving rights to the Negroes but on the vindication and enforcement of these rights against the former masters of slaves in sixteen states."

The legal shelter Congress erected for the ex-slaves rested on three great columns.

The Fourteenth Amendment:

No State shall make or enforce any law which shall abridge the privileges or immunities of citizens of the United States, nor shall any State deprive any person of life, liberty or property without due process of law, nor deny to any person within its jurisdiction the equal protection of the laws.

The Fifteenth Amendment:

The rights of the citizens of the United States to vote shall not be denied or abridged by the United States or by any State on account of race, color, or previous condition of servitude.

The Civil Rights Bill of 1875:

All persons within the jurisdiction of the United States shall be entitled to the full and equal enjoyment of the accommodations, advantages, facilities, and privileges of inns, public conveyances on land or water, theaters, and other places of public amusement; subject only to the conditions and limitations established by law and applicable alike to citizens of every race and color, regardless of any previous condition of servitude.

The Fourteenth Amendment, the Fifteenth Amendment, and the Civil Rights Bill were words on paper. The proof of the pudding would come literally in the eating and the riding and the balloting. When the lawyers got through with the words, these things became hedged about with prickly legal arrangements. A meal in a "white" restaurant, a ticket to a "white" opera house, a seat in a "white" railroad car: these became enormously complicated legal processes involving policemen, layers on layers of lawyers and judges and the expenditure of thousands of dollars on legal fees. It got so bad that almost everybody admitted that Negroes had certain legal rights, but almost no one could tell them where to go for redress. "When we seek relief at the hands of Congress," a Negro editor in Richmond, Virginia, said, "we are informed that our plea involves a legal question, and we are referred to the Courts. When we appeal to the Courts, we are gravely told that the question is a political one, and that we must go to Congress. When Congress enacts remedial legislation, our enemies take it to the Supreme Court, which promptly declares it unconstitutional." How did this situation come about? And why?

First, the why. The status of the Negro depended, to a great extent, on three fragile props: world public opinion, American public opinion and Nine Men in Black Robes. In the third and fourth quarters of the nineteenth century, the three props collapsed and the roof caved in. Europe, at the time, was embarking on "the Rape of Africa." America was involved in adventures with "little brown brothers" in the Caribbean. Everywhere, in this age, men were taking the blessings of white civilization to the natives. Everywhere, in these decades, men were shouldering "the white man's burden" of carrying tea, coffee, tin, and sugar back to the mother country.

America, moreover, was suffering from the prolonged hangover of the Hayes Compromise of 1877 which turned the ex-slaves over to the mercies of their ex-masters. Never before had men felt such a compulsion to believe in the innate inferiority of black and brown people. Men, Western men anyway, are so constituted that they cannot do wrong on a grand scale without believing that God or history is at their back. Science and the new discipline of sociology came to the rescue. Blood, the inkstands said, would tell. White men were superior and that was all there was to that. Nothing was more foolish than to attempt to enforce laws making brown and black people the equals of white people. White people would not stand for it, sir. Their "natural" "consciousness of kind" could not be curbed by laws and judges. "Stateways," Sociologist William Graham Sumner was saying, "cannot change folkways."

The Supreme Court was inclined to agree. In 1883, the Court declared the Civil Rights Bill unconstitutional. Ruling on several cases involving denials of equal rights to Negroes in inns, hotels,

railroads and places of public amusement, the Court said the Fourteenth Amendment forbade *states*, not individuals, from discrimi-
nating. In an eloquent dissent, Justice John Marshall Harlan dis-
agreed. The Court, he said, had gutted the Fourteenth Amendment
"by a subtle and ingenious verbal criticism." Railroad corporations,
inns, hotels and places of public amusement, he said, are instrumentalities of the state. "It seems to me that . . . a denial, by these
instrumentalities of the States, to the Citizen, because of his race,
of that equality of civil rights secured to him by law, is a denial by
the State, within the meaning of the Fourteenth Amendment. If it
be not, then that race is left, in respect of the civil rights in question, practically at the mercy of corporations and individuals wield-
ing power under the States."

As it turned out, Harlan was right. But this was no comfort to
Negroes who had to live with the majority decision which amputated the Fourteenth Amendment and spawned an epidemic of Jim
Crow laws. Tennessee had kicked off the modern segregation
movement in 1881 with a Jim Crow railroad law. Now, every
Southern state, beginning with Florida in 1887, enacted Jim Crow
railroad legislation.

Negroes protested bitterly. After the civil rights decision, protest meetings were held from Maine to Florida. Timothy Thomas
Fortune, the influential Negro editor, said Negroes felt as if they
had been "baptized in ice water." The polished John Mercer Langston told a full house at Washington's Fifteenth Street Presbyterian
Church that the decision was "a stab in the back."

Henry McNeal Turner, the fiery AME bishop, said the civil
rights decision was "barbarous." A former Union chaplain, he
never forgave the nation for what he considered "ungrateful" treatment of the Negro. "Years later," Lawrence D. Reddick has written, "when he felt that his last days on earth were near, he deliberately dragged himself off to Canada, in order not to die on
American soil."

Enter Booker T. Washington.

When Lee surrendered to Grant at Appomattox, Booker T.

Washington was a nine-year-old slave in Virginia. Seven years later, at sixteen, he entered Hampton Institute. Now, at twenty-eight, he was a comer, the president of Tuskegee Institute which he had built from the ground up, an educator who had been praised by whites for his "soundness" on racial matters and his innovations in industrial education. A year after the civil rights decision, Booker T. Washington traveled to Madison, Wisconsin, to speak to the National Education Association. The educators liked what he said.

"Brains, property, and character for the Negro," he said, "will settle the question of civil rights. The best course to pursue in regard to the civil rights bill in the South is to let it alone; let it alone and it will settle itself. Good schoolteachers and plenty of money to pay them will be more potent in settling the race question than many civil rights bills and investigating committees."

Eleven years later, Booker T. Washington turned up in Atlanta with the parable of the open hand and the separate but equal fingers. It was September 18, 1895. Atlanta was packed with people waiting for the opening of the Cotton States Exposition. Far away, in Gray Gables, Massachusetts, President Grover Cleveland was waiting to send the electric spark that would start machinery at the exposition.

In the Exposition Building, a large crowd of Negroes and whites was sweating through the opening speeches. Several whites spoke and then a man introduced "Professor Booker T. Washington." The Negro educator moved to the front of the platform. James Creelman, the famous correspondent of the *New York World*, saw "a remarkable figure; tall, bony, straight as a Sioux chief, high forehead, straight nose, heavy jaws, and strong, determined mouth, with big white teeth, piercing eyes, and a commanding manner. The sinews stood out on his bronze neck, and his muscular right arm swung high in the air, with a lead-pencil grasped in the clenched brown fist. His big feet were planted squarely, with the heels together and the toes turned out. His voice rang out clear and true, and he paused impressively as he made each point. Within ten minutes, the multitude was in an uproar of enthusiasm—handkerchiefs were waved, canes were flourished, hats were tossed in the air. The fairest women of Georgia stood up and cheered."

What was all the shouting about?

Metaphors, mostly—these and words millions were yearning to hear. Washington, whatever his limitations, was a man who could make a figure of speech shimmer and dance. He was working this day with the metaphors of the open hand and the empty bucket.

"A ship lost at sea for many days," he said, "suddenly sighted a friendly vessel. From the mast of the unfortunate vessel was seen a signal, 'Water, water; we die of thirst!' The answer from the friendly vessel at once came back, 'Cast down your bucket where you are.' A second time the signal, 'Water, water; send us water!' ran up from the distressed vessel, and was answered, 'Cast down your bucket where you are.' A third and fourth signal for water was answered, 'Cast down your bucket where you are.' The captain of the distressed vessel, at last heeding the injunction, cast down his bucket, and it came up full of fresh, sparkling water from the mouth of the Amazon River. To those of my race who depend on bettering their condition in a foreign land or who underestimate the importance of cultivating friendly relations with the southern white man, who is their next-door neighbor, I would say: 'Cast down your bucket where you are . . .'"

To whites, Washington offered the same advice. "Cast down your bucket . . . among the eight millions of Negroes . . . who have, without strikes and labor wars, tilled your fields, cleared your forests, builded your railroads and cities . . . the most patient, faithful, law-abiding, and unresentful people that the world has seen. . . ."

Suddenly Washington flung his hand aloft with the fingers held wide apart.

"In all things that are purely social," he said, "we can be as separate as the fingers, yet [he balled the fingers into a fist] one as the hand in all things essential to mutual progress."

The crowd came to its feet, yelling.

A "great wave of sound dashed itself against the wall," Creelman wrote, "and the whole audience was on its feet in a delirium of applause." When the din had subsided, Washington mentioned the unmentionable—social equality.

"The wisest among my race," he said, "understand that the agitation of questions of social equality is the extremest folly, and that progress in the enjoyment of all the privileges that will come to us must be the result of severe and constant struggle rather than of artificial forcing."

When Washington was done, waves and waves of applause dashed against the building. And the Negroes in the audience—did they applaud, too? At the end of the speech, reporter Creelman wrote in a prophetically chilling sentence, "most of the Negroes in the audience were crying, perhaps without knowing just why."

This speech, "the Atlanta Compromise," made Washington famous and set the tone for Negro leadership for some twenty years. Washington renounced social and political equality, temporarily anyway. What did he expect in return? Support for Negro education, Washingtonians say, an end to the maimings and killings and a square deal in the economic field. It didn't turn out that way.

Down went the buckets and up they came filled with brine. Economic discrimination continued. Lynchings and murders reached staggering heights. Caste lines hardened. Separate became more and more separate and less and less equal. Washington was not responsible for these things. But his "submissive philosophy," C. Vann Woodward has said, "must have appeared to some whites as an 'invitation to further aggression.' " Woodward, a white historian, added: "It is quite certain that Booker T. Washington did not intend his so-called Atlanta Compromise to constitute such an invitation. But in proposing virtual retirement of the mass of Negroes from the political life of the South and in stressing the humble and menial role that the race was to play, he would seem unwittingly to have smoothed the path to proscription." Rayford Logan, a Negro historian, hazarded "the guess" that Washington's philosophy "consoled the consciences of the judges of the Supreme Court."

Bessie Smith, pioneer blues singer, became a nationally known star in the twenties. She was born and reared in brutal poverty in Chattanooga, Tennessee.

George H. White, militant North Carolina politician, was the last of the post-Reconstruction Negro congressmen. His Congressional term ended in 1901.

"Separate but equal" water fountains in a Southern town indicate degree of discrimination in the Jim Crow system. Rash of Jim Crow laws were passed in first decades of the twentieth century.

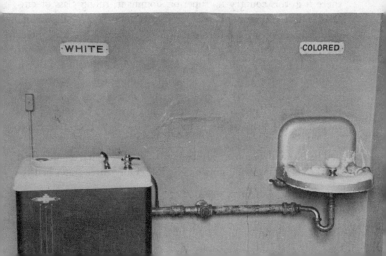

One year after Washington's Atlanta address, the Supreme Court rounded the fateful fork. In the case of *Plessy v. Ferguson,* the Court wrote into American law the doctrine of racial separation and classification. State laws requiring "separate but equal" accommodations for Negroes, the Court said, were a "reasonable" use of state police power. "The object of the [Fourteenth] Amendment," the Court added, "was undoubtedly to enforce the absolute equality of the two races before the law, but in the nature of things it could not have been intended to abolish distinctions based on color, or to enforce social, as distinguished from political equality, or a commingling of the two races upon terms unsatisfactory to either."

Justice Harlan was prophetic in his dissent. Laws requiring segregation, he said, fostered ideas of caste and inferiority and would lead to additional aggression against the rights of Negroes. "It is scarcely just to say that a colored citizen should not object to occupying a public coach assigned to his own race. He does not object, nor, perhaps, would he object to separate coaches for his race, if his rights under the law were recognized. But he objects, and ought never to cease objecting to the proposition that citizens of the white and black races can be adjudged criminals because they sit, or claim the right to sit, in the same public coach on a public highway. . . . in view of the Constitution, in the eye of the law, there is in this country no superior, dominant, ruling class of citizens. There is no caste here. Our Constitution is color-blind, and neither knows nor tolerates classes among citizens. . . . It is, therefore, to be regretted that this high tribunal, the final expositor of the fundamental law of the land, has reached the conclusion that it is competent for a State to regulate the enjoyment by citizens of their civil rights solely upon the basis of race. In my opinion, the judgement this day rendered will, in time, prove to be quite as pernicious as the decision made by this tribunal in the Dred Scott case."

The Plessy decision, as Justice Harlan predicted, led to additional aggression against the rights of Negroes. Only three states had required Jim Crow waiting rooms before 1899, but in the next three decades other Southern states fell into line. Only Georgia, before 1900, had required Jim Crow seating on streetcars. North Carolina and Virginia fell into line in 1901; Louisiana in 1902; Arkansas, South Carolina, and Tennessee in 1903; Mississippi and Maryland in 1904 and Florida in 1905.

A Jim Crow mania seized men. Driven by some deep, dark urge, they piled law on law. The laws came in spurts and waves. Each year brought some new twist or elaboration. Negroes and whites were forcibly separated in public transportation, sports, hospitals, orphanages, prisons, asylums, funeral homes, morgues, cemeteries. Mobile, Alabama, required Negroes to be off the streets by 10 P.M. Birmingham, Alabama, forbade Negroes and whites to play checkers together.

Unsuccessful attempts were made to create by law Negro and white residential districts and Negro and white blocks. When the Supreme Court struck down these attempts, the movement continued under the guise of restrictive covenants and gentleman's agreements.

Jim Crow sections grew up in almost every city and town— around Beale Street in Memphis and Cotton Row in Macon, Georgia. Jim Crow was busy, too, in the North. Here, the propulsive forces were the fears and phobias of poor white immigrants. Negro immigrants, in the early days, were scattered in several sections in Northern cities. Many Negroes, in fact, lived in close proximity to the rich whites they served as domestics. Gradually, the pattern shifted and predominantly-Negro sections came into being.

The founder of Chicago was Jean Baptiste Point du Sable, a Negro who got on very well with the Indians who had a saying: "The first white man to settle at Chickagou was a Negro." Later, when the whites displaced the Indians, life became a great deal more complicated. In the nineties, Drake and Cayton report, there were five thousand Negroes in Chicago and most of them were congregated "in a long, thin sliver of land, sandwiched between a well-to-do white neighborhood and that of the so-called 'shanty Irish.' "

There was a similar development in New York City. In 1890, the 23,000 Negroes in New York were clustered in several areas. Then, in 1903, a live-wire Negro real estate operator had a bright idea. He offered to fill the many vacancies in Harlem with Negro tenants. At first, James Weldon Johnson said, the whites paid little attention to their new neighbors. Then, as more Negroes moved in, a panic developed. The whites "began fleeing as from a plague. The presence of one colored family in a block, no matter how well bred and orderly, was sufficient to precipitate a flight. House after house and block after block was actually deserted." And thus, Harlem was born.

Meanwhile, in the South, Jim Crow building continued. Beginning with Mississippi in 1890, the South turned its attention to the Negro voter. How was it possible to disfranchise poor Negroes without disfranchising poor whites. The answer the South came up with was a wall with holes in it. The wall consisted of literacy and property tests and poll taxes. The holes, designed especially for illiterate, propertyless whites, were the understanding clauses and the "grandfather clauses." If a man's ancestors voted on or before a selected date in, say, 1866—a date on which unfortunately there were no Negro voters—then he could escape the other provisions. Or he could slip through the holes of "good character" and "understanding." If he could not read or write and if he were white, surely he had "good character." If the alphabet were foreign to him and if he were white, surely he could understand and explain an article of the constitution. But if he were black, the "read and write" and "understanding" clauses were jigsaw puzzles. The story is told of a Negro teacher, a graduate of Harvard, who presented himself to a Mississippi registrar. The teacher read the state constitution and several books. The registrar came up with a passage in Latin, which the teacher read, and a passage in Greek, which the teacher read, and pages in French, German and Spanish, all of which the teacher read. Finally, the registrar held up a page of Chinese characters and asked: "What does this mean?" The teacher replied: "It means you don't want me to vote."

By "grandfather clauses," literacy and understanding tests and white primaries, the Negro was excluded from the electorate. "Pitchfork" Ben Tillman, the South Carolina demagogue, said: "We have done our level best; we have scratched our heads to find out how we could eliminate the last one of them. We stuffed ballot boxes. We shot them [Negroes]. We are not ashamed of it."

These devices were extremely effective. In 1896, for example, there were 130,344 Negro voters in Louisiana. Negro voters were in the majority in twenty-six parishes. In 1900, two years after adoption of a state constitution with a "grandfather clause," the 5,320 Negro voters were a minuscule minority in every county.

The elimination of the Negro as an active element in the political life of the South coincided with an acute class conflict between poor whites and the old aristocrats. In the eighties and nineties, the long-subdued poor whites exploded in an orgy of agrarian agitation. The horde of talented, unscrupulous demagogues who came forth to do battle for them soon discovered that Negro-baiting was heady wine to millions whose sole distinction was white skin.

The uses of Negro-baiting did not go unnoticed by the aristocrats. When poor whites and poor Negroes temporarily submerged their differences and demanded basic economic reforms, aristocrats ran up the red flag of social equality and the Populist Revolt collapsed. Reunited under a flag of white supremacy, Southerners of all classes made solidarity an article of faith. Crossroads rang with tremolo references to White Womanhood and "our sacred institutions." Men stood on courthouse steps—a Tillman in South Carolina, a Vardaman in Mississippi, a Hoke Smith in Georgia—and gave Negroes hell. "The way to control the nigger," W. K. Vardaman told cheering crowds, "is to whip him when he does not obey without it, and another is never to pay him more wages than is actually necessary to buy food and clothing."

The crowds loved it. They whooped and hollered and slapped their thighs and the demagogues laid it on the line. And then what happened? Lynchings—naturally. In the peak years of the Terrible

Nineties, which Rayford Logan has called the low point of the Negro's status in America, a Negro was lynched somewhere every two days or so. Lynching became in C. S. Johnson's words "a hybrid of sport-vengeance," became in Myrdal's words a form of "witch-hunting," became in H. L. Mencken's words a diversion which often took "the place of the merry-go-round, the theatre, the symphony orchestra, and other diversions common to larger communities." Newspapers advertised lynchings in advance. Crowds came from afar on chartered trains.

As the decade wore on, as the Negro-baiting became more virulent, the crowds devised more tantalizing tortures. Victims were roasted over slow fires and their bodies were mutilated. And women, Negro and white women, were sometimes the victims.

Only a small percentage of the Negroes who died by the rope or in burning fires were accused of rape. Others were charged with testifying against whites in court, seeking another job, using offensive language, failing to say "Mister" to a white man, disputing over the price of blackberries, attempting to vote, accepting a job as postmaster and being too prosperous.

Pinned against the wall by lynchings, proscription and organized pogroms, with every man's hand raised against them, Negroes flopped about aimlessly, like fish caught in a net. Intolerably oppressed by conditions which they did not understand and which they could not control, they moved from here to there and back again, from one state to another, from one county to another, from the hills to the delta, from one miserable hut to another ten miles down the road. In the "Exodus of 1879," some 40,000 Negroes stampeded out of the South to the Midwest. Random movements continued throughout the period. A group left Alabama and went to Mexico and starved and came back again. Some went to Canada. Some went to Africa.

Negro leaders grasped at straws.

They organized, wrote resolutions and issued vague threats. Ida B. Wells, the intrepid woman editor who had walked the streets of Memphis with two guns strapped to her waist, organized the first effective opposition to lynching.

More than a million Negro farmers organized a Colored Farmer's Alliance and cooperated with the Populist Movement. Negro women organized the National Association of Colored Women.

The voice of Booker T. Washington was heard in the land. Work. Save. Pray. Clean up and paint up. Buy land and don't antagonize the white folk with fuzzy talk about social and political equality.

The National Afro-American Council called for a day of fasting and prayer. E. J. Waring, the first Negro lawyer in Baltimore, called for law suits. His idea was singularly modern. "We should organize the country over. Raise funds and employ counsel. Then, if an individual is denied some right or privilege, let the race make his wrong their cause and test the cause in law." Forty-eight years later, another Baltimore lawyer, Thurgood Marshall, would take this idea and make of it a thing of beauty.

There were some, in this age, who believed the time for talk was past. They wanted to fight fire with fire. When the Negroes of Clarksville, Tennessee, burned part of the town in retaliation for a lynching, the editor of the *Chicago Conservator* congratulated them.

There were some who wanted a Negro state. Edwin P. McCabe, the former state auditor of Kansas, attempted to set up an all-Negro state in the Oklahoma Territory. He had an interview with President Harrison, but the project never got off the ground.

Increasingly, in this dark age, the voice of collaboration was heard. Uncle Toms, "timid, cautious, despairing men," came forward and put themselves at the disposal of the ruling classes. Sir George Campbell, the distinguished British statesman, met a collaborator in Charleston. He was a Democrat who cooperated with the white Democrats—for a price. "His story," the shrewd Englishman said, "seemed to me a little too much as if it had been rehearsed. He tells very fluently how he was a slave, and how he was educated by his mistress; and how, after emancipation his master and mistress, being reduced to poverty, he supported them both, and eventually buried them both—he lays great stress upon the *burying*."

Fight, protest, run, organize, work, file suits, surrender—the babble of voices was stentorian. The babble continued and the Negro masses went to the wall. Here and there, a black hand reached for a straw and caught it. But for the millions, life was a shadowy nightmare of one-room huts and day-to-day danger.

To work from sun up to sun down for a whole year and to end owing "the man" $400 for the privilege of working; to do this year after year and to sink deeper and deeper into debt; to be chained to the land by bills at the plantation store; to wash away this knowledge with bad gin, to blot it out in an ecstasy of song and prayer; to sing, to pray, to cry; to bring forth a boy child and to be told one night that four thousand people are roasting him slowly over a hot fire and leisurely cutting off his fingers and toes; to be powerless and to curse one's self for cowardice; to be conditioned by dirt and fear and shame and signs; to become a part of these signs and to feel them in the deepest recess of the spirit; to be knocked down in the streets and whipped for not calling a shiftless hillbilly "Mister"; to be a plaything of judges and courts and policemen; to be black in a white fire and to believe finally in one's own unworthiness; to be without books and words and pretty pictures; to be without newspapers and radios; to be without *understanding*, without the rationalizations of psychology and sociology, without Freud and E. Franklin Frazier and *Jet;* to not know why it is happening; to not know that it had all happened before to white people and that Hitler would do it again; to not know where to go and what to do to stay the whip and the rope and the chain; to give in finally; to bow, to scrape, to grin; and to hate one's self for one's servility and weakness and blackness—all this was a Kafkaian nightmare which continued for days and nights and years.

And if a man protested, if he said enough, no more—what then? "And if any black was fantastic enough," W. J. Cash explained in *The Mind of the South*, "to run to the courthouse for redress for a beating or any other wrong, he stood a good chance (provided he was heard at all), not only of seeing his assailant go off scot-free, but of finding the onus somehow shifted to himself, of finding himself in the dock on this or some other count, and of ending by going away for a long time to the county chain gang and the mercies of persons, hand-picked for their skills in adjusting his sense of reality."

These chain gangs were real horror-houses. Sir George Campbell was told that chain gangs were often used as schools for undisciplined young Negroes who had grown up since slavery. As schools, in short, for servility. On the slightest pretext, unmanageable young Negroes were arrested, convicted and leased to private individuals and companies. In the turpentine camps and mining camps, on levees and railroad construction, manhood was worked and whipped out of them.

With chains welded to their bodies, waist deep sometimes in mud and slime, convicts toiled day in and day out. Fortunes were founded on their misery. Their quarters were unbelievably filthy. Vermin, investigators reported, crawled over their clothes and their bodies. And it was not unusual for a female prisoner and a male prisoner to be chained to a bed together at night. After a study of Southern chain gangs, Fletcher Green, a modern scholar, concluded that they had no parallel except in the persecutions of the Middle Ages and the concentration camps of Nazi Germany.

From this bitter soil came flowers. From the chain gangs and the cotton fields, from the Jim Crow sections of Memphis, New Orleans, Birmingham, Houston, and Macon, Georgia, came songs which went forth and told the world that America had at last created a new thing. Well-mannered, well-scrubbed young people went out from Fisk University and sang the old spirituals and the world sat up and took notice.

Could anything good come out of Jim Crow town?

Tattered characters in grimy clothes strummed guitars on the levees and in mean-looking bars or relieved their despair with bitter cries on the chain gang.

> *If I'd a had my weight in lime*
> *I'd a whupped dat captain*
> *Till he went stone blind.*

The music went back to the slave cabins and farther, back to the polyrhythmic complexity of the forgotten land—West Africa. The music was a melding of African, European, and American elements; of the spirituals and work songs; of cries and hollers; of "devil songs" and shouts and stomps; of slow drags, marches, funeral dirges, and hymns. It was a blend and yet it was new. A thing made in America by illiterate and despised Negroes. At the turn of the century, Buddy Bolden, the first great shouter, was making the bubbling notes in New Orleans. In 1900, a boy named Louis Armstrong was born and he went out into the world and played the music called Jazz. In Tennessee, a girl named Bessie Smith was born in brutal poverty and she went out into the world and sang the songs called the Blues. "Her blues," George Hoefer has written, "could be funny and boisterous and gentle and angry and bleak, but underneath all of them ran the raw bitterness of being a human being who had to think twice about which toilet she could use. You cannot hear Bessie without hearing why Martin Luther King doesn't want to wait any more."

Life behind the Jim Crow wall was more than singing and crying. Nine out of every ten Negroes lived in the South. They were living at the subsistence level, but they were making progress. There had been a dramatic rise in literacy. In 1865, when emancipation became a fact, about one in every twenty Negroes could read and write. Thirty-five years later, more than one out of every two could read and write.

There also had been a dramatic rise in the quality of Negro group life. The Negro church had become a solid and dynamic institution. Large numbers in almost every city belonged to the AME, the AMEZ, the Baptist and the CME churches. The secret fraternal orders, the Masons, Odd Fellows, Knights of Pythias and others, had laid the basis for Negro insurance companies. In 1898, S. W. Rutherford started the National Benefit Insurance Company. In the same year, C. C. Spaulding and others organized the North Carolina Mutual Benefit Insurance Company. Two years later, Booker T. Washington and others organized the National Business League. There were four Negro banks, sixty-four drugstores and

at least one millionaire. Charles P. Graves, president of the Gold
Leaf Consolidated Company, and the Montana and Illinois Mining
Company, was reported to be worth at least a million dollars.

By 1900, Negroes had more than $500,000 invested in funeral
homes. The Negro professional class had grown to more than 47,-
000. There were 21,267 teachers, 15,528 preachers, 1,734 doctors,
212 dentists, 310 journalists, 728 lawyers, 2,000 actors and show-
men, 236 artists, 247 photographers and one Negro congressman.

George H. White, the last Negro congressman of the post-
Reconstruction era, was a symbol of the shifting fortunes of the
four million freedmen who, by 1900, had become eight million. By
1901, almost all of the Negroes in Southern legislatures and city
councils had been eliminated. Now, in 1901, White himself was at
the turning of the fork. He had been elected to Congress from
North Carolina in 1896 and had been re-elected in 1898. But it was
clear by the middle of his second term that he would not be elected
again.

When White rose in Congress on a day in 1901, men shifted in
their seats to get a better look at him. For better or worse, they
would not be seeing his likes again soon.

White made the most of his last opportunity. He reviewed the
whole dreary story—the rise of the Negro to political power, the
undermining of Reconstruction, the gutting of the Fourteenth
Amendment and the birth of Jim Crow. Now, he said, the circle
had come full cycle.

And so it was time for goodbyes.

"This, Mr. Chairman, is perhaps the Negroes' temporary farewell
to the American Congress; but let me say, Phoenix-like he will rise
up some day and come again. These parting words are in behalf of
an outraged, heartbroken, bruised and bleeding, but God-fearing
people, faithful, industrious, loyal, rising people—full of potential
force."

> *Weel a-bout and turn a-bout*
> *And do just so*
> *Every time I weel a-bout*
> *I jump Jim Crow.*

10

Miscegenation in America

> *Nearly all our discussions of our own social order run upon questions of property. It is under the sex relation that all the great problems really present themselves.*
>
> WILLIAM GRAHAM SUMNER

S IN. Sex. Race.

The three words took deep roots, intertwined and became one in the Puritan psyche. In the famous sermon preached at Whitechapel in 1609 for Virginia-bound planters and adventurers, the minister fused the words in a stern admonition against miscegenation. From Genesis, he summoned the figure of Abram who left his country and his father's house and migrated to a land God had prepared for his seed.

"Abrams posteritie," the preacher said, mixing his races and his metaphors, "[must] keepe to themselves. They may not marry nor give in marriage to the heathen, that are uncircumcised. . . . The breaking of this rule, may breake the necke of all good successe of this voyage, whereas by keeping the feare of God, the planters in shorte time, by the blessing of God, may grow into a nation formidable to all the enemies of Christ."

It was easier said than done.

From the beginning, English colonists, following Abram's example, married and mated with Hagars—red and black. Even more distressing to the Puritan mind was the broad tolerance of the first Englishwomen who married and mated with Hagar's brothers. Proscription began early. In 1630, a bare twenty-one years after the Whitechapel sermon, one Hugh Davis was "soundly whipped before an assemblage of Negroes and others for abusing himself to the dishonor of God and the shame of Christians by defiling his body in lying with a Negro." Forty years later, white women were being whipped and sold into slavery and extended servitude for showing open preferences for Negro men.

Alarmed by widespread miscegenation, colonists from South Carolina to Massachusetts began a systematic campaign which ultimately made the Whitechapel sermon the racial policy of the land. Every instrument of persuasion—scorn, ridicule, sermons, whippings, banishments and laws—was used to teach white people that they should "not marry nor give in marriage" to Negroes. No amount of persuasion, however, could "keepe" whites to themselves. Miscegenation reached a peak behind the Cotton Curtain of slavery and continued after Appomattox.

Miscegenation in America started not in the thirteen original colonies but in Africa.* English, French, Dutch and American slave traders took black concubines on the Guinea coast and mated with

* The material in this chapter on miscegenation during the slavery period is based largely on James Hugo Johnston's doctoral dissertation at the University of Chicago, "Race Relations in Virginia and Miscegenation in the South, 1776–1860," Carter Woodson's article, "The Beginnings of the Miscegenation of the Whites and Blacks" in the *Journal of Negro History*, and A. W. Calhoun's study, *A Social History of the American Family*.

females on the slave ships. "The crossing of the two races," Robert W. Shufeldt wrote, "commenced at the very out-start of the vile trade that brought them thither; indeed, in those days many a negress was landed upon our shores already impregnated by someone of the demoniac crew that brought her over." It should be noted that many Africans and Europeans were themselves the products of thousands of years of mixing between various African, Asian, and Caucasian peoples.

In and around Jamestown and the Massachusetts of Cotton Mather, there was an extensive trade in genes. Socio-economic conditions in the early colonies encouraged racial mingling.

White men and women from England, Ireland, and Scotland were bought and sold in the same markets with Negroes and bequeathed in the same wills. As indentured servants bound out for five or seven years, these whites worked in the fields with Negro servants and lived in the same rude tenant huts.

A deep bond of sympathy developed between the Negro and white indentured servants who formed the bulk of the early population. They fraternized during off-duty hours and consoled themselves with the same strong rum. And in and out of wedlock, they sired a numerous mulatto brood.

When Negro servants were reduced to slavery, the Colonial governing classes redoubled their efforts to stamp out racial mixing. Miscegenation in this era was not only a serious breach of Puritan morality, but it was also a serious threat to slavery and the stability of the servile labor force. Dr. Lorenzo J. Greene said: "Sensing a deterioration of slavery if the barriers between masters and slaves were dissolved in the equalitarian crucible of sexual intimacy, they [racial purists] sought to stop racial crossing by statute."

As early as 1664, Maryland enacted the first antiamalgamation statute. It was an astonishing document. The statute was aimed at white women who had resisted every effort to inoculate them with the virus of racial pride; and the blunt preamble clearly stated the reasons which drove white men to the extremity of enslaving white women.

And forasmuch as divers freeborn *English* women, forgetful of their free condition, and to the disgrace of our nation, do intermarry with negro slaves, by which also divers suits may arise, touching the issue of such women, and a great damage doth befall the master of such negroes, for preservation whereof for deterring such free-born women from such shameful matches, *be it enacted:* That whatsoever free-born woman shall intermarry with any slave, from and after the last day of the present assembly, shall serve the master of such slave during the life of her husband; and that all the issue of such free-born women, so married, shall be slaves as their fathers were.

This law failed to stay intermarriage. Some women chose love *and* slavery; others were reduced to slavery by scheming planters who forced them to marry Negro men in order to reap the economic benefits accruing from the extended service of the mothers and the perpetual slavery of their children. A celebrated case revolved around Irish Nell, an indentured servant who came over with Lord Baltimore. When Baltimore returned to England, he sold Irish Nell to a planter who forced or encouraged her to marry a Negro named Butler.

Shocked by the practice of prostituting white women for economic purposes, Lord Baltimore used his influence to get the law repealed. The preamble to the new act of 1681 read:

Forasmuch as divers free-born *English*, or white women, sometimes by the instigation, procurement or connivance of their masters, mistresses, or dames, and always to the satisfaction of their lascivious and lustful desires, and to the disgrace not only of the *English*, but also of many other Christian nations, do intermarry with Negroes and slaves, by which means, divers inconveniences, controversies, and suits may arise, touching the issue of children of such free-born women aforesaid; for the prevention whereof for the future, *Be it enacted:* That if the marriage of any woman-servant with any slave shall take place by the procurement or permission of the master, such woman and her issue shall be free.

The new law was about as effective as the old one—which is to say, it was not effective at all. E. I. McCormac, the authority on white servitude in Maryland, said: "Mingling of the races in Maryland continued during the eighteenth century, in spite of all laws against it. Preventing marriage of white servants with slaves only led to a greater social evil, which caused a reaction of public sentiment against the servant. Masters and society in general were burdened with the care of illegitimate mulatto children, and it became necessary to frame laws compelling the guilty parties to reimburse the masters for the maintenance of these unfortunate waifs." In 1715, 1717 and 1728, the Maryland Assembly enacted new laws designed to control and stop the swirling tide of amalgamation in the colony.

Negro-white marriages, especially Negro male-white female marriages, were a problem in Virginia and other colonies. In 1691, Virginia restricted intermarriage. Similar laws were put on the books in Massachusetts in 1705; North Carolina in 1715; South Carolina in 1717; Delaware in 1721; and Pennsylvania in 1725. The laws generally extended the time of white servants who married Negro men or begat mulatto children. Free white men and women who contracted legal marriages with Negroes were fined, jailed or reduced to servitude; free Negroes who stepped across the color line were reduced to slavery or sold out of the province. Ministers and other persons who performed interracial marriages were required to pay fines of fifty pounds or so.

Private vigilante associations reinforced the edicts in some communities. The church and other institutions provided additional reinforcement. But nothing worked. Against the law in some communities, against public opinion in others, intermarriage and intermingling continued. Shortly after the enactment of Virginia's ban on intermarriage, Ann Wall was convicted of "keeping company with a Negro under pretense of marriage." The Elizabeth County court sold Ann Wall for five years and bound out her two mulatto children for thirty-one years. And "it is further ordered," the court said, "that ye said Ann Wall after she is free from her said master doe at any time presume to come into this county she shall be banished to ye Island of Barbadoes."

Another woman, a servant, ran afoul of the Whitechapel edict in Henrico County, Virginia.

Henrico County June 1, 1692
Information
Maj'r Chamberlaynes woman servant Bridgett by name for bearing a
base born child by a Negro.
Henrico County
Presented to ye grand jury for this County of Hen'co May 16; 1692 &
here recorded

Tests: Hen. Randolph, Vo; Cur.

Ye grand jury was busy, too, in Pennsylvania. As early as 1677,
a white servant was indicted for miscegenation in Sussex County.
The next year Chester County forbade intermingling. Among the
cases were the following:

For that hee . . . contrary to the lawes of the government and contrary to his masters consent hath . . . got with child a certain molato
wooman named swart Anna. . . .

David Lewis Constable of Haverford returned a negro man of his
and a white woman for haveing a baster childe. . . . the negro said
she intised him and promised him to marry him; she being examined,
confest the same . . . the court ordered that she shall receive twenty-
one lashes on her beare backe . . . and the court ordered the negroe
man never to meddle with any white woman more uppon paine of his
life.

In an unsuccessful attempt to stop intermingling, Pennsylvania
banned intermarriage in 1725. Forty-five years later, during the
glow of the Revolution, Pennsylvania repealed the ban on intermarriage. Thereafter, mixed marriages became common in Pennsylvania. Thomas Branagan visited Philadelphia in 1805 and averred that
he had never seen so much intermingling. "There are," he wrote,
"many, very many blacks who . . . begin to feel themselves con-
sequential. . . . will not be satisfied unless they get white women
for wives, and are likewise exceedingly impertinent to white people
in low circumstances. . . . I solemnly swear, I have seen more
white women married to, and deluded through the arts of seduction
by negroes in one year in Philadelphia, than for eight years I was
visiting [West Indies and the Southern states]. I know a black man
who seduced a young white girl . . . who soon after married him,

and died with a broken heart. On her death, he said that he would not disgrace himself to have a negro wife and acted accordingly, for he soon after married a white woman. . . . There are perhaps hundreds of white women thus fascinated by black men in this city, and there are thousands of black children by them at present."

Branagan contended that amalgamation was encouraged by well-to-do Philadelphians. "Many respectable citizens," he said, "who are reduced in temporalities; on their decease their poor orphans are bound out in gentlemen's homes, where the maid servants are generally white, the men servants are black, and the employers allow the blacks as many liberties as they think proper to take; and no distinction is made between the white girls and the black men. . . . It is a stubborn fact that there are more bound and hired white girls in rich men's houses, deluded by black men than anywhere else. If I were to give an account of the instances which have come to my knowledge to authenticate and demonstrate the assertion, it would make my readers shudder. . . ."

Several families in the Colonial period were broken up by adventures across the color line. A Westfield, Massachusetts, man won a divorce in 1750 on a complaint that his wife, Agnes, had borne a mulatto child for a Negro named Primus. The next year the Massachusetts legislature dissolved the marriage of Lois Way who had mothered a child by a slave named Boston. Another slave, also named Boston, won a divorce on a complaint that his wife, Hagar, "not having the fear of God before her eyes and being instigated by a white man has been guilty of the detestable sin of adultery and during the time of intermarriage was delivered of a mulatto bastard child begotten on her body."

Colonial newspapers yield additional evidence of race mixing.

American Weekly Mercury
   August 11, 1720

Runaway in April last from Richard Tilgman, of Queen Anne County in Maryland, a mulatto slave, named Richard Molson, of middle stature, about forty years old and has had the small pox, he is in company with a white woman . . . who is supposed now goes for his wife.

The *Pennsylvanian Gazette*
June 1, 1746

Runaway from the subscriber the second of last month, at the town of Potomac, Frederick County, Maryland, a mulatto servant named Isaac Cromwell, runaway at the same time, an English servant woman, named Ann Greene.

Aristocrats did not always obey the rules they made. Benjamin Franklin, it is said, was quite open in his relationships with black women. Carter Woodson, the careful historian, says Franklin "seems to have made no secret of his associations with Negro women."

Well-to-do people usually stopped short of legal marriage, but there is evidence that some threw caution to the wind. The following item appears in the will of John Fenwick, the Lord Proprietor of New Jersey. "Item, I do except against Elizabeth Adams of having any ye leaste part of my estate, unless the Lord open her eyes to see her abominable transgression against him, me her good father, by giving her true repentance, and forsaking ye Black ye hath been ye ruin of her; and becoming penetent of her sins; upon ye condition only I do will and require my executors to settle five hundred acres of land upon her."

God apparently did not open Elizabeth Adams's eyes. The granddaughter of John Fenwick was instrumental in establishing a settlement known as Gouldtown, where mulattoes intermarried with whites and accumulated considerable property.

Several well-known Negroes were products of unions between Negro men and white women. Lemuel Haynes, who was probably the first Negro to preach regularly to a white congregation, was the natural son of a white woman and an African. Haynes, a New Englander, later married a white woman, Bessie Babbitt. Benjamin Banneker, the astronomer and mathematician, was the grandson of Molly Welsh, a colorful Englishwoman who came to Maryland as an indentured servant.

White women continued to be a factor in American amalgamation in the plantation period. Kenneth Stampp, an authority on American Negro slavery, says white women were less involved in

amalgamation than white men but their role "was never negligible."
James Hugo Johnston, the authority on miscegenation in the
South, says white women are partially responsible for the existence
of American mulattoes.

With the rise of King Cotton and the plantation system, the
focus shifted from white women and Negro men to white men
and Negro women. The record is abundantly clear: *gentlemen of
the Old South did not prefer blondes*. Perhaps their nursery training had something to do with it. A. W. Calhoun, the authority on
the American family, suggests that the famous Black Mammy
played a central role in the psychological process that led to a fixa-
tion on Negro women and the parallel process of compensatory
glorification of white women.

"Close attention," he wrote, "should be given in the light of
modern psychology to the consequences upon white children of
constant association with members of the other race. . . . The
more subtle effects in the realm of the unconscious will suggest
themselves. White babies, for instance, commonly had negro wet
nurses, and it may be wondered whether in view of the psychic
importance of the suckling process there may not have been implanted in the minds of the southern whites certain peculiar attitudes toward negro women and whether this possibility may not
be a partial explanation of the sex tastes of the men of the Old
South."

Whatever the reason, the Old South abounded in wholesale
amalgamation—in casual rapes and concubinage, in polygamy and
polyandry, in prostitution and interracial incest. The moral results
of slavery, an old planter told Author Frederic Bancroft, "in its
most favorable aspects are unprintable." The printable part is
revealing. In most communities with a large slave population,
stories were common, W. J. Cash said, which ran to the tune, "the
image, my dear, the living image, of old Colonel Bascombe himself."

On this subject, the evidence is overwhelming.

Travelers mentioned it.

"As for the bugbear of amalgamation," E. S. Abdy wrote, "about which so much is said as to sicken every European who visits this country the only question he will ask himself when he sees its effect everywhere from Maine to Mexico is, will it be brought about by marriage or concubinage? Shall the future occupants of the New World owe their existence to virtue or vice?"

Planters admitted it.

"There is not a likely-looking black girl in the state," a planter told Frederick Law Olmsted, "that is not the concubine of a white man. There is not an old plantation in which the grandchildren of the owner are not whipped in the field by the overseers."

And planters' wives denounced it.

A planter's wife, one woman said, is the "chief slave of the master's harem." A sister of President Madison told the Rev. George Bourne: "We Southern ladies are complimented with the names of wives; but we are only the mistresses of seraglios."

In some cases, plantation amalgamation was the result of what Calhoun called "the master's right of rape." Threats, promises, the whip and the lash were used to subvert the morals of servile women. But force was not always necessary. The superior prestige and power of white men captivated some slave women. Mutual attraction played a part in other relationships. An additional factor was the indefensible position of a whole class of women whose only weapons were sexual ones. Some slave women apparently enjoyed the give-and-take of liaisons which involved direct and open competition with white women. The court cases of the period indicate that not a few slave women won these one-sided and dangerous contests.

In an 1828 divorce petition, a Virginia white woman complained that her husband "has deserted me, and is now in the city of Richmond or its vicinity with a colored woman in a state of open adultery."

Another woman, the mother of four children, complained that her husband had eloped with a comely slave girl named Cynthia, "and to facilitate his purpose, he stole a horse from the said Robert

Hoffman to carry the woman and her baggage." The man was captured and sentenced to three years in jail for stealing the slave woman—he got an additional four years for stealing the horse.

A Tennessee wife told the court that her husband was "in the habit of sitting by the fire with Polly after the laborers in the shop had gone to bed." Of like spirit and substance was the complaint of a South Carolina wife. Her husband, she said, "cohabited with his own slave, by whom he had a mulatto child, on whom he lavished his affection; whilst he daily insulted the complainant, and encouraged his slaves to do the same . . . That at dinner one day, he took away the plate from the complainant when she was going to help herself to something to eat, and said, when he and the negro had dined, she might."

The most astounding case, however, was filed in North Carolina. The petition alleged that the husband "insulted the petitioner by . . . repeatedly ordering her to give place to the . . . negro . . . and encouraged . . . Lucy to treat her also . . . that often he would, at night, compel the petitioner to sleep in bed with . . . Lucy. . . ." The petitioner said she was forced to accept a subordinate position in her own household.

Burning with love and paternal feelings, some planters went to great lengths in efforts to stabilize their relationships with slave women. Many slaveholders in Mississippi, Alabama, and Louisiana freed their mistresses and their mulatto children and sent them to Ohio, Indiana, and Pennsylvania. So many mulatto children were settled in Ohio that communities grew up at Tawawa Springs and other places.

Robert Purvis, the brilliant Negro abolitionist, was one of many mulattoes shipped north by penitent white fathers. The son of a Charleston merchant and a free Negro woman, Purvis was educated at Amherst. His father willed him a large amount of money and he lived a life of leisure in Byberry, a Philadelphia suburb. So fair that he could have passed for white, Purvis refused to abandon his mother's people and made an important contribution in the antislavery fight.

James Augustine Healy, the first Negro Roman Catholic priest in America, and the first Negro American to become a Catholic bishop, was another mulatto who received aid and encouragement from a white father. Born in Georgia in 1830 to an Irish planter and a mulatto slave, Healy was carried north in 1837 and placed in a Quaker School in Flushing, Long Island. He graduated from Holy Cross College in 1849 and was ordained a priest in 1854 at Paris' Notre Dame Cathedral. Returning to America, Father Healy worked his way up the hierarchy and was named Bishop of Portland, Maine, in February, 1875. The bishop's father, Michael Morris Healy, also aided other members of the family. ("His trusty woman Elisa" bore him ten children.) Michael Healy sent one of the girls and two more of his sons to the Long Island school. One of the younger boys, Patrick Francis Healy, became a Jesuit priest and served as president of Georgetown University from 1873 to 1882. Monsignor Healy is usually called the "second founder" of Georgetown.

It was not unusual for planters to will property to their mistresses and Negro children. Walter Robertson of New Bern, North Carolina, said: ". . . it is my will that my bosom friend, Ann Rose, for her long and faithful services, be immediately after my death put in possession of all my lands, slaves, household furniture, plate, stocks of horses and cattle, and every kind of real and personal estate which may belong to me. . . ."

Attempts to provide for "bosom friends" caused no end of trouble. White relatives often contested the cases and charged that slave women "had the influence over him of a white woman and wife."

Another charge was mental derangement. In at least one case, this charge backfired. A Kentucky court ruled in an 1831 case:

The fact that the deceased evinced an inclination to marry the slave, Grace, whom he liberated, is not a stronger evidence of insanity than the practice of rearing children by slaves without marriage; a practice but too common, as we all know, from the numbers of our mulatto population. However degrading such things are, and however repugnant to the institutions of society, and the moral law, they prove more against the taste than the intellect. *De gustibus non disputandum.* White

Bishop James A. Healy,
the first and only American
Negro to become a Roman
Catholic bishop, was the
son of an Irish planter and
a Negro slave. He was
named Bishop of Portland,
Maine, in 1875.

James P. Beckwourth, noted
trapper, was one of several
Negroes who rose to commanding
positions in Indian tribes.
Beckwourth became
a chief of the Crows.

men, who may wish to marry negro women, or who carry on illicit intercourse with them, may, notwithstanding, possess such soundness of mind as to be capable in law, of making a valid will and testament.

Nearing death, some slaveowners, being of sound mind, feared for the future of their Negro children. A Virginian was "impelled with blushes and confusion to own and acknowledge the cause that brings him forward on this occasion." The cause was a fairly common one. "Your petitioner believes and acknowledges himself to be the father of the said mulatto boy by a woman at that time the property of himself, and as his parent he feels great solicitude for his future welfare and liberty."

Not all masters were as solicitous. Frederick Douglass and Booker T. Washington received no help from their white fathers; nor did thousands of other mulattoes. Many planters sent their children to the cotton fields with their other slaves. Some planters even sold their own flesh and blood. Worse still was the aura of incest which hovered over some relationships between Negro sisters, white brothers and white fathers. In Virginia, in 1830, an attractive slave woman and her Negro lover, Patrick, murdered their master and attempted to destroy the body by burning the house. Several whites in the neighborhood testified for the slaves. The testimony speaks for itself:

. . . the deceased to whom Peggy belonged, had had a disagreement with Peggy, and generally kept her confined, by keeping her chained to a block, and locked up in his meat house; that he believed the reason why the deceased had treated Peggy in this way was because Peggy would not consent to [his solicitations], and that he had heard the deceased say that if Peggy did not agree to his request in that way, he would beat her almost to death, that he would barely leave the life in her, and would send her to New Orleans. The witness said that Peggy said the reason she would not yield to his request was because the deceased was her father. . . .

Not only slaveowners, but overseers, bachelors, city dwellers, and ministers were involved in what Calhoun called "the wholesale profligacy of the Old South."

Intermingling caused little comment in the lower classes of the

city. It was not unusual for poor white women to become involved
with Negro men; nor was it uncommon for poor white men to
live openly with Negro women. Some poor whites, in fact, vied
for the attentions and favors of well-to-do Negro women. In some
cases, poor whites contracted legal marriages with fair-skinned Negro women who had inherited money and property from their
white fathers.

Concubinage in most Southern cities was a luxury of the idle
rich. "Fancy Girls" (prospective concubines and prostitutes) were
sold openly in the major markets of the internal slave trade. New
Orleans and Frankfort, Kentucky, were the main markets for handsome quadroons and octoroons. The buyers were sports, debau-
chees, saloonkeepers, planters and wealthy bachelors.

In New Orleans, Charleston, and several other Southern cities
there were organized systems of concubinage. The placer system
of New Orleans was a respectable adjunct to the institution of marriage. The *placées*, stunningly attractive descendants of mulattoes
and whites, were well-educated and trained in the art of casual
domesticity. Young bachelors interested in a *placée* could shop at
the Quadroon Balls which were held at the Salle d'Orleans (which
later became a convent for Negro nuns) and other places.

Needless to say, some of the best men of the South patronized the
system. It was a saying: the best blood of the South runs in the veins
of the slaves. "Yes," a Virginian added, "even the blood of a Jefferson." It was widely said and believed in the slave period that
Jefferson had slave mistresses and slave children. His favorite mistress, the reports said, was "Black Sal." Fair-skinned with long hair
and Caucasian features, Sally Hemings played an important role
in several political campaigns. A favorite slave at Monticello, a
mystery woman who was seldom seen and often whispered about,
she was the butt of political jibes aimed at Jefferson. Thomas Moore
and William Cullen Bryant wrote poems about her and several
newspapers, including the *Richmond Examiner*, the *Richmond
Recorder*, the *New York Evening Post*, and the *Boston Gazette*,
speculated about her relationship with the author of the Declaration

of Independence. Pearl M. Graham wrote: "By the time he [Jefferson] turned the reins of government over to James Madison in 1809, Sally was the busy mother of several younglings who closely resembled Jefferson; poets were writing condemnatory verses; newspapers from Richmond to Boston were expressing disapproval: and in the taverns male voices were singing lustily, to the tune of Yankee Doodle, a popular ditty of the day." The song said:

> *Of all the damsels on the green,*
> *On mountains or in valley,*
> *A lass so luscious ne'er was seen*
> *As Monticellian Sally*

Pearl M. Graham and another scholar, W. Edward Farrison, have subjected the rumors and reports to modern research methods. Farrison, a professor at North Carolina College, was impressed by "the only absolutely authoritative source of truth concerning the paternity of Sally Hemings' children—from Sally Hemings herself. . . ." From her, he said, "the quiet stream of family history has flowed on through four generations." In September, 1948, Professor Farrison interviewed three sisters "who were obviously far from being full-blooded Negroes, each of whom was more than sixty-five years of age, and who traced their lineage directly to Sally Hemings through her daughter Harriet, who was born in May, 1801, and whose father those sisters had been told was Thomas Jefferson."

From a study of contemporary and modern sources, Miss Graham has proved, to her satisfaction anyway, that Sally Hemings bore Jefferson "at least four children, possibly six." The children, as listed by Jefferson under the name of Sally Hemings in his *Farm Book*, were:

> Hemings, Sally, 1773
> Beverly, 1798
> Harriet, May, 1801
> Madison, Jan. 1805
> Eston, May, 1808

Miss Graham also interviewed Sally Hemings' great-granddaughters. "These ladies descent," she wrote, "is further substantiated by the Mendelian Law of Heredity. I have been shown a daguerreotype of Mrs. Kenney—Harriet Hemings' daughter—which so closely resembles some of the portraits of Jefferson himself, painted in his middle years, that it could easily be taken for his own likeness, save for the fact that the daguerreotype process was unknown in his lifetime. All descriptions of Jefferson in his youth agree that his hair was of a sandy red color. Hair of this shade occasionally appears among the descendants of Harriet Hemings. Gertrude Harriet (Kenney) Watson was nicknamed by her mother "Jefferson hair Gertie because her own hair was of precisely this shade."

Jefferson was not the only famous American to wander across the color line. Patrick Henry, of "liberty or death" fame, reportedly fathered a Negro son, Melancthon. According to persistent reports, Alexander Hamilton, who was born in the West Indies, had some "Negro blood." "If Hamilton was not a Negro," Professor Maurice R. Davie of Yale University wrote, "he certainly brought two Negro sons into the world. One married a very light-colored wife; the other married into a white family and lived as white."

William Wells Brown, the Negro abolitionist, said that rumor had it that his mother was a daughter of Daniel Boone. Brown's white father, according to him, was a man "connected with some of the first families of Kentucky."

Better documented is the fascinating story of Thomas Hart Benton, the powerful U.S. senator, and Marcus B. Winchester, the first mayor of Memphis, Tennessee. J. D. Davis, a Memphis man who had a firsthand acquaintance with many of the things he related, told the story in his 1873 book, *History of Memphis*. Benton, it seems, came to Memphis with an attractive Negro woman named Mary and settled down to housekeeping. When he moved on to his future greatness, he gave the woman money and property and asked Winchester to guard her financial interests. One thing, Davis said, led to another and Winchester found himself madly in love. He took the woman to Louisiana, where the laws permitted intermarriage, and formally married her. On his return, he installed his bride in his palatial home on Front Street. People were indignant—naturally. Winchester's successor as mayor, Isaac Rawlings, was also an amalgamationist; but he was a much better politician. Davis wrote: "White men living with colored women was, I am sorry to say, quite common at that day. My old friend, 'Squire Isaac Rawlings, was not faultless, and it never set him back in the least with the very set who were most bitter against Winchester; but there was a difference—Rawlings' housekeeper was slave-born, and remained so, while Winchester's was born free, well-raised, and accomplished. Besides, Rawlings did not marry."

Another amalgamationist in high place was Colonel Richard Johnson, the Kentuckian who became the ninth vice-president of the United States. Johnson's mulatto mistress was the famous Julia Chinn. The couple had two daughters and Johnson married them off with style—to white men.

Southern white women were not blind; nor were they deaf and dumb. A great many seem to have considered their husbands exceptions to the rule. "Any lady," Frances Kemble wrote, "is ready to tell you who is the father of all the mulatto children in everybody's household but her own. These, she seems to think, drop from the clouds. My disgust sometimes is boiling over."

Many Southern women suffered in silence. Some, as we have seen, filed for divorce and named slave women as corespondents. Still others—the number is problematic—were involved in amalgamative ventures of their own.

The human passions "which motivated the man," J. H. Johnston wrote, "were also the passions of the woman of the South. . . ." He added: " . . . there is evidence that the birth of a mulatto to a white woman was not an uncommon affair."

Southern divorce records provide a surprisingly large amount of evidence. In a typical petition, a Virginia husband said that "about the close of the year 1803, his prospects . . . were darkened

by an occurrence the which he feels himself constrained with infinite regret to recount. His said wife being pregnant was at
the time delivered of a child, which was obviously the issue of
an illicit intercourse with a black man." Another husband said
that:

in the month of March, 1801, he intermarried with a certain Elizabeth
-----, a woman descended from honest and industrious parents, and of
unspotted character so far as your petitioner heard, or had any reason
to believe. Your petitioner lived with the said Elizabeth, with all the affection and tenderness that could possibly exist between husband and
wife, for about four months, when to the great astonishment and inex-
pressible mortification of your petitioner, the said Elizabeth was delivered of a mulatto child, and is now so bold as to say it was begotten
by a negro man slave in the neighborhood.

In 1825, the Virginia slave patrol found the wife of a prominent
citizen in "one of John Richardson's negro houses, in November
last after midnight—she got away." A witness in this case testified
that the slave and the planter's wife "lived together, almost as man
and wife."

In a North Carolina case, the petition alleged that the "husband
and wife had been married and lived together several years, until
about three or four months before the husband's death; . . . a
witness deposed, that, on the day of separation . . . as he was
going to the house, he met the plaintiff coming away in tears; . . .
the husband told him, that he had understood that his wife was
pregnant by a negro man, and he had driven the strumpet off, and
she should never live with him again. . . . a few months after the
separation, he filed a bill against her for a divorce for cause of
adultery with a certain negro ('slave') by whom she became pregnant of a child. . . . When the copy of the bill was served, it was
read to her by the witness, who asked her if it was so, and she
held up the child and said, it would show for itself; . . . the
witness . . . thought it was a negro child, and asked her if it were
not; and she replied, that she was not the first white woman that

negro had taken in—that, when he first came about her she hated him, but that, after a while, she loved him better than anybody in the world, and she thought he must have given her something. . . ."

Similar cases can be found in the records of all the former slave states. They were not at all uncommon, some witnesses said. John Rankin, who was a minister in slaveholding Kentucky, said: "Were it necessary, I could refer you to several instances of slaves, actually seducing the daughters of their masters. Such seductions sometimes happened in the most respectable families." A North Carolinian said: "Hardly a neighborhood was free from low white women who married or cohabited with free Negroes. Well can I remember, the many times, when, with the inconsiderable curiosity of a child, I hurriedly climbed the front gate to get a good look at a shriveled old woman trudging down the lane, who, when young, I was told, had had her free negro lover bled and drank some of his blood, so that she might swear that she had negro blood in her, and thus marry him without penalty. Since I became a man, I have heard it corroborated by those who knew, and I still see children of this tragic marriage, now grown men."

Unmarried women, some of them poor, some of them well born, were also implicated in the amalgamation of the period. J. H. Johnston made an exhaustive analysis of the cases of alleged rape in Virginia between 1789 and 1833. He concluded that ". . . the student who reads the evidence as submitted to the governor is astonished at the number of cases in which citizens of the communities in which these events transpired testify for the Negro and against the white woman and declare that the case is not a matter of rape, for the woman encouraged and consented to the act of the Negro." In twenty-seven of the sixty cases, judges recommended mercy or citizens sent petitions in favor of the Negro.

There is some evidence that white women continued to marry Negroes during the slave period. Census data confirm this unusual fact. In one county, Nansemond, Va., there were the following interracial couples in 1830:

Jacob of Rega, and white wife
Syphe of Matthews, and white wife
Jacob Branch, and white wife
Ely of Copeland, and white wife
Tom of Copeland, and white wife
Will of Butler, and white wife
Davy of Sawyer, and white wife
Stephen of Newby, and white wife
Amarian Reed, and white wife

All whites and all Negroes were not involved in amalgamative ventures. But many were, and the fact that they were has had a sharp impact on American family life. Certain it is that the white man's involvement with Negro women has cast a long shadow over his relationship with white women. A great many of his fears—of the Negro male and the white female, for example—were moulded in that dark (in the literal sense) episode. "It requires a special variety of obtuseness," Kenneth Stampp observed, "to be able to overlook the fact that miscegenation also had a sharp psychological impact upon the Negroes." At the very least, miscegenation sowed seeds of distrust and suspicion. Practically all Negro males bitterly resented the one-way prerogatives of the white male. On occasions, this bitterness flared into open and rather hopeless violence. To cite only one instance, a Mississippi slave murdered his overseer in 1859. The slave "introduced as a witness in his own behalf [his wife] who stated that . . . the overseer, had forced her, the witness to submit to sexual intercourse with him; and that she had communicated that fact to the prisoner before the killing took place." The court ruled that "adultery with a slave wife is no defense to a charge of murder."

There is evidence, too, that other slaves, males especially, resented women who found themselves in the classic slave position, limned by the late E. Franklin Frazier—"a wife without the confirmation of the law and a mistress without the glamor of romance." It is probable that the Negro male's resentment of past intimacies between Negro women and white males persists today in what the authors of *The Mark of Oppression* called "the uniformly bad relations between the [Negro] sexes on an emotional level."

During the slave period, mulattoes were born to Negro and white mothers in the North. Philadelphia was a major center of amalgamation. So were New York and other urban centers which received large numbers of poor immigrants from Europe. In neighborhoods like the notorious Five Points of New York City, immigrants and Negroes fought each other for bread and living space; but they also mated and married.

On the subject of amalgamation, the North was not too different from the South. There was a tendency to wink at backdoor matings (between Negro women and white men) and to disparage legal associations. William G. Allen, a Negro professor at Central College in McGrawsville, New York, kicked up a national storm when he married a white student. In 1853, Allen and his bride fled to England—one step ahead of an enraged posse.

North or South, backdoor or front door, miscegenation continued. After Appomattox, an increasingly large number used the front door. In 1866, in Vicksburg, Mississippi, a white Union officer married a Negro woman. In the same year, in the same city, the daughter and ex-slave of a planter applied for a marriage license and received instead a summons. They were arrested and the case was hushed up.

When the Black Republicans came to power, things changed in Mississippi and other Southern states. Mississippi dropped its law against intermarriage in 1870; Louisiana in 1870; Arkansas in 1874; South Carolina in 1872.

There was a great deal of camaraderie and mingling in the Reconstructed states—and, of course, there was some marrying and doubtlessly more mating.

A. T. Morgan, a planter from Ohio, summed up the spirit of the age when he blurted out to his brother: "Look me in the eye, ole polecat, I am anxious to see how you take it—there, steady now! . . . God willing, I am going to marry a 'nigger' schoolmarm."

God was willing—and the Reconstruction laws of Mississippi—
and Morgan, a state senator who later became sheriff of Yazoo
County, married Carrie V. Highgate in 1870. Another prominent
Mississippian who took advantage of the liberal laws of the age
was Haskins Smith, a "saddle-colored" member of the legislature
who married a young white girl named Ellen from Port Gibson.
How did Port Gibson take it? There was some grumbling, a white
contemporary said, "but I think the most sensible people in the
community concurred in the idea, that if she wanted to marry him
it was her business."

There are no reliable statistics on the number of obscure people
who married across the color line in Reconstructed Dixie. But
there is evidence that some did marry. An Irish contractor in
Claiborne County, Mississippi, made the following notation in his
diary:

Confirmation at Chadenel I was discusted to see *Joe O Brian* as god
father for Boys, he who has a lot of *Niger Bastards* & is now married to
a ½ Niger wife What a scandale to me.

"Discusted," many were; but some were in love. There were
several interracial marriages in South Carolina. A. A. Taylor, an
investigator for the Association for the Study of Negro Life and
History, reported: ". . . poor white persons, feeling that the new
order was permanent, braved the barriers of caste prejudice and
married Negroes."

In April, 1869, Bet Hancock, white, married Jim Gour in Tim-
monsville, South Carolina. A week later, C. P. Woods, a white
man from Beaufort, married Susan Ulmer. Two months later the
Charleston News ran, with disapproval, a social item on Paul Harl,
a Negro who married Josey Brennan in Fairfield County.

Edward King, a traveler in South Carolina, said there were
three or four instances in every county of white men married to
Negro women. He did not believe, however, that there were many
cases of white women married to Negro men; but he was wrong.
In 1879, when the Democrats renewed the ban against intermar-

riage, one of the strongest arguments advanced was that many white women were living in marriage with Negro men—twenty-five or thirty, the York County representative said, in his township alone.

One of the reasons for the founding of the Ku Klux Klan and other secret organizations was miscegenation among average people. Explaining the events which led to the founding of the Ku Klux Klan in his state, a North Carolina conservative told a Congressional investigating committee: "I do think that the common white people of the country are at times very much enraged against the negro population. They think that this universal political and civil equality will finally bring about social equality; there are already instances in the county of Cleveland in which poor white girls are having negro children."

When the whites returned to power, they immediately enacted laws against intermarriage. Mississippi, in a strange choice of language, declared such marriages "incestuous and void." There was a surprising amount of opposition when an intermarriage ban was proposed in the South Carolina legislature in 1879. One white representative said "it was preferable that our people should enter the marriage relation rather than live in concupiscence."

The legislature did not agree; the bill was enacted. Sixteen years later, when the intermarriage ban was written into the state constitution, Robert Smalls, a Negro representative, made a counter-proposal. He introduced an amendment which provided that any white person guilty of cohabiting with a Negro should be barred from public office and that the children of such unions should bear the name of their father and inherit property the same as legitimate children. The amendment caused consternation in the Assembly. A white representative found the spectacle enormously amusing. For the first time, he remarked, "the coons" had the dog up a tree. The antiamalgamation provision—without Smalls's amendment—was finally adopted, but not until the legislature had foundered on the delicate question of defining a Negro. A legislative committee suggested that a Negro was any one with one-eighth or more

"Negro blood." Some legislators thought one-eighth was too much and suggested a drop or two. This brought George Tillman to his feet. The record of debate contains the following statement:

. . . Mr. George Tillman stated, that he was very feeble, but that he felt compelled to say something on this subject. For one, he had felt ashamed when the delegate from Beaufort had clapped his hands, and declared that the coon had a dog up a tree. He was further mortified to see that the gentleman from Newberry . . . and the gentleman from Edgefield . . . goaded and taunted into putting into the constitution, that no person with any trace of negro blood should intermarry with a white person, and that for such marriage the legislature should provide punishment even beyond that of bastardizing children and adulterizing marriage . . . Mr. Tillman said . . . if the law is made as it now stands, respectable [white] families in Aiken, Barnwell, Colleton, and Orangeburg will be denied the right to intermarry among people with whom they are now associated and identified. At least one hundred [white] families would be affected to his knowledge. They had sent good soldiers to the confederate army, and are now landowners and taxpayers. He asserted as a scientific fact that there was not a full-blooded Caucasian on the floor of the convention.

Mr. Tillman put his finger on a sensitive spot. Passing—crossing of the color line by fair-skinned Negroes—started in the Colonial period and was institutionalized during the ante bellum period. In Louisiana, so many Negroes crossed over to the white race that white people today are exceedingly sensitive about the subject. "In Louisiana," Charles S. Mangum, Jr., says, "there has been so much infusion of Negro blood that it has been said that a marriage license would be refused only in cases where the admixture is evident from the appearance or other characteristics of the party making the application."

During the ante bellum period, there was much going and coming between races. As a result, courts oftentimes had to decide the delicate question of who was and who wasn't white. In some cases, the courts used professionals who claimed the ability to distinguish between fair-skinned Negroes and dark-skinned whites. Several cases in courts of almost every Southern state prove that some

persons with one-fourth or less "Negro blood" were legally passed
into the white race. A typical case, decided in South Carolina in
1843, was reported by Helen T. Catterall in *Judicial Cases Concerning American Slavery And The Negro*:

Johnson v. Boon . . . Report of Judge O'Neall: "tax execution . . .
was about to be enforced . . . against the relators, as free mulattoes.
They . . . obtained a prohibition nisi, on the ground [that they were]
free white men, but were ordered to declare in prohibition. . . . Thomas
and John, were in court, and submitted themselves to the inspection
of the jury . . . sister . . . was shown . . . I should say, was a quadroon. The father . . . Benjamin Johnson, (a white man) proved that
the relators were his children by Sally Johnson. She was the daughter
of Lydia Tan, by . . . a Dutchman, . . . her second husband. Lydia
Tan's mother was a white woman; her husband, Tan, was a colored
man. . . . On inspection, I thought Thomas and John very passable
white men. Thomas, particularly, had light or sandy hair, and a sunburnt complexion. . . . The relators . . . had always been regarded
as colored. . . . They associated with white persons, but never without
question. . . . Price proved that the relators *were colored.* . . . From
the proof, it seemed in the section where the relators were raised, that
little attention, in intercourse, was paid to the question whether the person *were or were not* colored. The jury . . . were told . . . Color
. . . was sometimes a deceptive test; that it ought to be compared with
all the circumstances . . . and if the jury were satisfied that the color,
blood, and reception in society, would justify them in rating the relators as free white men, they had a right to do so. . . . The jury *very
properly* found the relators to be free white men.

By legal and illegal means, a large number of Negroes have entered the white race. Charles S. Johnson, after a careful study of
population figures and other data, estimated that between ten thousand and twenty thousand Negroes pass into the white population
each year. The "white" descendants of these persons have held high
positions in American life. In his pioneering sociological study,
The Philadelphia Negro, W. E. B. Du Bois discovered several cases
of "white" Negroes. "Between 1820 and 1860," he wrote, "many
natural children were sent from the South and in a few cases their
parents followed and were legally married here. Descendants of

such children in many cases forsook the mother's race; one became principal of a city school, one a prominent sister in a Catholic church, one a bishop, and one or two officers in the Confederate Army." Other studies have indicated that several "white" bishops, legislators and other highly-placed persons were, in part, the descendants of Negro slaves. J. A. Rogers, a lay historian who has spent several decades studying *Sex And Race*, lists an impressive array of sources in support of his controversial contention that at least one President had a "Negro strain." When the President was asked about the charges, he reportedly replied, according to S. H. Adams's *The Incredible Era*, "How do I know . . . One of my ancestors might have jumped the fence."

Periodically, as in the Rhinelander case of the twenties and the more recent Torregano case in San Francisco, Americans are reminded of the large number of "white Negroes." Perhaps the definitive utterance on this subject was made in the thirties by *The Crisis* which chided whites for a public uproar over a passing case. "Lt. William J. French," the magazine said, "of the United States Army, who committed suicide recently, made an enviable record in the Army. It is now discovered that he had several drops of Negro blood, which seems to disturb some people. We shudder to contemplate the disturbance if all the Negro blood in this country stood revealed."

A complicating factor in the crazy quilt pattern of American miscegenation is the large-scale intermixture of Negro and Indian genes. American Negroes, Melville J. Herskovits wrote, "have mingled with the American Indians on a scale hitherto unrealized." Johnston said: "The Indian has not disappeared from the land, but is now a part of the Negro population of the United States."

Negro-Indian mixtures began in the Colonial period when both groups were held as indentured servants and slaves. In the absence of legal prohibitions, squaws took black husbands and braves took black wives. As the Negro population increased, whole Indian tribes, Gunnar Myrdal says, "became untraceably lost in the Negro population of the South."

Indian reservations in Virginia and other colonies were vast melting pots. Some tribes held Negro slaves with whom they intermarried; other tribes welcomed free Negroes and fugitive slaves who adopted breechcloths and moccasins, married Indians and went on the warpath against the white man. In several notable massacres, Indians killed every white man and spared every Negro. J. H. Russell thinks it is extremely significant that the Indians killed no Negroes in the Virginia Massacre of 1622. Much later, in Alabama, the Creeks spared Negroes in the Fort Mimms Massacre. "The Master of Breath," the Creeks said, "has ordered us not to kill any but white people and half-breeds."

In the Colonial period, Indians were awed by black people. Peter Kalm, who traveled in America in the middle of the eighteenth century, said Indians thought Negroes were "a true breed of Devils, and therefore they called them Manitto for a great while: this word in their language signifies not only God but likewise the Devil."

Several Negroes distinguished themselves in the Indians' vendetta with the white man and rose to commanding positions in the tribes. James P. Beckwourth, the noted Negro trapper, became a chief of the Crows. One of the leading Creek chiefs, Tustennuggee Emarthla or Jim Boy, was "a colored mixed." John Horse was a famous Seminole Negro chief. Among the distinguished Seminole Negroes was Abraham, a chief counselor who married the widow of a principal chief of the tribe.

Many Negro women married Indian braves. Of the two wives of Micanopy, the head chief of the Seminoles, one was a Negro-Indian. The beautiful Che-cho-ter (Morning Dew) was married to Osceola, the fabled Seminole warrior. Morning Dew's capture as a fugitive slave triggered the long and expensive Seminole War.

Black people were an integral part of the social life of the Creeks and Seminoles of Georgia, Alabama, and northern Florida. As slaves to the Indians and as fugitives slaves from the white man, Negro braves wore Indian garb and adopted the Indian way of life. Kenneth Wiggins Porter, an expert on Negro-Indian relations, has described the position of black people in the Seminole tribe. Negroes, he said, generally lived in separate villages and enjoyed equal liberty with the Indians. "Not only," he adds, "did the slaves occupy the economic position of favored tenants rather than that of plantation laborers, but also, politically, they were the counsellors—almost the rulers—of the Seminole nation. Their knowledge of agriculture and habituation to labor made them in large measure economically indispensable to their masters. The slaves could all speak English or Spanish, as well as Seminole, while their masters ordinarily knew only the native tongue; they consequently acted as interpreters—a role which could easily become that of adviser, especially since the Indians were accustomed to draw on the greater knowledge of the slaves for information as to the customs and institutions of the white man." Not all Negro Indians were slaves. It was very difficult, Porter said, "for an outsider to distinguish between the slaves, however obtained, of the Seminoles, and the runaway Negroes, sometimes styled 'maroons,' who had never put themselves under the protection of any master but who were living among the Indians in villages similar to those of the slaves."

Under the treaty of Fort Dade, which was put together "largely through the negotiations of the Negro, Abraham," most of the Seminoles were transported to Oklahoma. A basic condition of the final settlement was that black Seminoles would be allowed to accompany red Seminoles to the West. The surviving Seminoles in Oklahoma and Florida are very much mixed with Negro blood.

Since the turn of the century, the mixing of Negro, Indian, and Caucasian genes has followed unpredictable patterns. Sociologists believe there has been a sharp drop in interracial concubinage in the South which reached a post-Reconstruction high in some areas in the early part of the century. Indeed, in communities like the Mississippi Delta some white men became so attached to Negro mistresses that they abandoned white society and "went native." Herschel Brickell relates a story from this area which throws an interesting light on the post-Reconstruction mores of the Solid

South. A white man admitted that he had kept a Negro mistress for thirty years, but he indignantly denied that he favored "social equality." He had "never," he said hotly, "sat down to breakfast with her."

Clandestine relationships in the North probably were common in the twenties and thirties when it was fashionable to seek jazz and excitement in the Harlems of America. The extent of these relationships today is debatable; by their nature, they do not lend themselves to statistical analyses. The only thing that can be said with any degree of assurance is that casual relationships are probably a negligible factor in current amalgamation. Myrdal, Frazier and other students have pointed out that increasing knowledge of contraception renders most casual relationships sterile.

Accurate information on the number and extent of stable relationships is hard to come by—only four states keep records by race. Studies in Boston indicate that interracial marriages reached a top figure of about 5 per cent of all Negro marriages in 1914–1918 and dropped steadily to about 3 per cent in 1934–38. Although figures are lacking, there is a general feeling among sociologists that the rate started climbing again in the forties.

Within recent years, there has been a rather dramatic rise in the number of interracial marriages among artists, entertainers, bohemians, intellectuals and the personnel of interracial social agencies. Marriage clerks, social workers and counselors interviewed by *Jet* magazine in a recent survey said the trend is also on the upswing among ordinary people and is likely to continue with increasing integration. An interesting facet of this trend is the large number of white men marrying Negro women.

Some students believe there is an increasing acceptance of interracial marriages. In some areas, this acceptance is more apparent than real. Twenty-two states still forbid interracial marriages.*

---

* Several states have repealed antimiscegenation laws in recent years: Idaho (1959), Colorado and South Dakota (1957), North Dakota (1955), Montana (1953), Oregon (1951). The California Supreme Court ruled that state's antimiscegenation laws invalid in 1948.

Two states—Louisiana and Oklahoma—ban marriages between Negroes and Indians; and one—Maryland—provides for an unlikely
eventuality: Negroes are forbidden to marry Malays. Although
these laws are vague and in some respects contradictory (a Negro
in Alabama, for example, may not be a Negro in Indiana), some
courts have held that they do not violate the Fourteenth Amendment.

Fear of intermarriage plays a crucial but usually unstated role
in the contemporary dialogue over integration. A major factor in
resistance to residential, school and "social" integration is the deep
fear that "creeping miscegenation" will lead to the dreaded "*Cafe
au lait* Compromise"—an America which is neither black nor white.

"The ultimate appeal for the maintenance of the color line,"
Drake and Cayton wrote, "is always the simple, though usually irrelevant question, "Would you want your daughter to marry a
Negro?" To many white persons this is the core of the entire race
problem."

Would you want your daughter to—

The obvious answer—she can always say no—turns out, on inspection, to be no answer at all, for *fear of the answer* is the core of
the problem. The history of miscegenation in America teaches
that people can be legally separated by walls; but that history also
teaches that no wall can be built high enough.

The American white man and the American Negro are cases in
point: three centuries of miscegenation have had a decided impact
on both. In an article in the *Ohio Journal of Science*, Robert P.
Stuckert, of the Ohio State University Department of Sociology,
estimated that 21 per cent of American whites—one out of every
five—have African elements in their background. "Over 28 million
white persons," he wrote, "are descendants of persons of African
origin. Furthermore, the majority of persons with African ancestry
are classified as whites."

Wholesale miscegenation has had an even greater impact on the
American Negro. More than 27 per cent of a sample of 1551
American Negroes studied by Melville J. Herskovits had some

"Indian blood." Even more remarkable was the number of Negroes with white ancestors: 71.7 per cent. The percentage of mulattoes increases not only with additional Negro-white unions but also with additional "pure Negro"—mulatto unions. In Herskovit's sample, incidentally, only 22 per cent of the American Negroes were of unmixed ancestry. Bantu, Hottentot, Mandingo, Yoruba, Akan, Semite, Hamite, British, Irish, German, French, Spanish, Dutch, Creek, Choctaw, Seminole, Pequot, Marshpee—the American Negro is an extraordinary amalgam of different amalgamations. The end product of 343 years of miscegenation, he is also a constant reminder that nature is color blind.

11

From Booker T. Washington

to Martin Luther King, Jr.

If there is no struggle, there is no progress. Those who profess to favor freedom, and yet deprecate agitation, are men who want crops without plowing up the ground. They want rain without thunder and lightning. They want the ocean without the awful roar of its many waters. This struggle may be a moral one; or it may be a physical one; or it may be both moral and physical; but it must be a struggle. Power concedes nothing without a demand. It never did and never will. . . . Men may not get all they pay for in this world; but they must certainly pay for all they get.

FREDERICK DOUGLASS

WHEN HE WAS not at the White House with President Theodore Roosevelt or at Skibo Castle with Andrew Carnegie, when he was not in Julius Rosenwald's office or on H. H. Rogers' yacht, when he was not advising influential whites on "the Negro question" or lecturing Negroes on the need for self-help and self-improvement, Booker Taliaferro Washington rose at 6 A.M. and went to his pig pen.

A master psychologist who recognized and dramatized "the power of the pig" in the social life of American Negroes, Booker T. Washington made a point of personally tending his prize stock of Berkshires and Poland Chinas. Impeccably turned out in riding gear and fine leather boots, the educator slopped through the mud and checked the girth of his walking bundles of pork. If an idea struck him in the middle of the inspection, he summoned the stenographer who accompanied him almost everywhere and dictated a memorandum on race improvement. Then, mounting a favorite gray horse, he rode over the Tuskegee campus, inspecting the farms and buildings, dictating memorandums as he went.

While he rode, his aides were abustle. A research assistant was assembling facts and figures for his next speech; a personal assistant was processing confidential reports from agents in major Negro communities; another assistant was clipping stories from major newspapers; and a special aide was sorting incoming letters into four different stacks.

When Washington arrived at his office, everything of importance that had happened in Negro America in the preceding twenty-four hours was at his fingertips. Confidential reports from agents had been sorted and analyzed. Important letters—from the President and influential whites and Negroes—were ready for his perusal; letters and memorandums were ready for his signature. Deferential aides and assistants stood with pencils poised, awaiting his pleasure. With some impatience, with just a trace of harried haughtiness (he was humble only with influential whites), the ex-slave from Virginia pulled a chair to him and went to work.

From this office, for some twenty years, Washington practically ruled Negro America. Like a reigning monarch, he issued an annual message "To My People." He was the court of last resort on Negro political appointments in America and white political appointments in the South. No Negro institution, his critics said with only slight exaggeration, could get a substantial amount of money without his approval. He made and broke men and institutions with a word or a nod of his head and his silence, in the face of a request for "information," could ruin a career. He corrected messages of Presidents and said the word which made Confederates and sons of Confederates postmasters and federal judges. No other Negro in American history—not a Powell, not a Dawson—has ever felt quite so sure of himself as to send unbidden a memo like the following to an American President.

[A story in the *New York Herald* said] you have inaugurated a new policy which means the removal of all colored men from office in the South. This same dispatch was sent to several southern papers. The spreading of this falsehood in this manner has caused a feeling of bitterness among many colored people, and I am wondering whether it would not be wise to give out a line from the White House denying it. . . . *If you cared to make such a statement and wished me to look over it before you gave it out, I should be glad to do so.* [Emphasis supplied.]

In the critical years from 1895 to 1915, Booker T. Washington was the most prominent Negro in America. A conservative man, shrewd, hard-working and, some say, devious, Washington essayed a program of conciliation and racial submission. He refused to attack Jim Crow directly and urged Negroes to subordinate their political, civil and social strivings to economic advancement. By implication anyway, he accepted segregation and concentrated on a program of "industrial education."

Washington admirers say he was not the Thomist (from Uncle Tom) his critics said he was. That may be true, but it is extremely difficult to make out exactly what he was. It is true that he worked hard—behind the scenes—to make separate "equal" and that he sometimes condemned lynching. But his condemnations were often couched in extraordinary language. Always careful not to offend Southern public opinion, he blamed a revolting Mississippi lynching on the lack of education *of the Negroes who were lynched.* His classic condemnation, however, ran in this vein: "It is unreasonable for any community to expect that it can permit Negroes to be lynched or burned in the winter, and then have reliable Negro labor to raise cotton in the summer."

Almost everything Washington said or did was shot through with a certain irony. He bowed before the prejudices of the meanest Southerner, but he moved in circles in the North which were closed to all but a few white men. He told Negroes that Jim Crow was irrelevant, but he himself violated the law by riding first class in Pullman cars with Southern white men and women. And irony of ironies: he who advised Negroes to forget about politics wielded more political power than any other Negro in American history.

A story which Washington liked to tell himself underlines the paradox of his life. In 1901, he kicked up a storm in the South by dining at the White House with President Roosevelt and his family. Shortly afterwards, he ran into a poor white Southerner. "Say," the white man said, "you are a great man. You know, you're the greatest man in this country." Washington "protested mildly" and said that in his opinion the President was the greatest man in the country. "Huh!" the Southerner shot back. "Roosevelt? I used to think that Roosevelt was a great man until he ate dinner with you. That settled him for me."

Poor whites and rich whites worshipped at the feet of the ex-slave from Virginia. W. H. Baldwin, a prominent businessman, said: "I almost worship this man." Andrew Carnegie gave Tuskegee $600,000 in U.S. Steel bonds but on "One condition only—the revenue of one hundred and fifty thousand of these bonds is to be subject to Booker Washington's order to be used by him first for his wants and those of his family during his life or the life of his widow —if any surplus is left he can use it for Tuskegee." Andrew Carnegie added: "I wish this great and good man to be free from pecuniary cares that he may devote himself wholly to his great Mission."

Although Washington commanded enormous financial resources and had the active support of the most important white men in the country, he was backed against the wall by an idea. His refusal to make a direct and open attack on Jim Crow and his implicit acceptance of segregation brought him into conflict with a band of Negro militants led by two Harvard men. In 1901, William Monroe Trotter, an impetuous, headstrong Bostonian, opened the assault by founding the Boston *Guardian*. Trotter made a point of opening his office in the same building which had housed William Lloyd Garrison's *Liberator*. Like Garrison, Trotter demanded immediate equality. Booker T. Washington, he thundered, was a traitor to his race.

Two years later, another Harvard man, William Edward Burghardt Du Bois, published a book, *The Souls of Black Folk*, which, according to James Weldon Johnson, had a sharper impact on the Negro community than any other book published since *Uncle Tom's Cabin. The Souls of Black Folk*, a collection of essays written in a passionate, poetical style, divided the Negro community into two camps. Almost every literate Negro had to choose sides— for Du Bois or Washington. "Between these two groups," Johnson wrote, "there were incessant attacks and counter-attacks; the former [Washington camp] declaring that the latter were visionaries, doctrinaires, and incendiaries; the latter charging the former with minifying political and civil rights, with encouraging opposition to higher training and higher opportunities for Negro youth, with giving sanction to certain prejudiced practices and attitudes toward the Negro, thus yielding up in fundamental principles more than could be balanced by any immediate gains. One not familiar with this phase of Negro life in the twelve- or fourteen-year period following 1903 . . . cannot imagine the bitterness of the antagonism between these two wings."

The two wings were divided over words and attitudes. Du Bois was a throwback to the Frederick Douglass era of direct, militant action. He favored immediate social and political integration and the higher education of a Talented Tenth (of the Negro race) who would lead the masses out of the wilderness. In *The Souls of Black Folk* he attacked "The Tuskegee Machine" in an essay entitled "Of Mr. Booker T. Washington and Others." Du Bois contended that "manly self-respect is worth more than land and houses, and that a people who voluntarily surrender such respect, or cease striving for it, are not worth civilizing." He concluded: "So far as Mr. Washington preaches Thrift, Patience, and Industrial Training for the masses, we must hold up his hands and strive with him, rejoicing in his honors, and glorying in the strength of this Joshua called of God and of man to lead the headless host. But so far as Mr. Washington apologizes for injustices, North or South, does not rightly value the privilege and duty of voting, belittles the emasculating effects of caste distinctions, and opposes the higher training and ambition of our brighter minds,—so far as he, the South or the Nation, does this,—we must unceasingly and firmly oppose them."

With these words, W. E. B. Du Bois assumed command of the scattered forces opposing Booker T. Washington's program of conciliation and submission. Du Bois was, at the time, a proud, brown-skinned man of thirty-five, a little below medium height, erect, sharp-eyed and sharp-tongued—a reserved man with chiseled features and a Vandyke beard. He dressed carefully, carried himself well and was never seen without gloves and a cane. Du Bois was a descendant of Negroes, Frenchmen and Dutchmen, but "thank God," he reportedly said, "no Anglo-Saxon!"

Born in Great Barrington, Massachusetts, three years after the Civil War, Du Bois graduated from Fisk University, Harvard University and attended the University of Berlin. He returned to America in 1894, educated within an inch of his life, penniless but proud, holding himself aloof from the white immigrants—a lonely figure of terrible pride with a high hat, white gloves and cane. The young professor got a job at Wilberforce University in Ohio. One day he wandered into a prayer meeting at the school. The student leading the prayer meeting said, "Now, we will be led in prayer by Professor Du Bois." The blunt professor said, "No, you won't," and walked out. To make a long story short, Dr. Du Bois did not remain long at the African Methodist Episcopal School. He went to the University of Pennsylvania, where he made the pioneer socio-logical study, *The Philadelphia Negro* (1899), and then to Atlanta University where he organized a series of studies on Negroes.

During this period, Du Bois believed that truth, dispassionately presented, would set Negroes and whites free. But he soon changed his mind. There were, he recalled later, 1,700 Negroes lynched be-tween 1885 and 1894—"each death a scar on my soul." While he was at Atlanta University, an average of one Negro was lynched every week. It came to the young professor one day that "knowl-edge was not enough." Men, he concluded, must not only know but they must also act. Leaving his Ivory Tower, Dr. Du Bois went out into the world as a propagandist for truth. In *The Souls of Black Folk*, he cried out in Biblical fury: "Why did God make me an outcast and a stranger in mine own house?" Then, in one of the most brooding essays in the history of race relations, "On The Pass-ing of the First-born," he kissed the fire of his furnace. The essay, a memorial to a son who died shortly after birth, said:

He died at eventide when the sun lay like a brooding sorrow above the western hills, veiling its face; when the winds spoke not, and the trees, the great green trees he loved, stood motionless. . . . All that day and all that night there sat an awful gladness in my heart,—nay, blame me not if I see the world thus darkly through the Veil,—and my soul whispers ever to me, saying, "Not dead, not dead, but escaped; not bond, but free." No bitter meanness now shall sicken his baby heart till it die a living death, no taunt shall madden his happy boyhood. . . . Well sped, my boy, before the world had dubbed your ambition insolence, had held your ideals unattainable, and taught you to cringe and bow. Better far this nameless void that stops my life than a sea of sorrow for you.

Passionate in denunciation, bold in advocacy, Du Bois organized the first effective opposition to Washington. Aided by William Monroe Trotter, he organized Negro intellectuals and profession-als into a protest group, the Niagara Movement. This group held a secret meeting near Niagara Falls in 1905 and demanded the aboli-tion of all distinctions based on race and color. At its first national meeting, at Harpers Ferry in 1906, the Niagara Movement issued an address to the nation. The words were strong, vigorous, demanding. "We will not be satisfied with less than our full manhood rights. . . . We claim for ourselves every right that belongs to a free-born American—political, civil, and social—and until we get these rights, we will never cease to protest and assail the ears of America with the story of its shameful deeds toward us. We want full manhood suffrage, and we want it now, henceforth and forever."

To make sure no one missed the message, the group massed at dawn one morning and walked barefooted over the grass and rocks to the engine house in which John Brown made his last stand. As the sun rose in the east, the group—which included relatives of the Negroes who died with John Brown and Frederick Douglass' son, Lewis—sang the *Battle Hymn of the Republic*.

Aside from talking, the Niagara Movement did not—as Washington pointed out—accomplish a great deal. But the group did assail the ears of America; and the protesting made a great many people uneasy, including Booker T. Washington. And more—the talking and protesting laid the foundation for the National Association for the Advancement of Colored People, which merged the forces of white liberalism and Negro militancy.

Adam Clayton Powell said once that Negroes have never lost a race riot. Always after a riot, Powell said, white America discovers that there are oppressed Negroes in their midst. The 1908 riot which led to the founding of the NAACP was not a very big riot, as American race riots go; but it happened in Springfield, Illinois, in Abraham Lincoln's city. This fact horrified liberal America. William English Walling, a radical white Southerner, sounded the alarm with an article in *The Independent*. The article, "Race War in the North," appeared September 3, 1908. "Either the spirit of Lincoln and Lovejoy must be revived and we must come to treat the Negro on a plane of absolute political and social equality, or Vardaman and Tillman will soon have transferred the race war to the North."

Among the people who were stirred by Walling's appeal was a

Marcus Moziah Garvey, black nationalist leader
of the twenties, is led to prison by federal
agents. Garvey, who organized the first mass
movement among American Negroes, was
convicted of using the mail to defraud.

Federal troops from 101st Airborne Division escorted nine Negro children to classes at Little Rock's Central High School on September 25, 1957. Rev. Dunbar H. Ogden, president of Greater Little Rock Ministerial Association, said: "This may be looked back upon by future historians as the turning point—for good—of race relations in this country."

LITTLE ROCK CEN

young white woman, Mary W. Ovington. With Walling and other liberals, she conceived the idea of a national conference on the Negro question. The call for the conference was issued on February 12, 1909, the 100th anniversary of Lincoln's birth; and it was signed by prominent whites and Negroes—Du Bois, Bishop Alexander Walters, Oswald Garrison Villard and others. The conference convened on May 30, 1909, in the United Charities Building in New York City and immediately ran into trouble. The white liberals, who wanted to avoid an open break with Booker T. Washington, were uneasy in the presence of the Niagara militants. The whites were especially chary of William Monroe Trotter and Ida B. Wells Barnett who were more militant than Du Bois. During one stormy session, a Negro woman—probably Ida B. Wells Barnett—leaped up and shouted, "They're betraying us again—these white friends of ours." After a long and earnest debate, the breach was papered over and the new organization opened for business in a room in the *New York Evening Post* Building at 20 Vesey Street. Du Bois resigned his position at Atlanta University and joined the organization as Director of Research and Publicity. Although he was the only Negro officer, he gave tone and direction to the whole organization.

To the surprise of critics, the organization survived. Branches were established in Chicago, Boston and other urban centers. And *The Crisis*, under Du Bois' editorship, carried the battle to the enemy camp and stirred Negroes as they had never been stirred before. The association later succeeded in winning legal battles which banned the "grandfather clause" and residential segregation.

Another organization, the National Urban League, was quieter in its methods. Organized in April, 1910, in New York City, the League was an interracial organization which concentrated on the social problems of urban Negroes. It utilized the techniques of persuasion and conciliation. George Edmund Haynes, the first Negro to receive a degree from the New York School of Social Work, and Eugene Kinckle Jones were the first executive officers.

Still another organization, considerably to the left of the NAACP and Urban League, was William Monroe Trotter's National Equal Rights League. The league was blunter and less restrained than the NAACP. It was also an all-Negro organization, a reflection of Trotter's perennial distrust of white liberals.

Trotter, a brilliant, impetuous man, is a singularly neglected figure in Negro history. Like William Lloyd Garrison, Trotter was dictatorial, impulsive and impractical. Totally opposed to anything that smacked of compromise, he demanded absolute and immediate equality. When he couldn't get a whole loaf, he unhesitatingly turned down half a loaf. It was typical of the man that he consistently opposed Negro YMCA's and Negro social settlements. In a sense, his life was a long arc of failures; yet, in some respects, it was a splendid triumph. Alone, forgotten by friends, ridiculed by foes, he held fast to one obsessive idea: the complete integration of Negroes into every facet of American life. On his sixty-second birthday, on a night in April, 1934, he jumped or fell to his death from the roof of his boardinghouse in Boston.

Though his influence was discounted at the time, Trotter played an important role in re-establishing the Negro press as a dominant force in the Negro protest movement. In the pre-Civil War decade, Negro-edited newspapers like Frederick Douglass' *North Star* and Negro-edited magazines like David Ruggles' *Mirror of Liberty* had assumed leadership in voicing the aspirations and dreams of Negro Americans. After the Civil War, the influence of the Negro press diminished. There were, to be sure, vigorous Negro editors like T. Thomas Fortune and Calvin Chase; but the press, as a whole, was not as militant as the *North Star* and other periodicals of the abolitionist era.

During the twilight period between the end of Reconstruction and the founding of the NAACP, it became apparent to Negro Americans that they were not going to be integrated into the total fabric of American life. When white periodicals continued to insult Negro readers by playing up "Negro crime" and playing down Negro achievement, black Americans turned to an increasingly articulate Negro press for an interpretation of the world in which they lived. As the Negro public increased in literacy, the number of Negro papers increased. As the Negro public increased in militancy, the number of militant journals increased. In 1870, there were 10 Negro newspapers; ten years later there were 31; ten years later there were 154.

Trotter (with the *Guardian*), Du Bois (with *The Crisis*), and Robert Abbott (with the *Chicago Defender*), made the Negro press one of the dominant elements in the life of the Negro community. Since 1901, when Trotter founded the *Guardian*, the Negro press has played a crucial role in the development of the Negro community.

Under Du Bois' editorship, *The Crisis* became the first influential Negro magazine. Acidulous, sarcastic and witty, Du Bois pushed the Negro protest in his famous column, "As The Crow Flies." The magazine also used art work by Negro artists and presented stories on Negro achievement. Though nominally the organ of the NAACP, the magazine was something of a "rival" of the parent organization. Both *The Crisis* and *Opportunity*, the Urban League organ, published creative work by Negro poets and writers.

Working a different side of the street, Robert Abbott, the bold, imaginative Chicagoan, made a fortune with the *Chicago Defender*. He was quoted as saying that he aspired "to influence the actions of millions of our unseen and unknown fellows." More than Trotter, more perhaps than Du Bois, he proved what a large influence the Negro press could be. As we shall see, he was a major factor in The Great Migration which brought millions of Negroes to Northern industrial centers. Abbott's philosophy was simple and direct. "I have made an issue," he said, "of every single situation in which our people were denied their rightful share of participation." Proceeding on this plan, the *Defender*, the *Pittsburgh Courier*, the *Baltimore Afro-American* and other Negro newspapers became, in the words of Arnold Rose, "the Negro's weekly shot of racial adrenalin."

Trotter, Abbott, Du Bois, Eugene Kinckle Jones, and whites like Mary Ovington, Oswald Garrison Villard, Joel L. Spingarn and

Mrs. W. H. Baldwin were seminal figures in the diffuse movement which led to a partial mobilization of the energies of liberal America during the first two decades of the twentieth century. In the face of humiliations and discouragements which are scarcely conceivable today, they fashioned techniques and hammered out methods which carried the offensive to the conscience of America.

They were not immediately successful; no. In the first decades of the century, lynchings and discrimination were facts of life, like the mighty Mississippi. But the tide changed. Booker T. Washington himself seemed to be aware that the sun had set on submission. Before his death in November, 1915, he had moved considerably toward the position of his early critics. His final magazine article, printed after his death, was an open attack on segregation.

Washington and Du Bois dominated the headlines, but the great battles of life are not fought in headlines. In out-of-the-way places, without trumpets, millions of unsung Negroes laid firm foundations for the renewed spirit of assertion. A job gained, a house built, a word spelled, a new church, a new school: these were the contributions of millions of little folk.

In 1913, fifty years after the Emancipation Proclamation, Negro Americans licked their wounds and counted their gains. Giant celebrations were held at Jackson, Mississippi, New Orleans, Louisiana, and Nashville, Tennessee. Three states—New Jersey, New York, and Pennsylvania—appropriated money for fiftieth anniversary celebrations.

There was a great deal to celebrate. In 1913, Negroes owned 550,000 homes, operated 937,000 farms and conducted some 40,000 businesses. They had accumulated $700,000,000. More than 70 per cent of the Negro population was literate, a net gain of 65 per cent in fifty years. There were 40,000 Negro churches, 35,000 Negro teachers and 1,700,000 Negro students in public schools.

The voice of optimism was heard in the land. W. E. B. Du Bois said "the efforts of the Negroes since emancipation have been promising, and beyond what could be reasonably expected." Kelly Miller, the Howard University dean, was moved to write a poem, "I see and am satisfied." Another poem, "Fifty Years," was written by James Weldon Johnson:

> *Just fifty years—a winter's day—*
> *As runs the history of a race;*
> *Yet, as we now look o'er the way,*
> *How distant seems our starting place! . . .*

> *Courage! Look out, beyond, and see*
> *The far horizon's beckoning span!*
> *Faith in your God-known destiny!*
> *We are a part of some great plan.*

There was, to be sure, a need for courage in 1913. A wave of residential segregation laws was sweeping the South. In June of that year, Atlanta passed a law forbidding whites and Negroes to live in the same neighborhoods. In that same summer, the Woodrow Wilson Administration started segregating government employees in federal bureaus in Washington. Cleveland, Ohio, citizens were protesting the use of the word "darky" in the fourth reader of the public schools. And the Negroes of Greater New York were objecting to the use of the term "Nigger Brown" by department stores in advertising new colors in brown shoes. In Dixie, there was a wave of brutal murders. The NAACP reported that seventy-nine Negroes were lynched in the year of Jubilee.

During this period, there was a mood in Dixie which had no particular shape or texture. Now and then a letter came from the North, saying the air was freer and that jobs were available. The amorphous mood diffused and spread to the backwoods areas. Suddenly, in 1915, Negro America exploded in a Great Migration. Defense industries, hungry for labor, spurred the migration by sending labor agents into the South. The *Chicago Defender*, under Robert Abbott, crystallized the mood with headlines of welcome.

With cardboard boxes and brown bags smeared with the grease of fried chickens, with thin clothes pitifully inadequate for Northern winters, hundreds of thousands of Negroes hit the road. They came from the docks of Norfolk and Mobile, from the cotton fields of Mississippi, from kitchens and washtubs, from a thousand crossroads and hamlets, from Waycross, Georgia, and Shubuta, Mississippi, from Memphis, and Jackson, and New Orleans, and Little Rock. Almost two million of them came in the greatest internal migration in modern history.

Like the millions who came to America from Europe, like the thousands who went west in covered wagons, they were looking for a better life. Pushed by proscription and pulled by the lure of employment, they settled in the big industrial centers of the North.

During the first World War—the one that made the world safe for democracy—thousands of black immigrants were employed for the first time in factories. And thousands more—in the North and South—entered the Army. American Negroes furnished about 370,000 soldiers and 1,400 commissioned officers. A little more than half of these soldiers saw service in France. They made an enviable record. Negro soldiers fought at Chateau-Thierry, in Belleau Wood, in the St. Mihiel district, the Champagne sector and at Vosges and Metz. The first soldiers in the American Army to be cited for valor abroad were two Negroes, Henry Johnson and Needham Roberts.

Four of the outstanding regiments in the war were composed entirely of Negro enlisted men—the 369th, the 370th, the 371st, and the 372nd. Three of the regiments—the 369th, 371st, and 372nd—received the Croix de Guerre for valor and the fourth covered itself with distinction in battles in Argonne Forest. The 369th, the old Fifteenth Regiment of New York, was the first Allied unit to reach the Rhine. The regiment, which was under fire for 191 days, never lost a foot of ground, a trench or a soldier through capture. Equally gallant was the 370th, the old Eighth Regiment of Illinois. This regiment, which was officered almost entirely by Negroes, fought the last battle of the war.

For Negro America, World War I was a traumatic experience. Negro officers and soldiers were repeatedly humiliated. Negro soldiers trained for combat were forced into labor battalions or as-

Negro women have played important roles in the civil rights fight. Mary McLeod Bethune (left) was national figure in thirties and forties. Daisy Bates was key figure in Little Rock integration crisis.

B. T. Washington proposed program of temporary political submission.

W. E. B. Du Bois opposed
Washington, demanded
immediate integration.

Thurgood Marshall won a
series of important Supreme
Court decisions.

signed to menial duties as orderlies. Throughout the war, there were ugly conflicts between Negro and white soldiers and Negro soldiers and white civilians.

Especially galling was the attitude of the Wilson Administration. At the very beginning of the war, Colonel Charles Young, the highest-ranking Negro officer, was retired for "high blood pressure." Young dramatized his fitness by riding horseback from Ohio to Washington, but he was never assigned to combat duty.

Colonel William Hayward, commander of the famous 369th Regiment, said his troops were not allowed to accompany the Rainbow Division to France. He was told, he said, that black was not one of the colors of the rainbow. When Hayward's troops arrived in France, the American high command hurriedly assigned them to a French complement. Said Hayward: "Our great American general simply put the black orphan in a basket, set it on the doorstep of the French, pulled the bell and went away." Hayward named his unit: *"Les Enfants Perdus* (The Lost Children)."

In France, American authorities spent a large amount of time watching Negro soldiers and Frenchwomen. Brigadier General James B. Erwin issued an order which forbade Negro soldiers of the 92nd Division to speak to Frenchwomen. American military policemen arrested Negroes who were caught talking to Frenchwomen.

The whole campaign reached its height—or rather its depth— with an official order which was issued "from Pershing's headquarters" on August 7, 1918. The order was captioned: "To the French Military Mission Stationed with the American Army—Secret Information Concerning the Black American Troops."

Conclusion

1. We must prevent the rise of any pronounced degree of intimacy between French officers and black officers. We may be courteous and amiable with the last, but we cannot deal with them on the same plane as with the white American officer without deeply wounding the latter. We must not eat with them, must not shake hands or seek to talk or meet with them outside of the requirements of military service.

2. We must not commend too highly the American troops, particularly in the presence of [white] Americans. . . .
3. Make a point of keeping the native cantonment population from spoiling the Negroes. [White] Americans become greatly incensed at any public expression of intimacy between white women and black men.

Humiliated by a series of incidents, Negro troops reacted with sullen defiance. There occurred on a field near Metz on a day in 1918 one of the painful incidents of American history. Three thousand black men and six white officers of a Negro regiment were massed for an observance of Thanksgiving Day. They were requested to sing "My Country 'Tis Of Thee." The band played the introduction and the conductor raised his arm and there was utter silence. The 3,000 black men stood with their lips tightly closed. On that big, brooding field only six men sang "My Country 'Tis Of Thee"—and they were white.

In America, as in France, Negro Americans were being pushed to a point of no return. There were fifty-four lynchings in 1916 and thirty-eight in 1917. On July 2, 1917, white workers in East St. Louis, Illinois, turned on Negroes in one of the bloodiest race riots in American history. Estimates of the number of Negroes killed ranged from forty to two hundred. Nearly six thousand Negroes were driven from their homes.

The NAACP, which had been waging an increasingly effective campaign against lynching, organized a Silent Parade. On July 28, 1917, some 10,000 New Yorkers marched down Fifth Avenue in a silent protest against brutalities and lynchings. First came little children dressed in white. Behind the little ones came women, also dressed in white, and men, dressed in clothes of mourning. The little children carried signs:

THOU SHALT NOT KILL

MOTHER, DO LYNCHERS GO TO HEAVEN?

MR. PRESIDENT, WHY NOT MAKE AMERICA
SAFE FOR DEMOCRACY

A large streamer preceded the American flag. Sewn on the streamer were the words:

YOUR HANDS ARE FULL OF BLOOD

As a propaganda stroke, the parade was enormously effective. But it had no immediate effect on lynchers and rioters. In fact, lynching increased. There were sixty-four in 1918 and eighty-three in 1919. More disturbing than the number was the increasing sadism of the mobs. The Mary Turner lynching of 1918 was undoubtedly one of the most barbaric acts ever committed in a civilized country. Though pregnant, the Negro woman was lynched in Valdosta, Georgia. She was hanged to a tree, doused with gasoline and motor oil and burned. As she dangled from the rope, a man stepped forward with a pocketknife and ripped open her abdomen in a crude cesarean operation. "Out tumbled the prematurely born child," wrote Walter White. "Two feeble cries it gave—and received for answer the heel of a stalwart man, as life was ground out of the tiny form."

The next year, eleven Negroes were burned alive in six states. Then, before the returning veterans could catch their breath, America erupted in the Red Summer of 1919. Twenty-six race riots marred the beauty of that summer. The biggest riots were in Washington, Chicago, Omaha, Knoxville, Longview, Texas, and Phillips County, Arkansas. Six persons were killed and 150 were wounded in the Washington riots; fifteen whites and twenty-three Negroes were killed in the Chicago riots and 537 were injured. In Omaha, Nebraska, a white mob lynched and burned a Negro, hanged the mayor who tried to prevent the lynching and burned down the new county courthouse.

There was a new dimension in these riots. They were not all one-way massacres; some were, in fact, wars. Negroes fought back and some whites as well as some Negroes were killed. Some people found this fact exhilarating. A Washington, D.C., woman exploded with "fierce joy" when Negro men in that city took up guns in defense of their homes. She flung herself on the bed and flailed the pillows with her hands and cried out: "They're fighting, they're fighting, they're defending us."

Negroes were not only fighting; they were also thinking. A growing mood of pessimism, cynicism and despair gripped Negro America as the realization forced itself home that the war had not made America safe for democracy. Lester Granger, an angry young man of that day, recalled that he was disgusted by the "Wilsonian grandiloquence that smacked of sententious hypocrisy."

Another brilliant young man, Asa Philip Randolph, was criss-crossing the country making radical speeches. He had a set piece which never failed to break up a crowd. "I want to congratulate you," he would begin in rich broad "A" tones, "for doing your bit to make the world safe for democracy"—the crowd would snicker and Randolph would hurriedly drop his punch line—"and unsafe for hypocrisy." The Department of Justice didn't think it was funny. After a Cleveland meeting, federal agents arrested Randolph and jailed him for a few days.

During the dying days of the second decade of the twentieth century, two Jamaican-born Negroes viewed the American scene with increasing horror. The Red Summer of 1919 stirred Poet Claude McKay to a passionate sonnet of despair:

> *If we must die, let it not be like hogs,*
> *Hunted and penned in an inglorious spot,*
> *While round us bark the mad and hungry dogs,*
> *Making their mock of our accursed lot.*
> *If we must die, O let us nobly die. . . .*
>
> . . . .
>
> *Though far outnumbered let us show us brave,*
> *And for their thousand blows deal one deathblow!*
> *What though before us lies the open grave?*
> *Like men we'll face the murderous, cowardly pack,*
> *Pressed to the wall, dying but fighting back!*

The second Jamaican—a short, black spellbinder with a dandyish mustache and piercing, magnetic eyes—scoffed at pretty words. There is "No Law," he said, "but Strength; No Justice but Power."

What Negroes needed, he said, was an organization and a country. There was no hope of justice for a black man in America, he said; Negroes must return to the motherland—back to Africa.

Shrewdly exploiting the mood of pessimism, cynicism and despair, Marcus Moziah Garvey built the first mass movement among American Negroes. "Up, you mighty race," he thundered, "you can accomplish what you will." Using as a slogan, "Africa for the Africans at home and abroad," Garvey preached the gospel of a united Africa under the rule of black men. In the process, he recruited hundreds of thousands of black Americans in an extraordinary black nationalist movement. He gave his followers parades, uniforms and pageantry. He glorified everything black. God, the angels and Jesus were black, he said; and Satan and the imps were white. The bold Jamaican founded his own African Orthodox Church and canonized "the Black Virgin Mother." Urging Negroes to glory in their blackness, Garvey told them to "whiteball" undesirable applicants for membership.

Garvey reached his peak in 1921 when he declared the republic of Africa and designated himself provisional president. He surrounded himself with an African nobility, created Dukes of the Nile and the Niger.

Garvey talked big and dreamed big. James Weldon Johnson said Garvey collected more money (an estimated $10 million in one two-year period) "than any other Negro organization had ever dreamed of." He organized cooperatives, factories, a commercial steamship venture, the Black Star Line, and a private army.

Arrested in 1925 on a charge of using the mails to defraud, he was shipped to the Federal Prison in Atlanta. In December, 1927, he was deported to his native Jamaica. In 1940, his dreams shattered, he died in London. "That," commented Professor Albert Bushnell Hart, "is the difference between success and failure. Had Garvey succeeded in his undertakings he would have been uncontestably the greatest figure in the 20th century. Having failed, he is considered a fool."

Garvey was a product of an extraordinary era—the fabulous

twenties. During the years he strode the stage of Harlem, Negro artists poured out a stream of poems, plays and musical compositions. The era has gone down in history as the Negro Renaissance —a period of exceptional creativity by Negro artists and an equally exceptional receptivity on the part of the white public. The big names in the artistic awakening were Langston Hughes, Countee Cullen, Claude McKay, Jean Toomer and James Weldon Johnson. At its outer edges, the Negro Renaissance merged into the general giddiness of the age. During this period, no party was complete without at least one Negro intellectual. During this period, white America searched for the Garden of Eden in the Harlems of America. Langston Hughes was there. Let him tell you about it.

"It was a period," he wrote, ·"when local and visiting royalty were not at all uncommon in Harlem. And when the parties of A'Lelia Walker, the Negro heiress, were filled with guests whose names would turn any Nordic social climber green with envy . . . It was a period when at least one charming colored chorus girl, amber enough to pass for a Latin American, was living in a penthouse, with all her bills paid by a gentleman whose name was banker's magic on Wall Street. It was a period when every season there was at least one hit play on Broadway acted by a Negro cast. . . . It was the period (God help us!) when Ethel Barrymore appeared in blackface in Scarlet Sister Mary! It was the period when the Negro was in vogue."

It was a time of the Charleston and the Black Bottom, of *Shuffle Along* and Florence Mills, of bathtub gin and knee-high skirts, of black and tan on the South Side and Jim Crow clubs in Harlem. There was a night in the twenties when Al Capone went to a Negro Baptist church on Chicago's South Side to hear Clarence Darrow lecture on prohibition. There was a night in New York when Nora Holt, a blonde Negro entertainer, sang "My Daddy Rocks Me With One Steady Roll" at a bon voyage party for the Prince of Wales. When she finished, a prominent New York matron rushed up to her with tears in her eyes and said: "My dear! Oh, my dear! How beautifully you sing Negro spirituals."

It was *that* kind of era.

Carl Van Vechten took a long look at Harlem and named his novel, *Nigger Heaven*. There wasn't a chicken in every pot, but there was pork. Meat was cheap and homebrew was strong, Duke Ellington was at the Cotton Club and Satchmo was at the Sunset, God was in heaven and Father Divine was in Harlem. It was all a little precious and very daffy; and, in 1929, it seemed that it would go on forever.

The year started all right. Down in Atlanta, on January 15, a boy was born in a big frame house on Auburn Avenue and the proud parents named him Martin Luther King, Jr. Three months later, Oscar DePriest, the first Negro congressman in twenty-seven years, was sworn in as a representative from Chicago. In July, in 1929, *The Crisis* printed a message to American Negroes from Mahatma Gandhi. The Great Man said:

"Let not the 12 million Negroes be ashamed of the fact that they are the grandchildren of slaves. There is no dishonour in being slaves. There is dishonour in being slave-owners. But let us not think of honour or dishonour in connection with the past. Let us realize that the future is with those who would be truthful, pure and loving. For, as the old wise men have said, truth ever is, untruth never was. Love alone binds and truth and love accrue only to the truly humble."

In that year, in a time of merriment, it did not seem that the meek would inherit the earth. Bill Robinson was dancing up and down stair steps and people were singing "Ain't Misbehavin'." The new Negro congressman was saying he wasn't going to vote any more money to enforce the Eighteenth Amendment until something was done to enforce the Fourteenth and the Fifteenth. The South was threatening to secede again because Mrs. Hoover had had Mrs. Oscar DePriest in for tea—"a step," Senator Sheppard shouted, "[which was] fraught with infinite danger to our white civilization."

No—there was nothing unusual about 1929; it was an ordinary year. Babies were born and old men died. Funeral services for John Lisle, a Civil War veteran, were held at Charles Jackson's funeral home on the South Side. Robert Abbott and his wife returned from a four-month tour of Europe, and Chicago socialites held a glittering round of welcome home parties. In October, there was a new Louis Armstrong record, "When You're Smiling." The Gay Crowd let their hair down at a series of parties celebrating the October 26 football game between Tuskegee and Wilberforce. That same weekend the Harlem night club season went into high gear with the opening of the new revue at Smalls Paradise. Sunday came and Monday and Tuesday—and the bubble burst with the collapse of the stock market.

It took a while for the wound to bleed. On July 31, 1930, state auditors put a seal on Jesse Binga's big bank at 35th and State Street on Chicago's South Side. The word spread fast. Crowds gathered in the streets; grown men wrung their hands and some people cursed and cried. By August 16, three banks on Chicago's South Side had closed. The *Chicago Defender* urged its readers: "Don't Lose Faith." By August 23, however, the *Defender* had abandoned its chins-up attitude. The words were ominous, painful, and true.

GET FIXED

Times are not what they used to be. There is no use shutting our eyes to this fact. Prosperity has gone into retirement. . . . Our advice is for everyone to get something, and hold onto it. Get it in the city if possible, but, failing this, start toward the farm before the snow flies. . . ."

It was a long cold winter. For Negro America, the sun did not shine again until it came up in the wake of defense contracts spawned by the rising sun of Nippon.

During the Great Depression, Negro America, in the words of Lester Granger, "almost fell apart." There was a bitter bit of poetry: "The Negro, Last Hired and First Fired." Businesses tightened their belts and bade their Negro employees goodbye. Matrons cut their budgets and domestics went home and looked at empty larders. By 1935, about one out of every four Negroes in America was on relief. The need in urban areas was appalling. In Atlanta,

Georgia, 65 per cent of the Negroes were on public relief; in Norfolk, Virginia, the figure was 81 per cent.

In some areas, grown men stood on street corners and offered to sell their services for ten cents an hour. In some areas, slavery returned.

Faded newspapers and cold statistics tell a tale of appalling suffering and privation, of grown men crying and women wringing their hands in empty kitchens; of battered furniture standing on concrete curbs; of crowds protesting and Communists organizing the discontent; of white men coming with eviction notices and Republican mothers saying: "Run, boy; run and get the Reds"; of big government trucks cruising through Negro neighborhoods and dropping off navy beans and powdered milk; of a time of locusts and a mood of despair; of Mussolini invading Ethiopia; of Ethiopia stretching out her hand to the League of Nations and drawing back, the wits said, a nub; of Bessie Smith bleeding to death, probably because she was black and unlucky enough to have a car accident in Mississippi; of world-wide indignation over the rape convictions of the Scottsboro Boys on the testimony of two white women of uncertain reputation; of *Juden Verboten* in Berlin and "White People Only" in Birmingham; of people hoping and praying; of Eleanor Roosevelt saying what Thomas Jefferson said and acting like she meant it; of a night in June when Negro America danced in the street over the success of a prize fighter named Joe Louis; of a day in Berlin when Jesse Owens lectured to Hitler with his feet; of the poetry and pathos of *The Green Pastures* and the dignity of Richard B. Harrison's portrayal of "De Lawd"; of the AAA and the CCC and the Works Progress Administration; of the home of happy feet and Chick Webb; of Andy Kirk and his Clouds of Joy and the hi-de-ho of Cab Calloway; of Benny Goodman and a fad called Swing, and the Big Apple and Duke Ellington and Jimmy Lunceford and Count Basie; of Mary McLeod Bethune trudging up the White House drive, leaning dramatically on a dramatic cane; of Negroes becoming a part of official Washington;

of the Black Cabinet and "the race relations advisors"; of William Henry Hastie going off to the Virgin Islands as the first Negro federal judge; of the rising sun of India and Asia and the rising tide of color; of picket lines and boycotts in Chicago, New York, Cleveland, and Los Angeles; of "Double Duty Dollars" and "Don't Buy Where You Can't Work" campaigns; of a handsome young man named Adam Clayton Powell leading 6,000 Negroes to New York City Hall; of John Wesley Dobbs organizing and protesting in Atlanta and Rev. Maynard Jackson organizing and protesting in Texas; of the militance of John O. Holly in Cleveland and the protests of Rev. Clayton Russell in Los Angeles and Joe Jefferson in Chicago; of men, women and children marching in the streets; of Mary McLeod Bethune saying: "Be a Daniel. Take the vow of courage. Be militant!"

Faded newspapers and cold statistics tell another story, a story revolving around ballots and legal petitions. The Great Migration had forged a new set of political relationships in the North. At the beginning of the century, nine out of ten Negroes were living in rural areas in the South. By the middle thirties, however, millions of black immigrants were huddled in concrete ghettos in the great industrial centers of the North. Shrewd, tough-talking men like Edward Wright and William Dawson perceived that there was gold (politically speaking) in those ghettos. In 1928, Chicago Negro voters sent Oscar DePriest to Congress. Two years later, Walter White, the blond, blue-eyed executive secretary of the NAACP, organized a campaign which demonstrated beyond a shadow of a doubt that Negroes were an emerging political force.

It began in a prosaic manner. President Hoover nominated Judge John H. Parker for a spot on the Supreme Court. The NAACP made a routine check and turned up material which indicated that Parker had once opposed Negro suffrage. The NAACP asked Hoover to withdraw the nomination; Hoover refused. The NAACP rolled up big guns. Mass meetings were held; letters poured into Washington. Senators, who had been a trifle amused at the beginning of the campaign, began to feel the heat of political pressure. On April 21, 1930, the Senate refused to confirm the nomination.

It was an excellent campaign, boldly executed. It was also the beginning of a new day. The *Christian Science Monitor* called the Senate vote "the first national demonstration of the Negro's power since Reconstruction days."

Negro political power increased with a significant shift in political preferences. Since the days of Frederick Douglass, Negroes had clung stubbornly to the party of Emancipation—the Republican party. "The Republican party is the ship," Douglass said once, "all else is the sea." During the depression, Negro voters abandoned the ship and dived into the sea. It has been estimated that Franklin Delano Roosevelt received about one-fourth of the Negro vote in Northern cities in 1932. Eight years later, he received 52 per cent of the Negro vote in Chicago.

During the thirties, there was a stepped-up campaign in the courts. A young white man who turned down a million-dollar fortune was partially responsible for the increasing effectiveness of the NAACP's legal redress program. His name was Charles Garland. When Garland refused to accept an inheritance of a million or more dollars, the American Fund for Public Service was organized. "Once," James Weldon Johnson wrote, "when the Fund was being organized, "Mr. Garland lunched with us. He was an uncommonly handsome young man and extremely reticent. He turned his inheritance over merely with the request that it be given away *as quickly as possible, and to 'unpopular' causes, without regard to race, creed, or color.* In doing this, he made no gesture of any kind. He simply did not want the money, and refused to take it. He wished only to be left free to follow the life he had planned to live." Johnson added: "It was a strange experience to look upon a man in the flesh and in his right mind who could act like that about a million dollars."

Among the "unpopular" causes that benefited from Charles Garland's selflessness were the Urban League, the Brotherhood of

Sleeping Car Porters and the NAACP. The NAACP had been involved in court suits from its founding; it had succeeded in winning Supreme Court decisions banning the "grandfather clause," residential segregation, jury trials in an atmosphere of mob pressure and a Texas primary law. Its work, however, had been largely defensive. The money from the Garland Fund enabled the NAACP to plan a coordinated campaign and to hire a special counsel.

The NAACP hired Charles Hamilton Houston, a brilliant, tough-minded young graduate of Amherst and Harvard University. Houston had a vision. Negro lawyers, he felt, should be "social engineers." As vice dean of the Howard University Law School he had attempted to make Howard the "West Point of Negro Leadership." He had encouraged brilliant teachers like William Henry Hastie and promising students like Thurgood Marshall. Now, as special counsel of the NAACP, he planned a hedge-hopping campaign. Starting with the "soft underbelly" of Jim Crow—graduate schools—he planned to take case after case to the Supreme Court.

And so it began. The first case—filed on March 15, 1933, against the University of North Carolina—was lost on a technicality. In 1935, however, Thurgood Marshall persuaded the Maryland Court of Appeals to order the state university to admit Donald Murray. The next year—on December 8, in Montgomery County, Maryland—the NAACP began its long and generally successful campaign to equalize teachers' salaries.

Throughout the thirties, NAACP lawyers—Marshall, Houston, Hastie and others—leapfrogged across the country, arguing the subtleties of the Fourteenth Amendment. They won a great many cases, but they didn't get rid of Jim Crow. After losing a case, a state would simply set up an inferior law or journalism school at the Negro state college. One day in 1945, Houston's successor and protégé, Thurgood Marshall, decided that the time had come to "go for the whole hog."

The language—if not the decision—would have delighted that eminent hog-fancier—Booker Taliaferro Washington.

The "whole-hog" decision was not made in a vacuum. A great many things had changed in America; a great many things had changed in the world. After V–J Day, the Negro and the white man faced each other over a new set of relationships. The biggest and most obvious element in that change was World War II.

At the beginning, Negro Americans expressed deep skepticism about a second war to make the world safe for democracy. In a "letter to the editor" of the Raleigh *News and Observer*, a Negro observed: "The Negro races on earth are very suspicious of the white man's good intentions. This is very likely to be the last war that the white man will be able to lead humanity to wage for plausible platitudes." Another Negro, according to Gunnar Myrdal, said: "Just carve on my tombstone, 'Here lies a black man killed fighting a yellow man for the protection of a white man.'"

This mood of dissatisfaction, of bitterness even, erupted before Pearl Harbor. In an unprecedented show of unity, the NAACP, the National Urban League, Negro churches, sororities and newspapers asked America to put up or shut up. The demand was couched in insistent requests for fair play in defense industries, the armed forces and government apprenticeship programs.

Asa Philip Randolph fused the demands in a mammoth March on Washington organization. Unless Negro demands were met, Randolph said, 100,000 Negroes would stage a nonviolent march on Washington, D.C.

In some respects, Asa Philip Randolph is one of the most remarkable Negro leaders in American history. His March on Washington gambit was certainly one of the most brilliant power plays ever executed by a Negro leader, if not the most brilliant.

Born in Crescent City, Florida, in 1889, the son of an African Methodist Episcopal minister, Asa Philip Randolph is a tall, broad-shouldered man who has long championed nonviolent, direct action. "Nothing stirs and shapes public sentiment like physical action," he said. "Organized labor and organized capital have long since recognized this. This is why the major weapon of labor is the

STRIKE. . . . All people feel, think and talk about a physical formation of people, whoever they may be. This is why war grips the imagination of man. Mass demonstrations against Jim Crow are worth a million editorials and orations in anybody's paper and on any platform. . . . Mass social pressure in the form of marches and picketing will not only touch and arrest the attention of the powerful public officials but also the "little man" in the street. And, before this problem of Jim Crow can be successfully attacked, all of America must be shocked and awakened. . . ."

Randolph practiced what he preached. As we have seen, he went to jail in 1918 for shocking the sensibilities of federal agents with radical words about the first war for freedom. As a labor organizer, he fought the Pullman Company for twelve years and eventually won recognition for the Brotherhood of Pullman Car Porters. Now, as leader of the March on Washington Movement, he entered the arena against a wily political operator—Franklin Delano Roosevelt.

Roosevelt opposed the March on Washington. So did most white liberals. The march, they said, was impolitic and unwise. Mrs. Roosevelt and Fiorello LaGuardia called Randolph down to New York City Hall and tried to reason with him. Randolph was stubborn; the march, he said, was still on. President Roosevelt sent for Randolph and two of his powerful supporters, Walter White of the NAACP and T. Arnold Hill, acting executive of the National Urban League.

President Roosevelt sat behind his desk, flanked by the Secretary of the Navy and the Assistant Secretary of War. He was cordial, but cautious. He challenged the right of the group to put pressure on the White House. He was doing the best he could and he intended to do more; but there must be no pressure; the march must be called off.

Randolph was adamant. Unless something was done and quickly, he said, 100,000 Negroes would march on the White House.

The President: "We cannot have a march on Washington. We must approach this problem in an analytical way."

Randolph: "Then, Mr. President, something will have to be done and done at once."

The President: "Something will be done, but there must be no public pressure on the White House."

Randolph: "Mr. President, *something must be done now!*"

The argument grew heated. FDR switched suddenly.

"Phil," he asked in an obvious allusion to Randolph's beautiful diction, "What year did you finish Harvard?"

Randolph—who is not a graduate of any college—smiled; the tension relaxed.

President Roosevelt tried another tack. He turned to Walter White; he knew White, trusted him.

"Walter," he said, "how many people will *really* march?"

Walter White said, "No less than one hundred thousand." He recalled later that the President "looked me full in the eye for a long time in an obvious effort to find out if I were bluffing or exaggerating. Eventually, he appeared to believe that I meant what I said."

The President shrugged. "What do you want me to do?"

A. Philip Randolph said he wanted him to issue an Executive Order barring discrimination in war industries and the armed services. Seven days later, Randolph had his order: Executive Order 8802 which banned discrimination in war industries and apprenticeship programs. On the day the order was issued—June 25, 1941—Randolph called off the March on Washington. President Roosevelt later appointed a Fair Employment Practices Committee. Earl B. Dickerson, an attorney, and Milton P. Webster, a labor leader, served on the committee.

Throughout the war, Negro organizations peppered the government with complaints, demands and protests. There was a noticeable step-up in the protest movement. In 1943, for example, the Congress of Racial Equality was organized and staged its first sit-in demonstration in a restaurant in the Chicago Loop. An interracial organization with a program of direct, nonviolent action, CORE later staged successful sit-in programs in Baltimore and St. Louis.

The Negro press was a big factor in the protests of this period. The *Atlanta Daily World* (the first Negro daily published since Reconstruction), the Norfolk *Journal and Guide*, the *Courier*, and the *Defender* hammered away at racial injustices and indignities. These papers dispatched war correspondents to the European and Pacific Theaters and printed big headlines on discrimination and segregation. Robert L. Vann's *Courier* and Carl Murphy's *Afro-American* were particularly critical of discrimination in war plants and army camps. The *Courier* conducted a successful "Double V" campaign—for victory at home and victory abroad. The Negro press was so militant, in fact, that the government considered—and dropped—suggestions that Negro publishers be prosecuted for impeding the war effort.

In some respects, World War II was a carbon copy of World War I. There were many incidents between Negro soldiers and white soldiers and Negro soldiers and white civilians. In the summer of 1943, America exploded in the worst series of riots since the summer of 1919. Troops were called out to put down a riot which started when Negro workers were upgraded at a Mobile, Alabama, shipyard. Two persons were killed and martial law was declared in Beaumont, Texas, on June 16. Thirty-four persons died in the bloody Detroit, Michigan, race riot which started on June 20. Later that year, in August, there was a small riot in Harlem.

During the war, Negro soldiers fought in segregated units; but they fought for the first time in combat units in the Navy, Marine and Air Corps. A total of 1,154,720 Negroes were inducted or drafted into the armed services. After World War II and an increasingly strident campaign by Negro leaders, segregation was abolished in the armed forces. Randolph, incidentally, played a role in events which led to the issuance of an Executive Order which provided for "equal treatment and equal opportunity" in the armed forces. He had a heated conference with President Truman and threatened later to lead a mass civil disobedience campaign against the draft.

Another factor in the shift in Negro-white relationships was the

Martin Luther King, Jr., and his wife, Coretta, were received
by Indian Prime Minister Jawaharlal Nehru during 1959
visit. King and his wife visited India at invitation of the
Gandhi Peace Foundation.

Escorted by federal marshals, James H. Meredith registered at the University of Mississippi. Governor Ross R. Barnett precipitated gravest constitutional crisis since Civil War when he attempted to prevent Meredith's enrollment.

growth of mass media. Television made the South and the North, the Negro and the white man next-door neighbors. Negroes, with rare exceptions, were absent from TV screens and the pages of big magazines, but they received a favorable image in the columns of a bumper crop of new magazines (*Negro Digest, Our World, Headlines and Pictures*). The first and most successful publisher was a young Chicagoan, John H. Johnson, who started *Negro Digest* in 1942 and followed his initial success with *Ebony*, a monthly picture magazine, and *Jet*, a weekly news magazine. A cause and effect of the new climate of racial pride, these magazines dramatized the achievements of Negro Americans. Filled with colorful advertising displays and feature stories, *Ebony, Our World, Negro Digest* and other Negro periodicals played a part in the revolutionary reappraisal which Negro America made of itself between Pearl Harbor and Montgomery, Alabama.

Still another element in The Big Change was the power of money. Negroes had more money to spend, and they were demanding more for it. In the North and South, businessmen came forward to meet the demand. Banker L. D. Milton of Atlanta's Citizens Trust Company, C. C. Spaulding of North Carolina Mutual, Harry H. Pace and Truman K. Gibson, Sr., of Chicago's Supreme Life Insurance Company of America demonstrated that Negroes could hold their own in the corporate field. By taking the lead in capital accumulation, by hiring and training a cadre of clerks, accountants and executives and by providing community leadership, Negro businessmen made important contributions in this period. Some Negro businesses also fought for a desegregated society. In 1940, for example, Supreme Life, at the suggestion of General Counsel Earl B. Dickerson, became a party to the Hansberry-Lee case in which the theory of restrictive covenants was successfully challenged. Dickerson argued the case before the Court.

In this atmosphere of flux and change, a group of men sat down one day in 1945 in a room in Manhattan. The group, which included Thurgood Marshall, Walter White and William Hastie, decided that the time was ripe for an open attack on segregation. At a later meeting of NAACP lawyers, it was decided to frame petitions in a manner that would permit a direct attack on segregation if an opportunity presented itself.

Opportunity knocked in graduate school cases in Texas and Oklahoma. In the Texas case (*Sweatt v. Painter*), the state assumed that the NAACP was seeking a "separate but equal" law school. The legislature met, changed the name of the Negro state college to "Prairie View University" and adjourned without allocating funds for a law school building. When it became apparent that he was going to be able to launch an attack on segregation, Thurgood Marshall exploded in a sentence. Said he: "We got these boys."

After preliminary pleadings in the case, the state of Texas realized that the NAACP was attacking segregation. The legislature reconvened and appropriated $2,600,000 for a new Negro law school. But the damage had been done. Marshall presented expert testimony (from anthropologists and psychologists) that race was "an unreasonable classification" of students. On June 5, 1950, the Supreme Court handed down three decisions which undermined the legal structure of segregation. In the Sweatt case, the Court held that equality involved more than physical facilities. In the G. W. McLaurin case, the Court said that a Negro student, once admitted, cannot be segregated. In the Elmer W. Henderson case, the Court banned dining car segregation.

Building on this base, NAACP attorneys filed suits attacking segregation at the elementary and high school levels. When the cases reached the Supreme Court, Marshall—a big, loose-jointed man with a hooked nose and a constant frown—argued that segregation itself is discrimination. He asked the Court to ban state laws requiring "separate but equal" facilities for Negro and white schoolchildren. "Slavery," Marshall said, "is perpetuated in these statutes."

On Monday, May 17, 1954, the Supreme Court handed down its epochal decision. "We cannot turn the clock back to 1868," the Court said, "when the [Fourteenth] amendment was adopted, or even to 1896, when Plessy versus Ferguson was written. . . . We conclude that in the field of public education the doctrine of 'sep-

arate but equal' has no place." A year later, the Court ordered public school desegregation "with all deliberate speed."

The period between the Supreme Court decision and the dis-
patching of federal troops to Little Rock, Arkansas, was a Time of
the Tango—three steps forward and two steps backward. Baltimore, Louisville, and Washington initiated school integration; but
the Deep South breathed defiance.

Two months after the Supreme Court decision of 1954, a White
Citizens Council was formed in Indianola, Mississippi. The councils—one writer called them white-collar Ku Klux Klans—spread
across the South. Bankers, merchants and professionals joined and
swore resistance to school integration "by every lawful means."
The intellectual leader of the resistance was Tom Brady, a Yale-
educated circuit judge in Mississippi. What did Brady think of the
Supreme Court decision? The title of his book—*Black Monday*—
left little to the imagination. According to Brady, the decision was
a deep, dark plot which would lead to the "holoblastic tragedy"
of miscegenation. "Oh, High Priests of Washington," he cried out,
"blow again and stronger upon the dying embers of racial hate. . . .
The decision which you handed down on Black Monday has arrested and retarded the economic and political and, yes, the social
status of the Negro in the South for at least one hundred years. . . .
When a law transgresses the moral and ethical sanctions and standards of the mores, invariably strife, bloodshed and revolution follow in the wake of its attempted enforcement. The loveliest and
purest of God's creatures, the nearest thing to an angelic being
that tread this terrestrial ball is a well-bred, cultured Southern white
woman or her blue-eyed, golden-haired little girl."

Brady did not propose to obey the decision. "We say to the Supreme Court and to the northern world, 'You shall not make us
drink from this cup.' . . . We have, through our forefathers, died
before for our sacred principles. We can, if necessary, die again."

And so the war—it is not too strong a word—began. Skirmishes
were fought at Sturgis and Clay, Kentucky, where National Guard
units were called out to help little black children through the lines

of howling mobs. A mob prevented the enrollment of Negro students at Mansfield High School, Mansfield, Texas. The Tennessee National Guard was sent to Clinton to quell mobs demonstrating against integration. A dynamite blast destroyed Nashville's new Hattie Cotton Elementary School which had 388 white students and one Negro student.

Meanwhile, in the courts and legislatures, men were singing songs of "Massive Resistance," "Interposition" and "A Century of Litigation." Brief cases bulging with foolscap, Southern lawyers scurried from federal court to federal court in a skillfully-conducted rearguard action.

Enter Martin Luther King, Jr.

In Montgomery, Alabama, where the Negro had one of his finest hours, Martin Luther King, Jr., moved the struggle from the courtroom to the streets, from law libraries to the pews of the churches, from the mind to the soul. For twenty years, Negro leaders had been inching toward that fateful decision. In the thirties, in Harlem, Adam Clayton Powell made nonviolent noises. In Cleveland, Chicago and Los Angeles, depression crowds experimented with direct action. In the forties, Asa Philip Randolph said over and over again that the Negro protest wouldn't work unless it was a mass commitment. In the forties and fifties, CORE cleaned up downtown Baltimore and St. Louis with nonviolent sit-in campaigns and sent the first "Freedom Riders" into the South.

In 1955, Martin Luther King fused these elements and added the missing link: that which has sustained and bottomed the Negro community since slavery—the Negro church. By superimposing the image of the Negro preacher on the image of Gandhi, by adding songs and symbols with a palpable significance in the Negro community, Martin Luther King transformed a spontaneous racial protest into an awesome passive resistance movement with a method and an ideology. "Love your enemies," he commanded and servants straightened their backs and sustained a year-long bus boycott which, as King pointed out, "was one of the greatest [movements] in the history of the nation." The movement brought together laborers, college professors and doctors. More importantly perhaps, it fired the imagination of cooks in Chicago, porters in New York and long-suffering field hands in Mississippi.

A third-generation Baptist preacher, well read in philosophy, Martin Luther King, Jr., is of medium size and girth, brown-skinned, with a mustache and interesting eyes that slant upward slightly. Just twenty-seven years old when he burst upon the consciousness of Southerners, King has been likened—to his embarrassment—to Gandhi and Jesus Christ. Like Frederick Douglass, like Gandhi, like Jesus, he has an instinct for symbolic action—he knows how to dramatize truth.

The son of a militant Atlanta minister, M. L. the younger inherited a tradition of protest. His grandfather, A. D. Williams, helped lead a boycott against an Atlanta paper which spoke disparagingly of Negro voters. Rev. A. D. Williams was one of the leaders of a protest group which pressured into existence Atlanta's first Negro high school. The school was named for Booker Taliaferro Washington. Martin Luther King, Jr., attended Booker T. Washington High School and went on to Atlanta's Morehouse College.

In his introspective way, young King was wrestling with God. He wanted to be a preacher, but deep down inside he feared that the calling could not be intellectually respectable. Dr. Benjamin E. Mays, Morehouse's president, and Dr. George D. Kelsey, then chairman of the department of religion, changed King's mind. Their sermons, searching and profound with deep social significance, convinced him that there was a place in religion for light as well as heat.

In 1947, young King was ordained in his father's church in Atlanta. Later, at Crozer Seminary, near Philadelphia, he came upon a book that burned its way into his soul. The book, Walter Rauschenbush's *The Social Principles of Jesus*, opened a window on life for the young divinity student. So did a lecture by Mordecai Johnson, then president of Howard University, who related Gandhi's method of passive resistance to the struggles of submerged peoples everywhere.

Moving on to Boston University, where he received the Ph.D.

degree in systematic theology, Dr. King rounded another curve on the winding road to Montgomery. He met and married Coretta Scott, a Marion, Alabama, beauty who was studying voice at the New England Conservatory of Music. King took his books and his wife down to Montgomery, Alabama, and started preaching the social gospel to the members of the Dexter Avenue Baptist Church, which sits, like a nagging conscience, at the foot of the Alabama state capitol on Goat Hill.

Near this spot, at the old Exchange Hotel, William Yancey introduced Jefferson Davis, the new president of the Confederacy, with the words: "The man and the hour have met." Not too far from this spot, on December 5, 1955, Rosa Parks played midwife to a new man and a new hour. On an impulse, she decided suddenly that she wasn't going to obey an ancient custom which required Negroes to yield seats to white customers. Mrs. Parks, a seamstress, was arrested and the Negro community staged a one-day boycott in protest. The one-day boycott grew into a movement; the movement swept across the South.

Elected president of the Montgomery Improvement Association, the GHQ of the movement, King embarked on the formidable task of translating theory into practice. A car pool was organized; Negro professionals and maids were fused into an ongoing whole; regular pep meetings, with spirituals and hymns, were organized for the faithful. Skillfully utilizing the resources of television and mass journalism, King made Montgomery an international way station. For thirteen months, Negro Montgomery walked. Finally, on December 21, 1956, after a federal court order, the busses were integrated.

King moved later to Atlanta where he established a general headquarters for the Southern Christian Leadership Conference, a nonviolent direct action group whose influence is felt in every corner of the South. As chief spokesman, organizer and tactician of the passive resistance movement, King has traveled from two thousand to three thousand miles a week, explaining his nonviolent philosophy to Presidents, students and maids.

King advocates a four-pronged attack: direct nonviolent ac-

tion, legal redress, ballots and economic boycotts. He warns, however, that we "must not get involved in legalism, needless fights in
lower courts. That's exactly what the white man wants the Negro
to do. Then he can draw out the fight into what he has already
called a 'Century of Litigation.' The Court has spoken. The legal
basis of segregation has been destroyed. Our job now is implementation of the decision. We must move on to mass action."

A spiritual descendant of Frederick Douglass, who staged several
sit-ins on Massachusetts railroads, Martin Luther King, Jr., has
made a major contribution in the arena of mood. "The most important thing," he says, "is what has happened to the Negro. For
the first time, the Negro is on his own side. This has not always
been true. But today the Negro is with himself. He has gained a
new respect for himself. He believes in himself. World opinion is
on his side. The law is on his side and, as one columnist said, all
the stars in heaven are on his side. . . . The Negro is eternally
through with segregation; he will never accept it again—in Mississippi, Georgia or anywhere else."

King and the movement he led are partially responsible for this
interior change. One must be careful, however, not to overstate his
contribution. He built on the contributions of many men: W. E. B.
Du Bois, James Weldon Johnson, Walter White, Charles Houston,
Eugene Kinckle Jones, Lester Granger, Thurgood Marshall,
A. Philip Randolph, Roy Wilkins, Mary McLeod Bethune and
others—many others. Nor must we forget the contributions of the
artful infiltrators, the "Negro firsts" like William H. Hastie, Ralph
Bunche, B. O. Davis, Jr., Joe Louis, Jackie Robinson, Marian Anderson and Charles Richard Drew; the "Brown Guinea Pigs" like
Heman Marion Sweatt, Ossian Sweet and James Meredith; the path-
finders and schoolmasters like Mordecai Johnson, Benjamin E.
Mays, Carter G. Woodson, Charles S. Johnson and E. Franklin Frazier; and "the white hopes" like W. W. Alexander, Eleanor Roosevelt, Lillian Smith and Ralph McGill. Above all, King had the help
of impersonal socio-economic forces: the continuing migration and
the increasing political power of Negroes in the strategic industrial
states of the North and West and the burgeoning Negro vote in

the South; the power of money—the rise of the Negro middle class; the re-emergence of pride and a sense of roots and relatedness to the rising African states; and America's paradoxical position as a leader of "the free world" and a competitor in the Afro-Asian market place of ideas. These stones ground the movement. But, when all is said and done, they are still mere stones; the touch of an artist was required to give them life.

Creative leadership creates a climate in which other men come forward to lead. In the wake of Booker T. Washington came lesser men who lacked his skills but saw very well indeed that collaboration paid off (within certain narrow limits). For a generation or more, the bended knee and the bowed head were accepted techniques of leadership in some circles. In the wake of King came men and women who saw very well indeed that the masses would respond if only someone would lead.

King's influence was perceptive in Little Rock, where Daisy Bates outmaneuvered state and city officials and kept nine Negro children in a school which had become a battlefield. His influence was perceptive in Greensboro, North Carolina, where four North Carolina A. and T. students kicked off the Sit-in Age. His influence was palpable in the Jail-in Movement and the "Freedom Ride" Movement and the city-by-city operation of 1962 (Albany, Georgia; Englewood, New Jersey; Cairo, Illinois; Oxford, Mississippi).

The net result of this confluence of moods and militant men, women and children is a Second Reconstruction, a Reconstruction which ranges over the North and South. Reconstruction—Chapter II—assumed form and focus on September 25, 1957, when soldiers of the 101st Airborne Division escorted nine children into Little Rock's Central High School. It was the first time in eighty-one years that a President had dispatched American troops to the South to defend the constitutional rights of Negroes. There is a mother in Little Rock who will remember that hour until the day she dies. Mrs. Imogene Brown said: "It was the most beautiful thing I ever saw in my life and I'll never forget it." Another woman who will never forget the sight of soldiers with drawn bayonets escorting Negro children into an American school is Daisy Bates,

who was then president of the Arkansas NAACP. The day the soldiers came to her house for the children was sweet to her. It was
even sweeter to the children.

"The streets were blocked off," Daisy Bates recalls. "The soldiers closed ranks. Neighbors came out and looked. The street was
full, up and down. Oh! It was beautiful. And the attitude of the
children at that moment: the respect they had. I could hear them
saying, 'For the first time in my life I truly feel like an American.'
I could see it in their faces: Somebody cares for me—*America
cares.*"

As it turned out, the morning of the federal troops was also the
beginning of a protracted Cold War. Gov. Orval Faubus had attempted to prevent integration by cordoning the school with Arkansas National Guard troops who turned back Negro students.
When President Eisenhower federalized the National Guard and
sent federal troops to Little Rock, Faubus fell back to a second line
and continued a campaign of harassment and sniping. That he was
checkmated is due in no small part to the contributions of a svelte,
charming woman with a subtle sense of timing and a genius for
giving resolution to the minds and hearts of men and children.

Catapulted overnight into a complex struggle between federal
and state forces, Daisy Bates deployed her meager forces with consummate skill and artistry. When segregationists began a cruel campaign to drive the nine Negro children out of the school, she coun-
selled courage. The Negro students were shoved, kicked, elbowed
and pushed down steps. Can openers, slivers of glass, and sharpened
pencils were thrown at them. It was a deadly serious school war.
One boy threw a hangman's knotted venetian cord at one of the
girls—it missed. Another student was slugged from behind and
knocked out.

The tension was almost unbearable. Nerves, already taut,
snapped. A withdrawal was suggested. Daisy Bates pleaded and
persuaded; she explained the great moral and social issues involved.
The children and their parents decided to stick. It was an important decision. By remaining in the school, they dramatized the de-

termination of Negroes. The NAACP recognized the importance of the Little Rock turning point by awarding the Spingarn Medal to the nine Little Rock students and Daisy Bates. "We've got to decide," Daisy Bates said, "if it's going to be this generation or never."

There were students in North Carolina who were of like mind. On February 1, 1960, when four North Carolina A. and T. freshmen sat down at a lunch counter in a Woolworth store in Greensboro, they started an unprecedented student protest movement which shook the South to its foundations and set off social tremors that may affect race relations for years to come. Within three months, thousands of Negro—and some white—students were taking seats at "white" lunch counters and requesting service. If arrested, they submitted quietly. If attacked, they refused to fight.

The movement, patterned on the passive resistance techniques of Mahatma Gandhi, raced across the South. Chain stores, department stores, libraries, supermarkets, and movies were hit by demonstrations, picket lines and boycotts. By February 10, the movement had spread to fifteen Southern cities in five states. By September, 1961, more than one hundred cities in twenty states had been affected. At least 70,000 Negro and white students had participated. The Southern Regional Council estimated that 3,600 students had been arrested by September, 1961, and that at least 141 'students and 58 faculty members had been expelled by college authorities. The council said that one or more establishments in 108 Southern and border states had been desegregated as a result of sit-ins.

Far more important than the number of integrated cups of coffee served was the revelation of the mind and mood of the young. Most observers noted that the protests indicated a profound dissatisfaction with the pace of desegregation. The Southern Regional Council said the demonstrations made clear that "the South is in a time of change, the terms of which cannot be dictated by white Southerners." Carl Bair, president of the Montgomery, Alabama, Chamber of Commerce, was moved to utter strong words. Said he: "There's a revolution of the Negro youth in this nation."

Police in Albany, Georgia, removed Negro teen-agers from steps of Carnegie Library on July 31, 1962. Fifteen teen-agers were arrested after they knelt and prayed on the steps of the "white" library.

Roy Wilkins, executive secretary of the NAACP, Martin Luther King, Jr., and A. Philip Randolph, veteran labor and protest leader, clasped hands before the Lincoln Monument in Washington, D.C., and vowed to continue civil rights struggle.

Speaking from conscience to conscience, sit-in students raised embarrassing questions for almost everyone. Negro moderates were forced to re-evaluate their position. And the NAACP—which had been considered *very* radical—was forced to step up its pace. Roy Wilkins, NAACP executive secretary, said: "We have always used persuasion through various means of political and economic pressure, but now we're going to use it much more intensively than in the past because the membership has become restless over the slow pace of the Civil Rights proceedings."

A dramatic scene highlighted the personal nature of the sit-in challenge. A mother, weeping and moaning, confronted her daughter in the Tallahassee, Florida, jail. The mother offered to pay the girl's fine. The girl, who had been arrested in a sit-in demonstration, decided to remain in jail. She said: "Mamma, I love you. But I'm not free. And I'm not free because your generation didn't act. But I want my children to be free. That's why I'll stay in jail."

With the organization of the Student Nonviolent Coordinating Committee on April 15, 1960, the sit-in movement increased in effectiveness. SNCC (pronounced SNICK) was heavily involved in the Jail-in movement which started in Rock Hill, South Carolina, on February 6, 1961, when students refused to pay fines and requested jail sentences. The "JAIL, NO BAIL" movement spread to Atlanta and other Southern cities.

SNCC also played an important role in the "Freedom Ride" campaign which was initiated by thirteen CORE members who set out from Washington, D.C., on May 4, 1961, for an integrated bus ride through the South. Testing compliance with integration orders of the Interstate Commerce Commission and federal courts, the "Freedom Riders" crisscrossed the South. At several stops, they were beaten and manhandled. After a group of riders were attacked in Montgomery, Alabama, on May 20, 1961, Attorney General Robert Kennedy dispatched some six hundred United States marshals to the spot. Governor Patterson later declared martial law and called out the National Guard. The whole campaign converged on Jackson, Mississippi, where scores of riders were arrested.

On December 12, 1961, the "Freedom Ride" movement merged into a massive city-by-city assault which may prove to the pattern of the future. The arrest of twelve "Freedom Riders" in Georgia precipitated the militant Albany Movement—the general name for a coordinated, city-wide campaign by Martin Luther King, Jr., SNCC and some elements of CORE and the NAACP.

By July 22—the 100th anniversary of the day on which Lincoln submitted a draft of the Emancipation Proclamation to his Cabinet— the North as well as the South was embroiled in a deepening crisis. New Rochelle, New York, public schools had been desegregated by order of a federal judge. Suits challenging *de facto* segregation had been filed in more than a dozen Northern communities, including Chicago, Philadelphia, Newark, New Jersey and Kansas City, Kansas. And sit-ins had been staged in Chicago (schools and beaches), Cairo, Illinois (restaurants and recreational facilities), and Englewood, New Jersey (schools).

A complicating factor in the Northern protest movement was the presence of post-Garvey black nationalist groups like Elijah Muhammad's "Black Muslims." Muhammad, a slightly-built, Georgia-born organizer and religious exhorter, has fashioned a nationalist movement remarkably similar to Marcus Garvey's movement of the twenties. Like Garvey, Muhammad glorifies blackness and deprecates whiteness. Like Garvey, he has organized a string of cooperative business ventures. Muhammad, like Garvey, says there is no hope of justice for a black man in America. And, like Garvey, he has shrewdly exploited the pessimism, cynicism and despair of the masses in large urban centers. Muhammad champions separateness and a black state—in America. His followers are adherents of the religion of Islam. To indicate their distaste for the traditions of slavery, "Black Muslims" abandon their "slave-given" names (John Jones, Sam Washington) and adopt the letter X (John X, Sam X). The group has attracted national attention and the fiery devotion of an undetermined number of Negroes, principally in the large cities of the North and West. Other black nationalists groups received international attention in 1961 when they disrupted a

United Nations debate with a demonstration in favor of Patrice Lumumba, the slain premier of the Congo. Muhammad and other nationalist groups have been accused of preaching black supremacy.

The mood, the location and the birth rate of American Negroes give an ominous urgency to the contemporary dialogue over America's ancient problem. American Negroes, for the most part, are urban dwellers. Most Negroes outside the Deep South live in our twelve largest metropolitan areas—New York City, Los Angeles, Chicago, Philadelphia, Detroit, San Francisco-Oakland, Boston, Pittsburgh, St. Louis, Washington, Cleveland, Baltimore. Their power in these cities is growing; so are their problems; so are the problems of white people. Take Chicago, for example. There are almost 900,000 Negroes in the city. Soon there will be a million. By 1975, Donald J. Bogue said, there will be more Negroes in Chicago than whites (if present trends continue).

The problem is not peculiar to Chicago; nor is it a peculiarly Northern or urban problem. There are large Negro populations in Albany, Georgia (46%), Atlanta (38.3%), Washington (53.9%), New Orleans (37.2%), Memphis (37%) and other cities in the North and South. In a recent survey, *Fortune Magazine* pointed out that the salvation of the American city depends, to a great extent, on the rapid integration of the Negro into the total life of our civilization. "The city can be saved," Charles E. Silberman said in the *Fortune* article, "only if [America] faces up to the fact that the 'urban problem' is, in a large measure, a Negro problem. But the problem is more than just an urban problem; it is also the problem of all the United States, rural or urban, North or South. . . . Speeding the Negro's integration into American life . . . is the largest and most urgent piece of public business facing the United States today."

The urgency of this public business was underscored by the unsuccessful attempt to prevent the enrollment of James H. Meredith, a brave and mild-mannered Air Force veteran, at the University of Mississippi. Dredging up John C. Calhoun's discredited doctrine of interposition, mouthing the dead slogans of another Mississippian, Jefferson Davis, Governor Ross R. Barnett attempted to place state power between the university and the orders of a federal court. The attempt failed, but it precipitated the gravest federal-state crisis since the Civil War. Two white persons were killed in rioting on the university campus. More than twelve thousand federal troops, marshals and National Guardsmen were rushed to the campus to preserve order and to insure the implementation of court decisions.

The "Mississippi insurrection," ironically enough, marred centennial celebrations of the Emancipation Proclamation. The moral was obvious and observers were quick to point it out. Paul Guihard, the French reporter who was killed during rioting on the university campus, wrote in his last dispatch: "The Civil War has never ended." Martin Luther King, Jr., said President Kennedy faced the same situation in the Mississippi crisis which President Lincoln faced in the Civil War—"that of saving the nation." At bottom, King said, the issues were the same. Segregation, he added, "is nothing but a new form of slavery covered up with certain niceties of complexity."

Newspapers at home and abroad found ominous parallels between America's current crisis and the crisis of 1860. The *Süddeutsche Zeitung* of Munich, Germany, said President Kennedy, who ordered federal troops to Mississippi, and former President Eisenhower, who ordered federal troops to Arkansas, were convinced "that the dragon seed of slavery, abolished 100 years ago, would continue to flourish if it were not torn from the Southern soil with a hard hand." *L'Aurore*, the Paris newspaper, wondered if men had learned anything from history. From the Civil War? From Hitler? "Hitler, then, the paper concluded, "has not cured the world of racism? There are, then, in a country in a so-called model civilization, still people who distinguish between their kind according to the color of their skin."

On the eve of the 100th anniversary of the issuance of the Emancipation Proclamation, America was again at the turning of the fork. Again, as in 1863, Americans were grappling with the "dragon seed" of slavery. Again, as in the days of Lincoln, the Negro was at the center of a crucial national debate.

The terms of the debate were being dictated by a brooding militance on the part of the vast majority of Negroes; by anger, pessimism and despair on the part of a growing minority; by a realization on the part of an increasing number of whites that the salvation not only of the American city but also of American civilization depends, to a great extent, on a genuine confrontation with Thomas Jefferson's massive ALL.

By September 22—the 100th anniversary of the issuance of the preliminary Emancipation Proclamation—black men and white men were wrestling in the dusk of dawn and no man knew rightly the hour or the day of the coming of the sun.

12

The Bitter Harvest

". . . we shall pay any price, bear any burden, meet any hardship, support any friend, oppose any foe to assure the survival and success of liberty."

JOHN FITZGERALD KENNEDY

I T WAS A year of funerals and a year of births, a year of endings and a year of beginnings, a year of hate and a year of love.

It was a year of water hoses and high-powered rifles, of struggles in the streets and screams in the night, of homemade bombs and gasoline torches, of snarling dogs and widows in black. It was a year of passion, a year of despair and a year of desperate hope.

It was 1963, the one hundredth year of Negro emancipation and year one of the Negro Revolution.

In this year, which marked a fundamental forking point in the relations between black and white Americans, Negroes hurled themselves with a nonviolent spasm against the unyielding walls of the caste cage.

They surged through the streets in black waves of indignation.

They faced snarling police dogs and armored police tanks.

They were clubbed, bombed, slashed, murdered.

In scores of cities, North and South, there were riots and near-riots and small wars were fought in Cambridge (Maryland), Danville (Virginia), Savannah, and Birmingham. There were, all told, more than ten thousand racial demonstrations (sit-ins, lie-ins, sleep-ins, pray-ins, stall-ins) in this year, and more than five thousand American Negroes were arrested for political activities. The whole angry pageant of resistance and rebellion reached a pitch in the Red Summer of 1964, one of the most turbulent summers in American race relations.

By a strange irony of fate, this bubbling cauldron of discontent came to a boil during the centennial celebration of the Emancipation Proclamation. There were no indications in the first months of 1963 that America was moving towards its most serious domestic crisis since the Civil War. But there were disquieting omens. Negro ghettos were spreading like hot lava across the concrete crags of every metropolitan area; Negro unemployment was at a 1930 depression level; and Negro schools, the Supreme Court to the contrary notwithstanding, were separate and transparently unequal. In the North, there was gentle evasion of the spirit and letter of the Constitution; and in the South, there was open defiance. As the year of decision opened, federal troops were maintaining an uneasy vigil at the University of Mississippi. And police officers and black rebels of the Student Nonviolent Coordinating Committee (SNCC) were fighting grim guerrilla actions in the wilds of the Black Belt counties of southwest Georgia and central Mississippi.

There were, to be sure, signs of progress: glittering middle class oases in Chicago, New Orleans, and Los Angeles; Negro bureaucrats near the top levels of the Kennedy Administration and mushrooms of black Babbitts with new cars, new appliances and new hopes. But all this was vitiated by the creeping misery of the Negro masses and the mounting boldness of civil rights organizations. President Kennedy himself put his finger on the raw materials of revolt in a message to Congress on the eve of the centennial.

"The Negro baby born in America today," he said, "regardless of the section or state in which he is born has about one-half as much chance of completing high school as a white baby born in the same place on the same day—one-third as much chance of completing college—one-third as much chance of becoming a professional man—twice as much chance of becoming unemployed—about one-seventh as much chance of earning $10,000 a year—a life expectancy which is seven years less—and the prospects of earning only half as much."

The implications of all this were clear enough, and bad enough. What was worse was the dawning realization that this was the bitter fruit of one hundred years of patience. More and more people, as the weeks wore on, cast cold and disapproving eyes on sentimental celebrations of an emancipation that had not yet been achieved. More and more people, as Lincolnmania spread, cast about for a dramatic expression of the death of Negro hope and the death of Negro patience.

Wyatt Tee Walker, the tall, bold assistant to Martin Luther King, Jr., spoke for thousands of Negro activists. "We've got to have a crisis to bargain with," he said, adding: "To take a moderate approach hoping to get white help, doesn't work. . . . You've got to have a crisis."

And a crisis was what America got.

Centennial orators were declaiming, proclamations were being read and prayers were being spoken when the first shots of the campaign of 1963 were fired. On February 28, Mississippi racists made an abortive attempt to assassinate a young field worker of SNCC. Enraged SNCC workers converged on Greenwood, Mississippi, and organized a massive voter registration campaign. When the ides of March came, black men and white men were struggling in the drowsy streets of the Mississippi Delta town. Hundreds of native

Mississippians marched on the registrar's office and were ruthlessly repulsed by heavily armed officers and K-9 police dogs. The campaign attracted national attention when Dick Gregory, the militant comedian, went to Mississippi to lead the mass marches. Finally, after a great deal of hand-wringing, the Justice Department asked the federal courts to enjoin further harassment of the voter registration campaign.

The sounds of Greenwood—the whining of police dogs, the screams of demonstrators and the curses and counter-curses of policemen and adult onlookers—were still echoing in the minds of men when a second and larger front opened in Birmingham, Alabama. On Wednesday, April 3, Martin Luther King, Jr., stepped from an airliner and announced that he would lead racial demonstrations in the streets of Birmingham until "Pharaoh lets God's people go."

This was not, as some people believed, a precipitous move. The Pharaohs of Birmingham had long been on Martin Luther King's mind. King, as we have seen, had become a symbol of the renaissance of the Negro soul. He had led demonstrations in several cities in the early sixties, but he had not succeeded in making a dramatic breakthrough. As the Emancipation Proclamation centennial approached, King and his aides in the Southern Christian Leadership Conference (SCLC) cast about for an American Bastille, i.e., a key point that could yield more than a local or symbolic victory. With incredible boldness, King selected Birmingham, which was widely regarded as an impregnable fortress of bigotry. He felt, he said later, that "if Birmingham could be cracked, the direction of the entire nonviolent movement in the South could take a significant turn. It was our faith that 'as Birmingham goes, so goes the South.' "

King and the young activists around him drew up a battle plan for the proposed series of demonstrations. In a moment of prophetic genius, they designated the campaign, "Project C." And what precisely did the "C" mean? It was a shorthand symbol for a new concept: confrontation. There was no way then for King and his men to know that the project prophetically called "C" would lead Negro and white Americans to the brink of an eyeball-to-eyeball confrontation.

Project "C" was scheduled for the fall of 1962, but negotiations with the "white power structure" led to several postponements. By January, however, King was convinced that a showdown situation was necessary for racial progress in Birmingham and America. He therefore dispatched aides to Birmingham to secretly recruit workers and lay the groundwork for the most important racial demonstration since Nat Turner's blitzkrieg in Southampton County, Virginia.

The project began as scheduled on April 3, the day after Birmingham's municipal election. And it unfolded according to a brilliantly conceived plan tied to the major events of the betrayal, crucifixion and triumph of Jesus Christ. First, there were probes and scouting expeditions (sit-ins and picketing at downtown stores). For several days, little bands of demonstrators fanned out over the city, testing the strength of the police as patrols in the night test the main force of the enemy. Then, on Saturday, April 6, the campaign entered its second phase with a token street demonstration led by the Rev. Fred Shuttlesworth, the president of the Alabama Christian Conference, an SCLC affiliate. On the next day, Palm Sunday, there was the first reconnaissance in force and the first direct conflict between the main antagonists, *demonstrators* representing the Negro community and *policemen* representing the white community. The first contest was won hands down by the police. Aided by snarling police dogs, the policemen routed more than six hundred demonstrators.

With the shadow-boxing over, both sides dug in for a long and bitter campaign. Martin King directed his nonviolent army from a suite in the A. G. Gaston Motel in the heart of the Negro community. His aides moved out over the city, organizing nonviolent workshops and nightly mass meetings. Opposing King and his demonstrators was a force of policemen and firemen led by Eugene (Bull) Connor, a tough, chunky segregationist who had become a national symbol of Southern intransigence.

Demonstrators protesting segregation in Birmingham, Alabama, are dispersed by policemen. Demonstrations marked turning point in American race relations.

Some 250,000 Americans participated in the mammoth march on Washington demonstration on August 28, 1963. March was led by Asa Philip Randolph.

President Lyndon Baines Johnson distributes pens used in signing Civil Rights Bill of 1964. Among those receiving pens was Roy Wilkins of NAACP.

The main battleground of this improbable but nonetheless grim war was the Kelly Ingram Park, a square block of tall elms, concrete walkways and dirty green grass in the middle of the Negro business district. On one side of this park was the yellow brick structure of the Sixteenth Street Baptist Church. Every day, shortly after noon, demonstrators poured from this church and tried to penetrate the defenses of policemen and firemen deployed in depth around barricades two blocks away. The strategic objectives of the demonstrators were downtown stores and city hall. Fighting with their backs to the downtown section, policemen and firemen used high-pressure hoses and K-9 police dogs to drive demonstrators back through the park to the Negro church. Legal reinforcements were provided by a local judge who issued a sweeping injunction barring Negro protest marches.

On Good Friday, April 12, Martin Luther King, Jr., openly defied this order by leading a mass march of fifty or more disciples and some one thousand onlookers. Far from being intimidated by the symbolism of the day, "Bull" Connor moved swiftly, dispersing the marchers and arresting King and about fifty demonstrators.

So far, so good: all this—King's arrest and the increasing truculence of "Bull" Connor—was in the script; so apparently was the uproar that followed. From his Easter vacation headquarters in Palm Beach, President Kennedy phoned the Justice Department for "information." Kennedy later placed a personal call to Mrs. Coretta King to assure her of the safety of her imprisoned husband. The President's brother, Attorney General Robert F. Kennedy, bestirred himself, placing his crisis-weary civil rights staff on standby alert. Racial crises were, by now, routine to the Justice Department which issued statement No. 1: Burke Marshall, the assistant attorney general in charge of civil rights, announced that there was nothing the department could do at that juncture; but, he added pointedly, the Department was watching the situation closely.

There now occurred an incident that was not in the script. Eight leading white churchmen of Birmingham—Roman Catholic, Protestant, Jewish—denounced King as an interloper and urged "our own Negro community to withdraw support" from these "unwise and untimely" demonstrations.

This development, totally unexpected, proved to be a boon to the campaign. King, with the instinct for drama and the inventiveness of a great general, counterattacked with devastating thoroughness. From his cell, he answered his detractors in a memorable "Letter from a Birmingham Jail" that became a civil rights classic. Here are some excerpts:

You spoke of our activity in Birmingham as extreme. At first I was rather disappointed that fellow clergymen would see my nonviolent efforts as those of the extremist. I started thinking about the fact that I stand in the middle of two opposing forces in the Negro community. One is a force of complacency made up of Negroes who, as a result of long years of oppression, have been so completely drained of self-respect and a sense of "somebodiness" that they have adjusted to segregation, and, on the other hand, of a few Negroes in the middle class who, because of a degree of academic and economic security, and because at points they profit by segregation, have unconsciously become insensitive to the problems of the masses. The other force is one of bitterness and hatred and comes perilously close to advocating violence. It is expressed in the various black nationalist groups that are springing up over the nation, the largest and best known being Elijah Muhammad's Muslim Movement. This movement is nourished by the contemporary frustration over the continued existence of racial discrimination. It is made up of people who have lost faith in America, who have absolutely repudiated Christianity, and who have concluded that the white man is an incurable "devil." I have tried to stand between these two forces saying that we need not follow the "do-nothingism" of the complacent or the hatred and despair of the black nationalist. There is a more excellent way of love and nonviolent protest. I'm grateful to God that, through the Negro church, the dimension of nonviolence entered our struggle. If this philosophy had not emerged I am convinced that by now many streets of the South would be flowing with floods of blood. And I am further convinced that if our white brothers dismiss as "rabble rousers" and "outside agitators" those of us who are working the channels of nonviolent direct action and refuse to support our nonviolent efforts, millions of Negroes, out of frustration and despair, will seek solace and security in black nationalist ideologies, a development that will lead inevitably to a frightening racial nightmare.

What King was saying, in plain English, was that he was in Birmingham to stay and that Birmingham leaders had to fish or cut bait. Even as he wrote, events on the Birmingham streets added thunderous exclamation points to his stark eloquence. Day after night after day, Birmingham rang with the cries of demonstrators, the eerie whines of wolfish K-9 dogs, and the epithets of white policemen. Infinitely more menacing was the sullenness of Negro onlookers—unemployed adults and restless youth—who stood on the sidelines, waiting, watching, hating. On April 20, the day King posted bond and resumed direct command of the demonstrations, it was as clear as the statue of Vulcan on Birmingham's Red Mountain that the contest would go on until someone was knocked down or knocked out.

"Bull" Connor was a wily fighter who concentrated on wearing his opponents down. And he came dangerously close to succeeding. By May 1, the enthusiasm of the demonstrators was flagging and Connor was as close as he ever would be to a victory on points. Close to a thousand Negroes were in jail or out on bond and men were saying that "Bull" was unbeatable. Studying the situation, feeling the pulse of the wavering Negro community, King and his lieutenants decided that a truly audacious act was necessary. But what kind of act?

In the plush rooms of the Gaston Motel, King and his men weighed the dangerous alternatives. The hours stretched to midnight and beyond as the men talked, and tempers grew short. Under the circumstances, this was normal. For what King and his men were considering was nothing short of hair-raising. They were deciding, in a room filled with smoke, how far they were willing to go for freedom and how much they were willing to pay. It is easy, in retrospect, to say that the decision they finally made was brilliant. But the sun was hooded by clouds then and few men were willing to take the responsibility for the death of a child. Many men would say later that they made the big decision. But back there it was all in one man's hand. And history records that sometime before May 1, 1963, Martin Luther King, Jr., gave his assent to one of the most momentous decisions in the history of the Negro protest. He decided in love and, yes, in fear to commit thousands of children to the front lines of an explosive conflict involving nightsticks, snarling dogs and high-powered water hoses that could strip bark off an oak tree.

Events moved rapidly now. Mimeograph machines clanked and within hours leaflets were on the streets:

FIGHT FOR FREEDOM FIRST THEN GO TO SCHOOL. . . . Join thousands in jail who are making their witness for freedom. Come to the 16th Street Baptist Church now . . . and we'll soon be free. It's up to you to free our teachers, our parents, yourself and our country.

The Negro youth of Birmingham were awaiting the call; many of them, in fact, had demanded assignment to the front lines. Now they flocked to the yellow brick church on the edge of the battlefield, leaving public schools virtually empty. The day when the tide changed, the first day of massive use of Negro schoolchildren, was Thursday, May 2. It was a hot muggy day, with tempers and temperatures near the fever level. A little before noon, Negroes began to gather on the sidewalks along Sixteenth Street and Sixth Avenue. "Bull" Connor stood wide-legged, a straw hat pulled down over one eye, watching the gathering crowd and listening to the freedom songs coming from the Sixteenth Street Baptist Church where the students were gathering. Connor barked; firemen brought up three red pumpers; and blue-coated policemen shifted into position. All the while, firemen in dun-colored uniforms and knee-length slickers tinkered with the gadgets on the hoses, like violinists tuning up before a concert.

And then suddenly it happened: hundreds of singing, shouting, dancing youth burst through the door of the church and marched on the barricades. Some of them wriggled through and reached city hall and downtown street corners. The next day the same drama was repeated, and "Bull" Connor abandoned the amenities. Hundreds of teen-agers were bowled over by high-powered hoses and washed under cars like garbage. Policemen then waded in with clubs and dogs. Hundreds of youth were arrested and herded into detention cells at the jail and the state fairground.

The use of hoses and billy clubs and dogs on boys and girls, some of them no older than six, turned Black Birmingham into a volcano of swirling emotions. With a rush, the sentiment changed.

Pictures of snarling dogs sinking fangs into the flesh of black children produced a similar ferment in the world beyond Birmingham. Equally revolting, though oddly symbolic, was the picture of a white policemen standing triumphantly with his knee on the neck of a Negro woman.

Senator Wayne Morse (R., Oregon) told the Senate that the Birmingham spectacle "would disgrace a Union of South Africa or a Portuguese Angola." The *New York Times* commented editorially that the Birmingham "barbarities" were "revoltingly reminiscent of totalitarian excesses."

With pressure mounting for federal intervention, the Kennedy brothers acted, sending Burke Marshall to Birmingham to negotiate a settlement. Marshall initiated what he called a "dialogue" but the white power structure boggled on Negro demands for desegregation of facilities in downtown stores and upgrading Negro workers. What changed the power structure's mind was the increasing intensity of the demonstrations. On Monday, May 6, wave after wave of youthful demonstrators poured out of the Negro church and "Bull" Connor shouted to a police captain, "I told you these sons of bitches ought to be watered down." At a mass meeting that night, a King aide shouted dramatically: "War has been declared in Birmingham. War has been declared on segregation."

So it had; the next day the demonstrations reached an unprecedented intensity, and Birmingham tottered on the edge of social disorder. More than two thousand Negro youth participated in the demonstrations and thousands penetrated the police lines and

surged through the downtown area, singing freedom songs and
wandering through the stores of white merchants. When policemen
tried to disperse crowds in the Negro districts, sullen onlookers
pelted them with rocks and bottles in a riot that lasted more than
an hour.

That same day, Tuesday, May 7, Sheriff Melvin Bailey told an
emergency meeting of the Senior Citizens Committee, a group of
about seventy of the city's top industrial, commercial and professional leaders, that unless the demonstrations were ended it would
be necessary to impose martial law. The committee immediately
empowered a subcommittee to come to terms with the Negro leaders. After a night-long meeting in the home of a Negro insurance
executive, a tentative agreement was reached. At a press conference on Wednesday, May 10, Fred Shuttlesworth said, "The City
of Birmingham has reached an accord with its conscience." He announced agreement on a four-point program which called for the
desegregation of lunch counters, restrooms, fitting rooms and
drinking fountains "in planned stages within the next ninety days,"
the upgrading and hiring of Negro workers on a nondiscriminatory
basis in Birmingham businesses, the release of demonstrators (some
2,400 were arrested) on nominal bond and the establishment of a
biracial committee.

"Bull" Connor and other die-hard segregationists denounced the
agreement and called for a white boycott of merchants who accepted the agreement. On Saturday, May 11, the Ku Klux Klan
held a rally and cross burning in the suburbs to dramatize their opposition to "Martin Luther King, atheists or so-called ministers of
the nigger race." The grand dragons of Georgia, South Carolina,
Tennessee, and Mississippi offered condolences to the good white
people of Birmingham. "It is regrettable," one speaker said, "that
you are having these troubles. . . . King should be met with force.
King and Kennedy are worse than Castro. We need to go back to
the old-time religion time and the old-time Klan time. . . . In Atlanta, they're putting on a show about Cleopatra, and Cleopatra is
a black girl and she kisses a white boy. . . . You have just as much

civil rights as any Communist. There will be bloodshed in every state."

The meeting ended with a blessing from a minister.

"Heavenly Father we are grateful. . . . We know that these things cannot prevail, for they are of the devil. The terrible tide of black tyranny."

The crowd dispersed then and a voice on the microphone cautioned the Klan members to "drive carefully." A second voice said: "Run over any niggers you see." The first voice objected: "No, no. Wait till next year."

Someone, whether a Klansman or not, did not wait. At 10:45 on that night, the home of the Rev. A. D. King, brother of Martin Luther King, Jr., and a leader of the Birmingham Movement, was rocked by two dynamite explosions. Less than an hour later, the A. G. Gaston Motel, headquarters of the campaign, was heavily damaged by another bombing attack.

What happened next was rage—a blind, choking, mind-numbing rage. Thousands of Negroes surged through the streets, hurling rocks and bottles and shouting: "We'll kill you, white man, we'll kill you!"

Striking out blindly in an incoherent protest, the rioters burned a block of houses and stores, smashed police vehicles and attacked policemen and officers. For more than three hours, rioters—silhouetted by flames that leaped one hundred and fifty feet into the air—commanded the streets. Some fifty persons, including a policeman and a white taxi driver, were injured. By dawn on Mother's Day, a nine-block area was virtually devastated. President Kennedy immediately ordered federal troops into ready positions near Birmingham, but the disturbance in the ghetto of the city ended without further violence.

In a sense, however, the "disturbance" was just beginning. Birmingham was the end of an epoch in American race relations. Flames from that event leaped across the country, igniting inflammable material and welding Negroes of all ranks and creeds into one black livid mass of indignation. With a desperation born of a century of denial, black men went into the streets, screaming: "Freedom! Freedom! Freedom NOW!" In June and July, Birmingham-type demonstrations pushed scores of cities to the edge of civil war.

In Danville, Virginia, policemen, armed with submachine guns and armored cars, broke up a massive demonstration and waded in with billy clubs. After the march, some fifty demonstrators were taken to hospitals with broken heads and lacerations.

A month-long series of demonstrations in Savannah, Georgia, reached a climax in several pitched battles in the downtown area. When demonstrators lay down in the streets to stop traffic, officers, equipped with shotguns and bayonets, counterattacked with barrages of tear gas and concussion grenades.

The harshest encounter occurred in Cambridge, Maryland. A campaign for desegregation of public facilities in the Eastern Shore town led to an open confrontation between Negro and white skirmishers. Several persons were wounded in altercations which continued for several days. During the small war, bands of armed and angry men stalked each other in the shadows of the streets. On June 11, Cambridge abandoned the formalities and went to war. All through that night, there were sounds of warfare—careening cars, screaming men, shattering glass, sirens, yells and the short angry barks of rifles and pistols. At one point, two carloads of whites drove through the Negro section exchanging gunfire in what one eyewitness said was "virtually a Wild West gun duel." Major George E. Davidson of the State Police reported "shooting all over the city—almost on the scale of warfare." Cambridge's petite war ended with the arrival of the National Guard and the declaration of modified martial law. Attorney General Kennedy later called Gloria Richardson, the tough-minded leader of the Cambridge Negro community, and Mayor Calvin W. Mowbray, the leader of the white community, to the Justice Department where, like representatives of foreign powers, they signed a truce. The agreement later broke down and Cambridge remained under limited martial law for more than a year.

Meanwhile, another crisis heightened the tensions between Negro and white Americans. Medgar Evers, symbol and portent of the crisis, was a metaphor of an age of dying hope. Tall, heavy-set and stout-hearted, Evers was a native Mississippian who fought for America in World War II. After the defeat of Nazi racists, he returned to America to fight native exponents of the *Herrenvolk* creed. Evers knew, better than most men, the price of freedom. He had dodged bullets on the beaches of Normandy and in the foxholes of France. But this, as it turned out, was child's play compared to the Battle of Mississippi. Threats, floggings, bombings, blood, terror: all this was part of his daily life as field secretary of the Mississippi NAACP. Evers was in the forefront of every effort to crack the cotton curtain in Mississippi and he played an important role in the successful penetration of the defenses of the University of Mississippi. As the revolution reached new dimensions of strife in the spring of 1963, Evers went into the streets to lead a massive effort to desegregate public facilities in Jackson. More than seven hundred persons, including NAACP secretary Roy Wilkins, went to jail before the mass demonstrations ended. As a local man, Evers bore the brunt of white reaction to the street demonstrations and the boycott and voter registration campaign that followed. And in some way Evers perceived that the end was near. He had always known that death was possible, but now he turned around within himself and looked at the thing, telling a reporter: "If I die, it will be in a good cause. I've been fighting for America just as much as soldiers in Vietnam."

In the next few days, death was often on Evers' mind. He had a long talk with his wife, Myrlie, and he moved about the beleaguered streets of Jackson, so his friends remembered later, with the air of a man who *knows*. "I'm looking to be shot," he told a friend, "any time I step out of my car." To Gloster Current, an NAACP colleague, he was more explicit, saying: "Everywhere I go, somebody has been following me." It was Tuesday, June 11, just before midnight, when Evers dropped Current off after a mass meeting. "I'm tired," Medgar Evers said, ". . . I'm tired." So saying, as Current remembered it later, "he just held my hand and held it and held it."

Fifteen minutes later, Evers stepped out of his car in the driveway of his home. A white man, crouching in a honeysuckle thicket one hundred and fifty feet away, steadied himself, peered through the telescopic sight on a high-powered rifle, fired one bullet and ran. The bullet ploughed through Evers' body, slammed through a window and wall and came to rest in the kitchen of the house. Myrlie Evers ran outside, screaming. "Medgar," she said, "was lying there on the doorstep in a pool of blood. I tried to get the children away, but they saw it all. . . ."

A wave of revulsion ran through the ghetto. On the day of Evers' funeral, the accumulating tensions discharged in an ominous explosion. After the ceremony, which was attended by UN Undersecretary Ralph J. Bunche, Martin Luther King, Jr., and other notables, a group of Negro youth gathered near the funeral home. They stood silent for a moment and then they began to sing a Negro spiritual:

> *Before I'd be a slave*
> *I'd be buried in my grave*
> *And go home to my Lord and be free.*

The volume swelled, pulling others to the little knot of defiant mourners. In the sweltering heat, the crowd swayed, sobbed, shouted:

> *No more killin' here!*
> *No more killin' here!*

Suddenly the people began to move, oozing like an overflowing river toward the main business district. Somebody started to run and the crowd lurched forward, breaking through a blockade of policemen and storming to the edge of Capitol Street, which was filled with rural whites. A wall of blue-helmeted policemen halted the forward movement of the youth and slowly pushed them back towards the Negro district. For several minutes, the policemen and the Negro crowd dueled with epithets, nightsticks and lobbed bottles. Then John Doar, the No. 2 man in the civil rights section of the Justice Department, stepped into the no-man's land between the contending groups and succeeded in quenching the fire. But a white policeman said, menacingly: "He didn't stop it, he just postponed it."

This was the mood of both white and Negro Americans as Medgar Evers was lowered to his final resting place in Arlington Cemetery in Washington, D.C. And this mood forced President Kennedy to alter his civil rights strategy. Until that moment, Kennedy had pursued a sophisticated form of tokenism, appointing Negroes to highly visible and unprecedented posts in his Administration and damping down discontent with highly publicized feints in the halls of Congress. Kennedy's record at that juncture, compared with the record of his predecessors, was impressive; but judged by the demands of the time it was inordinately timid. The President and his brother, the Attorney General, had deep convictions on civil rights. But they wanted apparently to solve the problem without hurting anyone and without alienating Southern Senators who controlled key parts of the Kennedy domestic and foreign programs.

The failure of this policy was written in the blood of Jackson and the bombs of Birmingham. And Kennedy, who had a superb sense of history, shifted gears and proposed the boldest civil rights program ever sponsored by an American President. His first step came on the eve of the Evers assassination. After outmaneuvering the Alabama governor and forcing the registration of two Negro students at the University of Alabama, President Kennedy made a fourteen-and-a-half minute speech which may prove to be one of the most momentous acts of his career. For in this speech an American President said for the first time that segregation was morally wrong. "One hundred years of delay have passed," the President said, "since President Lincoln freed the slaves, yet their heirs, their grandsons are not fully free. They are not yet freed from the bonds of injustice; they are not yet freed from social and economic oppression. And this nation, for all its hopes and all its boasts, will not be fully free until all its citizens are free." The President concluded:

> We preach freedom around the world, and we mean it. And we cherish our freedom here at home. But are we to say to the world—and much more importantly to each other—that this is the land of the free, except for the Negroes; that we have no second-class citizens, except for Negroes; that we have no class or caste system, no ghettos, no master race, except with respect to Negroes?
>
> Now the time has come for this nation to fulfill its promise. The events in Birmingham and elsewhere have so increased the cries for equality that no city or state or legislative body can prudently choose to ignore them.
>
> The fires of frustration and discord are burning in every city, North and South. . . . We face, therefore, a moral crisis as a country and a people. It cannot be met by repressive police action. It cannot be left to increased demonstrations in the streets. It cannot be quieted by token moves or talk. It is a time to act in the Congress, in your state and local legislative body, and, above all, in all of our daily lives. . . .
>
> Those who do nothing are inviting shame as well as violence. Those who act boldly are recognizing right as well as reality. . . .

The President acted boldly, beginning a series of frank discussions with labor leaders, businessmen, religious leaders and civil rights leaders. On the day Medgar Evers was buried, he sent to Congress a civil rights bill which guaranteed equal rights in public accommodations, and gave the Attorney General power to file suits to force compliance with the Fourteenth and Fifteenth Amendments.

The fires of frustration and discord of which the President spoke leaped higher and higher in July and August, taking new shape and reaching new heights in the ghettos of the North. In city after city, Negroes used their bodies to halt work on construction sites and sprawled in the streets to stop traffic. They staged marathon sit-ins in the offices of the New York City mayor and the New York governor. More than seven hundred demonstrators were arrested in a month-long crisis in New York City. Hundreds more were arrested in Chicago, Philadelphia, and St. Louis. In Philadelphia, more than fifty persons, half of them policemen, were injured in three days of demonstrations at a construction site. The main objectives in the Northern campaign were increased employment of Negro workers in skilled trades and the ending of *de facto* segregation in public schools.

The months of July and August saw the completion of an anti-segregation consensus in the Negro community that became ever deeper and broader. Perhaps the most dramatic indication of the New Negro consensus was a Detroit mass march of more than two hundred thousand persons.

The upswelling of indignation forced established civil rights organizations to change their tactics. With the younger organizations (CORE, SNCC and SCLC) pre-empting headlines and hearts with bold, even flamboyant, action, the NAACP and the Urban League hurried to get into step. Meeting in an uproarious convention in Chicago, the NAACP called for a stepped-up campaign of direct action.

As various voices swelled the fast-rising chorus of the Freedom Now Movement, white liberals and moderates began, belatedly, to face racial reality. The governors of Kentucky, Indiana, Illinois, Minnesota, and California issued executive orders barring racial discrimination in certain limited areas. And church leaders started practicing, in a small way, what they had been preaching. Roman Catholic, Protestant, and Jewish church leaders issued strong statements urging racial justice. Far away in Rome, Pope Paul VI expressed keen concern over the struggle in the streets of America.

More importantly, priests, rabbis, preachers, and nuns appeared on picket lines and participated in demonstrations. Eugene Carson Blake, executive head of the Presbyterian church, underlined the central challenge of the age when he said: "Some time or other we are all going to have to stand and be on the receiving end of a fire hose." Blake and other Protestant, Roman Catholic, and Jewish clergymen were later arrested in an integration march on a segregated Baltimore amusement park.

The mammoth March on Washington was a visible expression of the new level of Negro militancy and white concern. More than two hundred and fifty thousand Americans—about sixty thousand of them white—participated in the August 28 demonstration. They came from points all over America, and from several overseas. They assembled in Washington on the grassy slopes of the Washington Monument and walked about a mile to the Lincoln Monument where they said with their bodies that the Negro had been waiting 100 years and 240 days and that he was still not free and that 100 years and 241 days were too long to wait.

For almost three hours, the multitude listened to speakers who demanded immediate passage of a civil rights bill and immediate implementation of the basic guarantees of the Declaration of Independence and the Thirteenth, Fourteenth, and Fifteenth Amendments.

In a memorable speech, Martin Luther King, Jr., etched the mood of the crowd. He came to the lectern late in the afternoon, when the shadows were long on the grass; he read for a time from a prepared text and then he began to improvise, speaking of a dream big enough to include all men and all women and all children.

"I have a dream," he said, over and over, and each elaboration evoked hysterical cheers.

I have a dream that one day this nation will rise up and live out the true meaning of its creed: "We hold these truths to be self-evident; that all men are created equal."

I have a dream that one day on the red hills of Georgia the sons of former slaves and the sons of former slaveowners will be able to sit down together at the table of brotherhood. . . .

This is our hope. This is the faith with which I return to the South. . . . With this faith, we will be able to work together, to pray together, to struggle together, to go to jail together, to stand up for freedom together, knowing that we will be free one day.

This will be the day when all of God's children will be able to sing with new meaning, "My country 'tis of thee, sweet land of liberty, of thee I sing. Land where my fathers died, land of the Pilgrim's pride, from every mountain side, let freedom ring."

And if America is to be a great nation this must become true. So let freedom ring from the prodigious hilltops of New Hampshire. Let free-

dom ring from the mighty mountains of New York. Let freedom ring
from the heightening Alleghenies of Pennsylvania! Let freedom ring
from the snow-capped Rockies of Colorado.

Let freedom ring from the curvaceous peaks of California!

But not only that; let freedom ring from Stone Mountain of Georgia!

Let freedom ring from every hill and mole hill of Mississippi. From
every mountainside, let freedom ring.

When we let freedom ring, when we let it ring from every village
and hamlet, from every state and every city, we will be able to speed
up that day when all of God's children, black men and white men, Jews
and Gentiles, Protestants and Catholics, will be able to join hands and
sing in the words of that old Negro spiritual: "Free at last! Free at last!
Thank God Almighty, we are free at last."

It was a magnificent evocation which called back somehow all
the old men and women who had that same dream and died dis-
honored—but it was only an evocation. Freedom did not ring.
There was a stillness on the hilltops of New Hampshire and in Birmingham there was hate. Eighteen days after the march, a car
careened past the Sixteenth Street Baptist Church and a hand tossed
a bomb. Inside the church, little black children were completing
the Sunday School lesson: Love thy neighbor. For an eerie second,
there was complete silence and then, with a rush of air and a deaf-
ening explosion, hate spoke. The ancient church crumbled in smoke
and fire and a man stood screaming in the debris: "Love 'em? Love
'em? *I hate 'em!*"

Four children died in the blast and twenty-one persons were injured. Later that day, two other Negro youth were killed, one by
a policeman.

And so the bitter harvest began.

A new mood, a mood made of acrid smoke and blood and dashed
hopes, rose from the ruins and moved across the mind of Negro
America. And the Freedom Movement began to inch toward the
dangerous and forbidden road of open and continuous self-asser-
tion. In a bitterly brilliant lament for the Birmingham Six, Wyatt
Walker asked: ". . . has the moment come in the development of
the nonviolent revolution that we are forced [to] literally im-

mobilize the nation until she acts on our plea for justice and morality. . . . Is the day far off that major transportation centers would be deluged with mass acts of civil disobedience; airports, train stations, bus terminals, the traffic of large cities, interstate commerce, would be halted by the bodies of witnesses nonviolently insisting on 'Freedom Now.' I suppose a nation-wide work stoppage might attract enough attention to persuade someone to do something to get this monkey of segregation and discrimination off our backs, once, now and forever. Will it take one or all of these?"

Yes, James Baldwin, the novelist and essayist, said: yes; it would take at least one of these and perhaps all. Calling for a Christmas boycott (national Negro leaders later vetoed the plan), Baldwin said Americans had forfeited the right to hide behind Christian rituals. He added: "If we don't move now, literally move, sit down, stand, walk, don't go to work, don't pay the rent, if we don't do everything now in our power to change this country, this country will turn out to be in the position, let us say, of Spain, a country which is so tangled and so trapped and immobilized by its interior dissension that it can't do anything else." Bayard Rustin, the theoretician of the revolution and the organizer of the March on Washington, added a defiant footnote, calling for "an uprising, nonviolently, in one hundred cities," an uprising which would "create a mountain of creative social confusion . . . until the government is forced to recognize us to carry on business."

The tempo of the Negro revolution changed now—nobody was playing. A rent strike began in Harlem and spread to other cities and a harsh, head-knocking integration campaign got underway in Chester, a Philadelphia suburb. More important as a harbinger of things to come was a massive school boycott in Chicago. Two hundred and twenty thousand children, about half of the enrollment, boycotted Chicago schools on October 22 as a protest against *de facto* segregation and the policies of Superintendent Benjamin C. Willis.

The period beginning with the bombing of the Birmingham church and ending with the Chicago school boycott marked still a new phase in the Negro Freedom Movement. Before Birmingham, the Negro Freedom Movement had been dominated by an elite group of well-trained nonviolent rebels who campaigned mainly in the South. Now the center of gravity shifted to the North and new groups—the angry young men of World War II and the Korean War and the so-called underclass, the permanently depressed strata of the Negro working class—entered the ranks, bringing with them the sharp black steel of a deeper discontent.

During this time of rising anger, the forces of reaction were not idle. So long as civil rights battles were fought on distant battlefields in faraway Birmingham and Mississippi, Northerners gave their assent. But when the fight came home, when Negroes poured into Northern streets demanding an end to *de facto* segregation in the schools and in the housing market, the Northern white community began to stiffen. There was, in fact, something akin to a white panic which was reflected in a precipitous drop in the popularity of President Kennedy.

Another reflection of the increasing hostility to Negro demands was the mushroom growth of a white resistance movement. In Chicago, Detroit, New York, Cleveland and other cities, whites began to organize in support of "neighborhood schools" and "community residential sections." Property owners associations in Chicago and Parents and Taxpayers (PAT) in New York held mass meetings and staged mass marches on city hall. In California and Illinois, real estate interests financed campaigns to force referendums on the issue of open occupancy. By January, millions of whites were organized in parents, taxpayers and real estate associations which Negro leaders called Northern counterparts of the White Citizens Councils of the South.

As white resistance spread in the North, racists moved to the offensive in the South. In Virginia, Alabama, Louisiana, and Georgia, Negro demonstrations were crushed with massive police repression. Virginia revived an old "John Brown statute" which made it a felony to incite Negroes "to acts of violence and war against the white population" and vice versa. Georgia followed suit, excavating an old slave era law which made insurrection a felony punishable by death.

In Alabama, officers crushed demonstrations with electric cattle prods and a liberal use of peace bonds. In Orangeburg, South Carolina, Negro demonstrators were summarily arrested and confined in barbed-wire compounds that resembled concentration camps. The height, or perhaps the depth, of this campaign came in Plaquemine, Louisiana, where officers bombarded a Negro church with tear gas grenades and fire hoses. Negro demonstrators said a state policeman with an electric cattle prod rode a horse down the aisle of the church at the height of the counterattack. The leading organizations of the Revolution—SCLC, SNCC and CORE—charged that Southerners were using "storm trooper tactics."

The net result of all this was a hardening of attitudes on both sides and a polarization of Negroes and whites into two mutually hostile groups. Another source of friction, deeper because less conscious, was the increasing weight of black power—and the increasingly hysterical attempts to circumvent the implications of that power. Sixty per cent of the population of Washington, D.C., forty-two percent of the population of Chester, Pennsylvania, thirty-eight percent of the population of Birmingham, twenty-three percent of Chicago, twenty-nine percent of Detroit—the Urban Negro, the main protagonist of the Negro Revolution, was, by 1963, the dominant social fact of almost every metropolitan community. And his strength—and his awareness of that strength—was increasing hourly by natural additions and migration from rural areas. Projections of population figures indicated that Negroes would be in the majority in Detroit, Philadelphia, Cleveland, and Chicago by the decade 1970–80. More disturbing to racists were predictions that Negroes would have comfortable majorities in at least seven of America's ten largest cities by the decade 1980–90.

These figures and the reality they reflected were at the root of the boiling ferment in the Negro ghetto and they told everyone with eyes to see and ears to hear that the salvation of America depended, to a great extent, on a genuine confrontation with Thomas Jefferson's ALL.

If this was not clearly seen in the summer of 1963, it was beginning to be clearly felt.

By November, in the North and South, men were quietly choosing sides for a confrontation many believed inevitable. And then for the second time in this eerie year a high-powered rifle spoke. The assassination of President Kennedy, who was riding in an open car in a Dallas, Texas, motorcade, shattered the gathering battle lines and restored, however temporarily, the broken ranks of American community.

President Kennedy's death, coming as it did in the middle of an emotional maelstrom not unlike the Civil War, called men's minds back to Lincoln and his deed and his manner of death. That this should happen in the United States of America on the one hundredth anniversary of the Proclamation of a President who died in a similar manner horrified Negro Americans who wandered, wailing, through the angry streets, bemoaning their nakedness. The young President, by a series of audacious acts, had captured the hearts of Negro Americans; and when he went to his grave, under circumstances and in a ceremony not unlike the Lincoln ceremony, Negro Americans played a highly visible role as honor guards and functionaries. Among the international who's who of mourners were Emperor Haile Selassie, resplendent in a uniform garnished with decorations and a chartreuse sash, and Martin Luther King, Jr., somber and thoughtful in a dark suit. Finally, on November 25, John Fitzgerald Kennedy was laid to rest in an Arlington Cemetery grave not too far from the grave of Medgar Evers.

The new President, Lyndon Baines Johnson, the first Southern-based President since Lincoln's successor, Andrew Johnson, moved swiftly to reknit the broken bonds of community between black America and the White House. Immediately after the funeral, he placed long-distance calls to civil rights leaders and asked their support. Then he went before Congress and asked for immediate passage of the Kennedy civil rights program, saying that "no memorial or eulogy could more eloquently honor President Kennedy's memory than the earliest possible passage of the Civil Rights Bill for which he fought. We have talked for 100 years or more. Yes, it is time now to write the next chapter—and to write it in books of law."

The President later conferred with James Farmer, executive director of CORE; Whitney Young, executive director of the National Urban League; and Roy Wilkins and Martin Luther King, Jr. King said he had made it clear to the President that the civil rights demonstrations would resume after the period of national mourning.

Two days after the end of the period of mourning, the demonstrations began in Atlanta, Georgia, with SNCC again leading the way. The momentum picked up in January and February with massive demonstrations in Princess Anne, Maryland, which became the first community in 1964 to deploy K-9 police dogs. There then followed a series of school boycotts in Harlem (464,000 absent in February and 267,000 absent in March), Cleveland (68,000 absent in April), Cincinnati (26,455 absent in February) and Chicago (172,350 absent in February).

The continuing conflict over *de facto* school segregation exploded in riots in Cleveland and Chester, Pennsylvania. In March, Negroes and whites fought a two-day duel in Jacksonville, Florida. A Jacksonville postman, a World War II veteran, spoke frankly of the rising tide of black rebellion. "I am ready to go to war for this country again," he told a reporter. "But I am also ready to go to war in this country. I am a peaceful man, but I can be moved."

What was moving Negro America was stark despair. Despite the demonstrations of 1963, despite repeated payments in blood and pain, despite the pious statements of liberals and moderates, despite Gandhi and King and Kennedy, very little had changed in America. "Colored" and "white" water fountains were still bubbling in Birmingham's City Hall; Negro schools were still separate and unequal; and craft unions were still excluding Negro workers.

Upon this stage, already crowded by social villains, came an onrush of new problems. The voices of opposition in the North became louder, and bolder, crystallizing in what mass media called "a white backlash of reaction." In letters to the editor, in mass marches, in rallies, white Americans struck back, blindly, at Negro activists. Perhaps the best indication of the depth of white fear was the success of Governor George Wallace, the Alabama segregationist, who won a stunningly large number of votes in the Wisconsin, Indiana, and Maryland Presidential primaries. Senator Barry Goldwater (R., Arizona), who voted against the civil rights bill, became the rallying point of the "backlash" after his nomination as the Republican candidate for President. Goldwater denied that he was a racist, but there was an undertone of anti-Negro hysteria in the Republican campaign against President Lyndon B. Johnson.

Fuel for the fire came from Congress where Southerners began a long filibuster on the civil rights bill. Although the bill was finally passed in a modified form, Negro resentment was exacerbated by Southern Senators who used the national arena as a sounding board for anti-Negro propaganda.

As a result of these events and others of similar tone and texture, a certain hope died in the Negro ghetto. Tangible proof of this was the rise of a new cadre of leaders who repudiated the tactics and programs of the established civil rights organizations and called for radical new departures. These leaders, who were in the forefront of the Northern school boycotts and demonstrations, were more political and less religious, more cynical and less conciliatory. They called for generalized expressions of disgust aimed at the whole white community—they called, in fact, for massive civil disobedience movements.

A shadow coming before the event was the threat of a dissident Brooklyn CORE group to bring New York City to a complete standstill through techniques of civil disobedience. Brooklyn CORE later precipitated the most acrimonious civil rights dispute since the beginning of the sit-in age by threatening to tie-up traffic with a stall-in (deliberately running out of gas on expressways) on opening day of the World's Fair. National CORE suspended the chapter and the city hastily adopted new laws designed to blunt the force of the stall-in. In the end, the plan fizzled, but national CORE dramatized Negro discontent with token civil disobedience demonstrations at pavilions inside the fair. After the first day of demonstrations, Norman Hill, the program director of CORE, said: "This marks the beginning of the hottest summer that has ever been seen in the United States."

Hill, as it turned out, was right. The Red Summer of 1964 reached an unprecedented peak of fury, dwarfing by comparison the summers of 1962 and 1963. In the summer of 1964, a barrage of events beat like a fusillade on the American mind. A small army of nonviolent demonstrators invaded the South and fought bitterly contested battles in the Black Belt Counties of Mississippi, Alabama, and Louisiana. There were riots and miniature civil wars on the streets of scores of cities in the North. All over America, during this troubled and chaotic summer and fall, men were in motion, singing, screaming, fighting, swept along by the dancing waves of passion and despair.

By the fall of 1964, black men and white men were wrestling in the dusk of dawn and no man knew rightly the hour or the day of the coming of the sun.

. . . And there wrestled a man with him until the breaking of the day.

And when he saw that he prevailed not against him, he touched the hollow of his thigh; and the hollow of Jacob's thigh was out of joint, as he wrestled with him.

And he said, Let me go, for the day breaketh. And he said, I will not let thee go, until thou bless me.

13

"We Cannot Escape History"

Epilogue

EVERYTHING HAS CHANGED in black-white America; and yet nothing has changed.

One hundred years ago, at a time of danger and doubt, Abraham Lincoln stood before Congress and pleaded for freedom for the slave in order to "assure freedom to the free." He added: "Fellow-citizens, we cannot escape history. . . . The fiery trial through which we pass will light us down, in honor or dishonor, to the latest generation."

The words are still relevant.

One hundred and thirteen years ago, in one of the Negro's perennial crises, Frederick Douglass warned that America's racial policy was "fraught with evil to the white man, as well as to his victims." He added: "*We* [Negroes] *are here*, and here we are likely to be. To imagine that we shall ever be eradicated is absurd and ridiculous. We can be remodified, changed, and assimilated, but never extinguished. We repeat, therefore, that *we are here*; and that this is *our* country. . . . We shall neither die out, nor be driven out; but shall go with this people, either as a testimony against them, or as an evidence in their favor throughout their generations."

The words are still relevant.

Today, 343 years after Jamestown, Negro Americans are still strangers in their own house. Today, 100 years after the Emancipation Proclamation, American Negroes are still permanent exceptions to the melting pot theory. Not only are they not melting, one writer said; but most white Americans are determined that they shall not get in the pot. To put the matter bluntly, the full privileges and immunities of citizens of the United States do not apply to Negroes—and they never have.

No honest balance sheet can ignore that painful fact.

The Negro's progress, when compared with the inferno of slavery, has been startling; compared with the progress of other minorities, that progress pales into insignificance. No Negro has ever been elected governor of an American state; no Negro has ever sat in a President's Cabinet; no black man, since 1870, has been elected mayor of a black-white American city. Negroes generally cannot live where they want to, work where they want to or die where they want to. And most of their children—North and South—are huddled in schools which are generally inferior to the schools maintained for white Americans. Negroes generally—and this is the heart of the matter—*are not dealt with as human beings* in their native land.

There has been progress—undeniably. But the progress is deceptive; in some cases, illusory. Take one index: the number of Negro judges. There are about seventy Negro judges in America, a 50 per cent increase in the last ten years. This sounds encouraging until you place it beside the total number of judges—between 5,000 and 8,000. There are now five Negro congressmen; in 1875 there were seven Negro congressmen and one Negro senator.

One must also consider the backwashes of centuries of denial and degradation. The systematic disruption of the Negro family in slavery and the years of migration and deprivation are partially responsible for a fantastic amount of family disorganization in large urban communities. Things are not what they seem, even in the economic field. Negroes made great gains between 1940 and 1952. Since 1952 and the series of "economic downturns" or recessions,

Negro workers have barely held their own. In some areas, there have been over-all losses since 1952.

Automation has made serious inroads on the security of unskilled factory workers.

Increasing complexity has largely negated the gains in literacy. Though basic illiteracy has virtually disappeared, there are indications that functional illiteracy (inability to cope with the requirements of a complex urban civilization) is increasing.

To repeat, no honest balance sheet can ignore these facts.

"Aye," Galileo is reported to have whispered after he was forced to back down on his belief that the earth moved—"Aye, but it does move!" The late Walter White used these words to illustrate the paradox of the Negro's stride forward. There are obvious and dramatic examples of forward movement. Negroes are in laboratories and factories where there were no Negroes before. There are manicured lawns and neat ranch houses in Crestwood Forest in Atlanta, in Chatham Field in Chicago, in Pontchartrain Park in New Orleans, in suburbs and middle-class neighborhoods all over America. Negroes have a total annual income of about twenty billion dollars. Their average family income is $3,233, about 55 per cent of the average family income of whites. There are 584,000 Negroes in professional and managerial occupations; 534,000 clerical workers; and 385,000 skilled craftsmen and foremen. About 233,000 Negroes are in colleges and professional schools. Negroes own about two million homes; they manage huge financial complexes like the Atlanta Life Insurance Company, the North Carolina Mutual Life Insurance Company and the Supreme Life Insurance Company of America.

The increasing political power of Negroes is reflected in the increasing responsiveness of the great political parties to Negro demands—in a series of Executive Orders which have placed the federal government on the side of the Fourteenth Amendment; in the passage of civil rights bills in 1957 and 1960.

Robert C. Weaver, an American Negro, has headed the Housing and Home Finance Agency; Negroes have served as assistant and deputy assistant secretaries of the Labor, State, Health and Welfare Departments. And Andrew T. Hatcher has held the strategic position of Associate Press Secretary at the White House. Since 1948, Negroes have been elected to governmental bodies in Nashville, Atlanta, Richmond and other Southern cities. And an Atlanta lawyer, Leroy R. Johnson, has served in the Georgia legislature.

There have been losses, but there have also been gains. The people have suffered, but the people have also endured. Martin Luther King, Jr., is right in a sense that transcends grammar and statistics. In his speeches to Negroes and whites, he quotes the ungrammatical truth of an old preacher.

> *Lord, we ain't what we oughta be,*
> *We ain't what we wanna be,*
> *We ain't what we gonna be,*
> *But thank God, we ain't what we was.*

Landmarks and Milestones

1492
Negro servants, slaves, and explorers came to the New World with the first Spanish and French explorers. Pedro Alonso Niño of Columbus' crew is identified as a Negro by some scholars. Negroes were with Balboa, Ponce De Leon, Cortes, Pizarro and Menendez.

1526
Negro slaves in first settlement in United States—a Spanish colony in area of present-day South Carolina—revolted and fled to the Indians, November.

1538
Estevanico (Little Stephen), a Negro explorer, led expedition from Mexico and discovered Arizona and New Mexico.

1619
History of Negro in English America began with landing of "twenty negars" at Jamestown, Va., August.

1624
William Tucker, first Negro child born in English America, baptized at Jamestown.

1641

Massachusetts became first colony to give statutory recognition to slavery, December. Connecticut followed in 1650; Virginia, 1661; Maryland, 1663; New York and New Jersey, 1664; South Carolina, 1682; Rhode Island and Pennsylvania, 1700; North Carolina, 1715; Georgia, 1750.

1663

First serious slave conspiracy in Colonial America, September 13. Servant betrayed plot of white servants and Negro slaves in Gloucester County, Va.

1664

Maryland enacted first antimiscegenation law to prevent marriages of Englishwomen and Negroes, September 20. Virginia banned interracial marriages in 1691; Massachusetts, 1705; North Carolina, 1715; South Carolina, 1717; Delaware, 1721; Pennsylvania, 1725.

1688

First formal protest against slavery in Western Hemisphere made by Germantown Quakers at monthly meeting, February 18.

1704

School for Negro slaves opened in New York by Elias Neau, a Frenchman.

1712

Slave revolt, New York, April 7. Nine whites killed. Twenty-one slaves executed.

1723

Massachusetts governor issued proclamation on the "fires which have been designedly and industriously kindled by some villainous and desperate negroes or other dissolute people as appears by the confession of some of them," April 13.

1730

Slave conspiracy discovered in Norfolk and Princess Anne counties, Va. Governor ordered white males to carry arms with them to church.

1739

Slave revolt, Stono, S.C., September 9. Twenty-five whites killed before insurrection put down.

1741
Series of suspicious fires and reports of slave conspiracy led to general hysteria in New York City, March and April. Thirty-one slaves, five whites executed.

1750
Crispus Attucks, hero of American Revolution, escaped from his master in Framingham, Mass., September 30.

1760
Richard Allen born a slave, Philadelphia, February 14.
Jupiter Hammon, New York slave who was probably the first Negro poet, published *Salvation by Christ with Penetential Cries*, December 25.

James Derham, who was born a slave in Philadelphia in 1762, is generally recognized as the first Negro physician in America. Derham learned the art while serving as an assistant to his physician master. In 1783, Derham bought his freedom and built up a large practice among Negroes and whites. By 1788, he was one of the top physicians in New Orleans. Dr. Benjamin Rush, a leading doctor of the day, said: "I have conversed with him upon most of the acute and epidemic diseases of the country where he lives. I expected to have suggested some new medicines, to him, but he suggested many more to me."

1770
Crispus Attucks was first of five persons killed in Boston Massacre, March 5. He is generally regarded as first martyr of the Revolution.
Quakers, led by Anthony Benezet, opened school for Negroes in Philadelphia, June 28.

1773
Massachusetts slaves petitioned legislature for freedom, January 6. There is a record of eight petitions during Revolutionary War period.
Phillis Wheatley's book, *Poems on Various Subjects, Religious and Moral*, published, the second book by an American woman.
First Negro Baptist church organized at Silver Bluff, S.C.

1775
First abolition society in United States organized in Philadelphia, April 14.
Negro and white minutemen fought at Lexington and Concord, April 19.

Negro patriots participated in first aggressive action of American forces, the capture of Fort Ticonderoga by Ethan Allen and Green Mountain Boys, May 10.

Negro soldiers fought at Battle of Bunker Hill, June 17. Two of heroes of day were Peter Salem and Salem Poor.

Horatio Gates, Washington's Adjutant General, issued general order banning Negro soldiers from American Army, July 10.

Council of general officers decided to bar slaves and free Negroes from American Army, October 8.

Continental Congress approved resolution barring Negroes from Army, October 23.

Lord Dunmore, deposed royal governor of Virginia, issued proclamation which promised freedom to male slaves who joined British Army, November 7.

General George Washington issued general order which forbade recruiting officers to enlist Negroes, November 12.

Alarmed by response to Dunmore proclamation, Washington reversed himself and ordered recruiting officers to accept free Negroes, December 31.

1776

Continental Congress approved Washington's order on enlistment of free Negroes, January 16.

Declaration of Independence adopted, July 4. Section denouncing slave trade struck out in deference to South Carolina and Georgia.

African Baptist Church organized Williamsburg, Va.

1777

Vermont became first American state to abolish slavery, July 2. By 1783, slavery was prohibited in Massachusetts and New Hampshire. Pennsylvania provided for gradual emancipation in 1780, Connecticut and Rhode Island barred slavery in 1784, New York (gradual) in 1799 and New Jersey in 1804.

1778

Rhode Island General Assembly in precedent-breaking act authorized enlistment of slaves, February.

After the disastrous winter of Valley Forge, Negroes—slaves and freemen—were welcomed into the American Army. There were Negro soldiers in the Revolutionary Army from every one of the original thirteen colonies. Most of the estimated 5,000 Negroes in the Revolutionary

Army fought in integrated units. Negro soldiers participated in practically all of the big battles of the war. They were at White Plains, Stillwater, Bennington, Bemis Heights, Saratoga, Stony Points, Trenton, Princeton, Eutaw, S.C., and Yorktown. Negro troops played important roles in the battles of Rhode Island, Long Island, Red Bank, Savannah, Monmouth and Fort Griswold.

1784
Death of Phillis Wheatley, Boston, December 5.

1785
David Walker, abolitionist, born free, Wilmington, N.C., September 28.

1787
Richard Allen and Absalom Jones organized Philadelphia's Free African Society, "the first wavering step of a people toward a more organized social life," April 12.

Continental Congress excluded slavery from Northwest Territory, July 13.

Prince Hall, Revolutionary War veteran, received charter from Grand Lodge of England for first Negro Masonic lodge in America, African Lodge No. 459, September 12.

Constitution approved by delegates at Philadelphia Convention with three clauses protecting slavery, September 17.

Boston Negroes, led by Prince Hall, petitioned legislature for equal school facilities, October 17.

First free school in New York City, the African Free School, opened, November 1.

1790
U.S. Population: 3,929,214. Negro population 757,208 (19.3%).

Jean Baptiste Point du Sable, French-speaking Negro from Santo Domingo, made first permanent settlement at Chicago.

1791
Haitian Revolution began with revolt of slaves in northern province, August 22.

Benjamin Banneker, mathematician and astronomer, served on commission which surveyed the District of Columbia.

1792
Joshua Bishop named pastor of First Baptist Church for whites, Portsmouth, Va.

1793

First fugitive slave law enacted by Congress, February 12. Act made it a criminal offense to harbor a fugitive slave or to prevent his arrest.

1794

Eli Whitney patented cotton gin which made Cotton King and increased demand for slave labor, March 14.

Absalom Jones and followers dedicated First African Church of St. Thomas in Philadelphia, July 17. Jones, an Episcopalian, was first Negro minister ordained in America.

Richard Allen and followers organized Bethel AME Church.

1796

Zion Methodist Church organized in New York City.

Boston African Society established with 44 members.

1797

Congress refused to accept first recorded petition from American Negroes, January 30.

Sojourner Truth born a slave on estate in Hurley, New York.

1800

U.S. Population: 5,308,483. Negro population: 1,002,037 (18.9%).

Antislavery petition presented to Congress on behalf of free Negroes of Philadelphia, January 2.

John Brown born in Torrington, Conn., May 9.

Nat Turner born a slave, Southampton County, Va., October 2.

Storm forced suspension of attack on Richmond, Va., by Gabriel and some 1,000 slaves, August 30. Conspiracy was betrayed by two slaves. Gabriel and fifteen of his followers were hanged on October 7.

1804

Jean Jacques Dessalines proclaimed independence of Haiti, second republic in Western Hemisphere, January 1.

Ohio legislature enacted first of Black Laws which restricted rights and movement of Negroes in the North, January 5. Several Northern states passed Black Laws. Three states—Illinois, Indiana, Oregon—had anti-immigration clauses in their state constitutions.

1805

Death of Benjamin Banneker, October 9.

William Lloyd Garrison born Newburyport, Mass., December 10.

1807

President signed bill which banned slave trade after close of year, March 2.

1809

Abraham Lincoln born Hardin County, Ky., February 12.

1810

U.S. population: 7,239,881. Negro population: 1,377,808 (19%).

Charles Lenox Remond, Negro abolitionist, born Salem, Mass., February 1.

1811

Louisiana slaves revolted in two parishes about 35 miles from New Orleans, January 8–10. Revolt suppressed by U.S. troops.

1814

Andrew Jackson issued proclamation at Mobile, Ala., calling upon free Negroes "to rally around the standard of the eagle" in the War of 1812, September 21.

Negroes fought in the land and water battles of the War of 1812. A large number of Negro sailors fought with Perry and Chauncey in the battles on the upper lakes and were particularly effective at the Battle of Lake Erie. Two battalions of Negro soldiers were with Andrew Jackson when he defeated the British at the Battle of New Orleans. Jackson issued his famous proclamation to Negro troops at New Orleans on December 18, 1814; "TO THE MEN OF COLOR.—Soldiers! From the shores of Mobile I collected you to arms; I invited you to share in the perils and to divide the glory of your white countrymen. I expected much from you, for I was not uninformed of those qualities which must render you so formidable to an invading foe. I knew that you could endure hunger and thirst and all the hardships of war. I knew that you loved the land of your nativity, and that like ourselves, you had to defend all that is most dear to you. But you surpass my hopes. I have found in you, united to these qualities, that noble enthusiasm which impels to great deeds."

1815

Henry Highland Garnet, minister, abolitionist and diplomat, born a slave in Kent County, Md., December 23.

1816

African Methodist Episcopal Church organized at Philadelphia convention, April 9.

Fort Blount on Apalachicola Bay, Fla., attacked by U.S. Troops, July 27. Fort, which was held by about 300 fugitive slaves and about 20 Indian allies, was taken after siege of several days.

American Colonization Society organized in hall of the House of

Representatives, December 28. Society was formed to transport free Negroes to Africa.

1817

Philadelphia Negroes held meeting at Bethel Church to protest against Colonization Society's efforts "to exile us from the land of our nativity," January.

Frederick Douglass, who has been called "the greatest American Negro," born Tuckahoe, Talbot County, Md., February.

Samuel Ringgold Ward, minister, abolitionist, author, born Eastern Shore of Maryland, October 17.

1818

Andrew Jackson defeated force of Indians and Negroes at Battle of Suwanee, ending First Seminole War which Jackson called "this savage and negro war," April 18.

1820

U.S. population, 9,638,453. Negro population: 1,771,656 (18.4%).

"Mayflower of Liberia" sailed from New York City with 86 Negroes, February 6. Ship arrived Sierra Leone, March 9.

Missouri Compromise enacted, March 3. Measure prohibited slavery to the north of southern boundary of Missouri.

1821

AMEZ Church formally organized at meeting in New York City, June 21.

1822

"House slave" betrayed Denmark Vesey conspiracy, May 30. Vesey conspiracy, one of most elaborate slave plots on record, involved thousands of Negroes in Charleston, S.C., and vicinity. Authorities arrested 131 Negroes and four whites. Thirty-seven were hanged.

Denmark Vesey and five of his aides hanged at Blake's Landing, Charleston, S.C., July 2.

Hiram R. Revels, First Negro U.S. senator, born free, Fayetteville, N.C., September 27.

1826

John Russwurm, first Negro college graduate, received degree at Bowdoin.

1827

First Negro newspaper, *Freedom's Journal*, published in New York City, March 16.

Slavery abolished in New York State, July 4.

1829

Race riot, Cincinnati, Ohio, August 10. More than 1,000 Negroes left the city for Canada.

Walker's Appeal, radical antislavery pamphlet, published in Boston by David Walker, a free Negro, September 28.

1830

U.S. population: 12,866,020. Negro population: 2,328,642 (18.1%). Negroes of Portsmouth, Ohio, forcibly deported by order of city authorities, January 21.

James Augustine Healy, first Negro Roman Catholic bishop in America, born to Irish planter and Negro slave on plantation near Macon, Ga., April 6.

First national Negro convention met at Philadelphia's Bethel Church with Richard Allen in the chair, September 20.

1831

William Lloyd Garrison printed first issue of the *Liberator*, January 1.

Nat Turner revolt, Southampton County, Va., August 21–22. Some 60 whites were killed. Nat Turner was not captured until October 30.

Nat Turner hanged, Jerusalem, Va., November 11.

1832

New England Anti-Slavery Society organized by 12 whites at African Baptist Church on Boston's Beacon Hill, January 6.

1833

Prudence Crandall, a liberal white woman, arrested for conducting an academy for Negro girls in Canterbury, Conn., June 27. Academy was later closed.

American Anti-Slavery Society organized in Philadelphia by Negro and white abolitionists, December 4.

1834

Slavery was abolished in British empire, August 1.

Since the Colonial period, Negroes have been hewers of the human spirit as well as wood. Benjamin Banneker, the astronomer and mathematician, produced the first scientific writing by an American Negro in his almanac which was issued annually after 1791. Banneker also wrote a dissertation on bees and put together what was probably the first clock made in America. It is said that a Georgia slave was partially responsible for the invention of the cotton gin. Jo Anderson, another slave, was a trusted helper of Cyrus McCormick while he was developing his reaping machine in Rockbridge, Va., in the 1830's. Henry Blair of Maryland was probably the first Negro to receive a patent for an invention. He took out a patent on a corn harvester on October 14, 1834. Equally inventive was Norbert Rillieux, a New Orleans machinist and engineer, who invented and got a patent on a vacuum cup which revolutionized sugar refining methods of his day. Between 1872 and 1920, Elijah McCoy of Detroit received over 57 patents for inventions on automatic lubricating appliances and other devices pertaining to telegraphy and electricity. Many of his inventions were used on locomotives on the Canadian and Northwestern railroads and on steamships on the Great Lakes. Perhaps the greatest of the early inventors was Jan E. Matzeliger who created the first machine for attaching soles to shoes, "the first appliance of its kind capable of performing all the steps required to hold a shoe on its last, grip and pull the leather down around the heel, guide and drive the nails into place, and then discharge the complete shoe from the machine." Matzeliger's patent was bought by the United Shoe Machinery Company of Boston which became a multi-million-dollar corporation. Matzeliger died in 1889 in obscurity.

1835

A Negro convention, meeting in Philadelphia, advised Negroes to remove the word African from the names of their institutions and organizations, June 1–5.

Antislavery pamphlets taken from mail at Charleston, S.C., and publicly burned, July 29.

Noyes Academy, an integrated school at Canaan, N.H., closed by mob violence, August 10.

1837

Elijah P. Lovejoy murdered by proslavery mob while defending his press in Alton, Ill., November 7.

Seminole Indian force defeated by American troops at Battle of Okeechobee, December 25. Negro chief, John Horse, shared command responsibilities with Alligator Sam Jones and Wild Cat.

1838

Mirror of Liberty, first Negro magazine, published in New York City by David Ruggles, a Negro abolitionist, August.

Frederick Douglass escaped from slavery in Baltimore, September 3.

Charles Lenox Remond began his career as antislavery agent. Remond was first Negro lecturer employed by an antislavery society.

1839

Samuel Ringgold Ward, Presbyterian minister, employed as lecturer by American Anti-Slavery Society.

Seminoles and their Negro allies shipped from Tampa Bay, Fla., to the West, February 25.

Robert Smalls, Civil War hero and Reconstruction congressman, born at Beaufort, S.C., April 5.

Liberty party, first antislavery political party, organized at convention in Warsaw, N.Y., November 13. Two Negro abolitionists, Samuel Ringgold Ward and Henry Highland Garnet, were among earliest supporters of the new political party.

1841

Blanche Kelso Bruce, only Negro to serve full term in U.S. Senate, born a slave at Prince Edward County, Va., March 1.

Frederick Douglass hired as lecturer by Massachusetts Anti-Slavery Society, August.

Slave revolt on slave trader "Creole" which was en route from Hampton, Va., to New Orleans, La., November 7. Slaves overpowered crew and sailed vessel to Bahamas where they were granted asylum and freedom.

1842

Robert Brown Elliott, Reconstruction congressman, born in Boston, Mass., August 11.

Capture of George Latimer in Boston precipitated first of several famous fugitive cases which embittered North and South, October. Boston abolitionists raised enough money to purchase Latimer from his master, November 17.

1843

Sojourner Truth, the first Negro woman to take the platform as an antislavery lecturer, left New York and began her work as an abolitionist, June 1.

At national convention of colored men in Buffalo, N.Y., Henry Highland Garnet made controversial speech in which he called for a slave revolt and a general strike, August 22.

Negroes participated in national political gathering for the first time at meeting of Liberty party convention in Buffalo, N.Y., August 30. Samuel R. Ward led convention in prayer; Henry Highland Garnet was member of nominating committee; Charles B. Ray was one of the convention secretaries.

1845

First Negro formally admitted to bar, Macon B. Allen, passed examination at Worcester, Mass., May 3.

1847

Dred Scott case began in St. Louis Circuit Court, June 30.

President Joseph Jenkins Roberts, a native of Virginia, declared Liberia an independent republic, July 26.

Frederick Douglass published first issue of his famous newspaper, the *North Star*, December 3.

1848

Free Soil party organized at Buffalo, N.Y., convention attended by several Negro abolitionists, August 9–10.

William and Ellen Craft escaped from slavery in Georgia, December 26. Ellen impersonated a slaveholder and William acted as her servant in one of the most dramatic slave escapes.

1849

Harriet Tubman escaped from slavery in Maryland, summer. She returned to South 19 times and brought out more than 300 slaves.

Benjamin Roberts filed first school integration suit on behalf of his daughter, Sarah, who had been denied admission to "white" schools in Boston, Mass., November. Massachusetts Supreme Court rejected the suit and established the controversial "separate but equal" precedent. Massachusetts legislature abolished separate schools on April 28, 1855.

Charles L. Reason named professor of belles-lettres and French at Central College, McGrawville, N.Y. "White" college had two other Negro professors, William G. Allen and George B. Vashon.

1850

U.S. population: 23,191,876. Negro population: 3,638,808 (15.7%).

Fugitive Slave Act passed by Congress as part of Compromise of 1850, September 18. Thousands of fugitive slaves fled to Canada.

1851

Negro abolitionist crashed into courtroom in Boston and rescued a fugitive slave, February 15.

At 18th annual meeting of American Anti-Slavery Society, Frederick Douglass broke with Garrison over the issue of moral force vs. political participation, May 7–9.

In Christiana, Pa., conflict, Negroes dispersed group of slavecatchers, September 11. One white man was killed and another was wounded.

Negro and white abolitionists smashed into courtroom in Syracuse, N. Y., and rescued a fugitive slave, October 1.

Abolitionist William C. Nell published *Services of Colored Americans in the Wars of 1776 and 1812*, the first extended work on the history of the American Negro.

1852

First edition of *Uncle Tom's Cabin* issued, March 20.

1853

William Wells Brown published *Clotel*, the first novel by an American Negro.

1854

Lincoln University, the first Negro college, founded as Ashmum Institute in Chester County, Pa., January 1.

Anthony Burns, famous fugitive slave, arrested by U.S. deputy marshal in Boston, May 24. Some 2,000 U.S. troops escorted him through the streets of Boston when he was returned to his master on June 3.

Kansas–Nebraska Act repealed Missouri Compromise, opened Northern territory to slavery, May 30.

James Augustine Healy, first American Negro Roman Catholic bishop, ordained a priest in Notre Dame Cathedral, Paris, June 10.

John V. DeGrasse, prominent physician, admitted to Massachusetts Medical Society, August 24.

1855

John Mercer Langston became first American Negro to win an elective office when he was elected clerk of Brownhelm township, Lorain County, Ohio.

1856

Booker Taliaferro Washington born a slave in Franklin County, Va., April 5.

Wilberforce University founded by Methodist Episcopal Church, August 30. University was later sold to AME Church.

1857

Dred Scott decision by U.S. Supreme Court opened federal territory to slavery and denied citizenship to American Negroes, March 6.

1858

John Brown held antislavery convention at Chatham, Canada, May 8. Twelve whites and thirty-four Negroes attended the convention.

The Escape, first play by an American Negro, published by William Wells Brown.

1859

Arkansas legislature required free Negroes to choose between exile and enslavement, February.

At secret meeting in stone quarry near Chambersburg, Pa., John Brown tried to recruit Frederick Douglass for his Virginia raid, August 20. Douglass advised Brown that the raid was ill-advised.

John Brown attacked Harpers Ferry, Va., with 13 white men and five Negroes, October 16–17. Of the five Negroes, two were killed, two were captured and one escaped.

John Brown hanged at Charlestown, Va., December 2.

John Copeland and Shields Green, two Negro members of John Brown's band, hanged at Charlestown, Va., December 16.

The last slave ship, *The Clothilde*, landed shipment of slaves at Mobile Bay, Ala.

1860

U.S. population: 31,443,790. Negro population: 4,441,830 (14.1%).

Abraham Lincoln elected President, November 6.

South Carolina declared "independent commonwealth," December 18.

NEGROES IN CONFEDERACY: Confederacy was first to recognize the Negro as a military factor in the war. As noncombatants, Negroes were muscles and backbone of rebel war effort. South impressed Negro slaves to work in mines, repair railroads and build fortifications, thereby releasing a disproportionately large percentage of able-bodied whites for direct war service. Small number of Negroes enlisted in rebel army, but few Negroes, if any, fired guns in anger. Regiment of 1,400 free Negroes received official recognition in New Orleans. This regiment, however, did no fighting; it later became, by a strange mutation of history, the first Negro regiment officially recognized by the Union Army.

NEGROES IN UNION ARMY: The 178,975 Negro soldiers in the Union Army were organized into 166 all-Negro regiments (145 infantry, 7 cavalry, 12 heavy artillery, 1 light artillery, 1 engineer). Largest number of Negro soldiers came from Louisiana (24,052), followed by Kentucky (23,703) and Tennessee (20,133). Pennsylvania contributed more Negro soldiers than any other Northern state (8,612). Negro soldiers participated in 449 battles, 39 of them major engagements. Sixteen Negro soldiers received Congressional Medals of Honor for gallantry in action. Some 37,638 Negro soldiers lost their lives during the war. Negro soldiers generally received poor equipment and were forced to do a large amount of fatigue duty. Until 1864, Negro soldiers (from private to chaplain) received $7 a month whereas white soldiers received from $13 to $100 a month. In 1863, Negro units, with four exceptions (Fifth Massachusetts Cavalry, Fifty-fourth and Fifty-fifth Massachusetts Volunteers and Twenty-ninth Connecticut Volunteers) were officially designated "United States Colored Troops (USCT)." There were few Negro commissioned officers; the War Department discouraged Negro applicants. The highest-ranking of the 75 to 100 Negro officers was Lt. Colonel Alexander T. Augustana, a surgeon. Some 200,000 Negro civilians were employed by Union Army as laborers, cooks, teamsters and servants.

NEGROES IN UNION NAVY: One out of every four Union sailors was a Negro. Of the 118,044 sailors in the Union Navy, 29,511 were Negroes. At least four Negro sailors won Congressional Medals of Honor.

1861

Confederates attacked Fort Sumter, April 12.

President Lincoln called for 75,000 troops. Loyal Negroes volunteered but were rebuffed. For almost two years, Negroes fought for the right, as one humorist put it, "to be Kilt."

Bull Run, a Union disaster, July 21.

Major General John C. Fremont issued proclamation freeing slaves of Missouri rebels, August 30. Lincoln nullified the proclamation.

School established at Fortress Monroe, Va., with a Negro teacher, Mary Peake, September 17. School laid foundation for Hampton Institute.

Secretary of Navy authorized enlistment of Negro slaves, September 25.

1862

President Lincoln, in message to Congress, recommended gradual, compensated emancipation, March 6.

Congress forbade Union officers and soldiers to aid in capture and return of fugitive slaves, thereby ending what one historian called the "military slave hunt," March 13.

Union and rebel forces fought bloody battle at Shiloh, Tenn., April 6–7.

Congress passed bill which ended slavery in Washington, D.C., April 16.

Three generals jumped gun and organized Negro regiments without official approval. David ("Black David") Hunter began organizing First South Carolina Volunteers, the first Negro regiment, on May 9; Jim Lane began organizing First Kansas Colored Volunteers during first part of August and Ben Butler issued call to free Negroes of New Orleans on August 22.

Gen. David Hunter issued proclamation freeing slaves of Georgia, Florida and South Carolina rebels, May 9. Lincoln revoked the proclamation.

Robert Smalls, a Negro pilot, sailed armed Confederate steamer, "The Planter," out of Charleston, S.C., Harbor and presented it to U.S. Navy, May 13.

Congress authorized President to accept Negroes for military service, July 17.

—Congress passed bill freeing slaves of rebels.

President Lincoln submitted draft of Emancipation Proclamation to his Cabinet, July 22.

President Lincoln received first group of Negroes to confer with U.S. President on a matter of public policy, August 14. He urged Negroes to emigrate to Africa or Central America and was bitterly criticized by Northern Negroes.

Secretary of War authorized General Rufus Saxton to arm up to 5,000 slaves, August 25.

Second Bull Run, another Union disaster, August 30.

Gen. George B. McClellan checked Robert E. Lee's advance at Battle of Antietam, September 17.

President Lincoln, in preliminary Emancipation Proclamation, warned South that he would free slaves in all states in rebellion on 1 January 1863, September 22.

President Lincoln discussed with his Cabinet acquisition of territory for deportation of free Negroes, September 23.

First Louisiana Native Guards, the first Negro regiment to receive official recognition, mustered into Army, September 27. Regiment was composed of free Negroes of New Orleans.

First Kansas Colored Volunteers repulsed and drove off superior force of rebels at Island Mound, Mo., October 28. This was first engagement for Negro troops.

President Lincoln, in message to Congress, recommended the use of federal bonds to provide compensation for states that abolished slavery before 1900, December 1.

1863

President Lincoln signed Emancipation Proclamation which freed slaves in rebel states with exception of 13 parishes (including New Orleans) in Louisiana, 48 counties in West Virginia, 7 counties (including Norfolk) in eastern Virginia, January 1. Proclamation did not apply to slaves in border states.

War Department authorized Massachusetts governor to recruit Negro troops. January 26. The Fifty-fourth Massachusetts Volunteers was first Negro regiment raised in North.

Two Negro infantry regiments, First and Second South Carolina, captured and occupied Jacksonville, Fla., causing panic along Southern seaboard, March 10.

Confederate Congress passed resolution which branded Negro troops and their officers criminals, May 1. Resolution, in effect, doomed captured Negro soldiers to death or slavery.

War Department established Bureau of Colored Troops, launched aggressive campaign for recruitment of Negro soldiers, May 22.

In ill-conceived assault on Port Hudson, La., two Louisiana Negro regiments (First and Third Native Guards) made six gallant but unsuccessful charges on rebel fortification, May 27. A Negro captain, André Cailloux, was hero of day.

Three Negro regiments and small detachment of white troops repulsed division of Texans in bitter, hand-to-hand battle at Milliken's Bend, La., June 7.

Union and rebel troops clashed at Battle of Gettysburg, Pa., July 1–3.

Union troops entered Port Hudson, July 9. With the fall of Vicksburg (on July 4) and Port Hudson, Union controlled Mississippi River and Confederacy was cut into two sections. Eight Negro regiments played important roles in siege of Port Hudson.

Hostility to draft and fear of Negroes, "the cause" of the war and potential competitors in the labor market, led to "New York Draft Riots," one of the bloodiest race riots in American history, July 13–17. Mobs swept through streets, murdered Negroes and hanged them on lamp posts.

Union troops, with First Kansas playing important part, routed rebel force after sharp encounter at Honey Springs, Indian Territory, July 17. Negro troops captured colors of a Texas regiment.

Fifty-fourth Massachusetts Volunteers, an all-Negro regiment composed of free Negroes of North, made famous charge on Fort Wagner in the Charleston, S.C., Harbor, July 18. William H. Carney, a Negro sergeant, won Congressional Medal of Honor for his bravery in the charge.

President Lincoln issued "eye-for-an-eye" order, warned Confederacy that U.S. would shoot a rebel POW for every Negro POW shot, and would condemn a rebel POW to a life of hard labor for every Negro POW sold into slavery, July 30. Order had restraining influence on Confederate government, though individual commanders and soldiers continued to murder captured Negro soldiers.

1864

Confederate troops decisively defeated three Negro and six white regiments and units of cavalry and artillery at Battle of Olustee, about 50 miles from Jacksonville, Fla., February 20.

Nathan Bedford Forrest, the Confederate general, captured Fort Pillow, Tenn., and massacred the inhabitants, sparing, the official report said, neither soldier nor civilian, black nor white, male nor female, April 12. Fort was held by a predominantly-Negro force.

Surrounded by a superior rebel force, First Kansas Colored Volunteers smashed through rebel lines and sustained heavy casualties at Poison Spring, Ark., April 18. Wounded Negro prisoners were murdered by Confederate troops.

Fighting rearguard action, six infantry regiments checked rebel troops at Jenkins' Ferry, Saline River, Ark., April 30. Enraged by atrocities committed at Poison Spring (above), Second Kansas Colored Volunteers went into battle shouting, "Remember Poison Spring!" Regiment captured rebel battery.

Ulysses S. Grant crossed the Rapidan and began his bloody duel with Robert E. Lee, May 4. At same time, Ben Butler's Army of the James moved on Lee's forces. Negro division in Grant's Army did not play a prominent role in Wilderness Campaign, but Ben Butler gave his Negro infantrymen and his 1,800 Negro cavalrymen highly visible assignments. Negro troops of Army of the James were first Union soldiers to take possession of James River (at Wilson's Wharf Landing, Fort Powhatan and City Point).

Two regiments of Negro soldiers, First and Tenth U.S.C.T., repulsed attack by famous rebel general, Fitzhugh Lee, May 24. Also participating in battle at Wilson's Wharf Landing, on bank of James River, were a small detachment of white Union troops and a battery of light artillery.

Nathan Bedford Forrest routed Union forces at Battle of Brice's Cross Roads, near Guntown, Miss., June 10. Brigade of Negro troops checked rebel advance and covered the retreat.

Grant outwitted Lee by shifting campaign from Cold Harbor to

Petersburg, June 15. Surprise attack by General W. F. ("Baldy") Smith succeeded but Smith hesitated and permitted rebels to reinforce their lines. General Charles J. Paine's all-Negro division spearheaded the attack, knocked mile-wide hole in Petersburg defenses, captured 200 of 300 rebels captured that day.

—Congress passed bill equalizing pay, arms, equipment and medical services of Negro troops.

Siege of Petersburg and Richmond, June 16—April, 1865. Thirty-two Negro infantry regiments and two Negro cavalry regiments were involved in siege. Negro troops were especially prominent in following engagements: Deep Bottom, August 14–16; Darbytown Road, October 13: Fair Oaks, October 27–28; Hatcher's Run, October 27–28.

In famous duel between USS "Kearsage" and CSS "Alabama" off Cherbourg, France, a Negro sailor, Joachim Pease, displayed "marked coolness" and won Congressional Medal of Honor, June 19.

General A. J. Smith with about 14,000 men, including a brigade of Negro troops, defeated Nathan B. Forrest at Harrisburg, near Tupelo, Miss., July 15.

Union exploded mine under rebel lines near Petersburg, committed three white and one Negro division and was soundly defeated, July 30. Negro division of Ninth Corps sustained heaviest casualties in ill-planned attack. Only Union success of day was scored by Forty-third U.S.C.T. which captured about 200 rebels and two stands of colors. Brave Negro sergeant, Decatur Dorsey of Thirty-ninth U.S.C.T., won Congressional Medal of Honor.

John Lawson, a Negro gunner on flagship of Admiral David Farragut, exhibited marked courage in Battle of Mobile Bay and won Congressional Medal of Honor, August 5.

William Tecumseh Sherman occupied Atlanta, September 2.

In series of battles around Chaffin's Farm in suburb of Richmond, Negro troops captured entrenchments at New Market Heights, made gallant but unsuccessful assault on Fort Gilmer and helped repulse Confederate counter-attack on Fort Harrison, September 29–30. Twelve Negroes won Congressional Medals of Honor on first day and one on second day.

New Orleans Tribune, first Negro daily newspaper, began publication as daily, in French and English, October 4.

Operating in support of Sherman, who was moving north after his "march through Georgia," mixed force (seven Negro and five white infantry regiments) attempted to establish foothold near Grahamsville, S.C., and was repulsed, November 30.

Largest all-Negro unit in history of U.S. Army, Twenty-fifth Corps, was established in Army of the James, December 3.

With mixed cavalry force which included Fifth and Sixth Colored Cavalry regiments, Major General George Stoneman invaded southwest Virginia and destroyed salt mines at Saltville, Va., December 10–29. The Sixth Cavalry was particularly brilliant in an engagement near Marion, Va.

In one of decisive battles of war, two brigades of Negro troops helped crush one of the South's finest armies at the Battle of Nashville, December 15–16. Negro troops opened the battle on first day and successfully engaged right of rebel line. On second day, Colonel Charles R. Thompson's Negro brigade made brilliant charge up Overton Hill. Thirteenth U.S.C.T. sustained more casualties than any other regiment involved in the battle.

1865

Robert E. Lee, with his back against the wall, recommended arming of slaves, January 11.

General Paine's Negro division participated in brilliant Fort Fisher, N.C., expedition which closed Confederate's last major port, January 15.

General Lee said it was "not only expedient but necessary" that Confederate Army use Negro slaves as soldiers, January 17.

Congress passed the Thirteenth Amendment which, on ratification, abolished slavery in America, January 31.

John S. Rock became the first Negro admitted to practice before the U.S. Supreme Court, February 1.

Henry Highland Garnet, first Negro to preach in the Capitol, delivered memorial sermon on abolition of slavery, February 12.

Rebels abandoned Charleston, S.C., February 18. First Union troops in city included Twenty-first U.S.C.T., followed by two companies of Fifty-fourth Massachusetts Volunteers.

Congress established Freedmen's Bureau to aid refugees and freedmen, March 3.

—Federal government chartered Freedmen's Savings and Trust Bank with business confined to Negroes.

Jefferson Davis signed bill authorizing use of Negro slaves as soldiers in Confederate Army, March 13.

Second Brigade of Second Division of all-Negro Twenty-fifth Corps was among first Union troops to enter Petersburg, April 2.

Fifth Massachusetts Colored Cavalry and units of Twenty-fifth Corps were in vanguard of Union troops entering Richmond, April 3.

Nine Negro regiments in three brigades of General John Hawkins' division helped smash defenses of Fort Blakely, Ala., April 9. Capture of fort led to fall of Mobile. Sixty-eighth U.S.C.T. had highest number of casualties in engagement.

Second Division of all-Negro Twenty-fifth Corps was one of units which chased Lee's tattered army from Petersburg to Appomattox Courthouse, April 3–9. Division and white troops were moving on Lee's trapped army with fixed bayonets when Confederates surrendered.

President Lincoln recommended suffrage for Negro veterans and Negroes who were "very intelligent," April 11.

Death of Abraham Lincoln, Washington, D.C., April 15.

Two white regiments and a Negro regiment, the Sixty-second U.S.C.T., fought last action of war at White's Ranch, Texas, May 13.

Negroes in Norfolk, Va., held mass meeting and demanded equal rights and ballots, May 11. Other equal rights mass meetings were held by Negroes in Petersburg, Va., June 6; Vicksburg, Miss., June 19; Nashville, Tenn., August 7–11; Raleigh, N.C., September 29–October 3; Richmond, Va., September 18; Jackson, Miss., October 7; Charleston, S.C., November 20–25.

Patrick Francis Healy, first Negro to win Ph.D. degree, passed final exams at Louvain in Belgium, July 26.

Thaddeus Stevens, powerful U. S. congressman, urged confiscation of estates of Confederate leaders and distribution of land to adult freedmen in 40 acre lots, September 6.

Thirteenth Amendment became part of U.S. Constitution, December 18.

White legislatures in former rebel states enacted Black Codes which restricted the rights and freedom of movement of freedmen, fall and winter.

1866

Fisk University opened, January 9.

Thaddeus Stevens proposed measure authorizing President to set aside land to be distributed to freedmen in 40 acre lots, February 5. Measure was defeated by vote of 126 to 37.

Civil Rights Bill passed over President's veto, April 9.

Race riot, Memphis, Tenn., May 1–3. Forty-six Negroes, two white liberals killed; about 75 wounded. Ninety homes, twelve schools and four churches burned.

Race riot, New Orleans, La., July 30. Thirty-five killed; more than one hundred wounded.

Edward G. Walker, son of abolitionist David Walker, and Charles L.

Mitchell elected to Massachusetts House of Representatives, the first Negroes elected to an American legislative assembly.

1867

Bill giving suffrage to Negroes in District of Columbia passed over President Johnson's veto, January 8.

Negro delegation, led by Frederick Douglass, called on President Johnson and urged ballots for ex-slaves, February 7.

Morehouse College opened, February.

First of series of Reconstruction Acts passed by Congress, March 2. Acts divided former Confederate states into five military districts under command of generals. Elections were ordered for constitutional conventions and freedmen were given the right to vote.

First national meeting of Ku Klux Klan, Maxwell House, Nashville, April.

Howard University opened, May 1. Talladega College also opened in 1867 and Atlanta University was chartered.

The Knights of White Camelia, a secret white supremacist organization, founded in Louisiana, May.

1868

South Carolina constitutional convention met in Charleston, January 14. This was the first assembly of its kind in the West with a majority of Negro delegates; seventy-six of the 124 delegates were Negroes.

William Edward Burghardt Du Bois born Great Barrington, Mass., February 23.

Hampton Institute opened, April.

Oscar J. Dunn, an ex-slave, formally installed as lieutenant governor of Louisiana, the highest elective office held by an American Negro, June 13. Negroes were later elected lieutenant governors of Mississippi and South Carolina.

First General Assembly of South Carolina Reconstruction government met Janney's Hall, Columbia, July 6. Eighty-four of the 157 legislators were Negroes.

Fourteenth Amendment became part of Constitution, July 28.

Death of Thaddeus Stevens, architect of Radical Reconstruction program, Washington, D.C., August 11.

Race riot, New Orleans, September 22. Other race riots in Louisiana in 1868 were at Opelousas, September 28; St. Bernard Parish, October 26.

1869

Ebenezer Don Carlos Bassett became minister to Haiti, April 16. Bassett was probably first Negro to receive an appointment in diplomatic service.

1870

U.S. population: 39,818,449. Negro population: 4,880,009 (12.7%).

Jonathan Jasper Wright became associate justice of South Carolina Supreme Court, February 2.

Hiram R. Revels succeeded Jefferson Davis as U.S. senator from Mississippi, February 25. Revels was first Negro in Congress.

Fifteenth Amendment became part of Constitution, March 30.

American Anti-Slavery Society dissolved, April 9.

First of series of Enforcement Acts (Ku Klux Klan Acts) put federal elections in hands of federal officials and guaranteed civil and political rights of freedmen through federal courts, May 31.

Governor Holden declared state of insurrection in two North Carolina counties, March 7 and July 8.

James W. Smith of South Carolina entered West Point, July 1. Smith, the first Negro student, did not graduate; he was separated June 26, 1874.

Joseph H. Rainey, first Negro in House of Representatives, sworn in as congressman from South Carolina, December 12.

Colored Methodist Episcopal Church organized Jackson, Tenn., December 16.

Robert H. Wood elected mayor of Natchez, Miss., December.

1871

Race Riot, Meridian, Miss., March 6.

Fisk Jubilee Singers began first tour, October 6.

President Grant issued proclamation against KKK in South Carolina, suspended writ of habeas corpus in nine counties, October 17.

1872

Paul Laurence Dunbar born Dayton, Ohio, June 27.

Charlotte E. Ray, first Negro woman lawyer, graduated from Howard University Law School, February 27. Attorney Ray, the first American woman to graduate from a university law school, was admitted to practice, April 23.

John Henry Conyers of South Carolina entered Annapolis, September 21. He later resigned.

P. B. S. Pinchback became acting governor of Louisiana on the impeachment of the governor, December 11.

1873

P. B. S. Pinchback elected to the U.S. Senate, January 15.

Colfax Massacre, Easter Sunday morning, Grant Parish, La., April 13. More than 60 Negroes killed.

Henry E. Hayne, secretary of state, accepted as student at University of South Carolina, October 7.

W. C. Handy born in Florence, Ala., November 16.

Richard T. Greener, first Negro graduate of Harvard University, named professor of metaphysics at the University of South Carolina, November. University had several Negro students and an interracial board of trustees.

1874

Death of Charles Sumner, militant advocate of Negro rights, Washington, D.C., March 11.

The White League, racist organization, founded at Opelousas, La., April 27.

Freedmen's Bank closed, June 29. Negro depositors had some $3,000,000 in the bank.

Patrick Francis Healy, S.J., Ph.D., inaugurated as president of Georgetown University, oldest Catholic university in America, July 31.

Sixteen Negroes taken from jail in Tennessee by hooded men and shot, August 26.

Coushatta Massacre, Coushatta, La., August 30. Several Negroes and Republican office-holders slain. Governor declared martial law.

Race riot, Vicksburg, Miss., December 7. Thirty-five Negroes killed.

President issued proclamation on violence in Mississippi, December 21.

1875

Civil Rights Bill enacted by Congress, March 1. Bill gave Negroes the right to equal treatment in inns, public conveyances, theaters and other places of public amusement.

Blanche Kelso Bruce entered U.S. Senate, March 5. Mississippi politician was only Negro to serve full term in Senate.

James A. Healy, first Negro Roman Catholic bishop in America, consecrated in Cathedral at Portland, Me., June 2.

Mary McLeod Bethune born Mayesville, S.C., July 10.

Race conflict, Yazoo City, Miss., September 1. Ten to twenty Negroes killed.

Race conflict, Clinton, Miss., September 4. Twenty to eighty Negro leaders and Negro Republicans killed.

Mississippi governor requested federal troops to protect rights of Negro voters, September 8. Request refused.

Conservatives won Mississippi election, November 2. "The Mississippi Plan"—staged riots, political assassinations and massacres and social and economic intimidation—was used later to overthrow Reconstruction governments in South Carolina and Louisiana.

1876

Senate, after three years of debate and controversy, declined to seat P. B. S. Pinchback by a vote of 32 to 29, March 8.

Race conflict, Hamburg, S.C., July 8. Five Negroes killed.

President issued proclamation commanding "Rifle Clubs" of South Carolina to disband, October 17.

President Grant sent federal troops to South Carolina, October 26.

Federal troops sent to Tallahassee, Fla., November 9.

Edward A. Bouchet received Ph.D. degree in physics at Yale University, the first Negro awarded Ph.D. by an American university.

1877

At conference in Wormley Hotel in Washington, representatives of Rutherford B. Hayes and representatives of the South confirmed an agreement which paved way for election of Hayes as President and withdrawal of federal troops from the South, February 26.

President Hayes appointed Frederick Douglass Marshal of District of Columbia, March 18.

Federal troops withdrawn from Columbia, S.C., April 10. Democrats took over state government.

Federal troops withdrawn from New Orleans, La., April 20. Democrats took over state government.

Henry O. Flipper graduated from West Point, the first Negro graduate, June 15.

1879

Death of William Lloyd Garrison, New York City, May 24.

Southern Negroes fled political and economic exploitation in "Exodus of 1879."

1880

U.S. population: 50,155,783. Negro population: 6,580,793 (13.1%).

1881

Frederick Douglass appointed Recorder of Deeds for District of Columbia, May 17.

Blanche Kelso Bruce appointed Register of Treasury by President Garfield, May 19.

Booker T. Washington opened Tuskegee Institute, July 4.

Tennessee kicked off modern segregation movement with Jim Crow railroad car law. Florida followed in 1887; Mississippi, 1888; Texas, 1889; Louisiana, 1890; Alabama, Kentucky, Arkansas, Georgia, 1891; South Carolina, 1898; North Carolina, 1899; Virginia, 1900; Maryland, 1904; Oklahoma, 1907.

1883

Death of Sojourner Truth, Battle Creek, Mich., November 26.

Supreme Court declared Civil Rights Act of 1875 unconstitutional, October 15.

1884

Race Riot, Danville, Va., May 19.

John Roy Lynch, former congressman, elected temporary chairman of Republican convention, became first Negro to preside over deliberations of national political party, June 3.

Death of Robert Brown Elliott, Reconstruction politician, New Orleans, August 9.

"Scramble for Africa" organized at international conference in Berlin, November 15–February 26.

1886

Carrollton Massacre, Carrollton, Miss., March 17. Twenty Negroes killed.

1889

Asa Philip Randolph born Crescent City, Fla., April 15.

1890

U.S. population: 62,947,714. Negro population: 7,488,676 (11.9%).

Mississippi constitutional convention began systematic exclusion of Negroes from political life of South, August 12–November 1. The Mississippi Plan (literacy and "understanding" tests) was later adopted with embellishments by other states: South Carolina, 1895; Louisiana, 1898; North Carolina, 1900; Alabama, 1901; Virginia, 1901; Georgia, 1908; Oklahoma, 1910.

1891

Lodge Bill, which provided for federal supervisors of elections, buried in Senate, January 22.

Chicago's Provident Hospital incorporated with first training school for Negro nurses, January 23.

1893

Walter Francis White born Atlanta, Ga., July 1.

Dr. Daniel Hale Williams performed "world's first successful heart operation" at Chicago's Provident Hospital, July 9.

1895

Death of Frederick Douglass, Anacostia Heights, D.C., February 20.

North Carolina legislature, dominated by Negro Republicans and white Populists, adjourned to mark the death of Frederick Douglass, February 21.

New Orleans Negro laborers attacked by whites, March 11–12. Troops called out.

Booker T. Washington delivered "Atlanta Compromise" address at Cotton Exposition in Atlanta, Ga., September 18.

1896

Supreme Court decision (*Plessy v. Ferguson*) upheld doctrine of "separate but equal," May 18.

1898

Death of Blanche Kelso Bruce, Washington, D.C., March 17.

Race Riot, Wilmington, N.C., November 10. Eight Negroes killed.

American troops, including Tenth Cavalry, drove Spanish forces from entrenched positions at La Guasimas, Cuba, June 24.

Tenth Cavalry made famous charge at El Caney and relieved Theodore Roosevelt's Rough Riders, July 1. Four Negro regiments in regular army were conspicuous in fighting around Santiago in Spanish-American War. Sixteen regiments of Negro volunteers were also raised during the war.

Bob Cole's "*A Trip to Coontown*," first musical comedy written by a Negro for Negro talent, produced.

1899

Edward Kennedy ("Duke") Ellington born Washington, D.C., April 4.

1900

U.S. population: 75,994,575. Negro population: 8,833,994 (11.6%).

Daniel Louis Armstrong born New Orleans, July 4.

Race riot, New Orleans, July 24–27. Several persons injured. Negro school and 30 Negro homes burned.

Death of James Augustine Healy, Negro Roman Catholic bishop, Portland, Me., August 5.

National Negro Business League organized at Boston meeting, August 23–24.

1901

Death of Hiram R. Revels, Holly Springs, Miss., January 16.

Term of George H. White, last of post-Reconstruction congressmen, ended, March 4.

Booker T. Washington dined at White House with President Roosevelt and was criticized in the South, October 16.

1903

Supreme Court decision upheld clauses in Alabama Constitution which disfranchised Negroes, April 27.

Publication of W. E. B. Du Bois' *The Souls of Black Folk* crystallized opposition to Booker T. Washington's program of social and political subordination.

1905

Group of Negro intellectuals organized Niagara Movement at meeting near Niagara Falls, July 11–13. Delegates from 14 states, led by W. E. B. Du Bois and William Monroe Trotter, demanded abolition of all distinctions based on race.

1906

Death of Paul Laurence Dunbar, poet, Dayton, Ohio, February 9.

Group of Negro soldiers raided Brownsville, Texas, in retaliation for racial insults, August 13. One white man killed, two wounded. President Roosevelt ordered discharge of three companies of 25th Regiment.

Race Riot, Atlanta, Ga., September 22–24. Ten Negroes and two whites killed. Martial law proclaimed.

1908

Thurgood Marshall born Baltimore, Md., July 2.

Race Riot, Springfield, Ill., August 14–19. Troops called out. Riot led to founding of NAACP.

Jack Johnson defeated Tommy Burns at Sydney, Australia, for heavyweight championship, December 26.

1909

NAACP founded, February 12. Call for organizational meeting was issued on 100th anniversary of Abraham Lincoln's birth.

Commander Robert E. Peary reached North Pole, April 6. Only American with Peary was man he identified as "my Negro assistant," Matthew H. Henson.

1910

U.S. population: 93,402,151. Negro population: 9,827,763 (10.7%).
National Urban League organized in New York, April.

1911

William H. Lewis appointed assistant attorney general of the United
States, March 26.

1912

First published blues composition, W. C. Handy's *Memphis Blues*,
went on sale in Memphis, Tenn., September 27.

1913

Death of Harriet Tubman, Auburn, N.Y., March 10.

1915

Supreme Court outlawed "grandfather clause," June 21.

Ku Klux Klan received charter from Fulton County, Ga., Superior
Court, July. Modern Klan spread to Alabama and other Southern states
and reached height of influence in the twenties. By 1924, organization
was strong in Oklahoma, California, Oregon, Indiana, Ohio. At its
height, it had an estimated 4 million members.

Great Migration began. Some 2,000,000 Southern Negroes moved to
northern industrial centers.

NAACP led protest demonstrations against showing of movie, *Birth
of a Nation*.

Association for the study of Negro Life and History founded by
Carter G. Woodson, September 9.

Death of Booker T. Washington, Tuskegee, Ala., November 14.

First Spingarn Medal, which is presented annually by NAACP to an
outstanding American Negro, was awarded February 2, 1915 to Biolo-
gist Ernest E. Just, who had conducted pioneering research on fertiliza-
tion, artificial parthenogenesis and cell division. Other Negro scientists
who have won the award include George Washington Carver, the agricultural chemist, and Dr. Percy Julian, the industrial chemist. Carver,
who was born of slave parents on a farm near Diamond Grove, Mo.,
about 1864, made 100 products from the sweet potato, almost 100 from
the pecan and 50 from the peanut. He also developed several products
from the clays of the South and was the first to use soybeans in paint
making. Dr. Percy Julian made a successful synthesis of the drug
physostigmine in 1935. The drug is used today in the treatment of glau-
coma. Dr. Julian's research work on the soybean led to the prepara-

tion of a male sex hormone, a weatherproof covering for battleships and a product which became the base of the famous Aero-Foam fire extinguishers which were used in World War II. Among other Negro scientists who have made basic contributions are Lloyd Hall, an industrial chemist who received over 80 patents on the preparation and curing of salts, spices and food products and Dr. William A. Hinton, who developed the famous Hinton test for detection of syphilis.

1916
Punitive force under Brig. Gen. John J. Pershing crossed Mexican border in pursuit of Pancho Villa, March 15. Two Negro regiments, 10th Cavalry and 24th Infantry, were part of American contingent.

1917
America entered World War, April 6.

Race riot, East St. Louis, Ill., July 1-3. Estimates of number of Negroes killed ranged from 40 to 200. Martial law declared.

Some 10,000 Negroes marched down Fifth Avenue, New York City, in silent parade protesting lynchings and racial indignities, July 28.

Race riot, Houston, Texas, between soldiers of 24th Infantry Regiment and white citizens, August 23. Two Negroes and 17 whites killed. Martial law declared. Thirteen members of regiment were later hanged.

Supreme Court decision struck down Louisville, Ky., ordinance which required Negroes and whites to live in separate blocks, November 5.

Jazz migration began. Joe Oliver left New Orleans and settled in Chicago where he was joined by Louis Armstrong and other pioneer jazz stars.

1918
Race riot, Chester, Pa., July 25-28. Five killed.

Race riot, Philadelphia, Pa., July 26-29. Four killed, 60 or more injured.

Armistice signed, ending World War I, November 11. Negroes furnished about 370,000 soldiers and 1,400 commissioned officers. A little more than half of these troops saw service in Europe. Three Negro regiments—369th, 371st and 372nd—received Croix de Guerre for valor. The 369 was first American unit to reach Rhine. Several individual Negro soldiers were decorated for bravery. First soldiers in American Army to be decorated for bravery in France were two Negroes, Henry Johnson and Needham Roberts.

Death of George H. White, ex-congressman, Philadelphia, December 28.

1919

First Pan-African Congress, organized by W. E. B. Du Bois, met Grand Hotel, Paris, February 19–21.

Race riots, Longview and Gregg County, Texas, July 13. Martial law declared. There were 26 race riots during the "Red Summer" of 1919. Six persons were killed and 150 were wounded in Washington, D.C., riot, July 19–23. Troops were called out to put down Chicago race riot which erupted on July 27; fifteen whites and 23 Negroes were killed and 537 were injured. Five whites and 25 to 50 Negroes were killed in rioting at Elaine, Phillips County, Arkansas, October 1.

1920

U.S. population: 105,710,620. Negro population: 10,463,131 (9.9%).

National convention of Marcus Garvey's Universal Improvement Association opened in Liberty Hall in Harlem, August 1. The next night Garvey addressed some 25,000 Negroes in Madison Square Garden. Garvey's black nationalist movement reached peak of its influence in 1920–21.

Emperor Jones opened at the Provincetown Theater with Charles Gilpin in the title role, November 3.

1921

Shuffle Along, first of a series of popular musicals featuring Negro talent, opened at the 63rd Street Music Hall, New York City, May 23.

Race riot, Tulsa, Oklahoma, June 1. Twenty-one whites and 60 Negroes were killed.

The Negro Renaissance, a period of extraordinary activity on the part of Negro artists and an equally extraordinary receptivity on the part of the white public, reached a peak in the twenties. Among the writers who contributed to the movement were Claude McKay, Harlem Shadows, 1922; Jean Toomer, Cane, 1923; Alain Locke, The New Negro, 1925; Langston Hughes, The Weary Blues, 1926; Countee Cullen, Color, 1925; James Weldon Johnson, God's Trombones, 1927.

Doctor of Philosophy degrees awarded for first time to Negro women —Eva B. Dykes, English, Radcliffe; Sadie T. Mossell, Economics, University of Pennsylvania; Georgiana R. Simpson, German, University of Chicago.

1922

Death of Colonel Charles R. Young while on expedition to Lagos, Nigeria, January 8.

Death of Bert Williams, New York City, March 11.

Louisiana governor conferred with President on Ku Klux Klan violence in the state, November 20.

1923

Governor said Oklahoma was in a "state of rebellion and insurrection" because of Ku Klux Klan activities, declared martial law, September 15.

Department of Labor estimated that almost 500,000 Negroes had left South during previous 12 months, October 24.

Runnin' Wild opened Colonial Theater, Broadway, October 29. Miller and Lyles production introduced Charleston to New York and world.

1924

Dixie to Broadway, "the first real revue by Negroes," opened at Broadhurst Theater, New York City, with Florence Mills in starring role, October 29.

Fletcher Henderson, first musician to make name with big jazz band, opened at Roseland Ballroom on Broadway.

1925

Ossian Sweet, prominent Detroit doctor, and others arrested on murder charge stemming from the firing into a mob in front of Sweet home in previously all-white area, September 8. Sweet was defended by Clarence Darrow who won an acquittal in second trial.

Louis Armstrong recorded first of Hot Five and Hot Seven Recordings which influenced direction of jazz, November 11.

1927

Supreme Court decision struck down Texas law barring Negroes from voting in "white" primary, March 7.

Death of Florence Mills, dancer and singer, New York City, November 1.

Duke Ellington opened at Cotton Club, December 4.

Marcus Garvey deported as undesirable alien, December.

1929

Martin Luther King, Jr., born Atlanta, Ga., January 15.

Oscar DePriest sworn in as congressman, April 15.

"Jobs-for-Negroes" campaign began in Chicago with picketing of chain grocery store on South Side, fall. The "Spend Your Money

Where You Can Work" campaign spread to New York, Cleveland, Los Angeles and continued throughout the Depression.

Collapse of stock market, October 29.

1930

U.S. population: 122,775,046. Negro population: 11,891,143 (9.7%). *The Green Pastures* opened at Mansfield Theater with Richard B. Harrison as "De Lawd," February 26.

President Hoover named Judge John J. Parker of North Carolina as justice of U.S. Supreme Court, March 31. The NAACP launched a nation-wide campaign against appointment. Parker was not confirmed by Senate.

Death of Charles Gilpin, actor, May 6.

1931

First of Scottsboro trials began in Scottsboro, Ala., April 6. Trial of nine Negro youths accused of raping two white women on freight train became cause célèbre.

1933

NAACP fired first gun in its attack on segregation and discrimination in education, filed suit against University of North Carolina on behalf of Thomas Hocutt, March 15. Case was lost on technicality when president of Negro college refused to certify scholastic record of plaintiff.

1934

Arthur L. Mitchell defeated Oscar DePriest, elected to Congress as first Negro Democratic congressman, November 7.

At conference in New York City, representatives of NAACP and American Fund for Public Service planned coordinated legal campaign against segregation and discrimination, October 26. Charles H. Houston, vice dean of Howard University Law School, was named to direct campaign.

1935

Joe Louis defeated Primo Carnera at Yankee Stadium, June 25.

Italy invaded Ethiopia, October 2–4. American Negro groups protested and raised funds.

Maryland Court of Appeals ordered University of Maryland to admit Donald Murray, November 5.

Swing Age began with commercial success of big bands. Late thirties were heydays of big bands of Chick Webb, Andy Kirk, Cab Calloway, Count Basie, Jimmie Lunceford and Duke Ellington.

National Council of Negro Women founded in New York City with Mary McLeod Bethune as president, December 5.

Langston Hughes' play, *The Mulatto*, began long run on Broadway.

1936

Atty. Charles W. Anderson entered Kentucky House of Representatives, January 11.

Jesse Owens won four gold medals at Olympics, Berlin, August 9.

NAACP filed first suit in campaign to equalize teachers' salaries and educational facilities, December 8. *Gibbs v. Board of Education* in Montgomery County, Md., was first of series of suits which resulted in elimination of wage differentials between Negro and white teachers.

Mary McLeod Bethune, founder-president of Bethune-Cookman College, named director of Division of Negro Affairs of the National Youth Administration.

1937

William H. Hastie confirmed as judge of Federal District Court in Virgin Islands, the first Negro federal judge, March 26.

Joe Louis defeated James J. Braddock for heavyweight championship, June 22.

Death of Bessie Smith, Clarksdale, Mississippi, September 26.

1938

Death of Joe (King) Oliver, pioneer Negro jazz star, Savannah, Ga., April 10.

First Negro woman legislator, Crystal Bird Fauset of Philadelphia, elected to Pennsylvania House of Representatives, November 8.

Supreme Court ruled that state must provide equal educational facilities for Negroes within its boundaries, December 12. Lloyd Gaines, the plaintiff in the case, disappeared and has never been located.

1939

Jane Matilda Bolin appointed judge of Court of Domestic Relations, New York City, by Mayor Fiorello LaGuardia and became the first Negro woman judge in U.S., July 22.

NAACP Legal Defense and Educational Fund incorporated as a separate organization, October 11.

1940

U. S. population: 131,669,275. Negro population: 12,865,518 (9.8%).

Richard Wright's *Native Son* published, February.

Virginia legislature chose "Carry Me Back to Ole Virginny" as state song, April. Song was written by Negro composer James A. Bland (1854–1911).

Death of Marcus Garvey, London, England, June 10.

The White House announced that Benjamin Oliver Davis, Sr. had been appointed brigadier general, the first Negro general in the history of the armed forces, October 16.

1941

Yancey Williams, a Howard University student, filed suit against the Secretary of War and other government officials, asked court to order them to consider his application for enlistment in Army Air Corps as a flying cadet, January 15.

The War Department announced formation of first Army Air Corps squadron for Negro cadets, January 16.

Mass meetings were held in 24 states to protest against discrimination in the national defense effort, January 26.

A Negro researcher helped save thousands of lives during World War II. Dr. Charles Richard Drew set up and ran the pioneer blood plasma bank in the Presbyterian Hospital in New York City. This bank served as one of the models for the system of banks operated later by the American Red Cross. On October 1, 1940, in response to a British SOS, Dr. Drew was appointed full-time medical director of the plasma project of Great Britain. As director of the first great experiment in the gross production of human plasma, Dr. Drew contributed many technical solutions. The report of the operation of this project served as a guide for later developments in the United States and Europe. When the project ended in 1941, Dr. Drew became the first director of the new project charged with the responsibility of setting up donor stations to collect blood plasma for the American armed services. He resigned three months later and became professor of surgery at Howard University. Under an American Red Cross ruling in World War II, Dr. Drew's blood, ironically enough, would have been segregated from the blood of white donors.

National Urban League presented one-hour program over nationwide radio network, urged equal participation for Negroes in national defense program, March 30.

Dr. Robert Weaver named director of section in Office of Production

Management devoted to integration of Negroes into the national defense program, April 18.

Bus companies of New York City agreed to hire Negro drivers and mechanics, April 18. Agreement ended four-week boycott by New York Negroes.

Supreme Court ruled in railroad Jim Crow case brought by Congressman Arthur Mitchell that separate facilities must be substantially equal, April 28.

President Roosevelt conferred with A. Philip Randolph and other leaders of the March on Washington Movement and urged them to call off a scheduled demonstration, June 18. Randolph refused, said 100,000 Negroes would march on Washington on July 1 to protest discrimination and segregation in national defense program.

President Roosevelt issued Executive Order 8802 which forbade racial and religious discrimination in war industries, government training programs and government industries, June 25. Randolph called off scheduled March on Washington same day.

Death of Ferdinand ("Jelly Roll") Morton, pioneer jazz pianist, in Los Angeles, July 10.

President Roosevelt appointed FEP Commission, July 19.

—First U.S. Army flying school for Negro cadets dedicated at Tuskegee, Ala.

Negro private and white military policeman shot to death on bus in North Carolina during fight between Negro and white soldiers, August 6. This was the first of a series of serious racial incidents (between Negro and white soldiers and Negro soldiers and white civilians) which continued throughout the war.

Dorie Miller of Waco, Texas, messman on USS "Arizona," manned machine gun during Pearl Harbor attack and downed four enemy planes, December 7. He was later awarded Navy Cross.

1942

Race riot, Sojourner Truth Homes, Detroit, February 28.

First cadets graduated from advanced flying school at Tuskegee, March 7.

Bernard W. Robinson, Harvard medical student, made ensign in U.S. Naval Reserve and became first Negro to win a commission in the U.S. Navy, June 18.

Group of Negro and white believers in direct, nonviolent action organized Congress of Racial Equality in Chicago, June. Group staged first sit-in that month in Chicago restaurant. National CORE organization was founded in June, 1943.

"Booker T. Washington," first U.S. merchant ship commanded by a Negro captain (Hugh Mulzac), launched at Wilmington, Del., September 29.

William L. Dawson elected to Congress from Chicago, November 3.

1943

William H. Hastie, civilian aide to Secretary of War, resigned in protest against Army's policy of segregation and discrimination, January 5.

Death of George Washington Carver, Tuskegee, Ala., January 5.

Porgy and Bess opened on Broadway with Anne Brown and Todd Duncan in starring roles, February 28.

Riot at Mobile shipyard over upgrading of 12 Negro workers, May 25. Troops called out.

President Edwin Barclay, first president of Negro country to pay official visit to an American President, arrived at White House, May 26.

99th Pursuit Squadron flew first combat mission, attacked Pantelleria, in Mediterranean Theater, June 2.

"Mexican Zoot Suit riots," Los Angeles, June 6.

Race riot, Beaumont, Texas, June 16. Two killed; martial law declared.

Race riot, Detroit, Mich., June 21. Thirty-four killed. Federal troops called out.

Lt. Charles Hall, Brazil, Ind., became first U.S. Negro flier to shoot down Nazi plane, July 2.

Race riot, Harlem, August 1-2.

Theater Guild presentation of *Othello* opened at Shubert Theater with Paul Robeson in title role, October 19. Production ran for 296 performances, set record for Shakespearean drama on Broadway.

Death of Fats Waller, Kansas City, December 15.

1944

Supreme Court (*Smith v. Allwright*) banned white primary, April 3.

United Negro College Fund incorporated, April 24.

Adam Clayton Powell elected first Negro congressman from East, August 1.

Anna Lucasta, starring Hilda Simms and Frederick O'Neal, opened on Broadway, August 20.

1945

First state FEPC law signed by New York governor, March 12.

B. O. Davis, Jr., named commander of Godman Field, Kentucky, July 1.

V-J Day, September 2. A total of 1,154,720 Negroes were inducted or drafted into the armed services.

One thousand white students walked out of three Gary, Ind., schools to protest school integration, September 18.

Irving C. Mollison, Chicago Republican, sworn in as U.S. Customs Court judge in New York City, November 3.

1946

Death of Countee Cullen, poet, New York City, January 9.

Race riot, Columbia, Tenn., February 26. Two killed, 10 wounded.

Col. B. O. Davis, Jr., assumed command of Lockbourne Air Base, March 13.

Mrs. Emma Clarissa Clement, Louisville, Ky., named "American Mother of the Year" by the Golden Rule Foundation, May 1.

William H. Hastie confirmed as governor of Virgin Islands, May 1.

Supreme Court banned segregation in interstate bus travel, June 3.

Death of Jack Johnson, Raleigh, N.C., June 10.

Race riot, Athens, Ala., August 10. Fifty to 100 Negroes injured.

Race riot, Philadelphia, September 29.

President Truman created Committee on Civil Rights by Executive Order 9808, December 5.

1947

CORE sent first "Freedom Rider" group through South, April 9.

Jackie Robinson joined Brooklyn Dodgers, first Negro in organized baseball in modern times, April 10.

Death of Jimmie Lunceford, Seaside, Oregon, July 13.

Archbishop Joseph E. Ritter said he would excommunicate St. Louis Catholics who continued to protest integration of parochial schools, September 21.

NAACP petition on racial injustices in America, "An Appeal to the World," formally presented to United Nations at Lake Success, October 23.

President's Committee on Civil Rights condemned racial injustices in America in formal report, "To Secure These Rights," October 29.

1948

Supreme Court decision (*Sipuel v. University of Oklahoma*) held that state must provide legal education for Negroes "as soon as it provides it for" whites, January 12.

First Lt. Nancy C. Leftenant became first Negro accepted in the regular Army Nurse Corps, February 12.

A. Philip Randolph told Senate committee that unless segregation and discrimination were banned in Universal Military Training and draft programs he would urge Negro youth to resist induction by civil disobedience, March 31.

Supreme Court (*Shelley v. Kraemer*) ruled that federal and state courts may not enforce restrictive covenants, May 3.

Death of poet Claude McKay, Chicago, May 22.

Oliver W. Hill elected to Richmond, Va., City Council, June 9.

Alabama and Mississippi Democrats bolted Democratic convention after adoption of "strong" civil rights plank, July 14.

President Truman issued Executive Order 9981 directing "equality of treatment and opportunity" in the armed forces, July 26.

A. Philip Randolph withdrew from civil disobedience group opposing Jim Crow in armed forces, August 18.

Ralph J. Bunche confirmed by United Nations Security Council as Acting UN Mediator in Palestine, September 18.

California Supreme Court held that state statute banning racial intermarriage violated Constitution, October 1.

1949

Congressman William L. Dawson approved as chairman of House Expenditures Committee, January 18. He was first Negro to head standing committee of Congress.

Paul Robeson, speaking at a Paris peace conference, said American Negroes would not fight against Soviet Union, April 20.

Wesley A. Brown became first Negro to graduate from Annapolis Naval Academy, June 3.

Jackie Robinson attacked Paul Robeson's statement in appearance before House Un-American Activities Committee, July 18.

Peter Murray Marshall of New York City appointed to American Medical Association's policy-making House of Delegates, August 8.

WERD, first Negro-owned radio station, opened in Atlanta, October 3.

William Hastie nominated for United States Circuit Court of Appeals, October 15.

Death of dancer Bill Robinson, New York City, November 25.

1950

U.S. population: 150,697,361. Negro population: 15,042,286 (10%).

Death of Charles R. Drew, Burlington, N.C., April 1.

Death of Carter Woodson, Washington, D.C., April 3.

Death of Charles H. Houston, Washington, D.C., April 22.

Gwendolyn Brooks awarded Pulitzer Prize for poetry, May 1.

Three Supreme Court decisions undermined legal structure of segregation, June 5. In Sweatt case, Court held that equality involved more than physical facilities. In McLaurin case, Court said that a student, once admitted, cannot be segregated. In the Henderson case, the Court knocked out "curtains, partitions and signs" that separated Negro dining car patrons from whites.

President Truman ordered armed forces to intervene in Korean conflict, June 27.

Negro troops of Twenty-fourth Infantry Regiment recaptured Yechon, Korea, after 16-hour battle, July 21.

Chicago Atty. Edith Sampson appointed alternate delegate to United Nations, August 24.

Ralph J. Bunche, former UN Mediator in the Palestine dispute, awarded Nobel Peace Prize, September 22.

1951

New York City Council passed bill prohibiting racial discrimination in city-assisted housing developments, February 16.

University of North Carolina admitted first Negro student in its 162-year history, April 24.

Z. Alexander Looby elected to Nashville City Council, May 10.

Death of Oscar DePriest, former congressman, Chicago, May 12.

Racial segregation in D.C. restaurants ruled illegal by Municipal Court of Appeals, May 24.

NAACP began frontal attack on segregation and discrimination at elementary and high school levels, argued that segregation was discrimination in cases before three-judge federal courts in South Carolina and Kansas, June. The South Carolina court, with a strong dissent by Judge E. Waites Waring, held that segregation was not discrimination, June 23. Kansas court ruled that the separate facilities at issue were equal but said that segregation *per se* had adverse effect on Negro children.

Pfc. William Thompson of Brooklyn, N.Y., awarded Congressional Medal of Honor posthumously for heroism in Korea, June 21. This was first grant of CMH to a Negro since Spanish-American War.

Governor Adlai Stevenson called out National Guard to quell rioting in Cicero, Ill., July 12. Mob of 3,500 attempted to prevent Negro family from moving into all-white city.

Twenty-fourth Infantry Regiment, last of all-Negro units authorized by Congress in 1866, deactivated in Korea, October 1.

President Truman named committee to supervise compliance with provisions against discrimination in U.S. government contracts and subcontracts, December 3.

Harry T. Moore, Florida NAACP official, killed and his wife seriously injured by bomb which wrecked their home in Mims, Fla., December 25.

1952

University of Tennessee admitted first Negro student, January 12.

Congressional Medal of Honor awarded posthumously to Army Sgt. Cornelius H. Charlton, Bronx, N.Y., for heroism in Korea, February 12.

Death of Canada Lee, actor, New York City, May 9.

Tuskegee Institute reported that 1952 was first year in 71 years of tabulation that there were no lynchings, December 30.

Death of Fletcher Henderson, arranger and bandleader, New York City, December 29.

1953

Supreme Court ruled that District of Columbia restaurants could not legally refuse to serve Negroes, June 8.

Albert W. Dent, president of Dillard University, elected president of National Health Council, June 19.

—Bus boycott began Baton Rouge, La.

Movement of Negro families into Trumbull Park housing project in Chicago precipitated virtually continuous riot which lasted more than three years and required assignment of more than 1,000 policemen to keep order, August 4.

President Eisenhower established 15-member Government Contract Compliance Committee to supervise antidiscrimination regulations applying to employers with government contracts, August 13.

Take a Giant Step, drama by Negro playwright Louis Peterson, opened on Broadway, September 24.

Rufus Clement, president of Atlanta University, elected to Atlanta Board of Education, December 2.

Hulan Jack sworn in as borough president of Manhattan, December 31.

1954

President Eisenhower nominated J. Ernest Wilkins of Chicago to be Assistant Secretary of Labor, March 4.

Supreme Court ruled that racial segregation in public schools was unconstitutional, May 17.

Dr. Peter Murray Marshall installed as president of New York

County Medical Society, first Negro to head component unit of American Medical Association, May 24.

First White Citizens Council unit organized in Indianola, Miss., July 11.

Death of Mary Church Terrell, Washington, D.C., July 24.

J. Ernest Wilkins represented Labor Secretary James P. Mitchell at weekly Cabinet meeting, August 18.

School integration began in Washington, D.C., and Baltimore, Md., public schools, September 7–8.

B. O. Davis, Jr., became first Negro general in Air Force, October 27.

Defense Department announced complete abolition of Negro units in armed forces, October 30.

Charles C. Diggs, Jr., elected Michigan's first Negro congressman, November 2.

1955

Marian Anderson made debut at Metropolitan Opera House as Ulrica in Verdi's *Masked Ball*, January 7. She was first Negro singer in the company's history.

Death of Charlie Parker, one of founders of modern jazz movement, March 12.

Bandung Conference of leaders of colored nations of Africa and Asia opened in Indonesia, April 18.

Death of Walter White, New York City, March 21. Roy Wilkins succeeded him as NAACP executive, April 11.

Death of Mary McLeod Bethune, Daytona Beach, Fla., May 18.

Supreme Court ordered school integration "with all deliberate speed," May 31.

E. Frederic Morrow appointed administrative aide to President Eisenhower, July 9.

Emmett Till, 14, kidnapped and lynched in Money, Miss., August 28.

Supreme Court in Baltimore case banned segregation in public recreational facilities, November 7.

Interstate Commerce Commission banned segregation in busses, waiting rooms and travel coaches involved in interstate travel, November 25.

Bus Boycott began in Montgomery, Ala., December 5.

—A. Philip Randolph and Willard S. Townsend elected vice-presidents of AFL–CIO.

1956

Home of Rev. Martin Luther King, Jr., Montgomery bus boycott leader, bombed, January 30.

Autherine J. Lucy admitted to University of Alabama, February 3. She was suspended February 7 after a riot at the university and expelled February 29.

Manifesto denouncing Supreme Court ruling on segregation in public schools issued by 100 Southern senators and representatives, March 11–12.

Singer Nat Cole attacked on stage of Birmingham theater by racists, April 11.

Supreme Court refused to review lower court decision which banned segregation in intrastate bus travel, April 23.

Bus boycott began in Tallahassee, Fla., May 30.

Federal court ruled that racial segregation on Montgomery city busses violated Constitution, June 5.

White mob prevented enrollment of Negro students at Mansfield High School, Mansfield, Texas, August 30.

Tennessee National Guard sent to Clinton, Tenn., to quell mobs demonstrating against school integration, September 2.

National Guard dispersed mob attempting to prevent school integration at Sturgis, Ky., September 6.

Louisville, Ky., public schools integrated, September 10.

Negro students entered Clay, Ky., elementary school under National Guard protection, September 12. They were barred from school, September 17.

Death of Art Tatum, jazz pianist, Los Angeles, November 5.

Supreme Court upheld lower court decision which banned segregation on city busses in Montgomery, Ala., November 13. Federal injunctions prohibiting segregation on the busses were served on city, state and bus company officials, December 20. At two mass meetings, Montgomery Negroes called off year-long bus boycott. Busses were integrated on December 21.

Home of Rev. F. L. Shuttlesworth, Birmingham protest leader, destroyed by dynamite bomb, December 25.

Birmingham Negroes began mass defiance of Jim Crow bus laws, 21 arrested, December 26.

Federal Judge Dozier Devane granted temporary injunction restraining city officials from interfering with integration of Tallahassee, Fla., city busses, said "every segregation act of every state or city is as dead as a doornail," December 27.

1957

Southern Christian Leadership Conference organized at meeting in New Orleans with Martin Luther King, Jr., as president, February 14.

Ghana became independent state, March 6.

W. Robert Ming, Chicago lawyer, elected chairman of American Veterans Committee, first Negro to head major national veterans organization, April 28.

Prayer Pilgrimage, biggest civil rights demonstration ever staged by U.S. Negroes, held in Washington, May 17.

Tuskegee boycott began, June. Negroes boycotted city stores in protest against act of state legislature which deprived them of municipal votes by placing their homes outside city limits.

Archibald Carey, Chicago, appointed first Negro chairman of President's Committee on Government Employment Policy, August 3.

Congress passed Civil Rights Act of 1957, August 29. This was first federal civil rights legislation since 1875.

Nashville's new Hattie Cotton Elementary School with enrollment of one Negro and 388 whites virtually destroyed by dynamite blast, September 9.

Rev. F. L. Shuttlesworth mobbed when he attempted to enroll his daughters in "white" Birmingham school, September 9.

President Eisenhower ordered federal troops to Little Rock, Ark., to prevent interference with school integration at Central High School, September 24.

—President made nationwide TV and radio address to explain why troops were sent to Little Rock.

Soldiers of 101st Airborne Division escorted nine Negro children to Central High School, September 25.

Order alerting regular army units for possible riot duty in other Southern cities cancelled by Army Secretary Wilbur M. Brucker, September 26.

Federal troops left Little Rock, November 27.

New York City became first to legislate against racial or religious discrimination in housing market with adoption of Fair Housing Practice Law, December 5.

1958

Clifton Reginald Wharton confirmed as minister to Rumania, February 5.

President Eisenhower ordered federalized National Guard removed from Central High School, Little Rock, May 8.

Robert N. C. Nix elected to Congress from Philadelphia, May 20.

Ernest Green graduated from Little Rock's Central High School with 600 white classmates, May 27.

Supreme Court reversed decision of lower court which had confirmed $100,000 contempt fine imposed by Alabama on NAACP for refusing to divulge membership, June 30.

Members of NAACP Youth Council began series of sit-ins at Oklahoma City lunch counters, August 19.

Martin Luther King, Jr. stabbed in chest by crazed Negro woman while he was autographing books in a Harlem department store, September 20. Woman was placed under mental observation.

1959

Death of Lester Young, New York City, March 15.

Raisin in the Sun, first play written by Negro woman to reach Broadway, opened at Barrymore Theater with Sidney Poitier and Claudia McNeil in the starring roles, March 11. Lorraine Hansberry's drama was first to be directed by a Negro—Lloyd Richards—in over half a century.

Mack Parker lynched, Poplarville, Miss., April 25.

Brig. Gen. B. O. Davis, Jr., promoted to major general, May 22.

Prince Edward County, Va., Board of Supervisors abandoned public school system in attempt to prevent school integration, June 26.

Death of Billie Holiday, singer, New York City, July 17.

Citizens of Deerfield, Ill., authorized plan which blocked building of interracial housing development, December 21.

1960

U.S. population: 179,323,175. Negro population: 18,871,831 (10.5%).

Four students from North Carolina A. and T. College started sit-in movement at Greensboro, N.C., five and dime store, February 1. By February 10, movement had spread to fifteen Southern cities in five states.

Race riot, Chattanooga, Tenn., at sit-in demonstration, February 23.

Alabama State College students staged first sit-in in Deep South at Montgomery, Ala., courthouse, February 25.

Police arrested some 100 students in Nashville sit-in demonstrations, February 27.

One thousand Alabama State students marched on state capitol and held protest meeting, March 1.

Alabama State Board of Education expelled nine Alabama State students for participating in sit-in demonstrations, March 2.

Pope John elevated Bishop Laurian Rugambwa of Tanganyika to College of Cardinals, first Negro cardinal in modern times, March 3.

Montgomery, Ala., police broke up protest demonstration on Alabama State campus and arrested 35 students, a teacher and her husband, March 8.

Police used tear gas to break up student protest demonstration at Tallahassee, Fla., March 12.

San Antonio, Texas, became first large Southern city to integrate lunch counters, March 16. Four national chain stores announced on October 17 that counters in about 150 stores in 112 cities in North Carolina, Virginia, West Virginia, Kentucky, Texas, Tennessee, Missouri, Maryland, Florida, Oklahoma, had been integrated.

Associated Press reported that more than 1,000 Negroes had been arrested in sit-in demonstrations, March 22.

Eighteen students suspended by Southern University, March 30. Southern University students rebelled March 31, boycotted classes and requested withdrawal slips. Rebellion collapsed after death of professor from heart attack.

Eighty-three Negroes indicted in Atlanta, Ga., on charges stemming from sit-in demonstrations at Atlanta, Ga., restaurants, April 15.

Student Nonviolent Coordinating Committee organized at meeting on Shaw University campus, April 15–17.

Race riot, Biloxi, Miss., after a wade-in by Negroes at local beach, April 24.

Home of Z. Alexander Looby, counsel for 153 students arrested in sit-in demonstrations, destroyed by dynamite bomb, April 19. More than 2,000 students marched on city hall in protest demonstration.

Consent judgment in Memphis, Tenn., federal court ended restrictions against Negro voting in Fayette County, Tenn., first voting case under Civil Rights Act, April 25.

President Eisenhower signed Civil Rights Act of 1960, May 6.

Elijah Muhammad, black nationalist leader, called for creation of Negro state at New York meeting, July 31.

Race riot, Jacksonville, Fla, after 10 days of sit-in demonstrations, August 27. Fifty reported injured.

Twenty Negro and white students staged kneel-in demonstrations in white churches in Atlanta, August 7.

Andrew Hatcher named associate press secretary to President Kennedy, November 10.

U.S. marshals and parents escorted four Negro girls to two New Orleans schools, November 14.

Death of Richard Wright, Paris, France, November 28.

Several thousand Negroes held two mass prayer meetings and marched on business district of Atlanta in protest against segregation and discrimination, December 11.

Two U.S. courts issued temporary injunctions to prevent about 700 Negro sharecroppers from being evicted from farms in Haywood and Fayette counties, Tenn., reportedly for registering to vote, December 30.

1961

Adam Clayton Powell became chairman of Education and Labor Committee of House of Representatives, January 3.

Riot, University of Georgia, January 11. Two Negro students were suspended, but a federal court ordered them reinstated. They returned to classes on January 16.

Jail-in movement started in Rock Hill, S.C., when students refused to pay fines and requested jail sentences, February 6. Student Nonviolent Coordinating Committee urged southwide "Jail, No Bail" campaign.

U.S. and African nationalists disrupted UN session on Congo with demonstration for slain Congo Premier Patrice Lumumba, February 15.

Robert Weaver sworn in as Administrator of the Housing and Home Finance Agency, highest federal post ever held by an American Negro, February 11.

Some 180 Negro students and a white minister arrested in Columbia, S.C., after antisegregation protest march on state capitol, March 2.

Atlanta Chamber of Commerce announced that Negro and white leaders had agreed on plan for desegregation of lunchroom and other facilities, March 7.

Clifton R. Wharton sworn in as ambassador to Norway, March 9.

Meeting place of National Civil War Centennial Commission shifted from Charleston to Charleston Naval Station after nation-wide controversy over segregated hotels in Charleston, March 25.

Thirteen "Freedom Riders," including national director of CORE, set out for bus trip through South, May 4.

Bus with first group of "Freedom Riders" bombed and burned by segregationists outside Anniston, Ala., May 14. Group was attacked in Anniston and Birmingham.

Mob attacked Negro and white "Freedom Riders" in Montgomery, Ala., May 20.

Attorney General Robert F. Kennedy dispatched some 400 U.S.

marshals to Montgomery to keep order in "Freedom Rider" controversy, May 20.

Governor Patterson declared martial law in Montgomery and called out National Guard, May 21.

Attorney General ordered 200 more U.S. marshals to Montgomery, May 22.

Twenty-seven "Freedom Riders" arrested in Jackson, Miss., May 24. On June 12, Hinds County Board of Supervisors announced that jail was overcrowded. More than 100 "Freedom Riders" had been arrested.

"Freedom Ride" Coordinating Committee established in Atlanta, May 26.

Judge Irving Kaufman ordered Board of Education of New Rochelle, N.Y., to integrate schools, May 31.

Wade-in demonstration at Rainbow Beach, Chicago, July 9, July 16.

James B. Parsons became first Negro appointed to federal district court in continental United States, August 9.

Southern Regional Council announced that sit-in movement had affected 20 states and more than 100 cities in Southern and border states in period from February, 1960, to September 1961, September 21. At least 70,000 Negroes and whites had participated in the movement, the report said. The council estimated that 3,600 had been arrested and that at least 141 students and 58 faculty members had been expelled by college authorities. SRC said one or more establishments in 108 Southern and border state cities had been desegregated as a result of sit-ins.

Federal Court was asked to order school integration in Chicago in suit filed by citizens, September 18. Suit was later dismissed.

Interstate Commerce Commission issued regulation prohibiting segregation on busses and in terminal facilities, September 22.

President Kennedy nominated Thurgood Marshall to U.S. Circuit Court of Appeals, September 23.

Purlie Victorious, a farce by playwright Ossie Davis, opened on Broadway, September 28.

Otis Milton Smith appointed to Michigan Supreme Court, October 10.

"Freedom Riders" attacked by white mob at bus station in McComb, Miss., November 29–December 2.

More than 700 demonstrators, including the Rev. Martin Luther King, Jr., arrested in Albany, Ga., as result of five mass marches on City Hall to protest segregation and discrimination, December 12–16. Arrests triggered militant Albany Movement which continued to stage antisegregation demonstrations in 1962.

Police used tear gas and leashed dogs to quell mass demonstration by 1,500 Negroes in Baton Rouge, La., December 15.

Supreme Court reversed conviction of 16 sit-in students who had been arrested in Baton Rouge, La., on "breach of peace" charge, December 11.

1962

Suit accusing New York City Board of Education of using "racial quotas" filed in U.S. District Court on behalf of Negro and Puerto Rican children, January 16.

Southern University closed because of series of demonstrations protesting expulsion of sit-in demonstrations, January 18–28.

Demonstrations against discrimination in off-campus housing staged by students at University of Chicago, January 23–February 5. CORE charged that university operated about 100 segregated apartment houses.

Lt. Commander Samuel L. Gravely assumed command of destroyer escort, USS "Falgout," January 31. Navy said he was first Negro to command U.S. warship.

Seven whites and four Negroes arrested after all-night sit-in at Englewood, N.J., City Hall, February 2.

Four Negro mothers arrested for staging sit-in at Chicago elementary school, February 2. Mothers later received suspended $50 fines. Protests, picketing and demonstrations continued for several weeks against *de facto* segregation, double shifts and mobile classrooms.

Suit seeking to bar Englewood, N.J., from maintaining "racially segregated" elementary school filed in U.S. District Court, February 5.

Bus boycott started in Macon, Ga., February 12.

Three Louisiana segregationists were excommunicated by Archbishop Joseph Rummel for continuing their opposition to his order for integration of New Orleans parochial schools, April 16.

Southern School News reported that 246,988 or 7.6% of the Negro pupils in public schools in 17 Southern and border states and the District of Columbia attended integrated classes in 1962, May 10.

Suit alleging *de facto* school segregation filed in Rochester, N.Y., by NAACP, May 28.

Sit-in demonstrations and passive resistance movement began in Cairo, Ill., June 26. Demonstrations against segregation in swimming pool, skating rink and other facilities continued for several months.

Rev. Martin Luther King, Jr., arrested in Albany, Ga., after antisegregation demonstration, July 10.

At least 161 Negroes jailed after demonstration in Albany, Ga., July

21. By August 1, almost 1,000 demonstrators had been arrested in the Georgia city.

Rev. Martin Luther King, Jr., jailed in Albany, Ga., July 27.

President Kennedy said city officials of Albany, Ga., should negotiate with Negro leaders, Aug. 1.

Police closed municipal parks and library in Albany, Ga., after integrated groups tried to use facilities, August 11.

Shady Grove Baptist Church burned in Leesburg, Ga., August 15.

About 75 ministers and laymen—Negroes and whites—from North arrested after prayer demonstration in downtown Albany, Ga., August 28.

Two Negro churches burned near Sasser, Ga., September 9. Negro leaders asked the President to put a stop to the "Nazi-like reign of terror in southwest Georgia."

Supreme Court Justice Hugo Black vacated an order of a lower court, ruled that the University of Mississippi must admit James H. Meredith, a Negro Air Force veteran whose application for admission had been on file and in the courts for 14 months, September 10.

Two Negro youth involved in voter registration drive in Mississippi were wounded by shotgun blasts fired through the windows of a home in Ruleville, Miss., September 11. James Forman, executive secretary of the Student Nonviolent Coordinating Committee (SNCC), asked the President to "convene a special White House Conference to discuss means of stopping the wave of terror sweeping through the South, especially where SNCC is working on voter registration."

Mississippi Governor Ross R. Barnett defied the federal government in impassioned speech on state-wide radio-television hookup, said he would "interpose" the authority of the state between the University of Mississippi and federal judges who had ordered the admission of James H. Meredith, a Negro student, September 13. Barnett said: "There is no case in history where the Caucasian race has survived social integration." He promised to go to jail, if necessary, to prevent integration at the state university. His defiance set the stage for the gravest federal-state crisis since the Civil War.

—President Kennedy denounced the burning of Negro churches in Georgia, supported Negro voter registration drive in the South, September 13.

Fourth Negro church burned near Dawson, Ga., September 17. Three white men later admitted burning the church. They were sentenced to seven-year prison terms for arson.

Governor Barnett personally denied James H. Meredith admission to the University of Mississippi, September 20.

U.S. Circuit Court of Appeals ordered Board of Higher Education of Mississippi to admit Meredith to the university or be held in contempt, September 24. The board announced that it would comply with the order.

Governor Barnett again defied the orders of the court and personally denied Meredith admission to the university, September 25.

—A Negro church was destroyed by fire in Macon, Ga. This was the eighth Negro church burned in Georgia since August 15.

Mississippi barred Meredith for the third time, September 26. Lieutenant Governor Paul Johnson and a blockade of state patrolmen turned back Meredith and federal marshals and officials about 400 yards from the gate of the school.

Governor Barnett found guilty of civil contempt of the federal court, September 28. United States Court of Appeals for the Fifth Circuit ordered Barnett to purge himself of contempt or face arrest and a fine of $10,000 a day.

Lieutenant Governor Paul Johnson found guilty of civil contempt of court, September 29. Court of Appeals ordered the official to purge himself of contempt or face a fine of $5,000 a day.

Large force of federal marshals escorted James H. Meredith to the campus of the University of Mississippi, September 30. President Kennedy federalized the Mississippi National Guard and urged Mississippians to accept the orders of the court in a radio-TV address.

—University of Mississippi students and adults from Oxford, Miss., and other Southern communities rioted on the university campus. Two persons were killed and 100 or more were wounded.

Some 12,000 federal soldiers restored order on the campus and in the town of Oxford, Miss., October 1.

—James H. Meredith, escorted by federal marshals, registered at the University of Mississippi.

—Edwin A. Walker, former major general in the U.S. Army, was arrested and charged with inciting insurrection and seditious conspiracy. Walker, who led federal troops during the Little Rock integration crisis, had called for "volunteers" to oppose federal forces in Mississippi. Witnesses said he led students in charges against federal marshals during the campus riot.

President Kennedy issued Executive Order barring racial and religious discrimination in federally-financed housing, November 20.

1963

Emancipation centennial protests began with massive voter registration campaign in Greenwood, Miss., March 1.

Martin Luther King, Jr., opened anti-segregation campaign in Birmingham, Ala., April 3. More than 2,000 demonstrators, including King, were arrested before campaign ended.

Rev. Fred L. Shuttlesworth announced agreement on limited integration plan which ended Birmingham demonstrations, May 10.

Bombing of motel and home of integration leader triggered three-hour riot in Birmingham, May 11–12.

Two Negro students, escorted by federalized National Guard troops and federal officials, enrolled at University of Alabama despite opposition of Governor George C. Wallace, June 11.

President Kennedy told nation in historic radio-TV address that segregation was morally wrong and that it was "time to act in the Congress, in your state and local legislative body, and, above all, in all of our daily lives."

Medgar W. Evers, 37, NAACP field secretary in Mississippi, assassinated in front of his Jackson home by segregationist, June 12.

Three thousand students participated in boycott of Boston public schools as protest against *de facto* segregation, June 18.

Civil rights group staged mass demonstrations at Harlem construction sites to protest discrimination in building trades unions, June 12–13. Demonstrations and marches were held in every major metropolitan area in June, July and August to dramatize Negro discontent over housing, school and job discrimination.

National Guard troops imposed limited martial law in Cambridge, Maryland, after open confrontations between Negro demonstrators and white segregationists, July 12.

W. E. B. Du Bois, scholar, protest leader and a founder of the NAACP, died in Accra, Ghana, August 27.

More than 250,000 persons participated in March on Washington demonstration, August 28.

Four Negro girls killed in bombing of 16th Street Baptist Church in Birmingham, Ala., September 15.

Some 225,000 students boycotted Chicago public schools in Freedom Day protest of *de facto* segregation, October 22.

John Fitzgerald Kennedy, 46, 35th president of the United States, assassinated in Dallas, Texas, November 22.

1964

Some 464,000 Negro and Puerto Rican students boycotted New York City public schools, February 3. More than 267,000 were absent during second boycott, March 16.

Sidney Poitier became first Negro to win "Oscar" as best actor of year, April 13.

New York police arrested 294 civil rights demonstrators at opening of World's Fair, April 22. Scheduled stall-in on highways and bridges leading to the fair failed to materialize.

U.S. Senate imposed cloture for first time on civil rights measure, ending Southern filibuster by a vote of 71–29, June 10. Civil Rights bill, with public accommodation and fair employment sections, was passed by Congress and signed by President Lyndon B. Johnson, July 2.

Race riot started in Harlem, July 18. Rioting spread to Negro ghetto in Bedford-Stuyvesant section of Brooklyn and continued for several days.

Race riot erupted in Rochester, N.Y., July 25. Governor Nelson Rockefeller dispatched national guard troops to city.

Race riot started in Jersey City, New Jersey, August 2.

Bodies of three civil rights workers discovered in crude grave on farm near Philadelphia, Miss., August 4. Three young men, two white and one Negro, had been missing since June 21. FBI said they were murdered on night of their disappearance by white segregationists.

Bibliography

Adams, Samuel. *The Writings of Samuel Adams*, ed. Henry Alonzo Cushing. 4 vols. New York, 1904–08.

Alexis, Stephen. *Black Liberator: The Life of Toussaint Louverture*. New York, 1949.

Aptheker, Herbert. *The Negro in the Civil War*. New York, 1938.

——. *The Negro in the American Revolution*. New York, 1940.

——. *The Negro in the Abolitionist Movement*. New York, 1941.

——. *American Negro Slave Revolts*. New York, 1943.

—— (ed.). *A Documentary History of the Negro People in the United States*, New York, 1951.

Armstrong, Louis. *Satchmo: My Life in New Orleans*. New York, 1954.

Ballagh, James C. *White Servitude in the Colony of Virginia*. Baltimore, 1895.

——. *A History of Slavery in Virginia*. Baltimore, 1902.

Bancroft, Frederic. *Slave-Trading in the Old South*. Baltimore, 1931.

Bancroft, George. *History of the United States of America*. 10 vols. Boston, 1866–74.

Bardolph, Richard. *The Negro Vanguard*. New York, 1959.

Barnes, Gilbert H. *The Antislavery Impulse, 1830–1844*. New York, 1933.

Barry, Williams. *A History of Framingham, Massachusetts*. Boston, 1847.

Barth, Heinrich. *Travels and Discoveries in North and Central Africa, 1849–1855.* 3 vols. New York, 1857–59.

Beard, Charles A., and Mary R. *The Rise of American Civilization.* 2 vols. New York, 1927.

Boas, Franz. *Race and Democratic Society.* New York, 1945.

Bond, Horace Mann. *The Education of the Negro in the American Social Order.* New York, 1934.

Bontemps, Arna, and Conroy, Jack. *They Seek a City.* New York, 1945.

Botkin, B. A. (ed.). *Lay My Burden Down.* Chicago, 1945.

Bradford, Sarah H. *Harriet, The Moses of Her People.* Auburn, 1897.

Bragg, George F., Jr. *Men of Maryland.* Baltimore, 1925.

Brawley, Benjamin G. *The Negro Genius.* New York, 1937.

———. *Negro Builders and Heroes.* Chapel Hill, 1937.

Brazeal, B. R. *The Brotherhood of Sleeping Car Porters.* New York, 1946.

Bremer, Frederika. *The Homes of the New World.* 2 vols. New York, 1853.

Broderick, Francis L. *W. E. B. Du Bois, Negro Leader in a Time of Crisis.* Stanford, 1959.

Brodie, Fawn M. *Thaddeus Stevens, Scourge of the South.* New York, 1959.

Brown, Sterling A. *Negro Poetry and Drama.* Washington, 1937.

———, et al (eds.). *The Negro Caravan.* New York, 1941.

Brown, William Wells. *Narrative of William Wells Brown.* Boston, 1848.

———. *The Black Man.* New York, 1863.

———. *The Negro in the American Rebellion.* Boston, 1867.

Buck, Paul H. *The Road to Reunion.* Boston, 1937.

Buckler, Helen. *Doctor Dan, Pioneer in American Surgery.* Boston, 1954.

Buckmaster, Henrietta. *Let My People Go.* New York, 1941.

Budge, E. A. W. *The Egyptian Sudan.* 2 vols. London, 1907.

———. *A History of Ethiopia, Nubia and Abyssinia.* 2 vols. London, 1928.

Butcher, Margaret Just. *The Negro in American Culture.* New York, 1956.

Butler, Benjamin F. *Butler's Book.* Boston, 1892.

Calhoun, A. W. *A Social History of the American Family.* 3 vols. New York, 1917.

Campbell, George. *White and Black.* New York, 1889.

Carroll, Joseph C. *Slave Insurrections in the United States, 1800–1865.* Boston, 1938.

Cash, Wilbur J. *The Mind of the South.* New York, 1941.

Catterall, Helen T. *Judicial Cases Concerning American Slavery and the Negro.* 5 vols. Washington, 1926–37.

Catton, Bruce. *This Hallowed Ground.* Garden City, 1956.

———. *The Coming Fury.* Garden City, 1961.

Chase, Gilbert. *America's Music.* New York, 1955.

Chicago Commission on Race Relations. *The Negro in Chicago.* Chicago, 1922.

Cohn, David Lewis. *The Life and Times of King Cotton.* New York, 1956.

Cornish, Dudley Taylor. *Negro Troops in the Union Army, 1861–65.* New York, 1956.

Cronon, Edmund David. *Black Moses: The Story of Marcus Garvey.* Madison, 1955.

Dabney, W. P. *Cincinnati's Colored Citizens.* Cincinnati, 1926.

Dana, Charles A. *Recollections of the Civil War.* New York, 1902.

Daniels, John. *In Freedom's Birthplace.* Boston, 1914.

Davidson, Basil. *The Lost Cities of Africa.* Boston, 1959.

———. *Black Mother.* Boston, 1961.

Davie, Maurice R. *Negroes in American Society.* New York, 1949.

Davis, J. D. *History of Memphis.* Memphis, 1873.

DeForest, John William. *A Volunteer's Adventures.* New Haven, 1946.

Detweiler, Frederick G. *The Negro Press in the United States.* Chicago, 1922.

Dollard, John. *Caste and Class in a Southern Town.* New Haven, 1937.

Donald, David. *Lincoln Reconsidered.* New York, 1956.

Donnan, Elizabeth. *Documents Illustrative of the History of the Slave Trade to America.* Washington, 1930–35.

Douglass, Frederick. *The Life and Times of Frederick Douglass.* Hartford, 1881.

———. *My Bondage and My Freedom.* New York, 1855.

Drake, St. Clair, and Cayton, Horace R. *Black Metropolis.* New York, 1945.

Drewry, W. S. *Slave Insurrections in Virginia, 1830–1865.* Washington, 1900.

Du Bois, W. E. B. *The Suppression of the African Slave Trade to the United States of America.* New York, 1896.

———. *The Philadelphia Negro.* Philadelphia, 1899.

———. *The Souls of Black Folk.* Chicago, 1903.

————. (ed.). *The Negro Church*. Atlanta, 1903.

————. *Black Reconstruction*. New York, 1935.

————. *Black Folk: Then and Now*. New York, 1939.

————. *Dusk of Dawn*. New York, 1940.

Dumond, Dwight L. *Antislavery*. Ann Arbor, 1961.

Dyer, Frederick H. *A Compendium of the War of the Rebellion*. Des Moines, 1908.

Eaton, Clement. *The Growth of Southern Civilization, 1790–1860*. New York, 1961.

Eaton, John. *Grant, Lincoln and the Freedmen*. New York, 1907.

Edmonds, Helen G. *The Negro and Fusion Politics in North Carolina, 1894–1901*. Chapel Hill, 1951.

Elkins, Stanley M. *Slavery, a Problem in American Institutional and Intellectual Life*. Chicago, 1959.

Embree, Edwin. *Brown America*. New York, 1931.

————. *13 Against the Odds*. New York, 1944.

Emilio, Luis F. *History of the Fifty-fourth Regiment of Massachusetts Volunteer Infantry*. Boston, 1894.

Eppse, Merl R. *The Negro, Too, in American History*. Chicago, 1939.

Fage, J. D. *An Introduction to the History of West Africa*. Cambridge, England, 1959.

Fairservis, Walter A., Jr., *The Ancient Kingdoms of the Nile*. New York, 1962.

Faulkner, Harold Underwood. *American Political and Social History*. New York, 1945.

Fauset, Arthur Huff. *Sojourner Truth*. Chapel Hill, 1938.

Feather, Leonard. *The Encyclopedia of Jazz*. New York, 1955.

Ficklen, John R. *History of Reconstruction in Louisiana Through 1868*. Baltimore, 1910.

Fleming, Walter (ed.). *Documentary History of Reconstruction*. 2 vols. Cleveland, 1906–07.

Foley, Albert S. *Bishop Healy: Beloved Outcaste*. New York, 1954.

————. *God's Men of Color*. New York, 1955.

Foner, Phillip S. *The Life and Writings of Frederick Douglass*. 4 vols. New York, 1950.

Forten, Charlotte. *The Journal of Charlotte Forten*, ed. Ray Allen Billington. New York, 1953.

Fox, William F. *Regimental Losses in the American Civil War*. Albany, 1889.

Francis, Charles E. *The Tuskegee Airmen*. Boston, 1955.

Franklin, John Hope. *From Slavery to Freedom*. New York, 1947.

Franklin, John Hope. *The Free Negro in North Carolina.* Chapel Hill, 1943.

——. *Reconstruction.* Chicago, 1961.

Frazier, E. Franklin. *The Negro Family in the United States.* Chicago, 1939.

——. *The Negro in the United States.* New York, 1957.

——. *Black Bourgeoisie.* Glencoe, 1957.

Freyre, Gilberto. *The Masters and the Slaves.* Translated by Samuel Putnam. New York, 1946.

Frobenius, Leo. *The Voice of Africa.* Translated by Rudolf Blind. 2 vols. London, 1913.

Gage, Thomas. *The Correspondence of General Thomas Gage,* ed. Clarence E. Carter. 2 vols. New Haven, 1931–33.

Gaines, Francis. P. *The Southern Plantation.* New York, 1924.

Gardiner, Alan. *Egypt of the Pharaohs.* London, 1961.

Garfinkel, Herbert. *When Negroes March.* Glencoe, 1959.

Garner, James W. *Reconstruction in Mississippi.* New York, 1901.

Garrison, W. P., and Garrison, F. L. *William Lloyd Garrison.* 4 vols. Boston, 1894.

Ginzberg, Eli. *The Negro Potential.* New York, 1956.

Gosnell, Harold F. *Negro Politicians, the Rise of Negro Politics in Chicago.* Chicago, 1935.

Gouldner, Alvin W. (ed.). *Studies in Leadership.* New York, 1950.

Greenberg, Jack. *Race Relations and American Law.* New York, 1959.

Greene, Lorenzo J. *The Negro in Colonial New England.* New York, 1942.

Guzman, Jessie P. (ed.). *Negro Year Book.* Tuskegee, 1947, 1952.

Handy, W. C. *Father of the Blues,* ed. Arna Bontemps. New York, 1941.

Hare, Maud (Cuney). *Negro Musicians and Their Music.* Washington, 1936.

Hayes, Lawrence J. W. *The Negro Federal Government Worker, 1883–1938.* Washington, 1941.

Henderson, Edwin B. *The Negro in Sports.* Washington, 1949.

Herodotus. *The History of Herodotus.* Translated by George Rowlinson. Chicago, 1952.

Herskovits, Melville J. *The American Negro: A Study in Racial Crossing.* New York, 1928.

——. *The Myth of the Negro's Past.* New York, 1941.

——. *Cultural Anthropology.* New York, 1955.

Higginson, Thomas W. *Army Life in a Black Regiment.* Boston, 1870.

————. *Travellers and Outlaws*. Boston, 1889.

Hirshon, Stanley P. *Farewell to the Bloody Shirt*. Bloomington, 1962.

Holland, Frederic M. *Frederick Douglass*. New York, 1895.

Hook, Sidney. *The Hero in History*. New York, 1943.

Hoskins, G. A. *Travels in Ethiopia*. 2 vols. London, 1835.

Hughes, Langston. *The Big Sea*. New York, 1940.

Humphreys, A. A. *The Virginia Campaign of 1864 and 1865*. New York, 1883.

Jahn, Janheinz. *Muntu*. Translated by Marjorie Grene. New York, 1961.

Jensen, Merrill (ed.). *American Colonial Documents to 1776*, in *English Historical Documents*, ed. David C. Douglass. London, 1955.

Johnson, Allen, and Malone, Dumas (eds.). *Dictionary of American Biography*. 22 vols. New York, 1928–1936.

Johnson, Charles S. *The Negro in American Civilization*. New York, 1930.

————. *Shadow of the Plantation*. Chicago, 1934.

————. *The Negro College Graduate*. Chapel Hill, 1938.

————. *Patterns of Negro Segregation*. New York, 1943.

Johnson, James Weldon. *Black Manhattan*. New York, 1930.

————. *Along This Way*. New York, 1933.

Johnson, Robert U., and Buel, Clarence C. (eds.). *Battles and Leaders of the Civil War*. 4 vols. New York, 1887–88.

Kardiner, Abram, and Ovesey, Lionel. *The Mark of Oppression*. New York, 1951.

Kemble, Frances A. *Journal of a Residence on a Georgian Plantation in 1838–39*. New York, 1863.

Kesselman, Louis C. *The Social Politics of FEPC*. Chapel Hill, 1948.

Key, V. O., Jr. *Southern Politics in State and Nation*. New York, 1949.

————. *Politics, Parties and Pressure Groups*. New York, 1942.

Kidder, Frederic. *History of the Boston Massacre*. Albany, 1870.

King, Martin Luther, Jr. *Stride toward Freedom*. New York, 1958.

Konvitz, Milton R. *Constitution and Civil Rights*. New York, 1947.

Korngold, Ralph. *Citizen Toussaint*. Boston, 1945.

————. *Thaddeus Stevens*. New York, 1955.

Lader, Lawrence. *The Bold Brahmins*. New York, 1961.

Leakey, L. S. B. *The Progress and Evolution of Man in Africa*. London, 1961.

Lerner, Max. *America as a Civilization*. New York, 1957.

Lester, John C. *The Ku Klux Klan*. New York, 1905.

Lewinson, Paul. *Race, Class and Party*. New York, 1932.

Lincoln, C. Eric. *The Black Muslims in America.* Boston, 1961.

Litwack, Leon F. *North of Slavery.* Chicago, 1961.

Locke, Alain. *The New Negro.* New York, 1925.

———. *Negro Art: Past and Present.* Washington, 1936.

Logan, Rayford. *The Negro in American Life and Thought: The Nadir, 1877–1901.* New York, 1954.

——— (ed.). *What the Negro Wants.* Chapel Hill, 1944.

——— (ed.). *Memoirs of a Monticello Slave.* Charlottesville, 1951.

Loggins, Vernon. *The Negro Author.* New York, 1931.

Lonn, Ella. *Reconstruction in Louisiana after 1868.* New York, 1918.

Lossing, Benson. *The Pictorial Field-Book of the Revolution.* 2 vols. New York, 1860.

Lugard, Flora Louisa. *A Tropical Dependency.* London, 1911.

Lynch, John Roy. *The Facts of Reconstruction.* New York, 1913.

Lynn, Annella. *Interracial Marriages in Washington, D.C., 1940–47.* Washington, 1953.

McCormac, E. I. *White Servitude in Maryland.* Baltimore, 1904.

McKay, Claude. *Harlem: Negro Metropolis.* New York, 1940.

McWilliams, Carey. *Brothers Under the Skin.* Boston, 1943.

Mangum, Charles S. *The Legal Status of the Negro.* Chapel Hill, 1940.

Martin, John Bartlow. *The Deep South Says "Never."* New York, 1957.

Martineau, Harriet. *Society in America.* 2 vols. New York, 1837.

May, Samuel J. *Some Recollections of Our Antislavery Conflict.* Boston, 1869.

Mays, Benjamin E., and Nicholson, J. W. *The Negro's Church.* New York, 1932.

Mazyck, Walter H., *George Washington and the Negro.* Washington, 1932.

Miller, John C. *Sam Adams: Pioneer in Propaganda.* Boston, 1936.

Miller, Kelly. *Race Adjustment.* New York, 1908.

Montagu, M. F. Ashley. *Man's Most Dangerous Myth: The Fallacy of Race.* New York, 1945.

Moon, Henry L. *Balance of Power.* Garden City, 1949.

Moore, George H. *Historical Notes on the Employment of Negroes in the American Army of the Revolution.* New York, 1862.

Moran, Charles. *Black Triumverate.* New York, 1957.

Morgan, A. T. *Yazoo.* Washington, 1884.

Murray, Florence (ed.). *The Negro Handbook.* New York, 1942, 1944, 1946–47, 1949.

Murray, Pauli. *States' Laws on Race and Color.* Cincinnati, 1951.

Myrdal, Gunnar. *An American Dilemma*. New York, 1943.

Nell, William C. *The Colored Patriots of the American Revolution*. Boston, 1855.

Nichols, Lee. *Breakthrough on the Color Front*. New York, 1954.

Nordhoff, Charles. *The Cotton States in the Spring and Summer of 1875*. New York, 1876.

Northup, Solomon. *Narrative of Solomon Northup*. Auburn, 1853.

Nowlin, William F. *The Negro in American Politics*. Boston, 1931.

Olmsted, Frederick Law. *The Cotton Kingdom*, ed. Arthur Schlesinger. New York, 1953.

Ottley, Roi. *Black Odyssey*. New York, 1948.

———. *The Lonely Warrior: The Life and Times of Robert S. Abbott*. Chicago, 1955.

Ovington, Mary White. *Portraits in Color*. New York, 1927.

———. *The Walls Came Tumbling Down*. New York, 1947.

Peck, James. *Freedom Ride*. New York, 1962.

Penn, I. Garland. *The Afro-American Press*. Springfield, 1891.

Phillips, U. B. *American Negro Slavery*. New York, 1929.

Pierson, Donald. *Negroes in Brazil*. Chicago, 1942.

Powell, Adam Clayton. *Marching Blacks*. New York, 1945.

Quarles, Benjamin. *Frederick Douglass*. Washington, 1948.

———. *The Negro in the Civil War*. Boston, 1953.

———. *The Negro in the American Revolution*. Chapel Hill, 1961.

———. *Lincoln and the Negro*. New York, 1962.

Quillin, Frank U. *The Color Line in Ohio*. Ann Arbor, 1913.

Record, Wilson. *The Negro and the Communist Party*. Chapel Hill, 1951.

Reddick, L. D. *Crusader without Violence*. New York, 1959.

Redding, Saunders. *The Lonesome Road*. Garden City, 1958.

Reuter, Edward B. *Race Mixture*. New York, 1931.

Rogers, J. A. *Sex and Race*. 3 vols. New York, 1940–44.

Rose, Arnold M. *The Negro's Morale*. Minneapolis, 1949.

Rousseve, Charles B. *The Negro in Louisiana*. New Orleans, 1937.

Rowan, Carl T. *Go South to Sorrow*. New York, 1957.

Ruchames, Louis. *Race, Jobs and Politics: The Story of FEPC*. New York, 1953.

Russell, John H. *The Free Negro in Virginia*. Baltimore, 1913.

St. James, Warren D. *The National Association for the Advancement of Colored People*. New York, 1958.

Sandburg, Carl. *Abraham Lincoln: The Prairie Years*. New York, 1926.

———. *Abraham Lincoln: The War Years*. 4 vols. New York, 1939.

Scott, Emmett J., and Stowe, Lyman Beecher. *Booker T. Washington, Builder of a Civilization*. Garden City, 1916.

Seligman, Charles G. *Races of Africa*. London, 1930.

Shapiro, Nat, and Hentoff, Nat (eds.). *The Jazz Makers*. New York, 1957.

Shoemaker, Don (ed.). *With All Deliberate Speed*. New York, 1957.

Siebert, Wilbur H. *The Underground Railway from Slavery to Freedom*. New York, 1898.

Simkins, Francis B., and Woody, Robert H. *South Carolina During Reconstruction*. Chapel Hill, 1932.

Simmons, William J. *Men of Mark*. Cleveland, 1887.

Simpson, George E., and Yinger, J. Milton. *Racial and Cultural Minorities*. New York, 1953.

Smith, S. D. *The Negro in Congress*. Chapel Hill, 1940.

Spencer, Samuel R. *Booker T. Washington and the Negro's Place in American Life*. Boston, 1955.

Spero, Sterling D., and Harris, Abram L. *The Black Worker*. New York, 1931.

Stampp, Kenneth M. *The Peculiar Institution*. New York, 1956.

Stearns, Marshall W. *The Story of Jazz*. New York, 1956.

Steiner, Bernard C. *History of Slavery in Connecticut*. Baltimore, 1893.

Sterling, Dorothy. *Freedom Train: The Story of Harriet Tubman*. Garden City, 1954.

Steward, Austin. *Twenty-Two Years a Slave*. Rochester, 1857.

Still, William. *The Underground Railroad*. Philadelphia, 1879.

Sydnor, Charles S. *Slavery in Mississippi*. New York, 1933.

Talley, Thomas W. *Negro Folk Rhymes*. New York, 1922.

Taylor, A. A. *The Negro in South Carolina During Reconstruction*. Washington, 1924.

Temple, J. H. *History of Framingham, Massachusetts*. Framingham, 1887.

Tindall, George B. *South Carolina Negroes, 1877–1900*. Columbia, 1952.

Torrence, Ridgely. *The Story of John Hope*. New York, 1948.

Truth, Sojourner. *Narrative of Sojourner Truth*. Boston, 1850.

Ulanov, Barry. *History of Jazz in America*. New York, 1952.

Villard, Oswald Garrison. *John Brown*. Boston, 1910.

The War of the Rebellion: A Compilation of Official Records of the Union and Confederate Armies. 128 vols. Washington, 1880–1901.

Ward, W. E. F. *A History of the Gold Coast*. London, 1948.

Warmoth, Henry C. *War, Politics and Reconstruction*. New York, 1930.

Washington, Booker T., and Du Bois, W. E. B., *et al. The Negro Problem.* New York, 1903.

Washington, Booker T. *Up from Slavery.* New York, 1901.

Weatherford, Willis Duke. *The Negro from Africa to America.* New York, 1924.

Weaver, Robert C. *The Negro Ghetto.* New York, 1948.

Wharton, Vernon Lane. *The Negro in Mississippi, 1865–1890.* Chapel Hill, 1947.

Wheatley, Phillis. *Phillis Wheatley: Poems and Letters,* ed. Charles F. Heartman. New York, 1915.

White, Walter. *Rope and Faggott.* New York, 1929.

———. *A Man Called White.* New York, 1948.

———. *How Far the Promised Land.* New York, 1955.

Williams, Eric. *The Negro in the Caribbean.* Washington, 1942.

———. *Capitalism and Slavery.* Chapel Hill, 1938.

Williams, George W. *History of the Negro Race in America, 1619–1880.* 2 vols. New York, 1883.

———. *A History of the Negro Troops in the War of the Rebellion.* New York, 1888.

Wilson, Joseph T. *The Black Phalanx.* Hartford, 1888.

Woodson, Carter G. *A Century of Negro Migration.* Washington, 1918.

———. *Free Negro Heads of Families in the United States in 1830.* Washington, 1925.

———. *The Negro Professional Man and the Community.* Washington, 1934.

———. *The History of the Negro Church.* Washington, 1945.

———. *The Negro in Our History.* Washington, 1947.

——— (ed.). *Negro Orators and Their Orations.* Washington, 1925.

——— (ed.). *The Mind of the Negro as Reflected in Letters Written During the Crisis, 1800–1860.* Washington, 1926.

Woodward, C. Vann. *Origins of the New South, 1877–1913.* Baton Rouge, 1951.

———. *The Strange Career of Jim Crow.* New York, 1957.

Work, Monroe N. (ed.) *Negro Year Book.* Tuskegee, 1914–15, 1918–19, 1925–26.

Writers Program, WPA. *The Negro in Virginia.* New York, 1940.

UNPUBLISHED STUDIES

Johnston, James Hugo. "Race Relations in Virginia and Miscegenation in the South, 1776–1860." Ph.D. dissertation, University of Chicago, 1937.

Risinger, Robert G. "Routine Slave Life in the Ante-Bellum South, 1830–1860." Master's thesis, University of Chicago, 1947.

PAMPHLETS AND SPECIAL SOURCES

American Anti-Slavery Society. *Annual Reports*. New York, 1834–39.

The Annals, American Academy of Political and Social Science, CXXX, November, 1928. Entire volume devoted to "The American Negro," ed. Donald Young.

The Annals, American Academy of Political and Social Science, Vol. 304, March, 1956. Entire volume devoted to "Race Desegregation and Integration," ed. Ira De A. Reid.

Bogue, Donald J. "Who Will Live in Chicago during the 1960's?" Address reproduced by Chicago Commission on Human Relations.

Civil War Papers read before the Commandery of the State of Massachusetts, Military Order of the Loyal Legion of the United States. Boston, 1900.
> Carter, S. A. "Fourteen Months Service with Colored Troops."
> Prescott, R. B. "The Capture of Richmond."

Congress of Racial Equality. *Cracking the Color Line*. New York, n.d.

Journal of Negro History. "Documents: Thomas Jefferson's Thoughts on the Negro," III (January, 1918).

———. "Documents: Letters of George Washington Bearing on the Negro," II (October, 1917).

Military Essays and Recollections: Papers read before Commandery of the State of Illinois, Military Order of the Loyal Legion of the United States. Chicago, 1894.
> Freeman, Henry V. "A Colored Brigade in the Campaign and Battle of Nashville."
> Furness, William Elliott. "The Negro as a Soldier."

National Association for the Advancement of Colored People. *Annual Reports*. New York, 1911–1961.

Ovington, Mary White. *How the National Association for the Advancement of Colored People Began*. New York, 1914.

Peabody, Andrew Preston. *Street Mobs in Boston Before the Revolution*. Pamphlet reprinted from *Atlantic Monthly* article. Boston, 1888.

Personal Narratives of Events in the War of the Rebellion, Soldiers and Sailors Historical Society of Rhode Island.

    Addeman, J. M. "Reminiscences of Two Years with Colored Troops." (Providence, 1880).

    Califf, Joseph M. "Record of Services of Seventh Regiment, United States Colored Troops." (Providence, 1878).

    Morgan, Thomas J. "Reminiscences of Services with Colored Troops in the Army of the Cumberland, 1863–65." (Providence, 1885).

    Rickard, James H. "Services with Colored Troops in Burnside's Corps" (Providence, 1894).

    Sherman, George R. "The Negro as a Soldier." (Providence, 1913).

Turner, Nat. *The Confessions of Nat Turner*, ed. T. R. Gray. Richmond, 1832.

United States, Department of Commerce, Bureau of the Census, various reports.

United States, Department of Labor. *The Economic Situation of Negroes in the United States.* Washington, 1962.

ARTICLES

Adams, Randolph G. "New Light on the Boston Massacre," American Antiquarian Society, *Proceedings*, V (1937).

Aptheker, Herbert. "Militant Abolitionism," *Journal of Negro History*, XXVI (October, 1941).

——. "Negro Casualties in the Civil War," *ibid.*, XXXII (January, 1947).

——. "The Negro in the Union Navy," *ibid.*, XXXII (April, 1947).

Baker, Henry E. "Benjamin Banneker, the Negro Mathematician and Astronomer," *Journal of Negro History*, III (April, 1918).

Bauer, Raymond, and Bauer, Alice. "Day to Day Resistance to Slavery," *Journal of Negro History*, XXVII (October, 1942).

Bell, Howard H. "Expressions of Negro Militancy in the North, 1840–60," *Journal of Negro History*, XLV (January, 1960).

Bennett, Lerone, Jr. "The King Plan for Freedom," *Ebony* (July, 1956).

——. "The South and the Negro: Martin Luther King, Jr.," *ibid.* (April, 1957).

——. "Daisy Bates: First Lady of Little Rock," *ibid.* (September, 1958).

——. "The Revolt of Negro Youth," *ibid.* (May, 1960).

Bigelow, Martha M. "The Significance of Milliken's Bend in the Civil War," *Journal of Negro History*, XLV (July, 1960).

Binder, Frederick M. "Pennsylvania Negro Regiments in the Civil War," *Journal of Negro History*, XXXVII (October, 1952).

Bond, Horace Mann. "Social and Economic Forces in Alabama Reconstruction," *Journal of Negro History*, XXIII (July, 1938).

Brisbane, Robert H. "New Light on the Garvey Movement," *Journal of Negro History*, XXXVI (January, 1951).

Brown, Sterling A. "Negro Folk Expression," *Phylon*, XIV (First Quarter, 1953).

Dufty, William. "A. Philip Randolph," *New York Post* (December 28, 1959–January 3, 1960).

Eliofson, Eliot. "African Sculpture," the *Atlantic* (April, 1959).

Farrison, W. Edward. "Origin of Brown's *Clotel*," *Phylon*, XV (Fourth Quarter, 1954).

Graham, Pearl M. "Thomas Jefferson and Sally Hemings," *Journal of Negro History*, XLIV (April, 1961).

Granger, Lester. "End of an Era," *Ebony* (December, 1960).

Greene, Lorenzo J. "Some Observations on the Black Regiment of Rhode Island in the American Revolution," *Journal of Negro History*, XXVII (April, 1952).

Greene, Samuel A. "The Boston Massacre," American Antiquarian Society, *Proceedings*, V (October, 1900).

Hansberry, William Leo. "Indigenous African Religions," *Africa Seen by American Negroes*. Paris, 1958.

Hartgrove, W. B. "The Negro Soldier in the American Revolution," *Journal of Negro History*, I (April, 1916).

Jackson, Luther P. "Virginia Negro Soldiers and Seamen in the American Revolution," *Journal of Negro History*, XXVII (July, 1942).

Lofton, James M., Jr. "Denmark Vesey's Call to Arms," *Journal of Negro History*, XXXIII (October, 1948).

Logan, Rayford. "Estevanico, Negro Discoverer of the Southwest," *Phylon*, I (Fourth Quarter, 1940).

Marshall, Thurgood. "An Evaluation of Recent Efforts to Achieve Racial Integration Through Resort to the Courts," *Journal of Negro Education*, XXI (Summer, 1952.)

Morrison, Allan. "A. Philip Randolph: Dean of Negro Leaders," *Ebony* (November, 1958).

Pei, Mario. "Swahili," *Holiday* (April, 1959).

Perkins, A. E. "Oscar James Dunn," *Phylon*, IV (Second Quarter, 1943).

Porter, Kenneth Wiggins. "Negroes and the Seminole War, 1817–1818," *Journal of Negro History*, XXXVI (July, 1951).

———. "Relations Between Negroes and Indians Within the Present Limits of the United States," *ibid.*, XVII (July, 1932).

———. "Florida Slaves and Free Negroes in the Seminole War, 1835–1842," *ibid.*, XXVIII (October, 1943).

Puttkammer, Charles W., and Worthy, Ruth. "William Monroe Trotter, 1872–1934," *Journal of Negro History*, XLIII (October, 1958).

Reddick, L. D. "The Great Decision," *Phylon*, XV (Second Quarter, 1954).

———. "The Negro Policy of the United States Army, 1775–1945," *Journal of Negro History*, XXXIV (January, 1949).

Rudwick, Elliott M. "The Niagara Movement," *Journal of Negro History*, XLII (July, 1957).

Silberman, Charles E. "The City and the Negro," *Fortune* (March, 1962).

Stafford, A. O. "Antar, the Arabian Negro Warrior, Poet and Hero," *Journal of Negro History*, I (April, 1916).

Turner, Lorenzo D. "African Survivals in the New World with Special Emphasis on the Arts," *Africa Seen by American Negroes*. Paris, 1958.

Walden, Daniel. "The Contemporary Opposition to the Political Ideals of Booker T. Washington," *Journal of Negro History*, XLV (April, 1960).

Weisberger, Bernard. "The Dark and Bloody Ground of Reconstruction Historiography," *Journal of Southern History*, XXV (November, 1959).

Wesley, Charles H. "The Negroes of New York in the Emancipation Movement," *Journal of Negro History*, XXIV (January, 1939).

Whitelaw, W. Menzies. "Africa," *Collier's Encyclopedia*. New York, 1953.

Wish, Harvey. "Slave Disloyalty under the Confederacy," *Journal of Negro History*, XXIII (October, 1938).

Wood, L. Hollingsworth. "The Urban League Movement," *Journal of Negro History*, IX (April, 1924).

Woodson, Carter G. "The Beginnings of the Miscegenation of the Whites and Blacks," *Journal of Negro History*, III (October, 1918).

NEWSPAPERS AND MAGAZINES

Afro-American (Baltimore)

Chicago Defender

Crisis Magazine
Ebony Magazine
Harper's Weekly
Negro Digest
New Orleans Tribune
New York Post
The New York Times
Pittsburg Courier
Southern School News

Index